Simple Rules for a Complex World

Simple Rules for a Complex World

R ICHARD A. E PSTEIN

Harvard University Press

Cambridge, Massachusetts
London, England

RECEIVED

MAR - 4 1996

MSU - LIBRARY

KF
385
. E67
1995

Copyright © 1995 by the President and Fellows of Harvard College
All rights reserved
Printed in the United States of America

Second printing, 1995

This book is printed on acid-free paper, and its binding materials have been chosen for strength and durability.

LIBRARY OF CONGRESS CATALOGING-IN-PUBLICATION DATA
Epstein, Richard Allen, 1943–
    Simple rules for a complex world / Richard A. Epstein.
        p.   cm.
    Includes bibliographical references and index.
    ISBN 0-674-80820-7
    1. Law—Economic aspects—United States.   2. Adversary system (Law)—
United States.   3. Lawyers—United States.   4. Social justice.   5. Simplicity
(Philosophy).   I. Title.
KF385.E67 1995
340'.1—dc20   94-40364
                    CIP

To the memory of Walter J. Blum,
friend and colleague, for whom, in law,
95 percent was perfection

Contents

Preface

The topic of this book has been a dominant theme in my legal research since I first started teaching law in 1968. Over that period of time I have taught or written in a large number of areas of public and private law. The particular plots and characters change quickly as one moves from subject to subject. Mastering these subjects requires the academic lawyer, like his practicing counterpart, to have a detailed working knowledge of a large number of cases, statutes, regulations, and practices. Without that level of knowledge, it is not possible to authoritatively answer any discrete legal problem. If my goal in this book were to exhaustively examine any single area of law, then, owing to the complexity of the law, it would be a far fatter book than it is, and far more limited in its choice of topics. I would be obliged to include in the book the full extensive scholarly apparatus of statutes and regulations, citations and quotations, notes and cross references. But that, quite simply, is not the goal of this volume. Instead I hope to act as an intellectual middle man between two cultures, and to lay bare some of the foundational difficulties in the modern law for readers without any specialized legal training and experience, but with more than a passing interest in the law. To make the book as readable as possible, I have largely suppressed the usual scholarly apparatus, citing only a few key references to the broader literature on specific topics.

The book is also written with a single strong message. There is too much law and too many lawyers. But it is not written as a breathless accusatory exposé of individual treachery or greed. It is a book about legal doctrine, and about social structures and the incentives that these legal doctrines help create. It does little good for one company, union, religious association, or charitable institution to abandon its lawyers if the organization will be beaten down by the lawyers who are hired by others. Yet if others are foolish enough to let down their guard by not engaging lawyers skilled in the art of litigation and persuasion, then these same organizations will do better to hire their own. We thus have yet another illustration of the now famous Prisoner's Dilemma game in which the ideal cooperative solution (fewer lawyers) cannot be obtained by isolated moves by individual social actors. Some collective method of control must take place. But what?

Here the nub of the problem is that the level of aspiration for law in the United States, and increasingly throughout the rest of the world, is simply too high. Ask most men or women on the street what the most important social problem today is, and they will answer that it is violence on the street, violence in the schools, and the loss of the sense of security that it entails. But how seriously can one take a legal system that devotes more of its intellectual ingenuity to identifying and correcting market failures resulting from asymmetrical and imperfect information in employment than to containing violence on the street? No one likes violence, and thus agreement on that issue tends to lead us to move on to more subtle questions that challenge and puzzle the intellect. But in so doing we then invent other situations which call for government intervention. We try to solve more and more problems by legal rules and fewer through voluntary accommodation. Often we do so because we are seduced by the dramatic forms of anecdotal jurisprudence: the ability to put before the camera the worker who is fired, the accident victim who is uncompensated under the current legal system. The implication is always that some new right has to be created to redress the evident hardship just portrayed.

Using law as an instrument for achieving perfect justice suffers from several major drawbacks. First, it diverts resources from the major questions of social order, and fritters away our precious moral authority on causes of far less weight and consequence. Second, focusing too much on the unhappy anecdote ignores the hidden benefits that voluntary transactions might have in other cases that produce not moving stories but inconspicuous successes. Third, the emphasis on law and regulation ignores the cumulative impact of independent systems of regulation on a single social institution. The employment contract may be able to survive minimum wage or maximum hour regulation, or discrimination and wrongful discharge suits, or health and safety regulation, or Social Security and Medicare taxes, or handicap access and the uncapping of mandatory retirement, or family leave and workplace safety, or unionization and collective bargaining. But is there any reason to think that real wages and job opportunities can rise in the face of all these regulations together, or that each new form of regulation can be justified without taking into account the regulations already in place?

By degrees, therefore, our extensive level of social ambition leads us to a very complex set of legal rules, one which only lawyers can understand and navigate, and then at very stiff fees. The virtue of simplicity, around which this book is organized, is never explicitly deprecated, but it does suffer from insufficient respect and appreciation. By degrees we find that private and public actors all must resort to the use of lawyers, or to administrators steeped in the law, in order to solve their individual problems—thereby creating additional problems for others. Yet it is hard to identify some discrete point that marks the triumph of legal complexity, much less to state how its triumph might be reversed.

In light of this situation, it occurred to me that to write a book that makes simplicity the hub of the wheel might help explain how we have come to the present impasse and what we can do to escape from its implications. In dealing with these issues, I have examined many of the detailed scholarly studies in these various areas, but have relied more on my sense of the field, acquired over twenty-five years of teaching and through innumerable meetings, conferences, workshops, classes, and, above all, lunches with colleagues and friends. The views expressed here rest as much on judgment as they do on precise empirical demonstrations. I hope that the arguments I have advanced are both accessible and plausible, and will lead my readers to reexamine some of their more cherished assumptions about the relationship between legal rules and social progress. I have for the most part tended to deal with subjects, such as property rights, employment relations, product liability, corporate liability, and environmental protection, that lie pretty close to the common law roots with which I began my own legal studies, and on which I continue to rely.

The proposals that I make are in many senses radical (perhaps too radical, or if not too radical then too reactionary, for most people) and heavily depend on the perception that cooperative ventures between individuals are better left to private ordering than to public control. One of the major intangibles that must be taken into account in organizing any legal system is the distribution and use of information. Quite simply, I believe that most people know their own preferences better than other people do. Accordingly, people are better able to act

in order to protect themselves and advance their own interests if given
the legal power to do so. The complexity of legal rules tends to place
the power of decision in the hands of other people who lack the necessary information and whose own self-interest leads them to use the
information that they do have in socially destructive ways. I am far
from advocating a move to a system utterly devoid of legal constraints
on individual conduct, although some might wish to describe my
views in so uncharitable a light. But it should be clear that while I
support innovation in technology and business, I think that perma-
nence and stability are the cardinal virtues of the legal rules that make
private innovation and public progress possible. To my mind there is
no doubt that a legal regime that embraces private property and freedom of contract is the only one that in practice can offer that perma-
nence and stability. Simplicity is yet another argument in favor of
strong private rights and limited government.

In reaching this conclusion, I have been heavily influenced by the
work of Friedrich Hayek, in particular his important manifesto, *The
Road to Serfdom*. Hayek's book first appeared in 1944, and has continued to be actively read and discussed in the half-century that has
elapsed since its publication. Hayek's major target was central planning, which in the context of the socialist calculation debates of his
time addressed the question of whether government officials could
ever acquire the information routinely imparted by prices to organize
product and labor markets. Today there is little general sentiment in
the United States or abroad in favor of the collective ownership of the
means of production that bore the brunt of Hayek's withering criticism. Instead the newer pattern is to preach the virtue of markets in
the abstract, and then to insist that government regulation of private
enterprises is necessary to correct the legion of supposed specific market failures that arise in complex modern institutions. Just such a
tempting argument might lead to the government domination of
health care in the United States.

In one sense I view this book as a reply to the argument that regulation is normally desirable even in circumstances where government
ownership of the means of production is not. In my view there is no
sharp dichotomy between government regulation of wages and prices,
on the one hand, and government ownership, on the other. Rather,
regulation takes certain elements from the owner's bundle of rights
and transfers them to the state, where they again fall prey to the same

difficulties that arose when central planning was defended on a grand scale. If the downfall of socialism comes from the inherent gaps in information available to public officials and from the inability of legal rules to constrain their self-interested behavior, the forms of modern regulation attacked in this book are subject to the same criticism. Hayek may well have been wrong, or at least incautious, when he insisted that markets could "spontaneously" evolve without the assistance of the state, but he surely was correct in noting the massive defects that pervade state planning. The government works best when it establishes the rules of the road, not when it seeks to determine the composition of the traffic. It is the vice of the Federal Communications Commission that it attacks the second task when it could confine itself to the deserved obscurity sufficient to discharge the first.

The philosophical roots for this book run deep, but the more proximate stimuli reflect change, circumstance, and good fortune more than any author should be happy to admit. Although simplicity has always been a theme in my legal writing, it first became prominent in a column I wrote for the *Wall Street Journal* with the title "Simple Rules for a Complex World" that appeared in June 1985. I did little more explicit work on this theme until I was approached by two people, Penelope Brook Cowen on behalf of the New Zealand Business Roundtable (and its indefatigable director, Roger Kerr) and N. Ray Evans on behalf of the Western Mining Company (and its president, Hugh Morgan), to make a speaking tour of Australia and New Zealand in order to talk about issues of liability and law reform that were of concern there. In particular they asked me to address questions of labor reform and tort liability. On a whirlwind tour of both countries in July 1990, I delivered a number of addresses, often hastily composed, on the topics covered in this book.

In the months that followed I reworked some of the transcripts of these talks into a group of articles that were published in Australia and New Zealand. It was suggested that I then compile the separate essays into a book on simple rules. The task has proved far more daunting than I had originally thought, and the book that follows has been substantially expanded and thoroughly revised at every point. In the early stages of the process, I was assisted by Penelope Brook Cowen, who undertook to make sense of the transcripts of the lectures that I delivered in New Zealand, and Roger Pilon of the Cato Institute, who read and annotated an earlier draft of the manuscript and pointed out in exquisite detail just how much work remained to convert a set of isolated lectures into a coherent volume.

Since that time I have talked about various aspects of the subject in lectures throughout the United States. In addition to giving talks at the University of Chicago, I have spoken on the issue of legal simplicity at the American Law and Economics Association, the Cato Institute, the Cumberland Law School in Samford University, the University of Kansas School of Law, the University of Michigan Law School, and the Yale Law School. I have also benefited from close and detailed readings of the manuscript from Robert C. Ellickson, Victor Goldberg, Lawrence L. Lessig, Fred S. McChesney, Richard A. Posner, and Mark Ramseyer. I owe a large debt of thanks to my three tireless research assistants who carefully corrected the various drafts of the book: Donna Coté, P. J. Karafiol, and Jay Wright. As usual I am grateful to my secretary, Katheryn Kepchar, for keeping up with the many revisions of the manuscript. I also want to give a word of thanks to Michael Aronson, Senior Editor in the Social Sciences at Harvard University Press, for spurring me on yet again toward publication, and to Nancy Clemente, Senior Editor at Harvard University Press, for the care and attention that she gave to editing the manuscript. Finally, over the years I have received financial support and moral encouragement from the John M. Olin Foundation, and its Executive Director, James Piereson, on this and on many other projects. To them a special note of thanks for help and support that extends over many years.

Chicago
August 15, 1994

Simple Rules for a
Complex World

Introduction

Too Many Lawyers, Too Much Law

The popular image of lawyers has not been favorable even in the best of times. However much the public at large rejoices in the transcendental value of the rule of law, it has never viewed the rule of lawyers with benevolence. Most people rightly have immense respect for their own lawyers, but distance from members of that profession does not make the heart grow fonder. As a group, lawyers are often condemned as greedy and opportunistic individuals who prey on the misery and misfortunes of others or as hired guns paid to perform wondrous deeds for the powerful, rich, and famous, while wreaking havoc on the public as a whole.

In recent years, casual empiricism senses an intensification of that sentiment: there are still more lawyers, too many lawyers, and suspicion and resentment of them. Perhaps we have not quite reached the level of anticommunist jokes: Q: What is the difference between capitalism and communism? A: In the former man exploits man; in the latter the reverse is true. But lawyer jokes must come in a close second. How else can one explain the raft of bad lawyer jokes that made the rounds even in my son Elliot's fourth-grade group at MacWillies Day Camp: Q: Why didn't the shark eat the lawyer? A: Professional courtesy. Or: Q: What are five lawyers at the bottom of the sea? A: A good start. Or: Q: What is your favorite law firm? A: Dewey, Cheatham & Howe. And what about the crude Miller Lite commercial where the determined rodeo cowboy lassoes and trusses up the "fat, rich tax

1

lawyer," to the evident satisfaction of knowing beer drinkers and the painful dissatisfaction of the state bar associations.

Lawyers do not like being the butt of popular jokes; nor should they (or is it we?). Just recently the American Bar Association has earmarked $700,000 to counter the negative image of lawyers; and Harvey Saferstein, the president of the California Bar Association, has undertaken a personal campaign against the jokes, which he believes have intensified over the past several years, only to be attacked as a defender of special privilege and a threat to the first amendment.[1] Yet campaigns will have no more effect than King Canute's efforts to hold back the tide. Failure to sway public opinion is one thing, but why are the popular perceptions so strong? Here the most disquieting answer is best: lawyers do a good job in serving the interests of their clients. The showboat trial lawyer who recovers a million-dollar verdict from the tire company for his drunk-driving client may receive a bad press; yet he does receive the approbation of the one person who really counts: his own client—who will recommend him to friends in a similar fix. Individual clients will rightly insist that lawyers take advantage of whatever opportunities the law gives them, and the entire canon of legal ethics requires the lawyer to do no less. When the legal system gives lawyers the room to wheel and deal, why should anyone be surprised that they take full advantage of it?

The reverberations are felt all the way down the line. These finely honed skills generate large fees that in turn translate into high salaries and partnership income—over $1,000,000 per partner in some firms.[2] Once the keys to success are clear, lawyers within the profession will retool or risk the loss of business; and young college graduates will decide whether their own personalities and temperaments suit the brisk practice of law. The ever increasing number of burnouts who complain about the pace will be replaced by fresh young legions eager for battle. The global uneasiness, the bad jokes, will do little to alter the shape and practices of the profession. The forces impelling lawyers and their clients to do the best they can *for themselves* within the rules of the game are too powerful for anyone to resist on an individual level. It is the rules of the game—the complex rules that undergird the modern legal culture—that should be the proper subject of public wrath.

Taken individually, many of these laws command wide public support, notwithstanding the larger intrusions to which they in part contribute. But the cumulative and interactive effects of these laws are hard to understand. Hence it is also hard to understand why these laws are wrong, and tempting to assume that tinkering at the edges—another paperwork reduction act here, another good government commission there—will leave us with the core of the modern regulatory state *shorn of* its excesses. But public patience on that score is wearing thin. Lawyers' humor, like gallows humor, is born of both resentment and impotence. It shows how difficult it is to quell the public nervousness about the rising influence of lawyers throughout the land.

The concern starts at the top: our current President and his wife are graduates of the Yale Law School; our Congress, state legislative bodies, and administrative agencies at all levels are populated with lawyers. All this is true: indeed 42 percent of the members of our House of Representatives are lawyers, as are 61 percent of our senators, compared with about 18 percent of the members of comparable bodies in other industrial countries.[3] But the increase in lawyers is everywhere, and in one sense at least the numbers do tell the story.[4] Between 1900 and 1970, lawyers as a percentage of the population were roughly constant at around 1.3 per thousand of population, a figure slightly below the number of doctors for that same period, 1.8 per thousand. After 1970 the percentage for both professions started to rise, but the increase for lawyers outstripped that for physicians, even though much of the increase in physicians could be explained by the increasing amount of subsidized care delivered through the Medicare and Medicaid systems. By 1980 lawyers and doctors were in a dead heat, at about 2.5 practitioners per thousand. By 1987 the lawyers had inched ahead and stood at 2.9 per thousand, compared with 2.76 per thousand for doctors. By 1990 lawyers stood at 3.0 per thousand and the percentage is still climbing. The overall effects are perhaps best summarized by two revealing statistics. Between 1960 and 1985 the population of the United States grew by 30 percent, while the number of lawyers increased by 130 percent.[5] More instructive, perhaps, between 1972 and 1987 the number of *Washington* lawyers increased fourfold, from 11,000 to 45,000.[6] The clear implication is that the internal composition of lawyers' work is changing as well, away from commercial transactions (which produce wealth) to politics (which transfers and diminishes wealth simultaneously).

There is one telling explanation for the continued entry of the ablest young Americans into the legal profession. The sharp increase in the number of lawyers has not been matched by any decline in the average income of lawyers. In fact in the years from 1960 to 1987, the average lawyer's income moved up and down in a band between $50,000 to $65,000 (in constant 1987 dollars) without any systematic direction. This stability of wages is notable given the enormous increase in the number of lawyers entering the profession after 1970. More striking perhaps, the mix within the pool of lawyers has changed in at least two ways. First, time has brought a steady sharp increase in the number of female lawyers in the pool (from about 1,000 graduates per year in 1970 to about 14,000 in 1985), while male graduates moved from about 15,000 in 1970 to a peak of about 25,000 in 1977, declining to about 22,000 in 1985. On average female lawyers have lower incomes than their male compatriots, most probably because of their greater commitment to family and children, although other explanations surely play a role. A breakdown of male wages before and after the shift suggests that the real earnings of lawyers are quite strong even with an increased supply of lawyers. Second, the average number of years of experience within the profession has declined sharply, going down from twenty-five years in the late 1960s to around thirteen or fourteen years in 1977–78, as a reflection of the huge influx, male and female, into the market in the preceding ten years. That number increased somewhat in the 1980s, but the wages retained much of their strength even though for individual lawyers earnings tended to peak at around twenty-seven years of experience and decline gradually thereafter.

It may well be that these heady numbers will not last forever, since the greater reliance on in-house lawyers for routine tasks promises, at least in the short run, to take salaries down a notch from the high levels that they reached in the late 1980s and early 1990s. Lawyers are out hunting for business, and are far more flexible and open about fee structures than they were even five years ago: straight hourly billing is less common, and a lower hourly fee in exchange for a piece of the money recovered is a common arrangement that admits of infinite variation. Younger associates now find that their probation periods are shorter than they were a decade or even five years ago, and even partners in this new competitive environment find themselves unceremoniously left without a job if they do not maintain their full quota of billable hours, usually in excess of two thousand per year. But even with the evident transformation of the legal profession, its overall size and influence continue to increase, as is reflected in the rising percentage of gross domestic product (GDP) devoted to legal expenditures in this period: from 0.6 percent in 1960 to 0.87 percent in 1980 to 1.39 percent in 1987.

These numbers reflect only the direct expenditures on legal services, and doubtless understate the percentage of GDP that is directed toward compliance with legal norms. The past twenty-five years have also witnessed a rapid expansion in the size and influence of law-related professions. Closest to home, paralegals play a far greater role today than ever before. Corporations defending themselves in mass tort litigation quickly learn that piecework for lawyers is a ruinous financial proposition, and thus implement new protocols that allow for the delegation of legal work to lower-paid professionals.

Yet it would be a mistake to assume that these overdue financial and structural reforms indicate a decline in the importance of law. Law and regulation heavily shape the contours of work in allied professions. Accountants do large amounts of tax-related and securities work. There has been a sharp increase in the number of trade associations (from 4,900 in 1956 to 15,000 in 1980 to 23,000 in 1994); at least one of these is a trade association whose members are trade associations. A raft of affirmative action compliance officers, environmental control experts, public affairs gurus, government relations consultants, and old-fashioned lobbyists do more than dot the landscape. And doubtless a far greater fraction of the time of ordinary managers, farmers, and entrepreneurs is spent in complying with government regulations. Many farmers now complain that they can farm only early in the morning or late at night, when government offices are closed. Otherwise they are hard at work negotiating permits and licenses (and, alas, subsidies) from a broad range of government officials. Likewise the business of designing new facilities has become far more cumbersome and costly after the passage of the Americans with Disability Act: the standard rule of thumb in universities is that compliance with the statute adds 20 percent to the total cost of new construction, and even more for the difficult renovations often required of existing structures. The 1.4 percent of GDP therefore constitutes a very low estimate of the extent of social resources that are controlled and regulated by law. More to the point, the halo effect is not constant in size over time, but itself doubtlessly accounts for a far larger percentage of GDP than in earlier years. And the effects of law are still larger than the effects of lawyers, for many regulations on the book can have powerful negative consequences even if they result in relatively little litigation that finds its way into the law reports, which have expanded apace.

The upsurge in demand for legal services of all kinds is best explained by the heavy increase in regulation that dates from the late 1960s and continues unabated to the present. The simplest measure of regulatory activity is provided by the turgid pages of the *Federal Register,* which contains the various rules and regulations put forth by the federal government. A simple table of some key years illustrates the growth in federal activity. The story here reveals the same inexorable expansion of law. The number of pages in the *Register* was small at the height of the New Deal, although it increased steadily over that period. The number of pages for appellate court cases was only somewhat greater. There was an understandable expansion in the *Register* during World War II, followed by a substantial contraction with the return of peace, but not quite to the prewar level. The amount of judicial work scarcely changed. The 1950s were a period of relative prosperity, and relatively little increase in pages on either front. The modern era thus began with the expansion of Lyndon Johnson's Great Society, for 1965 was the year after the passage of the Civil Rights Act and the year that brought Medicare and Medicaid onto the scene. In 1970 the Environmental Protection Act (EPA) was passed, and the Employee Retirement Income Security Act (ERISA), with comprehensive regulation of pensions, followed in 1974. The modern era was in full swing between 1970 and 1975, when two Republican Presidents, Richard Nixon and Gerald Ford, sat in the White House. Activity peaked with a flurry at the end of the Carter years, then went into a modest decline under Ronald Reagan (1986 saw the post-1970 low of 47,418 pages in the *Federal Register*). Output reached Carter-like levels under George Bush, and exceeded those under Bill Clinton. And a steady, but less erratic expansion in the amount of appellate litigation spanned the entire period. A genuine bipartisan effort! But virtually all this expansion has been driven by changes in the legal system rather than by any fundamental changes in the underlying population demographics. The amount of judicial activity was not much greater in 1960 than it was in 1940, if the numbers are adjusted for the popu-

Federal regulations and appellate court reports, 1936–1991

Year	*Federal Register* (pages)	*Federal Reports*[a] (pages)	GDP (billions, 1987$)	Population (millions)
1936	2,411	6,138	777.9	128,053
1940	5,307	7,161	906.0	132,457
1945	15,508	7,161	1,602.6	133,434
1950	9,562	8,184	1,418.5	152,271
1955	10,196	9,590	1,768.3	165,931
1960	12,792	10,549	1,970.8	180,671
1965	17,206	14,322	2,470.5	194,303
1970	20,036	22,512	2,873.9	205,052
1975	60,221	25,324	3,221.7	215,973
1980	87,012	32,026	3,776.3	227,722
1985	53,480	49,073	4,279.8	238,492
1990	53,618	45,893	5,522.2	249,924
1991	67,716	49,907	5,677.5	252,117

a. Appellate court reports, by volume publication date. District court reports went from 5,179 pages in 1936 to 42,727 in 1991.

lation, but the expansion of that activity was vastly greater than the increase in population or GDP thereafter.

It is relatively easy to understand why there is some increase in the number of lawyers given the increase in the population that they serve. The harder question is what to make of all these data which incontrovertibly indicate the large place of lawyers, and law, in our national life. One possibility is to put a rosy interpretation on the data. Just that approach receives a cautious endorsement from Robert C. Clark of the Harvard Law School, who offers explanations for the expansion in legal services that are either cancerous or relatively benign.[7] One cancerous explanation offered by Clark, and others, attributes the increase in law to the breakdown in the moral order. Where informal constraints break down, the law has to fill the gap, a regrettable but necessary countermeasure to the failure of families, schools, churches, and popular culture. Unfortunately, this explanation can all too easily be turned on its head if the failure of these dominant social institutions is regarded not as a bolt from the blue but as a consequence, at least in part, of more vigorous state intervention under the law. It is easy to think of other reasons why schools educate less well: they are saddled with requirements of compulsory unionization; they find it impossible to fire teachers or expel students without risking serious lawsuits; and they are subject to ever greater pressure from federal and state mandates on matters ranging from mainstreaming disabled students to overall supervision of the curriculum. No set of informal norms does well in competition with the harsher commands of the law. Although the precise patterns of influence may never be disentangled, the causation could well run both ways: the rise in law leads to a decline in morality, as well as the other way around.

A second cancerous explanation relies on yet another of the inevitable lawyer jokes, duly noted by Clark.[8] A single lawyer in town does not have enough to do. But once two lawyers are in town both will thrive. The intuition behind this quip is that lawyers who make their living through litigation shift wealth and waste wealth, but they do not produce wealth. Litigation, the preparation for litigation, and the avoidance of litigation are thus presumptive social evils until shown to be a social good. Although this explanation may account for some of the individual frustrations with lawyers, it hardly explains the explosive growth in legal services generally, or even in litigation in particular. Two or more lawyers have been around in small towns for a long time. To explain why litigation is more prevalent today, we need to look beyond their motivations to structural changes in the rules of the game.

Likewise, I think that Clark is correct to conclude that there is relatively little mileage in the third of his cancerous explanations, namely, that the conflict of interests between lawyers and their clients leads to an explosion in litigation. The source of the conflict here is well known and stems from the commonplace that a lawyer who works on a fee-for-service basis has an incentive to pad the hours, even when his additional work is of no benefit to his client. (Then again, a lawyer on a contingent fee arrangement may settle a case too quickly, a different but equally important conflict.) Clients of course seek to counter this tendency by monitoring the work of their lawyers, whether through checking references, demanding itemized billing, or resorting to in-house counsel. Yet precisely because these conflicts of interest between lawyer and client are so endemic, they cannot explain the explosive levels of growth of legal work over the last twenty-five or so years.

With these explanations to one side, it is possible to paint a bit rosier picture of the situation. Perhaps these increases are just a sign of the importance of legal services to those who receive them. The increase over the past thirty years in expenditures on computer services, home video movies, or recreational vehicles far outstrips those on legal services. However, there are clever ads, not gruesome jokes, about the Macintosh Power-Book, *Terminator 2,* and the Toyota minivan. Lower price and improved quality account for the increase in demand in a perfectly sensible fashion. Indeed, even the sharp increases in medical services (now edging toward 14 percent of GDP, up from 6 percent thirty years ago) deserve in part a benevolent interpretation. The advances in medical technology are such that physicians, hospitals, and a coterie of health care providers are now able to provide needed services and relief to an ever aging population. Why walk around with a slipped disk or a trick knee when innovative treatments are widely available? The shift in expenditures across sectors is in part a sign of increased wealth and better services, not just a sign of government foolishness, although there is a lot of that as well.

Likewise, advances in technology scarcely offer a suitable justification for the massive increase in the level of government activity. Increased technology surely allows government to supervise areas that it once had to leave unregulated: the FBI pursues a Clipper chip to audit communications over the Internet because it is far cheaper and more effective than old-fashioned wiretapping.[9] The ability to monitor trades on the stock exchanges to ferret out cases of insider trading, for example, depends on a level of computer power that did not exist over a generation ago. But that same power is available to the exchanges, so that if the regulation of insider trading were desirable,[10] it could be undertaken by the exchanges themselves. Likewise the increase in technological sophistication makes equipment easier and more user-friendly. It makes it easier for people to seek out and find contracting partners and for contracting partners to observe each other's behavior than in earlier times. It is now less necessary to herd workers into small places, where they can be directly supervised by management. Instead, the spread of information makes it possible for entrepreneurs to assemble teams tailor made for particular tasks, accounting for the large rise in temporary workers and small firms.[11] The dead time of workers in larger, more rigid firms can be mostly eliminated. The rise in technology therefore may increase the power of the state to regulate, but it hardly increases the need for that regulation. The explanation for that complexity must lie elsewhere.

Clark for one offers a benign explanation by citing the accelerating pace and complexity of international transactions.[12] But again the explanation is incomplete. Surely there is some truth to his observation that formal agreements are more important in transactions between strangers at a distance than they are in transactions between individuals who work in close proximity. That result has, for example, been borne out by Lisa Bernstein's excellent and detailed study of the diamond market,[13] which shows how greater levels of formality were introduced once the enterprise expanded beyond the Chasidic Jews in New York City to embrace Japanese and other Asian markets. Yet by the same token, her work shows that both before and after that expansion the members of the industry worked mightily to develop and refine internal methods of dispute resolution that precluded resort to the courts.

Other international transactions also respond to the demand for contractual clarity. But it would be quite a mistake to assume that most modern international practice involves the translation of private contracts into multiple languages. Massive amounts of litigation take place under the antidumping statutes, which act as though competitive injury to domestic firms represents some grave national emergency, instead of offering American consumers and other manufacturers (many of whom resell their goods abroad) opportunities to purchase superior goods at lower prices. Likewise the taxation of international transactions is an area of extraordinary complexity that has not been made any easier by successive layers of tax reform, often introduced for the most parochial of motives.[14] The expansion of global markets should, if anything, *reduce* the costs of legal services by increasing the range of choices that are open to all parties. The mind-boggling complexity of regulation—not international trade itself—makes this explanation more cancerous than benign.

Similarly, I think that Clark misses the mark when he says optimistically that the increased level of diversity and multiculturalism in the United States accounts for the increased levels of legal activity. That is surely correct as a descriptive matter, given the massive commitment to regulation that marks the American mindset. Diversity produces a greater difference in sentiment and demand in a population. Battles over legislation are likely to be more bitter and protracted given the conflicts between groups that are difficult to compromise and broker whenever a majority is in a position to expropriate wealth from a minority. Legislation, in a word, works best in homogenous societies where agreement on basic values reduces the overall level of conflict.

But, even with a nod to Lani Guinier,[15] no voting structures are able to counter the dangers of faction and polarization in a multicultural society. There is no way that rival groups can "take turns" in running the ship of state. Rather than struggling to devise costly voting systems that are likely to make matters worse, we should take the more profitable approach of working diligently to shrink the size of government so as to reduce the number of decisions that government must make. Once government can be made to stay its hand, small shifts in sentiment will lead not to a sudden shift of power from one faction to another, but to an expansion of opportunities within a marketplace. Small shifts in taste and power are followed by small shifts in the fortunes of the individuals who compete with each other, without the sharp discontinuities and endless logrolling that mark the pitched battles in the legislative arena. It is therefore not possible simply to say that diversity is a benign explanation for the expansion of legal services. The mistake here is to think that diversity works best with an expansion in the range and intensity of state activities, when precisely the opposite is true.

All these proposed explanations suffer from a common flaw of not looking closely enough at the changes in the composition of the laws that are on the books and the kinds of activities that they force lawyers and others to perform. Nor do these explanations, whether benign or cancerous, take into account some more empirical work that seeks to document the connection between the increased numbers of lawyers and the decline in productivity. Yet here some early returns bear notice. Stephen Magee and his colleagues have published a study which indicates that the optimal concentration of lawyers is about 60 percent of what we have in America today.[16] In Magee's view, each additional lawyer who is churned out by American law schools reduces the level of GDP by $2.5 million, a figure far greater than the presented discounted value of that lawyer's earnings, substantial though they may be.[17] In one sense, Magee's conclusion seems far too tame, for it suggests that 60 percent of the lawyers are needed when the number of lawyers was far below this level before the explosive growth of lawyers in the 1970s. It may well be that the turning point occurs even earlier than he suggests.

Nonetheless, most of the sharp criticism of Magee's evidence has come from those who believe, as Clark is inclined to do, that the increase in the number of lawyers is at most benign.[18] One line of criticism is that Magee is unable to develop any coherent theory of how lawyers could be so successful in their effort to prosper at the expense of the body politic. The large number of lawyers and their diverse interests make it unlikely that they could form a potent lobby in the halls of Congress. The difficulties of obtaining the needed coordination for the provision of the desired collective good seem too hard to overcome. In addition, it is difficult to assume that lawyers are so effective that they can advance their own interests while advancing those of the particular interest groups that they represent. Nor is it likely that the diversion of talent from other disciplines into the law (although the large number of students with sophisticated scientific training in my classes perhaps suggests otherwise) has depleted national productivity in other important areas.

The second set of objections to Magee's unhappy thesis is that the data are difficult to interpret because the definition and roles of lawyers vary widely across societies and because the occupational niches that lawyers occupy within our own society often vary enormously: lawyers do government affairs, public relations, financial training, and lots of other tasks because they have to receive a fine training in collateral disciplines in order to perform their job.

But although these objections may have some merit, they hardly seem decisive. The danger that arises from the large number of lawyers is attributable to the dangers that arise from a large number of laws, given the multiplier effect that new laws have on the activities of nonlawyers. We do not have to assume that lawyers were instrumental in the adoption of the passage of these rules. The political debates may well have taken the form that some additional legal expense is strictly necessary to combat the substantive evil which a civil rights, a welfare, or an environmental statute is passed to counteract. Many lawyers may oppose the passage of such laws. But whatever the origins of a particular statute, individual lawyers will be quick to seize on it if it will help their clients or help expand the size of their practice. The objection to the current legal system does not depend on any assertion that the morass is the distinctive creation of lawyers: others are free to take the blame. It is quite sufficient that strong commitments to ideas shared by the general public account for a law's passage. What matters is not why laws pass, but what they do to the overall productive strength of this country.

We therefore do not have to accept Magee's results as though they state the literal truth in order to be concerned with the issue that he raises. In addition, it is critical to note that Magee himself claims merely, with some false precision, that his judgments are good only at the margin: it is only the excess 40 percent of lawyers who are said to make the difference.[19] More generally, it seems as though the relationship between the number of lawyers and the levels of social productivity follows a bell-shaped curve: up to a certain point lawyers increase productivity, and beyond that point, productivity decreases as the number of lawyers increases. The empirical claim is that we have passed the point of positive returns from additional numbers of lawyers and lawyering services.

The shape of this curve makes good intuitive sense, for the same reasons that made the Laffer curve on taxation popular in the early Reagan years.[20] The argument was, and is, that tax revenues follow a simple pattern: up to a point higher rates increase revenue, but beyond that point, the negative impact that taxation has on production results in decreased revenues. The maximum level of tax revenues will therefore be collected at some intermediate level; so it is an empirical question whether the current level of taxes is too high or too low. Not to be ignored, however, is the proper social objective, which is not to maximize the amount of tax revenue for the government, but to maximize the level of social welfare for the community at large. In light of the additional burdens that any tax imposes on the operation of the economy, social welfare is best improved by keeping taxation at levels lower than those needed to maximize government revenue. It is better to quit too soon than to tax too long.

A bell-shaped Laffer curve also makes sense for the number of lawyers: a society with no lawyers is a society in which it is impossible to keep the social order or to organize any but the simplest business deals. Up to a certain point an increase in the number of lawyers is necessary to define property rights, to enforce contracts, and to run a decent system of criminal law and public administration. The initial increase in the number of lawyers thus facilitates the performance of these useful social functions. But as their (or, I should say, our) number increases further, lawyers assume very different roles. They occupy

Bleak House as the incarnation of the old expression that "justice delayed is justice denied." In addition, they stimulate a torrent of litigation which, far from encouraging production, perpetuates an endless cycle of wasteful and expensive transfer payments through litigation and regulation. The lawyer as litigator and the lawyer as dealmaker (deals with regulators, deals to beat regulators) both assume negative connotations. There is a manifest conflict of interest between the welfare of the legal profession and the welfare of the larger society, where the society needs fewer laws and fewer lawyers. As with taxation, the better result is to stop legal intervention before the legal peak is reached.

It is, of course, an empirical matter of when the curve starts to slope downward, but whatever the disagreement on the precise location of that point, there is, or at least should be, much agreement that we have crossed it even if we disagree with Magee's precise numbers. There are, in a word, too many lawyers, and the question is what should be done about it. The problem here is social, given the viselike hold of the Prisoner's Dilemma game. There are short-term private gains from hiring legal assistance, followed by undesirable consequences that ensue when the practice is made universal. Some collective method of control must take place, for it is fruitless to ask anyone to engage in the folly of unilateral disarmament. Still, that will only happen when legislation is repealed on as massive a scale as it has been introduced, and when judges take away from plaintiffs the legal rights created by earlier judicial decisions.

Although there are isolated instances of the contraction of legal claims, the general trend is quite in the opposite direction: more law. Our aspirations for what a legal system can do to improve social circumstances is simply too high. We try to solve more and more problems through legal intervention, and fewer through voluntary accommodation and informal practices. A kind of Gresham's law has set in, for the increased dependence on lawyers and legal proceedings renders the informal modes of doing business less effective. Any individual case may well present appealing reasons for some new statutory intervention (the adoption of family leave legislation is one recent battle),[21] but the combined or cumulative effect of countless legal innovations tends to be ignored in the ceaseless quest to adopt any single innovation. What appears noble in the individual case turns out to be dubious in the aggregate. By degrees, therefore, our extensive level of social ambition leads us to a very complex set of legal rules, one which only lawyers can understand and navigate, and then at very stiff fees. The virtue of simplicity, around which this book is organized, is never deprecated, but it does suffer from insufficient respect and appreciation. By degrees we find that private and public actors all must resort to the use of lawyers, or to administrators steeped in the law, in order to solve their particular problems.

Notwithstanding the enormous technical advances of the past generation, the prospects for American citizens have been flat at best. Wage levels have been roughly constant over the past several years, and perhaps have undergone a slight decline, especially for white men.[22] The prospects for improved job formation and higher wages are slight indeed, and there is in this country at least no general sense that children will lead richer and happier lives than their parents. Instead we try to find virtues in a philosophy of limits and sacrifice, without any clear sense that the deprivations of the moment will pay off in increased gains for the next generation. It could well be that we face sacrifice without end, and without apparent purpose. The promise of technology seems unlimited. The power of social arrangements to translate that improved technology into greater prosperity and greater happiness seems to be much in doubt.

The present malaise is not confined to the United States. There are strong signs that job formation has stalled in the European Community, and even the Japanese have discovered that it is impossible to give workers lifetime contracts in a down economy. The precise source of difficulties in these countries is surely not the same as our own; in a word, their mischief is more likely to be brought about by direct regulation, while in the United States the mischief is brought about by a combination of direct regulation and private litigation. But again the bloom is off the rose.

The strong undercurrent of social uneasiness should invite a fundamental reexamination of our collective ways of doing business. Yet whenever that prospect is mentioned, it is met with the same sense of distrust and uneasiness that greets the current situation. Even the failure and disintegration of socialism in Eastern Europe and the former Soviet Union has not led to a clear response to the next question: if government ownership of the means of production is so bad, why is government regulation of the private means of production so good? But it is just that question that has to be asked. We need a fresh start, which this book hopes to provide.

To understand something of how the legal system works and why it has gone so badly amiss, I shall organize this book around the theme of simple rules, and treat the increasing complexity of legal rules as a rough sign that something has gone badly astray. In Chapter 1 I shall therefore explain what I mean by simplicity (itself a fairly complicated conception) and its role in understanding the operation of a legal system. Thereafter in Chapters 3 through 6 I shall outline what I regard to be the substantive legal rules that are necessary to form a legal system that is both simple in its operation and durable enough to meet the demands of the complex modern society that it serves. In particular I shall try to show how traditional judge-made conceptions of common law are, if anything, more attuned to a complex modern world than to the simpler bygone age in which they were formulated. In so doing I shall offer functional explanations for the roles of individual autonomy, for the acquisition of private property, for the transfer of human and material resources under a regime of private contract, and for the protection of persons and property from aggression afforded by the tort law.

These first four rules constitute the law that is appropriate to some form of a minimal social state, and cover much of what a good legal system should desire. These rules are, however, not sufficient for a well-functioning legal system, for it is necessary as well to specify the limited circumstances under which private individuals and the state need not show an absolute respect for private rights, but should be allowed to force persons to surrender their property in exchange for some form of just compensation. None of these rules, however, makes peace with one of the persistent themes of modern society—the pervasive desire to engage in acts of redistribution, be it through direct transfers or mandated benefits that are imposed upon parties, typically employers in the private sectors. In Chapter 7 I therefore try to indicate both the perils of these forms of redistribution and some way, a flat tax, to allow them to go forward, but in a constrained and responsible way.

Thereafter in the second half of the book I discuss some applications of the general principles in certain areas of liability that have themselves been of general social concern. In Chapters 8 and 9 I deal with the many common contemporary restrictions on employment contracts. In Chapter 10 I discuss the more specialized topic of the liability for financial loss from professional negligence. In Chapters 11 and 12 I trace the evolution of product liability law. In Chapters 13 and 14 I turn to questions of corporate law, and in Chapter 15 I round out the discussion with an examination of environmental concerns. The book then concludes with the overview of alternative perspectives. I realize that there are many topics that this book could cover which are excluded from it, and for which the simple solutions that I advocate may not provide the full answers. There is only passing treatment of health care and education, both areas that suffer from massive levels of government involvement that have generated few if any associated gains. But it is not possible to tackle all the ills of the world in a single book, so I hope that concrete topics discussed here will provide a convenient framework that allows the analysis of similar topics that fall outside its direct scope.

I

Cutting through Complexity

1

The Virtues of
Simplicity

"Simple rules for a complex world" gives voice to an important social paradox. Everyone today agrees that the world has become more complex, and will become only more so in the future. The onrush of technology, the explosion of information and communication, the increase in population, and the constant migration of people across national borders are all phenomena that are so familiar and well documented that it is pointless to elaborate on them here. Alongside these general developments there has been a massive increase in the frequency and complexity of the legal rules that govern society. As a matter of individual self-survival, there is ample reason to become accustomed, perhaps inured, to the raft of complex legal rules that govern every aspect of human behavior. As a practical matter, the situation is not likely to change suddenly or soon. But the current situation is neither inevitable nor desirable. As a normative matter, the conventional view of the subject has matters exactly backward. The proper response to more complex societies should be an ever greater reliance on simple legal rules, including older rules too often and too easily dismissed as curious relics of some bygone horse-and-buggy age. Yet these rules have been cast aside in favor of approaches that at every turn frustrate the very human talents and initiatives they are supposed to protect and foster. My purpose in this book is to develop a set of simple rules capable of handling the most complex set of social relations imaginable, whether in the United States or anywhere else.

I therefore offer a set of universal prescriptions whose intrinsic desirability is not tightly bound to the controversies of our day or indeed to the legal and social environment within the United States. In one sense this view is decidedly unfashionable, for it is commonplace in writing about comparative law to stress the endless differences between the laws of one country and those of another. But the similarities in the underlying problems dwarf any differences in the responses to them. At the most general level, every society has to make choices between competing demands for scarce resources. In every society, the constraint of scarcity reflects itself in the self-interest of the individuals who compose it, while self-interest induces people to place themselves and their families and friends first—and everyone else far behind. To make matters more complex, that self-interest has both its good and its bad sides, again in all social settings. On the one hand, self-interest is often the source of high culture and great art, technological advance, intense effort, individual excellence, and a steady stream of reliable goods and services. On the other, self-interest is the source of theft, defamation, deceit, private intrigue, and abuse of office, both public and private. Thinking of ways to curb dangerous human impulses while allowing useful ones to flourish is a problem that confronts all societies in all ages, not just ours today.

The types of legal intervention best able to separate good human behavior from bad also show relatively little variation across cultures. Every system of law must address the acquisition of property, the limitations on the use of force, the enforceability of promises, the creation of state franchises and privileges, and the collection of taxes and the expenditures of public revenues. On issue after issue involving the use and limits of state power, it is easy to understand what is going on across cultures. Two people from different countries who share the same philosophical orientation find it easier to reach common agreement than two people from the same culture who do not. A free market enthusiast in the United States is far more likely to see eye to eye with a like-minded citizen of South Korea or Brazil than with the socialist who lives next door. It is really no surprise that Friedrich Hayek's classic, *The Road to Serfdom,* became the intellectual force behind the attack on socialist rule, even though most of its examples were based on the British experience with socialism half a century earlier.[1] The uses and problems of state regulation, the relationship between markets and politics, strike a responsive chord whenever and however these issues are raised. No impenetrable gulf of understanding separates the legal rules of one nation from those of another. It is no accident that the transplanted German Civil Code functions well as the basis of Japanese law, notwithstanding the enormous cultural differences between the two countries. The basic building blocks of all legal systems are largely the same.

Similarly, it goes without question that the expansion of government has taken place across the world, regardless of local differences in political practice or constitutional structure. With the decline of the socialist economies of the old Soviet Union and Eastern Europe, there is today (fortunately) very little support for the direct government ownership of the means of production. As a political theory today, the socialist remnant operates on a different level. At a personal level, it speaks to the alienation of the individual, stressing the need for caring and sharing and the politics of meaning. At a regulatory level, it seeks to identify specific sectors in which there is market failure and then to subject them to various forms of government regulation. It removes more and more activities from the private area by creating affirmative rights to housing, to education, to welfare, and to health care. The remnant of socialism works, as it were, on the installment plan, where it acts as a powerful counterpoint to the vision of the night-watchman state, chiefly concerned with the maintenance of public peace and order. In our revised set of social understandings, matters that were once regarded as subject to private decisions—land use before zoning laws or private negotiations before antidiscrimination laws—are everywhere on the agenda as proper subjects for public regulation.

SIMPLICITY ITSELF

In light of these recent developments, the common perception is that it is idle at best to long for a return to the imagined simplicity of some past gilded age. Criticisms of legal complexity are often greeted with a shrug by those who view the proliferation of legal rules as an unavoidable necessity, neither good nor bad in itself. This resigned pragmatic attitude toward simplicity is often reinforced by a conceptual ploy which claims that there really is no workable definition of simplicity in the first place. No one quite knows, it is said, how to define or measure legal simplicity. At the most basic level, this skeptical attitude is belied by successful movements of simplification that have taken place in previous generations. In the nineteenth century, both England and the United States witnessed enormous simplification of the system of land law; the technical forms used to transfer legal title and the cumbersome actions used to enforce it were swept away in a reform movement that produced simplified deeds and workable systems of public recordation which have successfully endured to the present day.

For simple pragmatic reasons, then, it seems most unwise to take the skeptical view that simple rules are a romantic pipe dream because of our collective inability to translate ordinary intuitions about simple rules into testable propositions. No definition will capture the subject with perfect certainty. But the opposite of simplicity is complexity, and it is possible to identify some of the critical elements that mark a set of legal rules as complex. Peter Schuck in his own study of legal complexity has sought to organize the field in a typically complex fashion, by reference to the four distinct variables that he regards as the markers of a complex set of legal rules: density, technicality, differentiation, and indeterminacy or uncertainty.[2] Dense legal rules are numerous and cover in minute detail all aspects of a given transaction: who may participate, what forms must be used; what terms are allowed; what approvals must be obtained. Technical rules are those which require a certain level of expertise to understand and apply. Ordinary citizens no longer can know whether they are in compliance with the law or are subject to its sanctions. Instead, they must take refuge and advice from highly paid professionals, most notably accountants and lawyers. The laws regulating business taxation, pension plans, and Social Security are both dense and technical. Indeed, these two characteristics often go hand in hand.

Differentiation in Schuck's terminology refers to the number of different sources of law that could be brought to bear in a given situation, often in an overlapping or inconsistent fashion. Thus federal, state, and local law all govern workplace injuries. Indeed, it is quite possible that more than one body of federal law will apply: workplace safety rules may require the use of buzzers at levels that the environmental regulations prohibit. Similarly, state and local landmark preservation statutes could prohibit the alterations that federal and state handicapped access statutes require; and the laws of collective bargaining could require a union official to take steps to protect current members of a bargaining unit only to run afoul of the antidiscrimination laws.

Numerous cases address the question of whether some federal statute has preempted (that is, displaced) some state or local law, a trend that shows no sign of abating. One common theme that runs throughout them is the extent to which a system of direct federal regulation works at cross-purposes with a system of private tort actions.[3]

Schuck's last test stresses the level of uncertainty that is generated in the effort to apply a given rule. The simplest rules by this test are those in which the answer to a single question of fact determines the legal outcome. Age requirements for voting or holding public office are usually offered as the simplest of simple rules because a single answer to an obvious question establishes legal rights and duties. On the opposite side of the ledger are those rules that are ever so much more common today: in order to decide whether a given product has a defective design, it is necessary to review a list of six, ten, or fifteen factors, all of which are relevant to the decision but none of which is decisive. In each case, both sides to the litigation are forced to play a game of "edges" in an inquiry that is structured to make it impossible to have dispositive answers to any question. Litigants therefore must seek to milk each factor for all that it is worth, and must recognize that an impressive victory scored on factor 4 could be wiped out by a calamitous defeat on factor 7. In essence, a question that necessarily has a yes/no answer—is the defendant liable to the plaintiff—is not governed by some simple on/off switch, but by a massive, costly, and uncertain inquiry.

Schuck has isolated most of the variables that we should regard as relevant to the question of whether certain legal rules are simple or complex. In good complex fashion, his list of relevant factors rules out any simple answer to the question of legal complexity, but hints at an array of rules that move from the very simple to the dauntingly complex—as befits our ordinary understandings of the subject. Yet oddly his list of factors does not direct its fire to perhaps the most critical relationship between the legal rule and the socially ruled: what is the cost of compliance, both public and private, with any given legal rule? Here the obvious connection is that the cheaper the cost of compliance, the simpler we can say the rule is, even if it is also at the same time foolish, perverse, and counterproductive.

In this area, first appearances can be deceiving: rules that look fearfully complex in fact may be quite simple in practice as long as it is easy to avoid their sting. Schuck cites the notorious and old common law rule against perpetuities as a vintage illustration of a complex legal rule: "No interest will be good unless it vests, if at all, within some life in being plus twenty-one years, with allowances for periods of gestation," is the classic statement of the modern rule. Nonlegal readers will not understand what this rule says or why it matters. Its full exposition took over five hundred pages in John Chipman Gray's classic nineteenth-century treatise on the subject; mastering the rule is a rite of passage that generations of property students would like to forget. At least one court has written that the failure to understand the rule is not grounds for legal malpractice. No layman will see the peril to the Republic in a gift (invalid under the rule) "to the first child of A (a living person) to pass the bar"—which could happen next Tuesday—and the unquestioned validity of a gift to "all the descendants of Prince Charles alive twenty-one years after the death of the last child of Prince Charles living at the time of this gift"—which could be a hundred years from now.[4]

It is not my purpose here to explain how the rule works, to illustrate its peculiar consequences, to explore its historical origins, to comment on the strength or weaknesses of its social justifications, or to propose some critical legal reform. Rather, it is to make one point about this rule that renders it simple: in practice it is easy for any lawyer to avoid its application. The rule looks to be a positive prohibition against the creation of certain kinds of gifts to living or unborn persons, and represents an incredible labyrinth for those unwary people foolish enough to fall within its grasp. But alongside the rabbit warren created by the rule runs a four-lane superhighway, open for all to travel, in the form of a standard savings clause, easily inserted into any will or deed, that will validate just about any conceivable gift that the harried testator or loving parent cares to make. In practice, therefore, the rule consumes few if any social resources, alters few if any private plans of gift or testation, invites no administrative response from judges or public officials eager to reassert their power in the face of private acts of evasion, and generates only academic disputes over possible reforms.[5] The utter absence of cut and thrust in this area is worlds apart from the web of income, estate, gift, and inheritance taxes that all too often engulf the most innocent of donative family transactions. In this arena each transaction (save those small transactions that fall outside the tax laws) must be shepherded through an ever changing legal thicket unless you just want to leave all your wealth to charity, or to the government. It follows therefore that the *minimum* condition for calling any rule complex is that it creates public regulatory obstacles to the achievement of some private objective. The mathematical rigor of the rule against perpetuities notwithstanding, the ready availability of the savings clause makes that rule a momentary distraction, a mere pussycat compared to modern forms of state regulation and taxation.

The availability of this safety hatch, then, makes the rule against perpetuities optional for property owners even though it looks prohibitory in form. In practice, the most ubiquitous legal safety hatch adds three words to the formal statement of any rule: *unless otherwise agreed.* Any rule that explicitly begins with these three words cannot in my view constitute a complex rule, for those who do not like what it provides will run and hide from its application. The escapees may well create private rules of conduct that are more complex than any the law could invent, as any member of a condominium association can attest. But why should we object if people want to make their own lives complex as long as they do not drag us down with them? And even here appearances are deceiving, for huge portions of modern contract law have little to do with setting the terms of the bargain between the parties. All too often the difficult problems arise when a straightforward business arrangement has to be made unduly complex in order to minimize the sting of regulation or taxation that no simple savings clause can deflect.

Even so, the phrase "unless otherwise agreed" does not obviate the need for all legal rules. "Unless otherwise agreed" is a workable strategy only where voluntary cooperation is a workable strategy. This rule cannot govern clashes between strangers over the acquisition and use of property; and it offers no safe haven from the coercive government powers of regulation and taxation. When the Internal Revenue Code supplies twenty-five different tax treatments for various forms of interest, then that legal regime is more complex than one which takes the blanket position that all interest payments are (or are not) deductible. If under one legal system a factory or summer home may be built without any prior government approval, then that system is simpler than one which requires approval by a local zoning board, which is in turn simpler than one which requires approvals by multiple tiers of state and federal regulators. In the world of government coercion— and it is a world that continues to expand—there is no "unless otherwise agreed" short of the unanimous consent of an ever longer list of interested parties: the private parties who initiate the transaction, the welter of interest groups that may oppose it, and the battalions of government officials who must approve its operation.

It is also a dangerous mistake to think of a rule as simple just because it is short. A legal rule that allows an employer to fire a worker only for "just cause" is not a simple rule, because the "unless otherwise agreed" option is not available, and the list of relevant considerations that helps determine which firings are for cause and which are not is almost endless. Likewise, any rule that says that individuals are entitled to automobile and health insurance as a matter of right is not a simple rule. The basic declaration of an affirmative entitlement necessarily requires some judgment as to how much insurance will be provided, what price will be charged, who will pay the subsidy, and what conditions allow for its discontinuation. The basic definition of the right is thus only the prelude to a whole host of subsidiary questions which cannot be resolved without extensive fact finding and legal interpretation. Indeed, any system of affirmative substantive rights is likely to be dogged by this difficulty.

Two more caveats are needed as well. First, the proposition that simple rules are best for a complex world does not imply that any simple rule could do the job. A rule that prohibits marriage or work is very simple in form, but disastrous in its social consequences. A less comprehensive rule that prohibits an employer from setting any fixed age for mandatory retirement looks on its face to be simple, but it is not for that reason alone desirable. People still have to be hired and fired. Therefore, when the firm can no longer resort to ordinary contractual solutions, then, ironically, more complex regulatory solutions will necessarily follow in their wake to determine whether workers can be demoted, receive salary cuts, be transferred, receive pensions, be eligible for on-the-job training, and so on down the line. The simple prohibition of one central contract term skews the rest, and it necessarily ushers in both a complex regulatory response and equally complicated responses from the regulated parties. None of that happens with the rule against perpetuities and its savings clause.

Second, some complex rules are both unavoidable, on the one hand, and not necessarily undesirable, on the other. The legal rules that regulate homicide must, in dealing with criminal intent, sort out gradations of purpose, intent, and knowledge; they must set the boundaries between murder, manslaughter, and killing by misadventure; and they must delineate the defenses in such cases: self-defense, provocation, abuse, insanity, and the like. The rules here are certainly complex by any conventional measure, and they could certainly benefit from a healthy dose of simplification.[6] Yet these are not the kinds of rules that I will study in this book. Historically, these rules are of very ancient origin, having long preceded the development of the regulatory state. More to the point, their impact on the day-to-day conduct of ordinary people is relatively slight, if only because the threshold condition for their application—the purposeful and premeditated killing of another person—is something that most people are able and eager to avoid in the conduct of their ordinary life. The criminal law of homicide thus provides its own safe harbor: don't kill anyone. In contrast, the rules regulating the use of property or the hiring and firing of workers, or even the selling of products or the buying and selling of companies, provide no similar haven. Rather these rules routinely intrude into the everyday lives of ordinary productive people, and are not directed to the destructive activities of a very small portion of the population. For my purposes at least, a complex rule is one that, in addition to meeting Schuck's criteria, has *pervasive application* across routine social activities, and is not directed solely to the dangerous activities of people who live at the margins of society. Legal complexity is not merely a simple measure of the inherent or formal properties of legal rules. It is also a function of how deeply they cut into the fabric of ordinary life.

With these qualifications, then, Schuck's four tests appear to provide a rough measure of the costs of private compliance, and hence of the relative measure of complexity, with which we have to deal. The fewer and the more accessible the inputs needed to make any legal decision, the simpler the legal system and, all other things being equal, the better its operation.

BEYOND SIMPLICITY

Even if simple rules can be distinguished from complex ones, why should anyone care? Why should anyone regard simplicity as an end in itself, instead of as a means to some greater end? Of course, simplicity does have the commendable characteristic that no one is against it; *ceteris paribus*, all persons, regardless of their position on the political spectrum, prefer a simple set of rules to a complex set. In principle,

even readers who disagree with my small-state, libertarian instincts
should accept at least this much of the analysis. The difficulties start
to mount with substantive claims that no simple rules can generate
the social benefits of complex ones. At this point much depends on
the choice of baseline or perspective. Relative to the state of nature,
any system of laws is complex; so the theme of simplicity would have
no independent or normative appeal. Instead, the preference would be
for rules that self-consciously maximize human happiness or welfare.
Today, however, we are as far removed from the state of nature as
can be imagined. Relative to the world as it now operates, simplicity
becomes a useful *test* for deciding whether or not a proposed legal
reform will *improve* human welfare, even if no set of incremental
changes could maximize it.

Within professional philosophical and economic circles, "utility"
has become the all-purpose placeholder for those goods and consequences that are desired, either by individuals or by collectives. Accordingly the maximization of social utility becomes the objective of
a sound system of legal rules. Although I have from time to time been
of different minds on this proposition, I have now made peace with
myself and believe that these consequentialist theories—that is, those
which look to human happiness—offer the best justificatory apparatus for demarcating the scope of state power from the area of individual choice.[7] Often this approach is dubbed the "efficiency" approach
to justice, but that term should be taken with a grain of salt because
it tends to overstate the purely economic portions of the analysis: in
ordinary discourse, efficiency involves the selection of means to ends,
but the task for a legal system is often the selection of the ends themselves.

THE GREAT TRADE-OFF BETWEEN ADMINISTRATIVE COSTS AND INCENTIVE EFFECTS

In setting up these ideal rules, however, legal simplicity has some role,
for it reduces the costs necessary to achieve any agreed-upon end. But
how much simplicity is required? To answer this question it is essential
to consider the great trade-off, namely, that between social incentives
and administrative costs.

To set the stage, administrative costs cover all costs necessary to run
the legal system. They include the costs that private parties must bear

in their efforts to bring themselves into compliance with the legal rules, by finding out what the law is, how it applies to them, what they must do to comply, and how they must demonstrate compliance to a regulator. These costs also include the public costs of enforcing legal norms. The direct costs of inspection, monitoring, and supervising are included, as is the general overhead for the legal system. Finally, I include in administrative costs the costs of *error* in operating the legal system. Where legal determinations are unreliable and uncertain, parties will be hurt when they are falsely charged and sanctioned for offenses they have not committed, or they will be allowed to escape charge and punishment when they actually violate a legal rule. The more complicated the legal rule, the greater the likelihood that these administrative costs, including error costs, will be high. A system of deterrence, no matter how laudable its objectives, is easily thwarted by incorrect factual determinations in individual cases. Thus if guilt and innocence are found at random, there is no incentive to comply with a rule, for incurring the costs of compliance carries with it no release from legal liability. And if there is an inverse relationship between guilt and the finding of guilt, then it will pay the rational actor to *violate* the law to minimize its sting.

Error therefore leads into the second set of costs, which deal with matters of individual incentive and resource allocation. Any legal rule does more than assign right and responsibility after the fact. It also shapes the behavior of the individuals who are subject to that rule; bad incentives lead to inferior allocations of resources, that is, lower levels of output for any given set of inputs. Yet reaching the optimum is never a straightforward task. Generally the first ambition takes its cue from the Hippocratic oath: avoid harm, that is, make sure that the law provides no incentives for individuals to engage in antisocial acts. Thus a rule which pays people to kill strangers would be simple in form and perverse in consequence, because individual advancement is directly tied to the creation of social mischief. A rule that punishes people who kill strangers does a better job of aligning individual conduct with social welfare; yet even here the selection of an optimal level of fines and punishments is no small detail. Excessive deterrence could forestall socially gainful actions. Insufficient deterrence could allow them to multiply beyond all reason. Minimizing the *divergence* between private and social costs is one of the main tasks for any sound legal system.

Yet finding the level of optimal deterrence is typically a matter of compromise. The legal system places strong prohibitions on torture and often on capital punishment, if only because of a genuine concern with the dangers of public abuse of power. That upper bound on criminal sanctions makes it impossible to preserve ideal proportionate deterrence for all criminal offenses. As the level of criminality doubles, the level of sanctions cannot double along with it. The problem does not go away if we reduce sentences across the board so that only the most heinous mass killers receive the death penalty. Adopting this strategy reduces the intervals in punishment until they are smaller than the incremental private gains from crime, so that the criminal could be better off by committing more serious acts: killing a second person may make perfectly good sense if it reduces the likelihood of capture without increasing the anticipated severity of punishment. Escaping cleanly from this double bind is not possible; so the question of optimal deterrence becomes yet another illustration of "second-best" theory: finding that compromise solution which causes the smallest level of social dislocation.[8]

What is true for criminal sanctions is true in every area. First-best solutions are rarely, if ever, possible; thus the beginning of wisdom is to seek rules that minimize the level of imperfections, not to pretend that these do not exist. No contract, no association is ever bullet proof: no matter what rights, duties, institutions, and remedies are chosen, in some circumstances they will be found wanting. Bad outcomes are therefore consistent with good institutions, and we cannot discredit these institutions with carefully selected illustrations of their failures. Counterexamples may be brought to bear against any set of human institutions. The social question, however, is concerned with the *extent* of the fall from grace. The fact of the fall should be taken as a necessary truth, not a shocking revelation. Perfection is obtainable in the world of mathematics, not in the world of human institutions.

Within this framework, therefore, the social function of law is to minimize the sum of the administrative (including error) costs and the costs associated with the creation of poor incentives for individual action. This formulation of the problem is a reasonably well-known one, for it lies behind Guido Calabresi's famous articulation of the purposes of the law of accidents: minimize the sum of the costs of accidents, the costs of their prevention, and the administrative costs of the system.[9] The reason that as a matter of first principle simplicity is not the sole goal of any sensible legal system is that it seeks to minimize only one set of costs—the administrative ones—without regard to the impact that this action will have on the other key variable: the incentives to human action.

To see what is at stake, let us start with a reductio ad absurdum. If simplicity is the only goal of a legal system, I can think of just two rules for determining the outcome of a lawsuit that would satisfy a criterion of ultimate simplicity. The first of these rules says that the plaintiff always wins. It's an uncomplicated rule, which can be applied in all cases. If you don't like that rule, there's always its mirror image, which says that the defendant always wins. That rule is equally simple, and it is equally capable of straightforward application. The first of these two rules would generate a litigation explosion that would leave even lawyers a bit leery of its consequences. Its administrative costs would faze even the most determined defender of justice through litigation. As for the second rule, the defendant always wins, it would by indirection force society to revert back to a Hobbesian state of chaos. After all, if the defendant always wins anyone could do anything, since all legal constraints would go by the boards. So when I urge the adoption of simple rules for a complex world, I cannot mean the *simplest* rules that human ingenuity can devise. Simple legal rules should, then, establish a presumption that can be overcome for good cause, not an absolute imperative that leads to untenable extremes. It is then necessary to identify those factors that drive us back to a certain level of complexity. A universal manifesto is thus reduced to a simple rule of thumb: When in doubt, choose the simpler of two alternatives.

The most simple social organization—that is, lawlessness—has two essential features. The first is there are no administrative costs: lawyers earn nothing; policemen earn nothing; nobody earns anything for providing any kind of public service. Nor are there any errors in making legal determinations. So far so good. But the second element is less pleasant, for there is also no restraint on asocial forms of private behavior. The central trade-off that must be examined at all times is this: does the creation of some administrative structure—hiring a police force, formulating rules, electing people to public office, or minimizing errors in enforcement—also create some desirable incentives for individual behavior such that the gain from *this* particular administrative expenditure is justified in terms of the overall improvement in incentive structures?

This formulation raises the obvious question, What counts as a social improvement? And to that I can give only one answer: The limitations that the legal rule places on each of us is smaller than the freedom it generates because like restrictions are placed on other individuals. The social welfare is just the composite of the welfare of separate individuals under alternative legal regimes. If a system costs each person $10 more to operate than its previous alternative, but generates $11 more in benefits for each person constrained by it, there is an allocative improvement that justifies the administrative costs. There are difficult cases where the size of the costs and benefits is hard to measure, and their distribution may be skewed in awkward fashion. But these difficulties are directed not to the fundamental question of whether some form of social control is necessary, but rather to the second-order question of how far that control should go. The basic desire for social improvements, even at some administrative cost, is the only argument that allows us to escape the brutish Hobbesian world. Some use of public force, funded by general taxation, will create desirable incentives well worth their administrative costs (including the costs of erroneous enforcement).

The basic trade-off between administrative costs and improved incentives for private behavior is always with us. The terms of that trade are not constant across all circumstances: how much more regulation is desired depends on how much is already in place, and on what we hope to achieve with the additional forms of social control. Although initially the inequality may point to the creation of a state, it surely does not always point to an inexorable expansion of public control. The balance of social convenience shifts with the change in public projects. Having set the state in place, we are faced with the question of which way to go next. Here it turns out that there are four basic possibilities. It is best to set them out clearly.

1. An increase in administrative costs will lead to the creation of superior incentive structures.
2. An increase in administrative costs will lead to the creation of inferior incentive structures.

3. A decrease in administrative costs will lead to the creation of superior incentive structures.
4. A decrease in administrative costs will lead to the creation of inferior incentive structures.

These four possibilities represent two easy and two difficult cases. There are genuine trade-offs in the first and fourth cases. With the first, we get better legal rules at a higher cost, and hence have to decide about the relative magnitudes of the costs and the benefits that further legislation brings. With the fourth, we face the same trade-off in reverse, and have to decide whether the savings in administrative costs is dissipated by the creation of inferior incentive structures. Again the question of relative magnitudes is inescapable. The second and third cases are kinder, for they yield easy results. The second case is the one universally to be avoided, while the third is to be universally embraced. If we can have better incentives for ordinary behavior at lower cost, who should be opposed?

These four alternatives shed light on the tortured modern legal situation: Too often we treat the second case as though it were the first, and aim to create more complex legal structures that in fact lead to inferior social outcomes, most typically by strangling well-functioning competitive markets for the provision of goods and services. Socialism, writ large, is the most powerful illustration of the second possibility. But many forms of regulation of land, goods, and services in the United States fall into that category as well. Additional public money spent on administration can completely muck up the system of production. Today we resort to more and more administrative controls and receive less and less in exchange. That unhappy state of affairs means that there is an enormous and welcome political opportunity for any political party which understands that by doing less government will achieve more. Getting rid of the administrative underbrush should clear the path to higher overall productivity. To the extent that there are real gains on both fundamental dimensions, everyone should be left far better off—except perhaps a lobbyist pushing or fighting special-interest legislation.

The basic problem, then, may be approached in two ways. In an ideal world, the decision as to whether any government program is desirable always boils down to the trade-off between incentives and administrative costs. In this context simplicity does not operate as a trump. The second approach situates the inquiry in the current social situation, where the biases toward overregulation make it unwise to accept the detached and agnostic view of legal simplicity that pure theory demands. Now the presumption should be set in favor of a simplification of legal rules. While the goal of a society without government may rightly be dismissed as utopian, the goal of a society with less government should be paramount. It is time to edge back toward the state of nature.

2

The Enemies of
Simplicity

Let us suppose for the moment that my critique of the modern regulatory state makes sense and that legal reform should proceed in the direction of simplicity. If so, then another paradox emerges: Why so little success in doing something about the situation? Why the constant push to legal complexity when its returns are so low, if not negative? In part the explanation lies in the inexorable pressure exerted by innumerable special-interest groups. But in addition, ideas are at work that lead the vast mass of disinterested people to keep a receptive ear open to the claims of regulation. In this context, I think that two of them deserve special attention. The first of these is the innocent but often fatal impulse to achieve perfect justice in the individual case. The second is the false belief that the complex forms of regulation which work within small, voluntary groups can be duplicated in larger, impersonal social settings. Both points need some explication.

PERFECT JUSTICE

The desire for justice in the individual case is one of the strongest forces shaping the operation of legal systems. A great deal of law is made or applied in the context of individual cases, before both judges and administrators. Within that framework, the stated function, as well as sworn duty, of the judge or administrator is to apply the general law to the facts of a dispute in order to reach the correct result.

An error in outcome is a miscarriage of justice which undercuts the moral authority of the law and reduces its effectiveness in the control of human behavior. It is therefore understandable that to avoid these injustices considerable resources are devoted to developing procedures that allow for the orderly presentation and evaluation of the relevant evidence.

The demand for justice is often regarded as sacred, as a good beyond price. Unfortunately, in one critical respect the thirst for justice is similar to the demand for any other desirable commodity. The demand for justice is subject to the law of diminishing returns. The initial improvements in the legal system come easily: the law can give all persons notice of the charges that are brought against them; it can give both sides an opportunity to present evidence and to cross-examine the witnesses for the other side. Implementing these common rules of natural justice will lead to major improvements in the legal system, relative to one that contains no procedural safeguards. But perfect justice demands more than incremental improvements in the operation of the system. It aspires to rooting out error in every individual case. Simple rules do not meet that exacting standard. At best they are only tests; and tests are rules of thumb that work most of the time, but are known and expected to fail some of the time. To adopt a simple rule therefore is to make an open acknowledgment that the rule cannot be perfect because it will generate an unjust outcome in at least one case, and doubtless in more. Even if we cannot identify which case that is, we know that the simple rule decisively thwarts the goal of perfection.

Complex rules avoid so gross and impolitic an admission up front. If the law can identify enough factors, can indicate the ways in which they should be taken into account, can specify the appropriate burden of proof, and can provide for the exhaustive collection of evidence, then maybe, just maybe, the legal system will reach the heady level of perfection to which it aspires. The upper potential of performance in a complex system is always higher than it is in a simpler system that confesses its weaknesses at the outset, and accepts not merely the possibility, but also the certainty, of bad outcomes and compelling counterexamples. Yet the gains from seeking perfection are an illusion, for with complexity come the opportunities for gamesmanship that will be part and parcel of social life so long as resources are scarce and individuals are motivated by self-interest. The relevant comparison between simple and complex rules should be conducted not in the language of aspiration, but in the language of realizable achievement. It is that more humble task which simple rules best discharge, for their relative cost-effectiveness and certainty forestall the vast amounts of intrigue brought into the legal system by the relentless, if naive, pursuit of perfection. The only question for the legal system is how it will make its errors, not whether it will make them. Simple rules are adopted by people who acknowledge that possibility of error up front, and then seek to minimize it in practice. Complex rules are for those who have an unattainable vision of perfection.

Several examples show the tension between simple rules and the search for perfection. Consider first the traditional rule that says that certain forms of contracts (such as those for the sale of real estate) are enforceable only if contained in a written document signed by the party against whom enforcement is desired.[1] The writing is only a formality; the true heart is the substantive agreement between the parties over the terms of the contract of sale. Insisting on the writing requirement necessarily dashes some legitimate expectations, for some people will back out of solemn oral engagements to sell property. A rule that dispensed with the writing requirement would never concede the injustice in a particular case, but would allow testimony by the aggrieved party about the terms and conditions of sale. In principle, it could achieve success in 100 percent of the cases. But the sad truth is that the great engine of cross-examination cannot keep pace with a prepackaged lie. Allowing oral contracts for the sale of land raises intolerable questions of whether certain conversations were a completed contract or merely a preliminary negotiation. Even if it is a completed deal, an oral contract leaves open serious questions as to what was agreed over subsidiary terms (who keeps the fixtures? which side has to arrange the financing? when may the buyer move in?). The writing requirement, announced in advance and well known by all professionals who work in the business, thus *channels,* to use the standard phrase, complex negotiations into safe paths. Perfect justice is not achievable, but the security of transactions is advanced, for the vast volume of routine real estate transactions moves along far more quickly and serenely with simple forms than with a labored inquiry into the manifestation of joint intentions.

The modest insights that dominate standard commercial practice should carry over to other areas of law, where the same trade-offs are often required. But too often the simple solution is disregarded in favor of complex solutions whose intrinsic unreliability offsets their ostensible substantive superiority. To give yet another example, the traditional Social Security law (which I would not defend in any of its substantive particulars) has long struggled with the question of how to take into account the asymmetrical positions of men and women. For years the law made no distinction between the contributions extracted from male and female employees, but it did make distinctions in determining who is entitled to payoffs under the fund. Until recently, one principle (whose wisdom could be debated) was that survivors' benefits were paid to widows without proof of dependency on their husbands; but the converse did not hold: widowers had to prove their dependency on their wives in order to be eligible for the same set of benefits.

So why the difference in approach? Here is not the place to question whether dependency is an appropriate tool for structuring Social Security benefits. In truth there is almost no connection between what any employee puts in and takes out of Social Security. The entire system is so riddled with anomalies that it works against the interests of men and women alike. (A sensible pension system would just allow the insured to designate a beneficiary and be done with it.) But if dependency is relevant, then differences in work and family patterns should make a difference. If, as Justice William Rehnquist concluded, fewer than 3 percent of men are dependent on their wives for support, proof in individual cases seems to be appropriate to avoid overpayment in 97 percent of the cases. If close to 90 percent of women are dependent on their husbands (a figure that is likely to continue to fall), proof of dependency adds extensive administrative costs while weeding out very few cases. The split rule may look inelegant, but it does tend to minimize the sum of the costs of administration and error in running a huge social system. It is perhaps for that reason that a sharply divided Supreme Court struck the scheme down on the ground that the discrimination between men and women was not justified by the administrative savings and greater reliability that it produced.[2] Now the Congress is in fact faced with a choice of vastly liberalized benefits or dependency hearings in a very large number of cases, and for what social end?

The insistence on inferior results is not confined to Social Security. Over and over, the courts and legislatures have decided that sex classifications must be ignored in determining such matters as pensions, automobile insurance, and drinking age because what everyone concedes to be a good fit is not perfect. Do we want a situation where women at eighteen are not allowed to drink beer because men of the same age are ten times more likely to drive under the influence of alcohol?[3] Or one where the insistence that men and women pay the same rates for automobile insurance, as in New Jersey and California, sends the insurance companies scurrying for female customers and makes them shun male applicants who would, if allowed, be willing to pay higher rates?

The modern rhetoric condemns all these classifications as stereotypes, and scarcely pauses to note that as statistical generalizations the basic propositions are true beyond a doubt. It is often said that the symbolic effect of these classifications can stigmatize and demoralize, and so it does in some cases. But losses of dignity are hardly eliminated when false overgeneralizations are adopted to ease the sting of true ones: there are also corrosive social losses, coupled with massive public cynicism, when everyone knows that the legal rule rests on factual assumptions at manifest odds with social reality. Indeed, one reason to prefer private to social decisions is that they can often go beyond a single characteristic in making their decisions. No public body could seek to individuate the drinking age beyond the obvious sex classification. But private insurance companies (except those constrained by regulation) can take into account territory, miles driven, type of vehicle, prior driving record, and a host of other variables before setting the rate. They thus provide a set of tools whereby over time the basic stereotypical features will gradually lose significance as other variables are added to the mix. No one should trumpet the differences that do exist as evidence of individual moral superiority. But by the same token, no one should ignore the genuine allocative dislocations that do take place when reliable, if imperfect, information is excluded by fiat from the decision-making processes of all institutions, both public and private.

This insistence on uniform rules raises yet another paradox. A rule that refuses to make sex-based distinctions, for example, appears on its face to be simpler than one which builds them in at ground level. But to this objection, there are two rejoinders. First, the refusal to make one strong distinction does simplify matters. Instead, the legal prohibition drives insurance firms to search for "neutral proxies" that are more numerous, less reliable, and more costly than the simple test that they displace. So the key questions become the numbers of miles driven per year, or the age of the car, or the number of accidents. These elements are always relevant in calculating rates, but too much of a good thing becomes a bad thing. Both good and bad drivers have accidents. Other variables, such as sex, do not become irrelevant simply because the accident history changes. To stress accidents and ignore sex (or age) is to countenance sharp swings in premiums not justified by all the available data. And it is to invite further complex maneuvers by companies who are barred from taking into account information that everyone knows has some predictive value. Often these strategies skirt the edges of the law, or cross the boundary into illegal territory. Yet when that illegality is detected, the misguided regulatory pressures that led to the illegal behavior are quickly forgotten, while the hue and cry once again rises for stricter regulations and heavier penalties. In the end, therefore, the rejection of one simple test creates powerful, if indirect, institutional incentives for the adoption of yet more complex rules.

Second, recall that the case for simple rules is not a case for no distinctions, or no rules. To ignore the significance of sex in matters of pensions and regulation is to cut ourselves off from information that has great predictive value for the behavior of large classes of individuals, even if it does not tell us much about any individual case. Often *one* critical distinction helps to organize large areas of social life, especially where there is no close proxy. Here it is not a case of getting the glass half empty or half full. We should celebrate tests that give us a 95 percent fit to their chosen end, and not bemoan the 5 percent of cases that stand between us and some unattainable perfection.

INFORMAL NORMS AND LARGE GROUPS

A second bias leading to the adoption of complex rules involves a hasty generalization from successful ordinary experience. Most individuals live much of their lives in settings with families and small groups whose operations are governed by an elaborate set of informal norms that are difficult to articulate and to write down. They often have little surface generality, and are bound to particular contexts, circumstances, and situations. The network of obligations for one family may be vastly different from the network adopted by another. There may be one division of responsibility for washing the dishes and another for paying the bills. Some small groups may be rigidly hierarchical while others may rely on a more equal distribution of power and responsibility. The distribution of tasks in any of these manifold settings may well appear to be unfathomable or irrational to persons outside the group, beyond the gravitational pull of the pressures that govern its collective life. But over a large percentage of cases the observed amalgam of practices leads to stable and prosperous relationships.

Why are these small groups often able to respond well to a complicated set of informal norms? First, to use the technical terminology of the modern welfare economist, there is a very high degree of interdependence in individual utility functions—each member of the group has to take to heart the interest of the other group members in making decisions. That is, within a family or small group, you are not dealing at arm's length with a stranger, but interacting with *preselected* people to whom you are bound, as the older lawyers used to say, by natural love and affection. If these relationships work well for the other people within the group, you will regard your life as being better for that reason alone; if they go badly, you will regard your life as being worse. In other words, there is a kind of benevolent interaction in which by helping somebody else you will be able to improve your own position as well. In practice, this interdependence reduces the amount of time family and group members have to spend keeping watch on each other, for they have fewer (not no) worries about sneaky behavior and underhanded conduct. A relationship of trust reduces the need for formal legal sanctions and protections. The conflicts of interest that are part and parcel of daily living are likely to be less intractable within a close-knit group than within a loose assemblage of strangers, dealing not from affection but at arm's length.

A second significant feature of small groups is that each member knows a lot about the people he or she cares about. People figuring out a course of action to pursue usually do not have to make a wild guess about what other people in the group desire or think. They have seen them in similar situations before; everyone knows who likes coffee black and who likes it with cream. That knowledge makes it possible to anticipate what others are likely to want and how they are likely to respond. It is then easier to engage in coordinated activities without first securing a formal agreement that might be appropriate in other settings. An outsider may find it difficult to understand the elaborate set of informal conventions that any group adopts, but that is scarcely of any importance for gauging its internal success. As long as the participants know what the informal norms require, group life can continue apace, without any external legal intervention. The internal group norms are complex; the legal norm is typically one of non-intervention in internal group affairs—the simplest rule of all.

Third, within small groups there is less of a problem than in large groups with asymmetrical payoffs to different individuals over the course of a single transaction. All parties are in the relationship for the long haul. If there is one particular deal in which one group member does better than the other, there is no need to worry about squaring the accounts forthwith. Because of the reciprocal interactions, it is likely that the person who wins one day will lose the next, and vice versa. As a result, there is less reason for anyone to pause to think about the distributive shares of a common venture, or winning and losing. It is sufficient to get on with the ordinary business of life, and the returns will even out over the long haul. The social rules for the division of gains and losses may be complex, but they are adopted by trial and error and modified by informal adjustment. In a sense, the rules are of uncertain authorship; they just "show up" without promulgation from some central authority. Their soundness is not measured by any external standard. Instead, a quiet incentive structure works to ensure their institutional success.

There is still the question of whether small groups can tyrannize over their own members. That is surely the case if these groups are allowed to exercise coercive powers over their members. But critical to the success of this informal system is that it lacks any sovereign power of its members. Those who do not like the group can leave or quit unless they obtain concessions that make staying more to their liking. This exit option is never cheap, but it becomes cheaper whenever group members think that they have received a raw deal. And it is far cheaper to quit a small group than it is to emigrate from the territory of an oppressive political entity, where the price for exit (if it is allowed at all) is the abandonment of property, friends, and attachments associated with the place that was once called home.

Within these limited and specialized settings, then, many forces bind people together without any express legal intervention from the state. The cooperation among group members will not necessarily endure all trials and tribulations. If some wrenching all-or-nothing choice arises (do we choose A or B as our head?), the informal peace-keeping mechanisms may well break down. That one decision may loom so large that long-term reciprocity becomes unable to balance the accounts between people on some later date. It is now or never, and the group that cannot settle its differences is likely to divide, often with bitterness: married couples may get a divorce; children may leave home; a club may disband. But over the wide range of routine day-to-day situations that constitute social life, these groups can and do rely on informal mechanisms of social control to keep themselves together. There is little if anything that any legal system could do to improve upon the delicate systems of sanctions and rewards that small groups are able to set for themselves.

The move from voluntary small groups to large political associations is a move from close connections to impersonal relationships. So profound a shift leads to major changes in the basic dynamics of the situation. The elements of trust and reciprocal dealing, the network of informal rights and informal sanctions, dwindle in effectiveness once that shift is made. Other mechanisms for decision must be found or invented. As the complex network of informal constraints inevitably breaks down, what ought to take its place?

The law could choose divergent strategies to respond to social problems in a world of countless strangers. One is to develop a complex network of detailed substantive obligations that mirror the elaborate set of informal norms used to hold smaller groups together. In essence, the law could create a command economy. It could try to figure out a social analogue to who does the dishes and who pays the bills—and call this a form of industrial policy. This approach treats an entire society as though it were a "family" writ large. Since the public family is far larger and more complex than any private one, the fair implication is that complex rules become strictly necessary for a complex society—just as the conventional wisdom claims. Someone must find a way to bring large numbers of people together under a common roof. And legal rules are the means by which that union can be achieved.

Yet the analogy does not hold, given the radical change in underlying conditions. First, the costs of monitoring the behavior of others becomes far higher, for as the size of the group expands the power of direct observation weakens. Yet by the same token the need for monitoring increases as well, for the bonds of reciprocity and interdependence are far weaker when faceless connections displace intimate relations. But the massive administrative costs of any precise system of public enforcement swamp whatever gains the system of regulation might in principle offer. The movement from small to large groups requires a shift from informal to legal sanctions. Legal sanctions cannot hope to perform at the same level of specificity and reliability achieved by informal sanctions in small groups. The movement from small to large groups cannot be accomplished by codification in laws of the informal standards of good conduct. As the tools of enforcement become more costly and cumbersome, a lower—and more realistic—level of aspiration becomes ever more critical.

That said, there is a second approach that promises far greater returns. It is to assume that the function of the law is to set the spheres of hegemony for each person. The insistence on the autonomy of the person, and on the dominance of private over collective property, is an effort not to promote greed and selfish behavior but to create many small separate domains in which informal norms can take over, at far greater precision and lower cost. A legal rule that calls for noninterference in the ordinary life of the family is one such rule. It recognizes that huge areas of personal behavior, from child raising, to sexual conduct, to financial affairs, are best regulated not by one collective response from the center, but by many smaller and autonomous groups pursuing their ends by means that they devise for themselves without popular or electoral approval. And similar rules can be developed for small groups. To the external world, the sign is "keep off." Within the membership, any number of different divisions of power and responsibility may be chosen by mutual agreement.

The systemic consequences of this second approach are desirable. As the frequency of these small islands increases, it becomes easier to organize lots of transactions between strangers, given the wide range of choices. The sting of exclusion in any individual case is offset by the increase in the range of choices in the aggregate. In contrast, when those diverse interests are required to fashion a collective decision by majority rule over their common destiny, political intrigue and factional strife can place massive strains on the political system. In trying to achieve so many ends for so many diverse and different people, the political system only ends up disappointing them all. It is in this sense regrettable that so many calls for multiculturalism instinctively demand greater government involvement in establishing the rules and symbols of social life. The differences in cultural views and elaboration will not be resolved harmoniously by political debate, even though they may be determined by fiat through majority rule. But no one should think that the outcomes that result from protracted political conflicts approximate those that come within a country mile of satisfying some ideal of unanimous consent. A system of limited government—one that does a few tasks well—is far more likely to achieve social harmony than a system of government that unleashes the warring impulses of clashing political forces.

The respect for autonomy leads to a welcome fragmentation of political power, which in turn goes a long way to protect the choices of a minority from the control of the majority. The diversity of informal rules and practices can be kept free of the leveling effect of any standardized legal system. But the initial strategy of breaking large problems into small ones does not answer one question, which is, how do members of different families and different groups interact with strangers? Here the situation changes because the postulates of trust and reciprocal benefits no longer hold. To illustrate, one of the basic precautionary rules about trading across national boundaries is: beware any transaction in which your trading party has *both* the goods and the money at the same time. With spot transactions, if the parties cannot square the accounts at the time, then they may never be able to square them at all down the road. Since the informal sanctions are too weak, other safeguards have to develop. Entire social institutions—escrow agents, brokers, middlemen of all sorts—have grown up to handle this one difficulty: what is the sequence of performance, as it arises in ordinary commercial transactions? But while self-help mechanisms are critical in dealing with these trades, matters are always made easier if the prospect of legal enforcement backs up the set of business sanctions that the parties are able to develop for themselves.

There is yet a second reason that transactions with strangers often take a form different from the form of those within an informal group. Within an informal group, it is usually inappropriate to resort to an explicit price system to allocate goods and services. Mary does not have to enter a winning bid in order to have an extra portion of ice cream, and Charles does not have to pay for the extra time he spends in the shower. Because the likes and dislikes of people are well known, it is possible to allocate the various benefits of family life by informal mechanisms that require each person to reveal something of his or her own desires and preferences, and to show why they should be entitled to special weight in the light of known differences in taste and temperament. Most people are very reluctant to reveal that kind of sensitive information to the butcher or the baker. Instead, one of the major objectives in transactions with strangers is to find rules for exchange, ones that do not require public disquisitions on private weaknesses. When you want to buy a loaf of bread, you are not eager to disclose your psychiatric vulnerabilities to a sales clerk. An impersonal relationship, a contract of sale that speaks to buyers and sellers generally, is a welcome development because it allows you to hand over the money and the clerk to hand over a loaf of bread in a cordial, but proper, fashion. It is for good reason therefore that many of the traditional legal rules simply postulate two persons, A and B, who are both anonymous and impersonal. In such arrangements, unlike family exchanges, generality is more important because it serves to facilitate the impersonal transactions desired by all. It is possible to formulate a set of rules by which people with widely divergent backgrounds can come together for some limited purpose and thereafter go their separate ways.

The two basic strategies for social organization thus look to very different decision procedures. The effort to specify elaborate rules for large and impersonal collectives runs into the major obstacle that each of many different groups will hold out for some special advantage of privilege that other groups will oppose. Majority rule allows one faction to impose its will on another, while a requirement of unanimity allows one group to hold out against the common will. The alternative strategy does not seek to gain either majority will or unanimous consent, or any mix between. Instead, it seeks to avoid both horns of the dilemma by creating separate zones of influence, where smaller groups are able to achieve through informal means greater cohesion and consensus, and to leave old groups and to form new ones when old alliances fail or become outmoded. As a society becomes larger and more diverse, the difference between these two approaches becomes more manifest. The level of social problems can only increase if the law responds to social diversity by lodging greater power in the center. A far better approach is to encourage the development of a network of voluntary transactions in which individuals deal on their own behalf with trading partners of their own choice. For the legal system to succeed at its task, it needs to adopt legal rules that are in harmony with its own intrinsic limitations. The question is what legal rules will allow the differences between public law and private association to flourish in responsible fashion. In the next section of this book, I seek to develop the simple rules which, rightly understood, and taken together, go a long way down that road.

II

The Simple Rules

3

Autonomy
and Property

My attack on the current accumulation of complex rules has thus proceeded without offering any principled alternative to it. Now I will put aside the critique of the here and now and develop an alternative framework capable of covering the same ground with far greater effectiveness and far greater simplicity than does the current plethora of rules and regulations. In making this claim, I realize that no set of rules will be perfect in its application; indeed, knowing when to quit is one of the driving forces behind a set of simple rules. Nonetheless even though there are some daunting exceptions, these rules do have the virtue of offering solutions for 90 to 95 percent of all possible situations. Never ask for more from a legal system. The effort to clean up the last 5 percent of the cases leads to an unraveling of the legal system insofar as it governs the previous 95 percent. No single, carefully constructed hypothetical case offers sufficient practical reason to overturn any rule that has stood the test of time.

So with due recognition to the powerful counterexamples to every general proposition, the simple rules are self-ownership, or autonomy; first possession; voluntary exchange; protection against aggression; limited privilege for cases of necessity; and takings of property for public use on payment of just compensation. In this chapter I deal with the first two of these rules, which are devoted to autonomy and to the acquisition of private property. The linkage between them is that they set the original position against which all subsequent voluntary and forced exchanges should be measured. The right set of rules governing control over one's person and the assignment of ownership of property play an indispensable part in any social system that seeks to maximize the welfare of its citizens. Yet the justification of these rules has too often been the subject of consistent attacks. Here I seek to explain their fundamental place in any sound legal system.

INDIVIDUAL SELF-OWNERSHIP

The first of the rules is one of individual self-ownership. If you go around the world trying to figure out who owns each of us, you would find nothing writ in stone which says that self-ownership is a necessary truth. To put it another way, to deny the proposition of individual self-ownership is not to engage in any logical self-contradiction. Slavery may be an evil system, but it is not internally inconsistent. Yet this system is vastly inferior to a position of self-ownership, and the comparison of the two has led many authors in the natural rights tradition to posit the moral necessity of self-ownership. John Locke, for example, took the view that we could properly say that each person owns his or her own labor. "Though the earth and all inferior creatures be common to all Men, yet every man has a property in his own person. This nobody has any right to but himself. The labour of his body, and the work of his hands, we may say, are properly his."[1] He treated his position as a moral postulate, and not as a conclusion derivable from some other premise by some independent argument.

The conclusory case for his decisive premise has led other writers, most notably those who see a larger role for state control over both human and natural resources, to challenge his view by taking still a third tack. The centerpiece of John Rawls's magisterial *Theory of Justice,* published in 1971, is, after all, the proposition that the individual ownership of natural talents and abilities should be regarded as "morally arbitrary"; that is, though they may be taken into account in some extended scheme of political deliberation, they are hardly to be accorded any bedrock status. According to Rawls the principles of justice require, first, an effort "to mitigate the influence of social contingencies and natural fortune on distributive shares" and, second, "an undertaking to regard the distribution of natural abilities as a collective asset so that the more fortunate are to benefit only in ways that help those who have lost out."[2] Rawls strikes a modern nerve by noting that the *value* attached to individual attributes is not solely a function of intellectual abilities or moral virtues: it is easy to imagine Mozart's obscurity if he had been born into other circumstances. What is true of the great and the famous may well be true of the rest of us. However much work and character count in this world, luck plays a part as well: I was born in Brooklyn on April 17, 1943, and the uprising in the Warsaw ghetto began two days later.

The question then emerges whether there is a way to approach the initial ownership of human talents and skills that avoids the clash of moral absolutes that has so dominated philosophical discourse in this area. I think there is, and it proceeds by a kind of reverse engineering, which asks what kinds of overall social consequences can be expected from the alternative systems of ownership and control over persons that might be devised. In working out this analysis, it is important to keep in mind that the relationship between administrative costs and incentive effects outlined previously applies here as well. Start with institutionalized slavery. It does not fare well relative to a system of individual self-ownership even by the criterion of administrative costs. A system of slavery requires that someone establish who has rights in which persons, and since this has never been done by contract, even when legal, then it must be done by conquest and capture, a system that is far bloodier, uncertain, and, yes, complicated than one that begins with individual self-ownership and requires *no* acts of acquisition for people to obtain certain ownership and control of their own labor.

It seems clear, however, that the sustained moral objection to slavery does not rest on the administrative complications of setting up the system and keeping it running, however severe these may be. Rather it rests on the indignities that it heaps upon those who are its victims. Stated in familiar terms, the inability of slaves to say no (save on pain of torture) to whatever is commanded of them creates terrible incentives for exploitation by the owner. To be sure, if the owner has an outright interest in the slaves, his behavior will be somewhat constrained in that excessive use of, or harm to, the slaves today will lead to an overall reduction in their long-term capital value. (The Spanish slave owners in South America were more brutal than our own because the slaves reverted to the Crown after a fixed number of years, so that it was in the owners' interest to exhaust their value prior to surrender.) But the extent of the constraint on the owner is far lower than that which exists in an employment relationship that requires joint consent at the outset and that normally preserves the worker's right to quit at will—a very different and far more credible threat. Under slavery the gains to the owner will systematically fall below the losses to the slave. Even if one could demonstrate some odd exception to the basic rule, a per se ban on slavery (and one backed up by massive moral conviction) is surely the right social response, *even if* we take into account the welfare of *both* the master and the slave. The concern with simplicity, then, does not begin to capture the social resentment of slavery, but it is certainly congruent with the overall outcome.

So what other alternatives are possible? We can quickly pass by a system in which no one is able to acquire any rights to his or her own person, for it is hardly better than a system of slavery, and may well be worse. In it, no actions are illegal because there is no clear conception of law, so that even the problem of order cannot be solved. The real issue today lies at the opposite pole. Rawls's uneasiness with natural ability and good fortune has led to the widespread belief that all talents and skills should be regarded as some form of collective asset, to which other individuals have at least some presumptive attachment. Yet here again the dual concern with administrative costs and incentive effects weighs heavily against any collective solution.

To start with the transactional objectives, any system that begins with the collective ownership and control of individual talents builds a form of institutional paralysis into the very fabric of social lives. So long as A does not own A's labor, the Lockean argument proceeds in reverse: A is no longer entitled to sell A's labor, and therefore has less of an incentive to improve it. Likewise, things that are made by his hands are no longer his either, but instead belong (if they are made at all) to that group which owns the labor in question. Finding those individuals or groups who are co-owners in A's labor is no easy task, because no general normative theory could rely on the happenstance of ethnic membership or national identity to establish the set of persons entitled to share in A's labor, and in whose labor A is likewise entitled to share. The Lockean theory instantly generates a decentralized market whose benefits are lost when each of us is able to sell labor only with the approval of some unascertained class of other individuals. In the resulting confusion, we would all starve, as Locke himself recognized, before anyone could renegotiate the original rights that people have in each other. We thus create an initial position in which individual holdouts and blockades could forestall all forms of productive activity.

There is another way to state this objection to the Rawlsian principle. What, if anything, could be done to purge individuals of any of the advantages that they receive by natural talents, social contingencies, and good fortune? To make some progress in that direction, it would be necessary to know how this world would look if all these elements were banished from human life. Of course, it is easy to knock out caste and privilege on Rawlsian grounds. But these quickly fall on Lockean grounds as well, given that they are an affront to the free, independent, and equal status that all individuals should have before the law. What is quite impossible to do is to develop any system of rectification for the unending series of social wrongs attributable to inferior talents, unwelcome social circumstances, and bad luck. Although it is possible to identify an individual aggressor, no single person bears the responsibility for someone else's want of natural talents, bad luck, or unfavorable circumstances. Therefore, the effort to displace a system that begins with individual autonomy requires complex systems of centralized controls that must deal with the onslaught of demands for special dispensation. Yet if everyone is a victim, who should be taxed to respond to the enormous requirements that are required once the autonomy position is called into question?

Against this backdrop the rule of self-ownership shows its comparative advantage. Even though talent, circumstance, and luck play a role in human behavior, we all are spared an enormous administrative burden if we mutually renounce any claim to these assets of others. A rule of self-ownership, far better than any of its alternatives, allows us to move on with the business of life. A rule of self-ownership selects the *single* person to be the owner of each person's natural talent, and picks that person who in the vast majority of cases tends to value those assets the most: each obtains control over his or her own body. At least for adults (and there are, of course, qualifications for children), the rule offers the shortest path from initial entitlement to productive human activity.

To be sure, this institutional arrangement has its disadvantages, given that everyone is made to renounce claims on the labor of others. But overall the losses are small. To see why this conclusion holds, it is useful to resort to the method that Rawls himself developed to explain why natural talents are a collective asset. Place people behind a veil of ignorance and ask them to choose between legal regimes when they have knowledge of the general characteristics of human behavior but none of their own specific place in the world. The point of the exercise is to remove favoritism from the equation and to induce people to make judgments that perfectly align their individual interests with those of the larger social groups. With slavery the outcomes are easy to predict. Ask anyone to choose between two worlds: in the first each person has a 50 percent chance of being an owner, but also a 50 percent chance of being a slave. In the second, each person has a 100 percent chance of self-ownership. Who would prefer the former to the latter, even if the two were equally costly to operate, which they are not?

Now do the same thought experiment with Rawls's complex system, in which everyone has some partial claim on the talents of every other person. Self-ownership excludes each from control over the others, whether in whole or in part, but the self-control that is obtained in exchange is well worth the price that is paid. Net advantage, not total perfection, is all that one can ask for in a world where scarcity is everywhere. The additional output that is obtained is a tangible advantage to the liberal system of rights, and is not inconsistent with some limited measure of social protection against bad circumstances and disaster, as supplied, for example, by charitable assistance to the needy, a practice that does not figure prominently in the Rawlsian scheme.

In this regard, it is somewhat instructive to note that although the autonomy principle is frequently attacked in economic affairs, it is often powerfully embraced in other areas of human endeavor. In medical ethics, for example, one critical question is whether a patient has the right to refuse treatment that others think to be in his or her interest. In dealing with this claim, the manifest tendency in both law and moral thought is to ignore the interdependence of persons and to resist any suggestion that friends and families (much less partners and creditors) should have a say in the decision, no matter how much their personal or economic fortunes depend on the outcome. Likewise, there is a commendable refusal to hold that individuals are incompetent to deal with these decisions, even when the complex medical issues tax the depleted physical and emotional resources of the individual patient. There is at best an odd discontinuity between recognizing the individual's right to control matters of life and death, against the claims of others, and simultaneously endorsing collective control of talents and abilities in ordinary circumstances. Indeed, the only real exception to the principle of self-determination in medical affairs concerns the prohibition of active euthanasia, and its kindred prohibition of assisted suicide, both of which have rightly come under increased attack in recent years, notwithstanding the asserted interest of the state in the preservation of human life. The reason for the dominance of the autonomy principle is not any belief that people live in small social islands uninfluenced by and unconcerned with the interests and the behavior of others. It is that no other principle matches power with interest to the same degree.

The wisdom of this initial assignment of property rights in persons—the autonomy principle—is underscored by the consequences for human happiness and productivity that it generates over a very broad class of decisions vital to the welfare of each person as an individual. This rule establishes at very low cost a rule of ownership over all labor—and removes the need for any ministry of health to make decisions on matters of life and death, or any ministry of labor to assign people to particular tasks. In all affairs, decentralization of ownership necessarily follows from the principle of self-ownership. Its functional roots are so powerful that it should be treated as a moral imperative, even though the most powerful justification for the rule is empirical, not deductive.

First Possession

The second rule is directed toward the acquisition of property. Once it is accepted, we can abolish still other government ministries. Here again, the common law established a rule which, with some important theoretical qualifications, works in probably 80 to 90 percent of cases. It certainly applies with greatest soundness to land and chattels, our two most important assets. It is important to understand both why this rule works so well in many common cases and what limitations in practice nonetheless remain.

The simple rule is this: you take what you can get. It has the appearance of being a very egotistical rule. In the history of both Roman and Anglo-American law, it was called "natural occupation" or "first possession" for land or "the rule of capture" for wild animals and material things. The rule starts from the assumption that in the original position no person owns anything that is external to the self. But the world could not stay in that condition lest everyone perish from hunger. The transition from nonownership to ownership takes place unilaterally by individual acquisition. If somebody went out and grabbed something, then the rest of the world had to suffer, which is how collectivist critics of the rule have always put the matter. That is, however, the least favorable light in which to cast the issue.

The classical justification for this position, the Lockean theory of labor, hardly does anything to quell the critic. Why should a person become the owner of a natural resource when, as Locke said, he "mixes" his labor with it? In some cases the labor may constitute the largest amount of value in the thing, but that is by no means a necessary truth: those who remove oil from the ground may become instant millionaires by sheer good fortune and the labor and skills of other people. In any event, the prior question is why any person has the right to mix labor with external resources, and that challenge may be met only by reasoning in a circle, by showing that labor has already been added to the thing. If allowed to add labor at all, the person should at most get a lien on the common property equal to the value added by the labor in question. The unearned increment could still remain part of the commons, shared by all alike. There is much to commend in a system of labor, but it explains merely how individuals are entitled to the increase in value of the things that they do own, not why they own them in the first place.

The better explanation for the common law rule of individual ownership looks not so much at some magical relationship between the owner and the thing owned as at the systematic social consequences that are generated by the choice of different legal rules. Initially, it is clear that any rule will have its drawbacks, and the obvious objection to the first-possession rule is that it encourages a certain level of individual selfishness—grasping and greedy behavior. But as was evident from the discussion of the rule of individual self-ownership, a proposed rule can be subject to a strong objection and on balance still be socially desirable. To evaluate this, or indeed any other rule, it is necessary first to ask what other rule you could put in its place. One possibility is to have a rule that adopts the same basic form but with one small change in detail: a rule of *second* possession, whereby the second person who comes onto land or across a thing is the person who owns it, so that the race no longer goes to the swiftest, but to the merely speedy.

A rule of this sort has never been tried, but before it is dismissed out of hand as a straw man, it is important to understand why it is an invitation to social disaster. The only way there can be a second possessor is for there to be a first possessor beforehand. But who would undertake so dubious an honor of initial possession if the expenditure of private resources only creates a situation that allows someone else to capture the spoils? Rigorously enforced, this rule would have a damning incentive effect, for nothing could ever be subjected to private ownership. Of course, there could be efforts to evade the rule: you could ask a friend to take possession of something for an instant in order to set the stage for your triumphant entry, and you could reciprocate on some other occasion to even matters out. But if the second-possession rule were respected, a practice of this sort should rightly be condemned as a sham, given that the collusive behavior makes you a first possessor after all. Even if collusion were allowed, why require a complex set of side agreements, which may all too easily go astray?

It is possible to offer more complex variations of the first-possession rule. Thus one option is to conduct a lottery of sorts, wherein each member of the group (however defined) receives a certain number of tickets. The first possessor gets more tickets than anyone else and thus a greater chance to receive the prize at the end of the day. A system of this sort is now in use in the National Basketball Association draft (where players cannot be held in common), whereby the worst team in the league obtains the largest number of chances in the lottery, but not the automatic rights to the first player.[3] Yet this lottery is adopted by contract within a close-knit league, and its justification is to reduce the incentives of losing teams to throw games in order to obtain the highest draft choices in the following year. There are no similar incentive problems with respect to unoccupied land in the state of nature and no obvious ranking system on which to found the lottery. The complex system thus produces administrative drag without allocative gain, and is outperformed on both counts by the simpler system that treats possession as the root of title.

Yet there is no necessary reason to remain with some variation of the first-possession rule. But to depart from it requires embracing some regime of centralized authority—some strong system of state allocation—to decide how to parcel everything out to everybody over the face of the globe. Yet when it is needed most, any conceivable state is likely to be weak, or at best able to exert only partial control over a small portion of the earth's surface. When conditions are primitive, when survival is at issue, when transportation and communication are virtually nonexistent, it is whistling in the dark to believe that any form of central control could allocate natural resources among members of disparate cultures living thousands of miles apart. The state (or clan or tribe) that could not even make arbitrary assignments of property rights could hardly be expected to organize a sophisticated auction designed to sell natural resources to the user that values them most. It is difficult to conceive of who could conduct an auction in a world devoid of money and the rudimentary rules of exchange.

At this point the discussion of the first-possession rule takes the same path as the previous discussion of autonomy. It is one thing to defend the rule against its critics. It is quite another thing to argue that the rule enjoys the status of some necessary truth, which it does not. Like the autonomy rule, the first-possession rule imposes costs on those who are excluded. But also like the autonomy rule, it provides compensating benefits—most notably, the security of possession— that justify its place in the social order. The rule also allows for decentralized control of material resources at a low overall cost. Those who are unable to acquire goods by first possession are able to acquire them by purchase financed by money, goods, or land that they acquire from the use of their own labor. Since two individuals can make gainful exchanges without the participation of the rest of the world, the overall size of the gain is so large that we need not trouble ourselves over its distribution. Quite simply, the gains from the use or exchange of a very broad class of resources are higher than the losses others bear from exclusion. It is again an empirical matter, not a deductive one.

Precisely because the justification for the rule is empirical, it is possible to state something of the limits of its desirability, given the familiar trade-off between administrative simplicity and desirable incentives. A rule that allows the first possessor ownership of the soil is not likely to lead to a premature exhaustion of the fields. The owner who stakes out a bit of land can then decide how and when to cultivate it and when to let it lie fallow. Indeed, the long-term time horizons give the right incentives against overuse. One of the standard justifications for property rights self-consciously makes use of an agricultural metaphor: he shall reap only where he has sown. Simple boundaries enforceable at low administrative costs create optimal incentives for use.[4]

In dealing with wild animals, however, the same happy scenario may well not play out, for the hunter of a single buffalo or beaver gets all the gains from the animal captured but bears only a tiny fraction of the loss in the size and stability of the herd. A system of hunting territories is more expensive to administer than a first-possession rule applied to individual animals, so when consumption of animals is low there is really no reason to switch property regimes.[5] But when there is an external jolt to the system that stimulates demand—such as the arrival of French fur traders in Canada in the early eighteenth century—the system of first possession will yield to a different system of ownership. Exclusive hunting rights over discrete territories became the order of the day for fur-bearing animals that did not migrate across territories. In essence a somewhat more complex system of property rights (although one marked by clear borders) displaced the older rule when technological pressures created new demands that in turn justified greater restraints on individual choice. Yet here too the system was not one of centralized collective ownership by government. It was a movement to separate territories, each with private owners who now had the right incentives to trade off the value gained from present and future captures.

BREAKING THE CHAIN OF TITLE

A first-possession rule, be it for animals or territories, does not guarantee its own enforcement. Although modern lawyers tend to think of the law of property as concerned with land-use control and planning permits, the dominant concern in ancient legal systems was with dispossession through war and social unrest.[6] In a perfect world, a first-possession rule suffices because all subsequent transactions will be in accord with the rules of the game. But in a world filled with private violence and political corruption, it often happens that the great chain of title is broken beyond recognition. At this point, the familiar problems of the second best arise: As an administrative matter, it is most difficult to deal with remote events which authenticate title under a rule of first possession. Pragmatic considerations therefore tend to lend greater weight to recent events in order to stabilize relations for the future even if it is not possible to rectify the wrongs of the past. A complete legal system therefore has to confront two problems that an ideal system could ignore: title by adverse possession or prescriptive right is the first; relative title is the second. Each requires some explanation.

Title by Adverse Possession or Prescriptive Right

The problem of title by prescription or adverse possession arises when one person has unlawfully taken property from another and then continues to occupy it for a long period of time. At what point, if any, do the prescriptive rights of the wrongdoer ripen into a title that is good against the original owner? As a matter of justice the first answer one is tempted to give to that question is *never:* Why should anyone profit from his own wrong? And how can the mere passage of time convert the wrong of dispossession into a lawful act? But in practice all legal systems have adopted statutes of limitations to cope with the problem, so that if suit is not brought within some fixed number of years the property is lost—a simple rule that is far preferable to the more complex case-by-case determination that seeks to examine the mental states and the behavior of both the dispossessor and the dispossessed. Some rule of this sort is essential, first because it protects those titles that *are* valid from false suits brought by others, and second because it again creates a single owner needed to bring property back into the stream of commerce: who will purchase or improve land when someone else may be able to snatch it away?

Matters of prescriptive title become far more complex in cases where it was legally impossible for the original owner to bring the suit, as is the case in many of the Eastern European countries that have just emerged from communist rule. Here the conflicts of interest that are created are excruciating. On one side are the countless tales of deliberate dispossession of innocent people. On the other side stand the claims of innocent occupants who insist that too many years have gone by to undo past injustices without creating greater injustices in their stead. And standing outside the claims of the parties is the question of whether any society can go forward when uncertainties about legal title make any future deployment of land precarious.[7] The case is surely hard under any view of the world, and the responses in different countries have been far from uniform. On balance, however, the correct decision is to bar restitution in kind, leaving open the possibility of paying some compensation, however inadequate, for the property taken.

What has to be avoided above all is a case-by-case adjudication of a set of complex claims which will leave even the *winners* (to say nothing of the innocent losers) of particular suits hobbled by nightmarish legal uncertainty when they wish to deal with their reacquired property. It is not as though rectification can isolate one case and ignore all the others, for although that is a convenient and safe assumption for random cases of misconduct, it does not hold when systematic acts of injustice have taken place. The most obvious point is that acts of injustice do more than redistribute wealth among parties: they destroy the processes whereby wealth is formed and transmitted. There is less to go around than would otherwise have been the case, and no system of compensation can possibly offset the losses from two generations of abuse and neglect. The party who wins in one case may be able to collect something from the state treasury, but will be forced to help fund the claims that countless others can and will bring against the state. And all will suffer from the legal uncertainties over title in the decades necessary to identify and resolve these claims. Only part of that difficulty can be avoided by demanding redress from individual wrongdoers. Many of them have died, and have left their property to the next generation, or sold it to third parties, or both. The present possessors of the property are likely to have improved it substantially, but could not document either the cost or value of the improvements made.

There comes a point when the injustices are so frequent and widely distributed that the only choice is to correct all of them or to correct none. The choice seems clear. The dual concern with administrative costs and incentive effects normally protects vested rights. But in these strained situations, it flips over and tolerates the new set of holdings notwithstanding their illegitimate origins. At the very least, one needs a simple categorical rule of no restitution in kind of land to its prior owners. Even efforts to award compensation in individual cases seem counterproductive, and the best that can be done is to strip those few persons who still retain their ill-gotten gains of their booty, which can then be returned to the public treasury. And if this result seems, as it is, highly unsatisfactory, one lesson can still be learned. So central is the concern with stability of possession that heavy investments should be made to ensure that no violations of that principle occur in the first place. Prevention here dominates rectification. In ordinary times, one of the quiet heroes of the modern law is those boring systems for the registration of land titles that reduce to the vanishing point the likelihood of erroneous dispossession of real property.

Relative Title

The second major challenge to a system of first possession arises when neither claimant has the best claim to the disputed property. Thus if C takes property from B, which B has taken from A, A may surely recover the property from either B or C. In a world of perfect enforcement, this outcome would always happen, so that the problem of relative title would never arise. But the world has too many frictions to be called a perfect place. Therefore, if A has left the scene, what are the relative positions of B and C, when neither is the first possessor of the property? One possibility is to say that all illegitimate titles are of equal weight. Such a rule economizes on administrative costs, but the allocative consequence of that position is disastrous, for it means that once the rules of ownership are violated no form of civil order can be retained. B cannot recover from C, but in the next round neither can C recover from D, the thief who steals from him, and so on down the line. A single fault within the system destroys forever the possibility of maintaining civil order.

To meet this difficulty, courts uniformly hold that C cannot defend her possession against B by showing the better right of the third party, A (the so-called *ius tertii*), in any suit brought by B. Under this system, title becomes a relative notion, so that prior in time becomes higher in right, with first in time being just a special case of a general principle. With the passage of title, all higher claimants will either bring their suit or have their action barred by the passage of time, so that we are once again left with a single person vested with all the attributes of a common law owner.

The rules of property thus have a two-part structure with some considerable elegance. In the initial stage, first acquisition is best, and sets the stage for all subsequent voluntary transactions. But once an error has committed, then statutes of limitations force the wronged party to speak up or forever hold his peace. Yet unless and until the wronged party comes forward, the present possessor is immediately endowed with all the attributes of an owner as against the rest of the world. In ordinary situations this system is both sensible and durable. It is only in those cases where the wrong has been committed and the process of redress has been barred that we are forced to make the kinds of impossible judgments that now arise in Eastern Europe. If only the simple rule of first possession had been respected throughout!

COMMON PROPERTY

Thus far the rule of first possession creates a close analogy between the rules for the protection of individual liberty and the rules for the acquisition of property. Yet the range of natural resources is far broader than the range of differences between persons, and there is no guarantee that a rule of private property will necessarily dominate a rule of common or open property for all resources. The mix between property which is held in common and property that is reduced to private ownership is, indeed, as old as the law itself. The Romans, for example, began their discussions of property with the assertion that by the natural law, the air, running water, the sea, and consequently the seashore were things that were "common to all."[8]

Introducing forms of common property at the ground floor of the classical legal system cannot be viewed as the opening wedge of the modern welfare state, so the question is whether my general theories can accommodate not only private property obtained by first possession, but also forms of public property characterized by equal access, regardless of time, for short-term use. Here the Roman approach was to appeal to natural law, as if there were some permanent and necessary answer to the question of how property should be allocated and assigned. Yet if the judgments in favor of a first-possession rule (like those in favor of personal autonomy) turn less on deduction and more on empirical regularity, there is no reason to think that some theory of necessary or natural truth will be better able to account for those forms of property that are held in common, that is, those which offer open access to all people at once. The question is how to explain the existence of two strongly different types of property within the same legal system.

To solve the puzzle, it is again useful to revert to the trade-off between administrative costs and incentive effects that should shape any legal regime. First, the administrative costs of running a system in which property is held in common are not always as high as they might first appear. The system does not give the state power to decide who shall use common assets, and in what proportion; it is not some nascent version of zoning or permit system. Second, it deals well with the question of incentives and behavior. Recall that the basic empirical judgment for land and for personal property was that the benefits of a system of use and exchange justified in the long run the costs of exclusion that were imposed on others. But the relative magnitude of these costs varies sharply as we change the underlying nature of the resource in question. Thus a first-possession rule applied to running water in principle would allow one person to block off an entire stream and claim its contents for herself by the naked act of possession. Yet that decision reduces the value of the water to that which it would have in a large thermos bottle. Lost would be the value for sustaining fish, plants, and wildlife; lost too would be its value for navigation; and gone also would be its value for recreation and aesthetics. The ancient maxim that says that "water ought to flow where it does flow" is a very simple-minded but accurate way of saying that the site-specific, "going concern" value of a viable river or lake is far greater than its value, as it were, in liquidation as barrels of rainwater. Keeping the property common in its original position preserves that value in a way that any system of acquisitive possession could destroy.

But it is one thing to preserve value and it is quite another to maximize it. There is no reason why all the water in a river should be kept there because most of it should. Some portion of the water could well be used for drinking, caring for animals, or nurturing crops. And the earlier systems allowed for this form of mixed use by permitting riparian owners to take for their own use *limited* amounts of water for such domestic and agricultural uses. Locke's effort to justify this outcome under the labor theory of value fails here as it does for the first-possession rule for land and other forms of property. If labor were the decisive element, then the more one worked the more water one could remove. His theory therefore explains only the basic right, but not its inseparable limitation. As before, he fails to explain what gives only certain persons, riparian owners, the right to remove only some water. As before, his mistake is to seek an answer to the question in the mysterious relationship between the owner and the thing.

A far better approach is to look at the systematic welfare consequences of the rule. Allowing limited private use of water works in accord with another rough but reliable empirical generalization. The marginal gain from private use of some water is greater than the marginal loss to the body of water, so long as these private uses are sharply constrained. The system therefore seeks to maximize the sum of the in-stream and out-stream uses of water. It permits exclusive use when its external costs are low, but limits it where these costs turn out to be high, and does so under a customary regime that operates at reasonably low cost and without extensive centralized control. The system is, to be sure, somewhat more complicated than the rules that apply to land. But we should expect that, since water is a more complex resource than land, the benefits to A are far less separable from its costs to B. Rules that create separate castles must yield to those which structure both common and private use.

Given this basic situation, many of the features of the legal regime for land are no longer appropriate for water.[9] First possession is the first rule to go. All riparians have an equal and limited right to withdraw water regardless of how far back they can trace their land titles. Free alienation is next to go: the sale of water rights may proceed only appurtenant to the sale of the riparian land, otherwise the sustainable property of a river would be destroyed by excessive withdrawals for the benefit of nonriparian lands or programs. The perpetual nature of possession goes as well. In-stream uses of water are short-term, not perpetual; going up and down a river does not give one the right to squat on any portion of it, and recreational uses are likewise limited by time and circumstance. The absolute nature of the property rights quickly also disappears. The owners of land may exclude all others and hold their property inviolate. The owners of water have to share and share alike, and must reduce their take proportionately during the dry season. Ideally, one would like to have a system in which the least valued uses are ended first. But in a system where trades are difficult to establish, it is simply too difficult to make individualized judgments of who needs the water more and why. Again the simpler rule of thumb has displaced the more accurate measurements of values.

This entire web of rights and duties is also closely bound to certain forms of rivers and certain kinds of technologies. It works best in regions where water is in abundant supply (so that wells are an alternative source) and in-stream uses of the water (fishing, swimming, boating, and so on) are valuable. Let the external circumstances change and the system of legal rights will change as well, notwithstanding the natural and timeless nature of property rights so praised by Justinian. Thus the rise in technology during the nineteenth century required adjustments in the system of property rights to allow the creation of mills along rivers.[10] The lack of in-stream uses for certain western waters gave rise to a system of prior appropriation, which resulted in virtually all the water being used for irrigation. These differences in property rights are not simply random or uncertain. They respond to the constant pressures to create the right incentives for productive behavior at low administrative cost. Their durability over time is a good test for their social usefulness. The next question is how one can build the remainder of the legal system on its initial foundation of property rights.

4

Contract

My first two rules have done a good deal to create order in the legal landscape. The first rule gives people control of their own lives; the second assigns each external thing an owner. The system satisfies at least the minimum concerns with formal equality, for everyone is entitled to use his or her own endowments and to search for the acquisition of particular things. Whatever the fortunes of individuals might be, the structural advantages of this system remain, for the common law rules of personal autonomy and individual ownership necessarily decentralize control of both human and material resources. No single person, no select group of individuals, can decide who is going to own what things or who is entitled to deal with whom on the transfer and use of labor or talents.

Very often, however, the lot we are given by nature, or have acquired by taking possession, is not the lot we wish to have in the end. We therefore need some way of altering the control of various resources so as to enhance their value to all people simultaneously: hence the critical role of voluntary exchange. We can begin by stressing the standard economic observation that there is sometimes an enormous difference between value in exchange and value in use, both for labor and for natural resources. To illustrate, a computer might be worth $100 if used by its present owner. But it could be sold for $125 in the marketplace, and yield $150 in benefits to its new owner. The use value to the present is below the exchange value, which in turn is below the use value to the buyer. If trade is blocked, potential gains for both buyer and seller are destroyed, without any offsetting social benefit.

There is, of course, no reason to believe that all goods have greater value in exchange than in use. Sometimes you can use what you own better than your neighbor. This is why every house in town is not graced with a "for sale" sign by the front door. But sometimes your neighbor, or some total stranger, can make better use of your house than you can, which is why *some* houses happen to be for sale. The basic mechanism of contract is very simple, powerful, and universal. It essentially involves your surrendering something that you value in exchange for something else that you value even more. If both sides allow the trade to occur, there will be an enormous increase in overall well-being, unless there are some systematic losses to third parties, an issue best deferred until dealing with the fourth simple rule. What is even better is that this one simple idea of gains through trade is capable of infinite repetition. What is purchased in one transaction can be reworked, repackaged, and resold in another transaction. As long as the mutual gain condition is satisfied at every stage, there is no reason to place any artificial limitations on the number of times people can rely on this one rule. One good idea beats a thousand bad ones.

Acquisition through voluntary contract is not sufficient to construct the entire system, for it does not answer the problem of infinite regress: If I have acquired my title through you, how have you acquired your title? And if you have acquired it through X, then how has X acquired hers? And so on. The postulate that each person owns his or her own person, and through it his or her own labor in the initial position, cuts through the regress and establishes a strong foundation for the subsequent system of voluntary exchange. The principles here are perfectly general. First apply the property rules of self-ownership and first possession; next apply the general rules of contract with respect to the endowments so acquired; and afterward apply the tort laws to see that no impermissible actions of aggression took place. Specialized bodies of real estate law and labor law simply fall out of these general considerations, without any special edict or legislative command. The common law achieved a very high level of coherence and universality with its very few generative principles of rights and duties.

These contractual exchanges also work to mitigate some of the apparently individualistic excesses of a system of first possession. Not only do contracts allow us to trade our own labor or things that we have acquired; they also allow us to trade or share things that we will acquire at some future time. If a hunting party decides to divide a future catch by single members among the group, then the transaction is perfectly valid even though the voluntary exchange takes place prior to acquisition. The duty to transfer is just deferred until after acquisition. Just that form of contract is made by the members of a crew of a whaling vessel. Likewise, if a family or social group imposes strong status obligations on its members, the first possessor is bound to share his catch in accordance with the applicable rule. And in feudal systems the land acquired either by conquest or by original occupation can be parceled out to members of the group in exchange for obligations of loyalty and support—a pattern of social organization adopted in widely diverse cultures.[1] Properly understood, the only function of the first-possession rule is to exclude strangers from the property acquired. Where there are gains from cooperation and sharing, the rule of voluntary exchange allows for the consensual conversion of individual to common ownership. The two rules work together and should be evaluated together.

ABSTRACTIONS AND PERSONS

The logic of mutual gain from voluntary exchange is perfectly general. It rests only on the self-interest of individuals in a world of scarcity. It is not particular to one culture, one time, or one set of values. Most important for these purposes, the logic of exchange is not role specific. It does not speak about one set of rules for employers and another for employees, or one set for landlords and another for tenants. It does not create one set of rules for people who are rich and powerful and another set for those who are frail or meek. Instead, the law speaks about two hardy standbys in all contractual arrangements: A and B. These people are colorless, odorless, and timeless, of no known nationality, age, race, or sex. These people are self-conscious abstractions known to be false as representations of people in the world, and useful precisely because they are so detached from any grubby set of particulars. A and B (and their friends C to Z) are surely ubiquitous, yet only occasionally make contact with the hurly-burly world of commerce that they are meant to describe.

There is a cold, practical logic behind this remorseless search for abstractions. The common law theory was that as long as you know there is an A and a B, you have all the information necessary to figure out their *self*-definition of social roles by contract. It does not matter to the law (although it surely does to the parties) that both are equal partners or that one side to the agreement is the employer and the other is the employee. These relationships, these categories, are not imposed upon private persons through the operation of the law; these roles are freely chosen by individuals acting within the system. A decides to work for B, and B agrees to work for A. Each remains free to assume other roles in relation to other parties. There is no inconsistency in A's working for B in one transaction and hiring C in a second. There is no inconsistency in A's owning one house, renting another, and holding a mortgage on a third. The patterns of social life are determined not by some powerful central authority, but by the repetitive and independent decisions of thousands of separate individuals pursuing their self-interest. There is no final pattern of jobs or contracts that is simply just, proper, or fair solely because of the way it looks. The pattern that emerged was justified solely by chasing down the "chain of title" for each original transaction.[2]

This massive oversimplification of the social universe treats all persons as though they are as fungible as the letters of the alphabet, and thus ignores or rejects every effort to force the common law to take into account the difference between an individual worker of limited means and a huge industrial corporation. The major attack on this common law system castigates its refusal to recognize differences in role and status that were, and are, apparent to all who care to look at the operation of the legal system. The reformers want to dismiss the common law approach as a pitiful caricature of the rich tapestry of social interactions, and to replace the slippery generalities of contract, property, and tort with a far more reticulated set of rules that takes into account known and particular differences in social roles and institutional contexts. The earlier forms of antidiscrimination law were content, for example, with a general prohibition against refusing to hire or promote because of race, sex, or nationality. But the more modern variants, most notably the Americans with Disabilities Act, contain detailed rules that regulate what may be asked or done at each stage of the employment process: what questions may be asked about medical history, what assistance must be supplied, what structural accommodations must be made, and so on down the line. The attack on the common law seeks to make the applicable rules more sensitive to the dominant features of social relationships.

Now why should any analyst or legal system try to disregard evident social truths and speak only of abstract As and Bs when specific information about context and role is indispensable for understanding how individuals behave and markets operate? To answer this question, it is necessary to step back from matters of detail in order to focus again on points of general principle. It is true that all individuals differ in natural endowments, in personal ambitions, in social roles, and in institutional expectations. But there is one thing that each of them wants and wants just because each is an A or B: *more*. We may not be able from a disinterested perch to answer the question "more of what?" or to explain why more of this is preferred to more of that. Indeed, on many occasions people are unable to articulate to themselves why they want more of one commodity or good than they do of another. But regardless of these gaps in knowledge, we do know that people who have more can always end up with less by giving away some of what they have to any number of eager recipients, from relatives to charitable institutions. But people with less can only end up with more by one of two routes: force or exchange (broadly construed to include not only barter but gifts).

This characteristic of wanting more is universal. It applies with equal force to both greedy and rapacious firms and self-interested individuals. Indeed, wanting more is not a characteristic for which we should want to condemn people. The desire for more is one of the few features that is indispensable for human progress and advancement. The right question to ask is not why we want more. It is how are we prepared to go about getting the more that we all want.

There are only two kinds of games (two patterns of behavior) that people can play in a world in which everyone desires more and fears ending up with less. The first game is to get more for yourself by taking it from someone else. The second is to get more by entering into a voluntary exchange with another person. All ostensible independent third cases (for instance, state regulation or private misrepresentation) are essentially only variations on either coercion or consent. In light of these general truths, the argument for thinking about legal relationships in terms of the lifeless As and Bs runs as follows: Each A and B has certain initial endowments: these are then augmented by things which are acquired through first possession or voluntary exchange. When A enters into a voluntary arrangement with B, this constant pressure to end up with more instead of less implies that two critical inequalities are simultaneously satisfied. The first inequality says that when A surrenders anything (be it labor or material goods) he will value it less than the thing that he receives in exchange. The second inequality says that when B surrenders anything she will value it less than the thing she receives in exchange.

Taken together, these inequalities have enormous social significance. They imply that all voluntary exchanges are *positive-sum* games for the participants. Exchange does not merely transfer physical or intangible assets. It increases human satisfaction by matching assets with the persons who value them most. That proposition holds regardless of how A and B received their initial endowments. It holds even if we as analysts have no strong theory of value which explains why A wants to order his preferences in one direction and B wants to order hers in another. So long as we know that all As and all Bs desire more, there is sufficient warrant for allowing voluntary exchange to take place. *Both* sides are better off than they were before.

Theft arises when one person takes something without the consent of the other and with no intention of making compensation. It is at best a constant-sum game, for what one party gains the other necessarily loses. In truth, thefts typically consume wealth, given the resources used to obtain or block these forced transfers. Although the transaction is likely to be to the thief's benefit, it will not be to the benefit of his victim. The exact size of the gains and losses cannot be identified in the abstract for each particular transaction, but in general there is good reason to believe that the thief's private gains will be smaller than the victim's private losses. Indeed, in those cases where the thief could make better use of the thing taken, the transfer of ownership can take place by ordinary sale. The key lies in the incentive structures: if the transaction is allowed, the thief need only compare his costs of arranging the theft with the value he derives from it. There is no particular reason to take into account the value that the owner (if that term could still be used) attaches to the thing. If the costs of theft are 10, the value to the thief is 50, and the value to the original owner is 100, the thief will decide that $50 - 10$ yields a gain of 40. But if the losses to the owner are taken into account, then the social value of the transaction now equals 100 lost to the owner, less the 40 gained by the thief, or −60. Theft is likely to be a *negative-sum* game. The conclusion is not universal, for in some cases the value to the thief could be greater than the value to the owner. But in these circumstances a voluntary sale can typically be arranged.

This negative pattern of theft therefore is likely to be the dominant one, for if it just happened that routine thefts produced systematic gains, we would be hard pressed indeed to explain the uniform condemnation of the practice in all societies. If thefts promised net gains on average, then the only concern would be with the distribution of gains and losses from any individual transaction. But surely there would be no reason to incur the costs of legal protection against the predator, for we would be in that happy zone where we could both lower administrative costs and improve incentives. In the absence of any trade-off, the appropriate remedy for theft would be not punishment, but an invitation to the victim to practice the same art, for the greater good of the whole. If one gains on each transaction, then it is good to have as many transactions as possible: if only the transfer of wealth had the same desirable social consequences as its creation!

Thus far I have emphasized how simple and impersonal legal rules are sufficient to define and organize markets. There is, however, a sense in which it *does* matter who A and B are after all, even in a world of voluntary exchange. If it turns out that there is only *one* A sitting there with a monopoly position, while there are lots of Bs who are pretty close substitutes for each other, A is going to be in an exceedingly strong position with respect to any particular B. B can't go anywhere else to find a substitute A, while A can pick and choose among a large array of more or less identical Bs.

Given this initial distribution of roles, it is instructive to try to figure out how the pattern of exchanges will evolve. To do so, it is necessary to know the *threat position* of each party, that is, what that party can do to better his lot, unilaterally acting on his own, when there is no bargain to be made with some other person. (Theft is so damaging because if unrestrained the thief's threat position is to take everything.) That threat position will be exceedingly strong for A, who can choose from an array of Bs. But it will be weak for each B, who has to deal with A if there is to be any agreement at all. We can be pretty confident that in a world of one A and many Bs, A will end up with a very large proportion of the gain that comes out of any A-B agreement. The strength of a common law system, and the weakness of centralized systems of regulations, relate directly to the ratio between the As and the Bs in any market. The common law's decentralized system of original ownership rights in the person helps ensure, both by natural selection and by migration, that many As and Bs will operate in any organized market. The common law allows *no one* to say "only I can enter this side of a market." "Free entry in open markets" is a necessary corollary of the basic common law rules of self-ownership and voluntary exchange.

THE MANY AND THE ONE

The institutional implications of the use of these simple rules are both clear and striking. No government, no group of individuals with special privileges or franchises, will be able to preclude entry on either side of the market. With this condition in place the uniqueness of any A or B vanishes. Many people, all self-selected, can choose to occupy any particular social role. Accordingly, all persons have a reasonably good threat position vis-à-vis the rest of the world. If you do not wish to do business with me, there are lots of other people in the world to whom you (and I) can turn. It follows that the naive A and B model is extraordinarily robust if two assumptions are satisfied: (1) multiple players and (2) mutually advantageous exchanges.

By starting from this very modest material, the law can facilitate (not compel, but facilitate) sizable productive interactions which will continue to expand over time and transactions until they embrace all individuals who possess the minimum capacity to engage in contracting at all. The system goes forward in a benevolent fashion because the exchanges are mutually beneficial. Otherwise the parties would not choose to enter into them. We don't have to know *why* any given exchange will prove beneficial for a particular person. It is quite enough to know that, given the external manifestation of consent, this will be the case. The legal system can flourish from voluntary exchanges whose content it does not fully understand. Indeed, it must take just this tack if it is to function effectively at all. Otherwise the risk is that each transaction will require some formal and public demonstration of its intrinsic merits for the parties as a precursor to its legal validity. In such a world the good outcome is that the agreement goes forward, but only after some cost is incurred; the bad outcome is that the transaction is vetoed by a government agent who does not understand the full range of relevant costs and benefits and who has no incentive to presume their existence. Either scenario is worse than one of unimpeded exchange; so the supervised arrangement can be put to one side even if we optimistically believed that intelligent administrative decisions would drive out uninformed ones. The background knowledge of the uniform incentives moving self-interested parties is a more reliable guide to their interests than any public vetting of their deal.

Nonetheless, if we step out of our skeptical mode, it is possible to say something about the forms of voluntary exchange that should emerge over time, namely, that there will be sorting by role—specialization in the market. To defend that conclusion we need one additional assumption, which is as critical as it is accurate. We must assume that there is some natural variation across people over a wide range of different dimensions. The obvious ones will be such things as height, weight, and intelligence. But other less obvious attributes will be critical as well, such as attitudes, skills, and taste. We may not know exactly how these attributes are distributed, but we can say with perfect confidence that all people are not concentrated at a single point on the distribution: people do not have identical heights and weights, and so too with their other natural endowments, characteristics, and abilities. The biology and the sociology of the situation make us confident that some people will be better at some things, and others at other things. The dimensions of these differences can be quite subtle and important, and some of them may escape the external analyst while they are instinctively understood by people inside some particular segment of the market. It seems clear (given the behavior of professional gamblers and traders) that some people are better than others at managing risk, while others may be better at executing complex transactions. The first could become traders and the second brokers, both in the same financial marketplace.

Similarly, within a contractual arrangement those people who are better at bearing risk may become owners and employers, while those who are less willing and able to bear it may be quite content to take the fixed salary and greater security associated with employee status. Nor is there any reason why employment relationships must be divided along stark and rigid lines. It is possible to incorporate commissions and bonuses into hiring arrangements that reflect some complex system of risk sharing between the parties. The parties can mix and match risk to their hearts' content while the *law* of contract continues to treat A and B as placeholders instead of persons.

As the process runs its course, there is a slow transformation in the way in which the world operates. We start with isolated and undifferentiated As and Bs, but some of the As start coalescing and some of the Bs start coalescing. Certain powerful asymmetries in role start to emerge; with time we can see the variegated world that we observe today, filled with complex organizations and individual entrepreneurs, much as in evolution we see organisms of different sizes filling the various niches available in nature. At every stage, the observed social complexity is reached by a process of self-definition, not of external compulsion. And each transaction, each link in the chain, is a positive-sum game for its participants.

The Standard Limitations on Contractual Freedom

The case in favor of freedom rests on the postulate of mutual gains through trade. The rationale for the institution provides the essential clue for its limitation. When bargaining takes place in settings where mutual gain is not the probable outcome, there is sufficient warrant for the law to step in to set that transaction aside. Transactions will never go forward when both sides expect to lose; consequently the greatest danger lurks when one side to the bargain is made better off by an exchange that is likely to make the other side worse off.

That win/lose outcome is identical to the one created by theft. The task therefore is to weed out those transactions that operate as the unilateral imposition of one party's wishes upon the other party. Physical duress is the paradigm case. It arises when A forces B to enter into a contract with the threat that he will inflict physical harm on her if she does not. Any exchange so coerced will leave B better off than she was *after* the threat was made, but the benchmark used to gauge the social desirability of the exchange is B's welfare *before* A made his threat. A may stand to gain only 10 units of welfare. But without legal intervention, he will be prepared to expend 9 units of effort, whether B's loss is 1 or 100. If it were 1, then an ordinary exchange would be easy to organize, for B would agree to A's terms. So theft is likely to take place when B's loss is 100 instead of 1. And thus most such transactions yield the same negative-sum outcome as theft. There is little social cost associated with a ban on the use of duress, which is found in all legal systems.

Duress is hardly the only ground for setting contracts aside. Infancy, insanity, undue influence, fraud, and misrepresentation are universally recognized as reasons for refusing to enforce contracts, or for undoing their effects once they have been performed. Allowing these escape hatches from contractual obligations is fully consistent with, and indeed necessary to, the operation of free markets as we understand them. Each filters out important subclasses of agreements for which the assumption of mutual gain from exchange is not likely to hold.

The dangers of infancy and insanity are easy to see. As a general matter, people who labor under any major form of incompetence are incapable of making the comparisons required to enter into profitable exchanges, and are known to be such. Competent people can easily steer clear of incompetents, so there is little hardship in banning transactions that are likely to be win/lose transactions. Cases of undue influence are often more difficult to categorize. These transactions usually involve people whose capacities are limited by illness or old age or who have to participate in complex commercial transactions that are outside their usual ken, or both. Is B likely to benefit from a bargain with A when she does not receive independent advice from some third party whose sole loyalty is to her?

The dangers of fraud, or indeed any misrepresentation, are not limited to incompetents but can arise in any transaction. If goods worth $10 are represented by a seller as being worth $12, then the buyer who pays $11 ends up worse off for having traded under false information. Misrepresentation blocks the mutual gain, and is all the more likely to occur when deceit is practiced. The hardest cases to evaluate are those where either side or both sides make mistakes not induced by the other party, sometimes when neither party knows the truth. A variety of solutions have been proposed to place the risk on the party better able to avoid it, which usually means that the loss is borne by the party that makes the mistake unless the other side knows of the error and "snaps up" an offer that is too good to be true. But this matter is truly complicated, and tends to arise only infrequently, both in standard product and labor contexts. Any class of routine contracts is not likely to fall prey to some pervasive and unknown mistake: the business pressures for clarification, correction, and standardization are just too powerful. Ironically, only the committed *opponents* of laissez faire are bold enough to claim that the principle of freedom of contract is so absolute that this class of defenses is excluded. The sensible advocates of laissez faire all recognize that the power of contract lives and dies with the presupposition of mutual gain for self-interested parties on which it rests, and tailors the class of defenses to reflect that fundamental proposition.

THE COUNTERATTACK ON CONTRACTUAL FREEDOM

The central debate over freedom of contract arises over the extent to which the concerns of duress, misrepresentation, and incompetence can be extended beyond the cases of their origins. The fear of incompetence in particular transactions leads to a more systematic preoccupation with exploitation whenever the parties have different levels of skill or knowledge. Physical duress becomes the abuse to which economic duress is compared. And back of this widespread disquiet lies the common conviction that certain transactions should be banned or limited because they seek to make commodities out of things that should not be traded at all. I consider these common efforts to expand the limitations on freedom of contract under three separate heads: exploitation, economic duress, and commodification.

Exploitation

The first frontal attack on the principle of contractual freedom seeks to generalize from the cases of incompetence beyond infants and insane people. Those so disabled will normally not enter into labor or commercial markets at all. Instead they are, and should be, represented by their natural guardians, such as their parents, or by special guardians appointed by either the family or the state. Any effort to assume that ordinary individuals are similarly incompetent, however, is fraught with totalitarian dangers. Workers who are competent to participate in union politics and union elections, to marry and raise families, to participate in public affairs should not be deemed incompetent to bargain directly with employers if they so choose. Individuals who are normally entitled to buy and sell homes and businesses can negotiate rent with a landlord. Indeed, if workers and tenants are so incompetent, why let them vote or participate in political affairs, activities that require them to address matters far more complex than filling a shopping cart at the local supermarket? Matters of incompetence are therefore only tangential to the smooth operation of ordinary markets.

The modern attacks on freedom of contract try to resurrect the concern with the exploitation of incompetence in a somewhat different form, namely, one of positional or status dominance. Labor markets cannot be trusted because the employer holds all the high cards in negotiation while the individual worker holds none. The employer is said to have great wealth and considerable cunning. An isolated worker in the labor market is said to possess neither. The contract, therefore, is said to have a predictable and inexorable result. The employer dictates the terms of the contract. Some legal protection of employee interests is said to be necessary to redress inequality of bargaining power and employer exploitation. Similar arguments can be made with respect to real estate rental markets or consumer markets.

To understand what is wrong with this familiar position, it is critical to disaggregate two different conceptions that travel under the single banner of market power. On the one hand, market power could be treated as synonymous with wealth. On the other, it could be said that market power is synonymous with a lack of rivals on your side of the market. The first conception is mistaken, if only because wealth has its disabilities as well as its advantages. If known by the other side it could lead, for example, to a demand for higher wages when workers think that the employer can pay more. Or it might lead to lower wages if the workers think that employer wealth reduces the likelihood of employer default or bankruptcy. As a matter of principle, there is no obvious direction of wealth's effects on bargaining behavior. There are countless illustrations of successful executives at large firms being lured away to run their own show at smaller rival companies. The exodus in talent from IBM that led to its 1992 shake-up is only one illustration of a more general phenomenon. The key element for exploitation is not wealth, but the absence of rivals.

The argument about exploitation can be addressed by still another thought experiment. Assume that a perfectly rational employer who possesses the power to dictate terms now seeks to maximize her gain through contracting. Assume that a worker, capable of being exploited, has a relatively lower income. What bargain is likely to take place? If the theory of exploitation is correct, the outcome should leave the worker worse off than before and the employer better off. Yet so long as employee consent is required, why expect exploitation to take place? The worker, however desperate his position, still has the option (denied to a slave) to refuse the offer that is made, and that unilateral action will allow him to escape the exploitation in question. What incentive is there to bargain one's self into more abject poverty? It hardly matters that the wealth of the two parties is wildly unequal before the transaction begins. If the exchange is voluntary, both sides will ordinarily benefit from the transaction. The worker's ability to withhold consent stands as a strong bulwark against any form of exploitation. Indeed, any public effort to insist that the worker get some specific share of the gains will not only increase the costs of running the system, but preclude some gainful transactions that would otherwise take place—again inferior incentives at higher administrative costs.

The argument about exploitation is surely no stronger when cast in the analogous language of inequality of bargaining power. Thus assume that an employer could "dictate" the terms of trade in the marketplace. What would we expect to see the contract look like? The answer is that the employer would never stop pressing her advantage. If it turned out that the employer could dictate terms, why would she offer a wage of 10 if she could drive it down to 9; and why would she settle for 9 if she could drive it down to 8? The logic of dictation leaves the employer no reason to stop until, without mercy, she has extracted the last bit of advantage. When the process comes to a halt, we should observe people working for employers at a zero wage, and we don't. If firms can exploit workers, then retailers can exploit their customers, so that it is unnecessary to offer cash discounts, free exchange privileges, and volume discounts. Start with these oft-repeated assumptions, and there is no stable or discernible equilibrium with wages or, for that matter, prices in any relevant market. Yet the theory of exploitation notwithstanding, we have long observed positive wages for labor and finite prices for goods. Worker earnings place a budget constraint on worker purchases in a straightforward commonsense manner. The idea of inequality of bargaining power, the idea of dictation, fails the most decisive test: it has no *descriptive* power.

What does inequality of bargaining power mean? The intuition is not wholly without economic roots. In practice, there is a better way to explain it that gets away from the all-or-nothing characterizations of the standard account. Many contracts between workers and employers will endure over a long period of time. In many cases, the employer will gain some special advantage from dealing with a familiar and trusted employee. By the same token, an employee will gain an advantage from dealing with a familiar and trusted employer. Thus, even if labor contracts are terminable at will, it does not follow that they will be terminated as a matter of course at the end of each working day. The question of inequality of bargaining power then responds to this question: When there are special gains from trade, that is, supracompetitive returns, to be shared by two individuals, who gets the lion's share—the employer or the employee? In essence it is possible to construct an index from 0 to 100, where each point represents a percentage of the surplus captured by one side. Bargaining power for both sides is equal when each side captures half the surplus. If one side can capture, say, 60 percent, then it has bargaining dominance by a three to two ratio.

The critical question is what percentage of the surplus will be captured by each side. The short answer is nobody can be sure how the gains will be divided. Indeed, the outcome could well vary from case to case. More to the point, there is no theoretical reason to believe that the employer has any systematic advantage in capturing surplus, and the opposite may well be true. An employer may have more to lose if a single worker is able to halt an important process, so that the employer may yield first to avoid the prospect of a far greater loss. Again, an employer has to bargain through agents, while an employee often bargains on his own account. It is an open question whether an agent's professional bargaining skills will prove decisive when she is giving away someone else's money and the worker is giving away his own. Again an agent has to make offers to many workers at a single time. The worker only has to worry about himself. It is well known that when employers make standard buy-out offers to reduce the size of the workforce, these are often accepted by the workers whom the employer would most like to keep. Yet it is simply too difficult to calibrate the offer to take into account individual differences in need.

Guessing the actual allocation of surplus in any individual case is virtually impossible, so the matter remains resistant to any empirical estimation. But even with all the doubt, one thing does remain clear—you can count on both sides getting at least a competitive return, one for capital and the other for labor. The question of inequality of bargaining power goes *not* to the issue of how you divide up the beef, but *only* to the question of dividing up the gravy. Contrary to the popular conception, there are limits to the advantage that either employer or employee can obtain from pressing a bargaining advantage. The worker will leave if wages are reduced below the competitive level, and the employer will fire the worker if the wages soak up the full profit from the venture. Once again, zero wages and infinite prices are just a fairytale. To repeat, for an understanding of labor markets it is the second definition of market power—the lack of rivals—that is critical. There are very powerful forces in these marketplaces that determine what wages will look like.

The parallels exist elsewhere. Housing markets are normally quite "thick" since everyone from the owner of an apartment complex to the owner of a two-flat is a potential renter. The open market thus sets the background for competitive rentals. But even against this backdrop, some elements of monopoly power appear. When leases expire, renegotiation pits a single landlord against a single tenant. Typically, it is in the interest of both landlords and tenants to renew, to capture the gains specific to their ongoing arrangement. The precise division of the gain is hard to determine, and in some cases negotiations will break down. But in those cases where the renewal takes place, it is simply a mistake to assume that the landlord has gotten the lion's share of the profits unique to the transaction. Tenants, both individual and commercial, can be skillful bargainers as well. If the landlord follows the common strategy of offering a new lease at the same percentage increase charged incoming tenants, much of the problem is averted. There is little that state intervention can do to avoid the familiar frictions of contract renewal and negotiations. But the one thing government should never do is to increase the size of the stakes in the renegotiation game by stifling new entry.

Economic Duress

Another form of attack on competitive markets seeks to extend the moral force of physical duress to cases of economic duress. Some forms of economic duress do partake of the same logic as the use of force. Suppose that A and B have entered into a contract under which A is obliged to do certain work for B, but A refuses to perform unless B pays some additional money for the work. Here the threat of breach of the first contract is the functional substitute for the use of force. In the easiest case, A simply demands a price alteration that makes the overall deal a loser for B. To counter that threat, B must be allowed either to promise and then to resist payment, or to pay and then recover the excess. Otherwise, the law will no longer protect security of exchange. Even so, the question of economic duress in cases of renegotiation can be unavoidably complex when it is not clear which party is in breach. Thus suppose that some fishermen are dispatched to Alaska with a promise that they will be paid a certain amount for catch. If they do not follow through with the work, the entire catch will be lost.[3] If they insist on additional compensation before fishing, it looks as though there is a form of economic duress, equivalent to the stock example of the cleaner who refuses to return garments to their owner unless an additional fee is paid. But suppose now that the nets supplied by the shipowner are inferior to those required by contract; now the response of the fishermen appears to be an effort to offset a contractual wrong in the other direction, and not a crude effort to exploit a bilateral monopoly situation in which each side has to deal with the other. Yet in some cases both forces may be at work, and no rule, simple or complex, is able to deal with the full range of cases calling for midcourse contractual correction.

Yet it is important to keep this form of duress in perspective, since the problem is of ancient lineage and unavoidable in many business settings. Any decision on whether to require the firm to honor its promise has only small consequences for the overall operation of the economy. The critical point is that this form of duress must be sharply distinguished from a very different phenomenon that bears the same name. Economic duress, if it refers only to hard bargaining under conditions of scarcity, does not make one party worse off after the interaction than before. The omnipresence of scarcity (which is distinguishable from the narrower common law category of necessity) is a reason to expand, not limit, the scope of contractual freedom. Without scarcity, no one would care about improving incentives or reducing administrative costs: why bother if there is always enough wealth to go around? As long as the practice of contracting expands the use of resources, why incur any administrative costs to correct an imagined set of economic difficulties? The class of transactions that ought to be set aside on the grounds of economic duress is an empty set—another categorical and simple rule.

Once the broad idea of economic duress is placed to one side, the entire case for mandatory minimum terms in labor contracts is exposed as wholly misguided. It thus becomes unwise for the state to say that a certain minimum wage should be imposed as a matter of law, or that certain contractual forms, such as the contract at will, should be ruled out of bounds, or that certain institutional and organizational arrangements, such as mandatory collective bargaining and family leave arrangements, should be imposed as a matter of course. It also becomes impossible to condemn the entire system of market arrangements as inherently coercive. The simple rule is to disregard all claims of economic duress, save in the limited sense outlined above.

Commodification

A third argument against freedom of contract, made most often in the context of labor markets, is frequently cast in very heroic terms. Its most vivid statement comes in the Clayton Act of 1914, which declared that the "labor of a human being is not a commodity or article of commerce."[4] That theme has been seized upon by the forces for regulation everywhere. The argument is that labor is simply not an article of commerce, not a simple commodity, to be traded like any other. There are some very great difficulties with that argument, both descriptive and normative.

The first point is that under the common law position labor becomes a commodity or an article of commerce only if its owner chooses to make it such. People are allowed, not required, to sell their labor, just as they are allowed and not required to sell their homes. People who prefer to keep house, raise a family, do volunteer work, pursue hobbies, or travel may do so, as long as they have the resources to support themselves. No potential employer can commandeer any person into taking a job. Markets feature voluntary exchange, not forced labor.

Yet most people both want and need to work. For them, if labor is not an article of commerce, then what is it? One answer might be that labor is "sacred"—carefully preserved outside the mainstream of commerce, much like religious institutions. But even the most stalwart defenders of organized labor have no use for that definition, which is ruinous not only for future employers but also for laboring men and women. If labor is outside the scope of commerce, then it cannot be sold on any terms at all, even those which give employees wages above competitive levels. Calling labor sacred is to say it cannot be traded at all, to the advantage of no one. Yet what is desired by invoking this phrase is a very different end: the monopolization of labor markets through collective bargaining or similar arrangements. And so it was that the Clayton Act provided that unions were not, in legal contemplation, conspiracies in restraint of trade, as they were sometimes considered before its passage.

The idea of placing labor "beyond commerce" overstates the case of what is desired. Almost everyone is willing to trade labor; the only question is what are the terms on which it will be traded. It is clear that labor will be traded on terms different from those applying to other kinds of commodities mainly because people are willing to sell their services, by the hour, but are not willing to sell themselves into slavery—even if such were legal. In dealing with ordinary goods, however, with houses and other kinds of real estate, an outright sale which changes ownership from one side to the other is perfectly appropriate. One does not have to rely on external conceptions of what is and is not a commodity for trade to make a judgment that people acting in ordinary markets will generate types of trades in labor that are on terms different from those governing the trades that they generate in goods and in land. Indeed, the sure sign of dysfunctional regulation in, for example, housing markets is rhetoric about fundamental goods and basic needs so important that their provision must be guaranteed or at least regulated by the state.

This description of the law of the role of exchange has looked at the question of exchange only from the vantage point of gains and losses to the parties. Its basic structure has been a two-stage approximation: first recognize the logic of mutual gain through exchange, and next look at those practices that lead to contractual formations that are likely on balance to falsify that assumption in some particular case. A full analysis of the social welfare from private contracts cannot take into account only the gains and losses of the parties to a transaction; it must also make some assessment of the effects that this agreement will have on third parties. In this respect, however, contractual freedom is best understood as a subset of individual freedom, which is also subject to limitations devised to take into account the welfare of third parties. These external limitations on freedom of contract constitute an important qualification that is best taken up in connection with the fourth simple rule, that of protection against external aggression through the operation of the tort law.

5

Torts

The fourth rule deals with how to protect the things that you have. This rule forms the basis of the law of tort. In its crudest and simplest form, the irreducible core of this body of law can be succinctly expressed: "keep off." This two-word rule accurately describes the historical and intellectual thrust of much of the common law: to prevent trespass to land, larceny, murder, rape, and (by extension) infringement of patents—and indeed interference with the exchange relationships between parties. It is amazing how much, even in this age of heightened sensitivity to sexual harassment, you can learn about interactions between strangers by remembering to keep your hands to yourself. That precept was drummed into us as little children as one of those homespun homilies that make the world go round. But that rule also turns out to track the deep philosophical principle of respect for the autonomy of other individuals. This rule allows people to use, and use productively, the things they own without your being able to impose your will on them. And you will have the same freedom relative to them.

To see why this regime makes sense, it is necessary only to rephrase the inquiry I first posed concerning the rules for autonomy and property. Would you rather live in a world where each person could routinely block the use that others made of their own property, or in one where each person could use her property as she sees fit? There is no universal or a priori answer to that question, but there is a neat distinction to be made between the harms prohibited and the harms allowed. The prevention of force will generally work to the mutual advantage of all parties, while the prevention of competition—itself a form of harm to competitors—will have the opposite consequences. It is the difference between a negative-sum game, in which the total amount to be distributed to the players is reduced when unbridled force destroys the products of human labor, and a positive-sum game, in which all improve their positive through trade.

Even after the basic "keep off" norm has been established, other subsidiary questions must still be addressed. Answering them often presents a graphic choice between a simple rule and some more complex alternative. The primary objective of the tort law is to allow people to live in peace (if not in harmony) with each other. It enforces the separate domains in which all of us, singly, can live our own lives as we see fit. But however sensible this goal, a subsidiary question is whether all invasions of someone else's person or property should give rise to a legal right to redress.

With respect to the intentional infliction of harm, the conclusion is too clear to require extended discussion. If harms may be routinely inflicted on purpose, the rules of protection are gutted from the outset, and autonomy and property quickly tumble. To be sure, there are occasions when a person is justified in inflicting deliberate harm: self-defense and disciplinary action head the list. But even in such cases the conduct should not exceed the bounds of justification. The use of force in self-defense may not exceed its end of self-protection, and in civilized society even the innocent party may be forced to forgo self-help and rely on the uncertain remedies provided by the law when the harm inflicted is out of proportion to the benefit obtained: concealed spring guns, activated when their wires are tripped, cannot be used, for example, to defend mere property, especially property of trifling value.[1]

NEGLIGENCE AND STRICT LIABILITY

A more troublesome inquiry arises with regard to accidental injuries. Here there is rightly no sentiment in favor of a rule that removes all cases of bodily injury or property damage from the protection of the law. Rather, the critical choice is whether a defendant's responsibility should turn strictly on the fact of physical invasion or whether a defendant is properly chargeable only if the accident was one that could have been avoided through the exercise of reasonable care. Ordinary intuitions on this question are hopelessly divided, for some say that whoever inflicts physical injury should pay for the harm so caused, while others say that no legal remedy is appropriate unless the defendant's conduct fell below some socially determined standard of care. In legal parlance, this debate is said to be the debate between strict liability and negligence. Both legal principles have commanded wide allegiance over time, and each has been subject to searching criticism.

What causes the inability to reach consensus on so recurrent a social question? One way to understand the difficulty is to observe that usually judgment is rendered after the fact, when it is too easy to select a general principle because you already know your position in a particular dispute. It is much harder to determine your substantive commitments from behind the veil. Suppose that you did not know whether you would be the victim or the injurer in some subsequent accident, but you had equal chances of assuming both roles. Which rule of liability would you choose? This question yielded an emphatic answer when the question posed a choice between protection against the intentional infliction of harm or a free-for-all in which everybody could use force with impunity. There the burden of the restriction is more than compensated for by the security it provides. But this same veil of ignorance device speaks far less clearly on the duty to compensate for the subclass of accidents not avoidable by the exercise of reasonable care.

To see why, assume first that we live in a universe in which judges and juries can, costlessly and without error, determine whether or not the defendant exercised the appropriate level of care. Further assume that all individuals have the psychological presence of mind to make rational choices, that is, choices which advance their individual self-interest in whatever legal and social environment they find themselves. At this point it becomes virtually impossible for anyone to make an intelligent choice between the two legal rules, whether that person is motivated by the narrowest form of self-interest or the highest level of social concern, from behind a veil of ignorance.

A word of explanation is in order for this counterintuitive result. First we must define the idea of "due" or "reasonable" care in the law of negligence. For years the English judges spoke of the behavior of "the man on the Clapham Omnibus." But that is not a formulation that travels well outside England, or even south London. In the search for higher and more workable levels of generality, judges referred first to the behavior of the reasonable man, and more recently to that of the reasonable person. Jury instructions commonly speak of unreasonable risks created by, of course, the unreasonable conduct of the defendant. But that formulation only pushes the inquiry to another level, without resolving it. How do we know what the reasonable person does, or should do?

Answering this question often requires some refinement of the concepts of peril and precaution. One possible way of defining negligence, dating at least from Roman times, is to say that it is what results when you do not take the same level of care with the affairs of others that you would bring to your own affairs. In an effort to make this test more operational, some have suggested that negligence involves the failure to take common precautions against obvious risks, where the exact formula for striking the balance is left unspecified. The historical nuances of the negligence formula are subtle and varied, but in modern discussions the intuition behind the test is captured in a simple formula first articulated by Judge Learned Hand.[2] Under the Hand formula, the question of due care depends on the outcome of a cost/benefit analysis that expressly turns on three related variables: the first of these is the probability of an injury if a precaution is not taken—call that P; the second is the anticipated magnitude of the loss if the injury does occur—call that L; and the third is the cost of the precaution necessary to avoid the injury in question—call that B.

At this point it becomes possible to formulate the due care question in a way that is consistent with, but not compelled by, ordinary intuitions on the subject: If $P \times L$ is less than B, the accident is not worth preventing, because the precautions in question cost more than is gained. Certainly, if we abstract from the question of liability, and assume that any ordinary person must ask whether to take certain precautions against *self*-inflicted harm, some informal calculation of this sort is exactly what this person would undertake, assuming (as seems plausible) that he wishes to advance his own self-interest. It is therefore certainly not unprincipled for the legal system to ask a similar question about accidents involving two or more people. Indeed (to return to the initial assumptions), where the costs of perfectly determining the value of these three relevant variables is zero, the law has devised a perfect filter for handling such accident cases. Only those accidents that should have been avoided require compensation; the others will not. Since the rule is universal, everyone will benefit from it equally, and it looks therefore as though the law has stumbled upon an optimal rule—one that cannot be beaten.

But it is a rule that can be tied. Suppose now that the law chooses to dispense with the negligence inquiry and to hold defendants strictly liable for all harms that they inflict. It does not follow that no accidents will take place because all accidents are compensable. There is still the question of the interaction of the three critical variables, B, P, and L. Although the law may no longer command a jury to evaluate the inequality formed by these three terms, a rational defendant will undertake that basic inquiry with (let us for the moment cheerfully assume) the same costless perfection as our previous judge and jury. What is more, a person who makes the right calculations will prefer paying for those accidents that are too expensive for him to avoid. Here again, there is little reason to quarrel with the outcome, for in reality it is the same as that under negligence: just those accidents which should be avoided are avoided. All that differs is whether the accidents that could not be avoided at reasonable cost will be compensated: with strict liability the answer is yes. As with the negligence rule, under strict liability there is no deviation between what precautions would have been taken if the same person had been both injurer and victim. Everyone will enjoy at the outset the same level of wealth and utility under the one rule as under the other. And lest the payment of compensation be regarded as an end in itself, recall that first-party insurance against a wide class of injuries and risks is always available to meet any pressing financial needs of an injured party. Both rules are therefore optimal, which is why it is so hard for ordinary mortals to use their moral intuition to choose between them, and why first-year law students are generally unfamiliar with the distinction at the outset of their studies.

Thus far the equivalence in outcomes between the two systems depends on forming judgments behind the veil of ignorance in a world in which the cost/benefit standard of the negligence law can be perfectly defined and effortlessly applied. But we clearly know that these assumptions have to be false. If the rules of negligence were as precise as I have so far assumed, no accident would ever generate any liability, for the rational defendant would always have minimized his costs by taking all cost-effective precautions. But instances of negligence are commonplace, and some significant fraction of these depends on the psychological and informational difficulties that render my initial austere, not to say wishful, assumptions problematic at best. Yet once I relax these strong assumptions, the choice between the two rules will depend on an issue somewhat foreign to ordinary intuitions: what should be done when I trade my foolhardy, perfect-world assumptions for a more realistic environment in which gathering and interpreting information is difficult at every stage of the process, for individual actors, for judges, and for juries.

At this point it is possible to revert to the central heuristic trade-off that defines the case for simple rules: making any distinction always consumes administrative resources, and so it must be justified by some improvement in overall incentive effects. Here the negligence system will normally cost far more to operate than a regime of strict liability: collecting and interpreting information on the critical three variables is likely to be an exercise in frustration. Probabilities are normally best estimated over a series of similar recurrent events, and many accidents will (at least arguably) have some distinctive features, which require the jury to rely on crude hunches, ordinary experience, and sophisticated expert testimony that never comes cheap. Similarly, determining damages for injuries cannot be done by consulting a price list in a supermarket, for the task requires a detailed understanding of the cumulative effect of the forgone pleasures of living, medical expenses, and lost earnings, not only in the case as it occurred, but as it might have been anticipated when the defendant made his decisions to act. Finally, the costs of untaken precautions are often buried in some more complex set of decisions: one precaution might have reduced some accidents but increased the likelihood of others; another precaution might have been more unpleasant to live with but more effective to operate. The negligence system requires all these calculations to be made on the public record, and for what purpose—since the incentives for safe conduct are, as best we can determine, as good with the strict liability rule as with the negligence system?

It might be said in opposition that the negligence system offers one administrative advantage over the strict liability alternative, namely, that it reduces the number of legal disputes that do require adjudication by weeding out from the legal system cases of unavoidable accidents. But this supposed filter is likely to be very porous in cases involving strangers, for whenever there is an accident, it will be possible after the fact to point to something that went wrong. Since the calculations are often on the knife's edge (P = 0.01, L = $1,000, B = $11, no negligence; P = 0.01, L = $1,000, B = $9, negligence), there will be few cases clean enough for the filter to work. The level of complexity per case therefore dominates any culling effect of the negligence system.

An important lesson can be learned from this exercise. Efforts to refine and apply strong moral intuitions often lead to inquiries with a distinct economic cast, where the focus of the inquiry is to do the right cost/benefit calculations. But this implicit acquiescence in cost/benefit thinking does not require making cost/benefit analyses as part and parcel of the legal rules. Quite the opposite, achieving the efficient social outcome often requires that the legal rules *consciously* avoid making any explicit reference to cost/benefit analysis. Instead, the rules should measure the good or bad in conduct by the *output* (did A hit B or not; did A or B have the right of way), and leave it to the parties to determine how to maximize their own welfare within the legal constraints so established. Rules that force people to treat strangers as they treat themselves (as the strict liability rule does) will usually be far superior to any more refined legal rules that seek in a public forum to re-create or evaluate the types of decisions that rational actors did make, or should have made, before the fact. The endless refinements of the law of negligence add little to the quality of the decisions generated by the legal system. Here is yet another instance where what is simple is also best.

Harms Caused Jointly

Thus far I have considered only those accidents where one person has inflicted harm upon a stranger. Implicit in that discussion is the assumption that only one person caused or could have avoided the harm in question. But some of the most vexing problems of harms to strangers involve issues of joint causation, where the conduct of two or more parties is in some measure responsible for the injury at hand. (The parallel issue in the law of contracts arises when both parties are in breach.) In a strict liability system, it may well be that A and B hit each other, so we cannot say that one party moved and the other did not. Or, within a negligence system, it could have been that both sides failed to take precautions which, together or singly, could have avoided the harm in question. How should those cases of joint responsibility be resolved?

Start with the common case where the two parties responsible for the harm are the plaintiff and the defendant. One solution, much favored by the earlier common law judges wedded to a negligence system, was to use the negligence of the plaintiff to excuse the negligence of the defendant. The rule has an obvious simplicity. It can be defended on the ground that it avoids the expense of many lawsuits, and tiptoes around the delicate question of apportionment of damages that would otherwise have to be addressed. But to ordinary intuitions, this result seems unfair, and to the more economically minded it seems arbitrary and inefficient as well. Why should legal responsibility for bad conduct turn on the fortuity of who was injured in a head-on collision? And why should the legal system impose incentives on plaintiffs while giving defendants a free pass? It is just sentiments of this sort that have led most commentators and judges to embrace some system of apportionment in cases of joint responsibility regardless of how that responsibility is defined.

But the apportionment question merely leads to further inquiry— apportionment in accordance with what principles? Under the banner of comparative negligence, the modern cases and commentary have all opted for refinement. Try to figure out the percentage of responsibility from 0 to 100 in each case. On its face this looks like a simple inquiry. Indeed, the instructions to the jury usually state no more than that the loss to the plaintiff should be apportioned in accordance with the fault of the parties. Yet this is another instance where short is not simple, for working out the particulars will entail an extensive trial without any clear norms to guide its conduct. In some cases, an inquiry may focus on a comparison of the causal inputs by the two parties. If the use of force is the source of liability, greater use of force should result in greater liability. In other instances the approach is to measure the level of departure from the applicable standard of care. If large deviations are more culpable than small ones, the law should assign responsibility in the same proportions. In a world of reliable information, these exotic requirements might be worth undertaking. In fact, if you could exactly measure the percentage of deviation from the applicable standard, perfect apportionment would be possible. But in the crude world of legal administration, these analytically rigorous formulas are neutralized by the utter inability to supply the necessary data.

Here again the two parts of the basic inquiry yield a suggestive result: *divide by two*. Once it is established that both parties are responsible for the injury, then split the losses evenly. This rule has neither subtlety nor refinement, but it fulfills the ideal of apportionment and is far easier to administer than the common alternatives. Any greater precision could be justified only if it entailed some clear gain in the incentives it creates. But each effort to place greater responsibility on defendants only removes proportionately the incentives the plaintiff has for good behavior. It is impossible to know whether any change in legal outcome improves or reduces the overall result, even if we assume that parties can chart their behavior with knowledge of the precise course of a harm that has yet to occur. After the fact, people will make elaborate arguments to place the blame on the other side, but in most cases the upshot is that their efforts will cancel out, so that apportionment will be bunched about the 50 percent mark. That being so, the extra effort yields only a small variation from the automatic rule of an even split. So the entire struggle is hardly worth the candle, even if there is the occasional appellate decision that shows a radical split in liability.[3] Furthermore, for routine automobile collisions where both sides are in violation of the traffic rules, an even division of losses avoids recourse to sophisticated formulas whose cost far exceeds their utility.

Sometimes it is possible to introduce constrained modifications of the basic rule. Thus in one oft-litigated question, the issue is how to apportion fault where the plaintiff's sole misconduct is the failure to fasten a seatbelt. In this context, the 50 percent solution seems too harsh on plaintiffs, if only because much of the total harm might have occurred whether the belt was worn or not. But it does not follow that we must abandon the ideal of *wholesale* determinations simply because the 50/50 rule is out of phase. Seatbelt cases are quite common, and it may well be that a routine reduction of 25 percent of the total damages better approximates justice in this important and well-defined subclass of cases.

Yet those cases aside, most often the rule of even division works well in the bewildering array of jointly caused accident cases. Striking confirmation of the soundness of this approach comes from the law

of admiralty, which allocated the responsibility for collision losses at
sea under the divided damage rule until 1975, when the Supreme
Court displaced the older rules by adopting a pure comparative negligence rule in United States v. Reliable Transfer Co., Inc.[4] The facts of
that case show the difficulty of making such comparative judgments.
There the fault of the Coast Guard was its failure to maintain a break-
water light at a dangerous stretch of water. The fault of the captain
was the foolish decision to pass another ship in the channel during
the storm, when he knew that the light was not functioning. The trial
court thought that 75 percent of the fault lay with the captain, owing
to his rashness in setting the ship's course. Yet his decision was made
under conditions of serious uncertainty, while the Coast Guard could
have eliminated all the subsequent risk and uncertainty (by easy compliance with a simple and noncontroversial norm). The negligence of
both sides was necessary for the accident, and the care of either side
would have cured it. How then does one compute this ratio, or defend
it if challenged in another court? The Supreme Court found that the
75/25 percent split between the captain and the Coast Guard was appropriate, but even if this case was rightly decided, in how many other
cases could this claim of accurate division be made? (It seems highly
likely that the Court was looking for a clean set of facts in order to
strike down the older rule.)

The earlier admiralty practice is of special weight because it arose
in a close-knit community in which all the players—all professionals—were necessarily located behind the veil of ignorance, for when
the rule was announced, they could not tell whether it was in their
short-term interest in any particular case. The use of this customary
practice therefore reflected an implicit industry consensus that more
refinement of the damage split would do little to prevent accidents,
and much to complicate the administration of the law. It is hardly a
source of comfort that the rule was abandoned not because of any
general dissatisfaction with it on the part of the maritime community
but because of the disapproval of its rough nature by judges looking
in from the outside. The appeal to perfect justice once again is allowed
to disrupt the search for less subtle, but more hardy legal rules.

The principle of equal division, then, affords the best legal response
to the problem of joint responsibility. One further advantage to this
approach is that it allows easy generalization to still more complex
situations where three or more persons are responsible for the harm:

pro rata responsibility. If three defendants have harmed an innocent plaintiff, and all are solvent, then divide the loss by three. If the plaintiff is also at fault, divide by four and allow a recovery of three fourths of the loss. Matters become more difficult when one of the defendants is insolvent, but here too a simple response seems to work well: divide the loss attributable to the insolvent parties pro rata among the others. The rule of equal division becomes by easy stages a rule of apportionment: yet another simple rule for a complex world.

In this discussion of tort law I have focused thus far on harms inflicted on strangers. One striking feature of the modern law is that interactions with strangers now constitute a much smaller portion of the total cases than they did in earlier days. Medical malpractice and product liability cases, for example, arise out of contractual situations. At this point you might think that the simple rules of tort outlined above would carry the day in ordinary private disputes: after all, why shouldn't what makes sense between strangers also make sense between trading partners? But the correspondence is far from perfect: sometimes the rules of allocation resemble the strict liability rules (as with warranties for the replacement of defective goods), and sometimes they resemble the rules of negligence (as with the laws of medical malpractice).

What then should be the legal response to personal injury or property damage that is embedded in some form of a consensual arrangement? The problem has become an important one and arises whenever medical treatment results in medical injury, or when a visitor slips on a wet floor, or when goods are lost or damaged in shipment. Here again simple rules are useful in navigating a complex world. Consider first the relevant domains of contract and tort law. Between the parties, contract should dominate tort, and private decisions should dominate public commands. Yet the inveterate modern tendency is the reverse: tort dominates contract, and coercion dominates consent. So expanding the scope of the positive law violates the simplest rule of all—"unless otherwise agreed"—and invites courts to fashion legal regimes for the parties that they would never fashion for themselves. But it is far wiser for courts to follow a more modest course of action: to enforce agreements instead of overriding them. Private parties have better information about the relevant costs and benefits even if they cannot articulate their reasons with the conviction of a learned professor. In repetitive transactions, they have strong incentives to reach the correct result, if only by trial and error. If they adopt a contractual rule that achieves that result, then they can make both sides better off by shifting the price, up or down, in favor of the party that is asked to bear the increased portion of the risk. It is therefore a mistake to look at the terms governing loss allocation in isolation and to assume that if they are not in balance the entire agreement is suspect.

Second, in seeking to minimize the losses from destruction or accident, the parties typically take one leaf from the basic tort analysis of interactions between strangers. Their explicit economic concerns *never* lead to the voluntary adoption of an explicit cost/benefit formula that follows the lines of Learned Hand's famous formula, whose transactional weaknesses I discussed above. Quite the opposite, they make a systematic effort to avoid the informational problems of this approach. Consider these examples.

In cases involving the warranties for defective goods, the standard contract provisions are those of strict liability, but they are usually subject to explicit limitations on the extent of liability: fixed damages are paid or, more often, the seller assumes the obligation to repair or replace the goods in question, as long as they have been damaged in ordinary use. The last part of the formula is important to control the buyer's conduct (just as it is in cases involving strangers). The first part of the formula allows for the liquidation of liability (that is, it reduces liability to some fixed figure or easily applied formula) while offering the product buyer some confidence that the goods in question will conform with the stated warranties. Here the liability is strict because the ratio of defective to safe products is very low, and the likelihood of correlation between the seller's negligence and injury is usually very high. In most cases, this simple rule does as good a job in regulating the joint affairs of the parties as any other.

When the context shifts to personal injuries resulting from medical malpractice, however, we find no private agreements that adopt a strict liability rule. Instead, the principles of negligence dominate virtually every discussion of the question. But it is not the negligence of the Hand formula. It is the negligence standard which asks whether the defendant's practice has been in accordance with the custom of the profession or some significant portion thereof.[5] The use of this reactive standard, which continues to dominate current cases, does not represent a blindspot in the thinking of judges. Rather, their commendable restraint rests on a range of considerations that renders this rule, relative to its alternatives, an efficient one for allocating loss.

The standard of trade custom measures up well against both prongs of the great trade-off. Its administrative costs, relative to an unbounded cost/benefit inquiry, are low, for experts in the field can give voice to the relevant standards. And it encourages physicians to take difficult cases because they know that they will be judged by attainable standards. Nor is there any reason to fear that the customary standard will undermine initiatives for medical research. Breakthroughs in technology and treatment need carrots, not sticks. They stem from efforts to create new techniques to respond to demands for better outcomes and lower risks from patients and physicians alike, not from the prospect of crushing liability for an unfortunate misstep. Professional advancement, public recognition, financial profit, and personal satisfaction and curiosity are what drives innovation and research. The proper office of the tort system is to control avoidable blunders under existing technology, and that function will be compromised if it is assigned any more ambitious role.

Nonetheless, the standard has been attacked chiefly on the ground, in Learned Hand's words, that "a whole calling may have unduly lagged in the adoption of new and available devices," without any explanation as to why it would have any incentive to do so or, indeed, any convincing illustration that it did.[6] Nor is it easy to overcome this gap, whether real or imagined. The legal system that tries to construct its own cost/benefit analysis would fall (and occasionally has fallen) prey to a thousand traps for judge and jury alike. The most famous occasion when a court sought to override the customary standard involved the simple question of whether it was prudent to test for glaucoma in nonsymptomatic patients under the age of forty.[7] The court's own cost/benefit analysis was filled with doubtful assumptions about the anticipated severity of harm; it failed to correct the relative frequency figures by taking out the symptomatic cases; it did not consider the very high rate of false positives in the testing procedures, and the costs of further tests; and it assumed that the test was riskless in its application on the supposition that it was always properly performed. Its own cost/benefit analysis was inferior to that generated by the customary medical standard. It is hard enough to make medical decisions for purposes of treatment. It is well nigh impossible to make them for purposes of litigation, when no long and difficult set of decisions would be invulnerable to legal attack after the fact. The customary standard may lack the ostensible rigor of a cost/benefit analysis, but it is far cheaper to apply, and less capable of being misapplied or abused.

Invoking custom, however, is not the only way to avoid the clutches of a cost/benefit analysis. It is also possible to revert to the strict liability rule of paying for all harm caused. But strict liability will not work here, even if it works in other contexts. Quite simply, the success of that rule depends in large part on the assumption that most accidents between strangers, and most instances of defective products, are avoidable by the exercise of reasonable care. If the assumption were otherwise, the administrative burdens of the broad strict liability rule would be vastly increased by the large number of cases brought into the legal system when nothing could sensibly have been done to alter the outcome. The argument made earlier was, quite simply, that in cases involving strangers negligence principles should be rejected because they remove very few cases from the system while imposing heavy administrative costs on the large number of cases that remain.

The balance of convenience, however, shifts radically in the medical malpractice context. Here we know (from common experience to be sure, but know nonetheless) that many adverse consequences from dangerous surgery or aggressive drug treatment will result even from the best of all possible care. Indeed, the best surgeons may have the highest failure rates because they treat the most difficult cases. In this environment, the disadvantages of the strict liability rule are manifest: large numbers of cases are brought into the system, and all of them require a complex causal inquiry that seeks to apportion the responsibility for medical injury between the underlying disease condition and the medical treatment. The administrative burdens are high and the improvement in incentives is wholly absent, and is probably negative if the best doctors are so besieged with litigation that they refuse to handle certain kinds of cases (such as those in which there have already been previous unsuccessful surgeries) or abandon certain areas of expertise altogether.

The medical custom functions like the boundary conditions that can be observed in trespass cases. Those harms that result from compliance with the practice lie with the patient; those that result from noncompliance lie with the physician. That simple rule is not so simple as it sounds, but it is far simpler than any open-ended cost/benefit analysis, for in principle it offers a sharp up-or-down response that meets the needs of a liability system that also has to make up-or-down decisions. The customary standard thus strands far fewer delicate cases at the boundary than does any ordinary cost/benefit analysis. The two factors—administrative costs and incentive effects—that point to a strict liability rule in the context of cases involving strangers therefore lead to the customary care standard in medical cases. A single theory is able to account for critical discontinuities in the law regulating personal injuries.

A short digression: Why the recurrent crises in medical malpractice? And why a set of costs estimated at around 2 to 3 percent of the total health bill, far greater than the comparable costs in any other industrial society? One part of the explanation lies in the subtle erosion of the customary care standard. The customs have been forged in an environment in which defensive medicine has become an implicit social norm. As long as some medical practitioners have a genuine fear of liability, they can raise their own internal standards to respond to their heightened perception of risk. But once they do it, their new standard can be invoked against other practitioners who hold a different view. What ensues is a race to the bottom where the views of the most cautious wing of the profession set the standards for everyone else. Custom then becomes corrupted by external pressures.

At this point, the need for contractual correction becomes paramount, but remains practically unavailable. Since medical malpractice is regarded as a branch of tort law, the parties do not have freedom to set limits on damages by contract or to choose at the outset of the physician-patient relationship to settle their disputes through arbitration instead of litigation. In many cases, the legal subrules on matters of causation tend to treat harms from underlying disease as though they were medical injuries. The use of tort law, not contract rules, stifles the prospect of voluntary private correction of a wide range of uneducated judicial guesses. When judges become more concerned with providing compensation after the fact to the injured parties than with maximizing joint welfare before the fact, it is easy to get the wrong outcome, even if the customary standard is largely preserved.

It should not be supposed that the customary norm for medical malpractice is easily universalizable. That customary norm, for example, has been widely rejected in dealing with workplace injuries.[8] Although the law of workers' compensation is today a regulatory scheme (and the weaker for it!), in its origins, the system was contractual. The system was first adopted in the (unionized) mines and railroads in the middle part of the nineteenth century, when the formal tort law often allowed an employer to escape all liability by claiming that the worker had assumed the risk. This system of workers' compensation shares with the law of product warranties and medical malpractice the avoidance of any explicit use of a cost/benefit formula. But it also avoids any use of the traditional tort standard of strict liability or of the medical malpractice alternative of customary care. Instead, the usual rule, then as now, apportions liability in accordance with previously stipulated damages for injuries arising out of and in the course of employment, wholly without regard to the level of care taken by the employee, except in (rare) cases of willfully self-inflicted injuries.

Here too a strong economic logic drives the system. In those industries where accident rates are likely to be high, it pays to set up some special system for both the prevention and the compensation of losses. The costs of setting up the system can be spread over a large number of cases. The coverage of the workers' compensation system is in fact broader than the coverage offered by the strict liability rules of the tort system, for the worker need make no showing that the employer did anything wrong or, indeed, did anything at all to cause the injury. It is enough to show that the injury occurred on the job. There is still the need to regulate the plaintiff's conduct, for the willful misconduct rule covers only rare and egregious acts, too small a fraction of the overall system to be of general consequence. In this context, *low* damage awards operate as an effective check on the plaintiff's misconduct because they implicitly assign some fraction of the loss to the injured party, and thus give workers a strong incentive to monitor safety. Through the use of arbitration to run the system, a strong sense of industry practice can grow up to handle recurrent cases. Even in the early days of workers' compensation the rules allowed for compensation for those occupational diseases peculiar to particular industries and not normally suffered by members of the population at large.

Here again the efficient solution seeks by indirection to address the question of costs and benefits, but shies away from any explicit incorporation of the negligence calculus into the rules of liability. The pattern here is far from accidental, and results in relatively simple rules of liability for injury with desirable incentive effects. But it also gives rise to a note of caution. The choice of these rules is heavily industry-specific, which makes them poor candidates for second-guessing by courts and by legislatures. Also the financial problems with modern workers' compensation systems have origins similar to those of medical malpractice. The legislative increases in basic coverage and in compensation levels have undercut the effectiveness of the original contractual design.

HARMS TO RELATIONAL INTERESTS

The focal point of any system of tort law is its protection of person and property from physical invasion. But that protection can be extended in accordance with simple principles of law, as actions for loss of consortium by spouses and children of injured parties demonstrate. In this connection, two other torts—interference with prospective advantage and defamation—show how that expansion can usefully take place. Often, the use of force is directed not to the individual actually harmed, but to other people with whom that person wishes to trade. The use of force against A's potential trading partner normally inflicts losses on A as well, who had every reason to expect to profit from the exchange. The recognition of a cause of action for the interference with this "relational interest" preserves the exchange system and has long been recognized by the law of tort. Thus a schoolmaster is entitled to bring an action against a competitor who frightens off his pupils with a show of force, but he is not allowed to bring an action against the competitor who offers these same pupils lower tuition— unless they are already bound by contract with the first schoolmaster.[9]

Viewed in its general form, the distinction between force and competition is as clear in this area as the distinction between theft and voluntary exchange, for both are subsets of the same overall system. Only if we allow each person to examine his own place *selectively* do we find countless exceptions, all based on self-interest, to this general proposition. It is the all-or-nothing nature of the choices allowed that keeps individual egotism from running wild. People will choose competition for all and force for none if they are denied any preferred position for themselves.

In many cases, these relational interests are threatened not by acts but by words. The law of defamation addresses the harms inflicted when the defendant publishes (orally or in writing) to a third party false words about the plaintiff, which tend to disparage the plaintiff in the eyes of that party. It is commonly said that the law of defamation is concerned with the protection of reputation, which is analogous to the protection of physical integrity. Within limits that analogy is correct, but it should not be thought that reputation is some form of lifeless abstraction with no human consequences. Reputation, often in the form of business good will, involves the likelihood that others will interact or trade with you. When somebody uses false words to damage that reputation, the loss equates exactly to that in the previous cases—anticipated gain, social or economic, for others.

In protecting reputation, the law must decide whether actions for defamation lie only for deliberate lies or extend as well to falsehoods innocently uttered. Here of course it is important *not* to allow actions for *true* statements that injure reputation (save for information acquired in confidence), for true negative statements only correct reputations that are not deserved in the first place, and thus produce gains to the hearers of the statement that should not be ignored in any social calculus. But *false* statements both injure the plaintiff and mislead third parties, and thus have on balance a negative social value. Clearly, then, legal intervention is justified, because false words offer a close analogy to external aggression. It is most unlikely that a general audience will, or could, bring suit for the diffuse harms that they suffered. So a direct action by the target of the defamation has to do service for this host of smaller injuries.

Once the class of protected interests is expanded, what about the basis of liability? On this score, the common law opted for the strict liability standard for these false words. The soundness of that conclusion can be seen in the progeny of the Supreme Court's decision in New York Times v. Sullivan, which held that false words spoken of public officials (later extended to public figures) are actionable only if they were uttered with actual malice, that is, with knowledge that they were false or in reckless disregard of their truth or falsity.[10] The ability to damage reputation almost with impunity has led to the unfortunate result that powerful media defendants escape the obligation to correct or acknowledge past errors by showing that their mistakes resulted at most from inattention or neglect. Here the *contraction* of liability complicates litigation by injecting the issue of motive and knowledge into all cases, and simultaneously weakens the incentives for fair and accurate reporting. The simpler common law rule of strict liability on matters of fact does a better job of reconciling the different issues involved in defamation cases.

Harms That Should Not Be Compensated

A remaining question is how far the concept of harm may be expanded within the framework of the tort law. In particular, two sorts of harms have as of late been put forward as candidates for legal protection. The first arises when people take offense at what other individuals say or do, even when no force or fraud is involved. The second is harm that results from competition in open markets, where competitors are able to undersell their rivals, even those who have enjoyed entrenched positions in the basic market. In both of these situations, it is quite pointless to insist that the harms sustained by offended bystanders and disappointed competitors are not real: these people are worse off in virtue of the losses that they have sustained and feel keenly and deeply. To give legal protection against these forms of harms is to undertake an enormous expansion of the legal system. People's sympathies in individual cases might incline many to start down this road even if they are not quite sure how far they are willing to go. But the temptation should be resisted: for these types of harms, the only correct legal response is the simple one of no compensation.

Once again, consider a categorical situation from behind the veil of ignorance: Suppose that you do not know whether you will give offense or receive offense; or suppose that you do not know whether you will be a disappointed or successful competitor, or perhaps the purchaser who wishes to choose between them. What rule would you want to protect your own interest? The private losses from force and fraud were associated with social losses, but the same cannot be said in either of these cases. On matters of offense, consistent application of the principle means that if you cannot practice your religion because it offends me, then I cannot practice my religion because it offends you. As a confident empirical generalization, one can say that both sides lose more than they gain, so that a mutual renunciation of religious or personal freedom costs more than it provides—except of course where the exercise of religious belief comes in conflict, as it too often does, with the independent prohibition on force and fraud. The same caution should sound on issues of lifestyle and attitude. Nothing is more necessary than for everyone to recognize that there are limits on the extent to which personal preferences can govern the conduct or attitudes of other individuals. As a rule of thumb, the more you care about these issues, the more leery you should be of overreaching into the private domains of others.

Similarly, the constant appeals to competitive injury as a source of private relief are also misguided. If Japanese cars are better than American ones, American firms should improve their products, not impose tariffs and import quotas on their foreign rivals. If Southwest Airlines reduces its prices so that American Airlines and United Airlines are forced to respond, the last thing that is needed is an extravagant Texas lawsuit that claims this business practice is a form of unlawful predation, *even if* the jury arrives at a correct no-liability verdict. The language of predator and prey is best applied to lions stalking antelopes. It only operates as a misleading metaphor when applied to economic conflicts between strangers or economic competition between rival firms. Once again, the per se rule of no compensation is appropriate in all such cases. Unlike the harm ensuing from the use of force and fraud, the private loss in these contexts is not a reliable proxy for any form of social loss. As a first approximation then, the principle of force and fraud sets the appropriate limits on the extent to which one person may complain of the action of a stranger.

To summarize, the four rules that I have described so far establish what some might call a libertarian synthesis. They describe a world with strong and well-defined rights in persons and property, complete freedom of exchange, and powerful protection against external threats. On this last score, the most obvious points of separation between people are physical boundaries. Yet those rules will not be able to cover all the relevant situations in which redress of individual grievances is used to promote some overall standard of social welfare. To flesh out the system, it is therefore necessary to find other boundaries that work when barriers to physical invasion do not, and it is just there that the rules of custom and the prohibition of false statements by strangers take such strong hold. This synthesis has much durability, but unfortunately the real world is not quite this simple. We must think not so much about the "dark" side of this system as about its limitations. In doing so, we must take account of two other rules: the rule of necessity and the rule of just compensation, in both the private and the public arena.

6

Necessity, Coordination, and Just Compensation

The basic ground rules set out in the previous three chapters go a long way toward establishing a stable legal order largely impervious to variations in behavior, custom, and practice within and across societies. Individual autonomy, coexisting systems of private and common property, free exchange and protection are not some fleeting ad hoc requirements tied to any given level of technology or any current set of social beliefs. The inevitable differences across time and culture are easily taken into account by changing the *content* of the substantive agreements made within the basic framework. Since ordinary agreements respond to variations in local conditions, the emerging patterns of social behavior can differ profoundly across societies that are bound by the same set of legal rules.

All this is not to say, however, that these rules offer a complete solution to the legal problems of any given society. They do not, for they miss one important set of issues in both the private and the public law. These four basic rules together assume that voluntary transactions can produce gains from trade once the initial endowments in labor and property are set by law. In essence, the major impediment to a well-functioning system is the use of force against strangers, augmented in lesser degree by the use of false words. The protection against aggression and defamation and the enforcement of contracts are the major legal job in such a system. In practice, however, a second set of obstacles requires a fresh response. Thus in Chapter 4, I noted that voluntary contracts work best when there are multiple actors on both sides of the market. But more remains to be said about what should be done if entry on either side of the market is not possible, that is, in cases of *bilateral monopoly*, where A must do business with B and B must do business with A in order for either to gain. Of course, the best solution is to allow entry, so as to obviate these dangerous confrontations. But although that approach will work in some settings, it will hardly work in all, for there are some situational monopolies that the law does not create, and whose occurrence it cannot prevent. In those circumstances—which first arose in cases of necessity—controlling aggression is but one side of the coin. The other side of the coin is the problem of *coordination* when one party is in a position to *hold out* against the other for a huge portion of the potential gains from any contract. Here the task is to minimize the total distortions from two problems that often work at cross-purposes with each other. How might this be done?

PRIVATE NECESSITY

When critics seek to undermine a universal regime of free contracting, they typically offer a number of powerful counterexamples that echo on the single theme of necessity. Suppose you are in the desert and a man nearly dead of thirst staggers up to you and begs for something to drink. You say, "Sure, I'll give you something to drink. It cost me a dollar to get this glass of water for you, so a million dollars (which we both know you have) will be the contract price. You pay me that much, and you will be better off because you will be alive. Oh, by the way, I'll be better off, too, because a million dollars is more than the cost to me of producing the glass of water." The standard, strong-willed libertarian will say that this contract is as good as any other, given the mutual gains from trade.

Those of us who are a little bit more tempered in our beliefs will generally recognize, as did the common law in England and the United States, and the earlier Roman law, that the basic rules of property will normally be suspended in the face of necessity.[1] This necessity exception is narrowly defined to cover only those cases where there is imminent peril to life or to property. Where it is in place the owner of the water cannot on strict principle use force to defend his water against the demands of the stranger consumed with thirst. Indeed, necessity inverts the usual relationship between owner and stranger, for the party in need is entitled to use force in order to wrest the water from its owner. Similarly, a ship's crew caught in a storm may use force to take refuge at a lakeside dock, and a traveler caught in a storm may take refuge in a barn or, perhaps (if there be no peril to the owner), in a dwelling house as well.

The necessity principle carries with it, however, a correlative duty: just compensation to the owner. When A has an enormous "holdout" advantage over B, where the thing that B needs as a matter of life and death can be provided at very low cost, the rule is: "take now *and* pay later." But when all is said and done, B's duty is circumscribed: pay the ordinary market value for the bottle of water, or the rental value for the dock, and perhaps a little extra to compensate A for the loss of control. The rights of property are attenuated, but respected, by this compromise solution. It is not as though the stranger in need can treat the water as though it were unowned or its owner as a resource devoid of rights. The compensation is designed to leave the owner indifferent between the state of affairs where she is left alone and one in which the property is taken for use by another. It is a simple rule, moreover, that prevents the party in need from overstating his needs or from taking more than is required. The just compensation principle also has the desirable effect of reducing the level of resistance from the owner, who now is assured that the stranger's necessity will not become her private loss.

The just compensation solution thus addresses both sides of the coin: it allows but limits aggression, and it neutralizes the advantages of the holdout position. To see the logic of this solution, it is instructive to apply the same test that has guided us thus far. Before the event, would you rather have the absolute right to exclude under all circumstances, only to be excluded by others? Or would you rather be subject to the duty to admit in cases of necessity, especially if you received just compensation, if you could compel others to accept you under like necessities?

The opponents of the private necessity rule fear that its incorporation into the legal system will swamp the basic system of property rights that makes ordinary voluntary exchanges possible. The basic rules of property, contract, and tort are all hard-edged. Necessity, it is claimed, perches us at the top of the slippery slope. But it does no such thing when correctly applied. Not only is it improper to say that ordinary shortages of commodities give rise to situations of necessity, but it is even improper to expand the concept of necessity to cover the housing shortage after the 1906 San Francisco earthquake, the shortage of lights in the 1965 New York City blackout, or the lack of chainsaws and electric generators in Charleston after the devastation of Hurricane Hugo. In all these cases, the concept of necessity should not be invoked, even if there is some temporary increase in the price of needed equipment and commodities after the onset of a major disaster.

All these extended versions of necessity differ in a palpable way from the crisis of the starving man in the desert or the ship in imminent peril of being capsized in the storm with all hands aboard. In San Francisco, New York, or Charleston, multiple sellers and buyers populate each market even after disaster has struck. Although a sudden shift in demand may move prices rapidly upward, there is no particular reason to believe, even in the short run, that some nonprice system will do a better job of responding to external shock than the entry of new sellers into an open market. The turmoil that follows widespread social dislocation does not simply present situations comparable to the stark cases of necessity where the privilege is recognized. In its most distinctive aspect, however, such a crisis requires the coordination of the efforts of thousands of independent people, many of whom are driven by a strong sense of fear and a strong need for survival. It is quite impossible to allow people to take the equipment owned by others for their own use in the hope that the correct level of compensation at some future time will be tendered in exchange. The sheer risk of protracted violence should caution against unleashing this orgy. If the usual requirements of voluntary exchange are observed, the sharp upward movement in prices will serve as a powerful magnet to introduce new supplies from unsuspected quarters that will quickly bring prices back down toward their pre-crisis level.

The results can be stunningly quick. San Francisco had a viable rental housing market within a month after the earthquake, but was unable to respond nearly as rapidly to its housing shortage at the end of World War II. For its part the New York housing market still faces chronic shortages fifty years after rent control was introduced in response to wartime housing shortages.[2] The prices for needed equipment in Charleston came tumbling down within several days after the storm struck.[3] It also helps that charitable assistance is often made widely available (no one worries that people are feigning need when their houses are flooded by a hurricane). In addition, steady customers often receive favorable price terms from retailers who are moved by some intrinsic sense of fairness or by a desire to obtain the gains of long-term relational contracts.

The necessity defense should therefore be confined to the strict bilateral monopoly situation, where the prospect of entry does erode the monopoly position of the dominant player. It should not be, and has not been, expanded to undermine the importance of security of exchange. It should be evident that the necessity exception, however indispensable, is not cut from the same cloth as the rules on fraud and duress. Yet by the same token, necessity should be kept radically distinct from woollier conceptions of economic duress or unequal bargaining power based on differential wealth. Necessity stems from the bilateral monopoly position in which one person has a dominant holdout position that undercuts the effectiveness of the bargaining process.

JOINT OWNERSHIP BY MISTAKE

Bilateral monopoly problems also arise in situations that at first glance look far removed from these necessity cases. But when necessity appears in yet other guises, the combination of take and pay also provides a sensible solution. For example, one very important set of questions in Roman and common law involves the arcane topics of accession, specification, and confusion:[4] the classical heads of law when the labor or property of two persons is mixed together *by mistake*. Some measure of the great historical importance of the subject is the amount of space these topics receive in the classical treatments of the issue. Justinian's *Institutes* devotes twice as many pages to these questions as it does to the law of sale, a vastly more important commercial subject, but oddly enough one of less theoretical importance because it falls so neatly under the rules of voluntary exchange. In contrast, these problems cry out for legal solutions that require an enlargement of the basic repertoire of legal rules beyond the four rules of autonomy, acquisition, exchange, and protection.

The basic problem is easily set out. A owns some property—say a piece of wood—which B uses to make a statue. The question is who owns the statue and why. If A and B are in agreement as to the ultimate ownership of the statue, then ownership follows the agreement: ordinary contracts work to assign title. If B steals the wood from A, generally A gets back the statue, because no person is allowed to profit from his own wrong. Requiring B to surrender the wood, and thereby to sacrifice his labor, is one cheap way to deter theft by encouraging B to use his own wood. The difficulties come when B by innocent mistake comes into the possession of the block of wood. It may be that A has left her block in B's house by mistake, or that a third person delivered it to B instead of A. Then B carves the statue thinking in good faith that the block is his own. Now that each party has made a contribution to this inadvertent joint venture, who keeps the statue, and why?

This question is far more subtle than might first appear. One possible solution is to return the block of wood to A, who owns it (along with the shavings). But that solution forces a transfer of B's labor to A, in violation of the autonomy principle that accords to each person control of his own labor. So to protect B's labor the statue should stay in his hands. But now A has lost her wood without receiving anything in return. This last clause gives the clue to the classical solutions to the problem of a mistaken, innocent, and irreversible combination of inputs from two parties into a single thing: follow the lead of the necessity cases. One party takes the property or labor of the other, but pays compensation. The explanation? The mixture of the goods creates a bilateral monopoly situation between A and B, blocking a return to the status quo ante where A owns her (unaltered) block of wood and B owns his (now expended) labor. Perhaps the law could treat the two parties as partners in a common venture in proportion to their inputs, but that solution forces two strangers into the fiduciary obligations of co-owners against their will—not the kind of obligations that should ever be imposed without consent. Just compensation for transfer of rights becomes the preferred solution. It respects the inputs of both innocent parties while allowing them to go their separate ways, as they could before the unfortunate mix-up took place.

But who gets to keep the thing, and who is forced to settle for the just compensation? No single, categorical answer covers the enormous range of cases, but some guidelines light the way. The most important rests on the difference between market and subjective value. A's block of wood is a fungible commodity. Apart from the unfortunate mix-up, it is highly unlikely that she had any special attachment to it, or could explain why she bought it, and not another of like grade and quality. The statue is a unique work of art whose value is highly uncertain. Awarding the statue to B, and requiring the payment for a substitute board to A, is clearly preferable to giving the statue to A, and then making ticklish evaluations of the value added to the statue by B. Since it is most improbable that A would be the one person to buy the statue if B had made it out of his own materials, the classical solution has yet another advantage: it tends to award the thing to the party who values it most. In essence, for a low administrative cost (that of finding out the value of the block of wood) the law imposes a forced purchase that leaves A an equivalent to her block of wood and B as well off as if he had carved the statue from his own block of wood. An elegant and simple solution to a tricky problem.

It should not be supposed, however, that all cases of accession and confusion are that simple to resolve. Where A innocently builds her improvements on B's land, it is far from clear who should end up the owner of the combined entity. Modern inclinations on this issue might favor a transfer of the title of the (fungible) land to A. Historically, however, the rule was the other way, perhaps because the formalities necessary to secure a transfer of land (permanent, valuable, and unique) were highly elaborate, while labor could be hired under simple consensual contracts. It is better to avoid forced transfers of land without the necessary formalities, and better to give the good faith improver (for such is what A was called) the incentive to stay off B's property by limiting her rights. This subject gives rise to many other variations, which it is not necessary to recount here: for example, A and B could contribute inputs that are used by C. The key point is that the rule of takings under conditions of necessity (now understood to be bilateral monopolies) upon payment of just compensation became an indispensable part of any system of private law from its earliest moments.

DIVORCE

Another area that gives rise to the same formal problem of private law is divorce.[5] Although there is an abundance of possible mates, parties seeking a divorce have no such luxury: each can obtain that divorce only from the current spouse. That simple one-on-one situation is the source of all the difficulties in fashioning the right set of rules. A rule that allows one party to divorce at will does little to protect the party to the marriage who invests first in the relationship: in classical settings, although less so today, the wife who has worked at low-paying jobs to put her husband through professional school. To allow him to divorce at will is to permit him to reap the benefits of her labor, much as if A were allowed to keep a statue B carved out of A's materials.

Alternatively, a rule that requires mutual consent between the parties is one that invites an impossible holdout situation. The party who wants to get out of the marriage could be asked to surrender everything in exchange for freedom; that is the situation under Jewish law, where a religious divorce, or "Get," takes place only with joint consent. Its dramatic possibilities have become fodder, with appropriate supernatural overtones, for an incident on the TV show *L.A. Law* (the husband unconscionably holds out for full title to the marriage home, only to see it destroyed by fire after the wife capitulates). By process of elimination, there is some gravitation to a system where the divorce takes place as of right, upon payment of just compensation for the release—alimony and support.

In this regard, the modern tendency to create flexible rules—the so-called principle of equitable division—of alimony, child support, and property division only introduces a limited version of the holdout problem by the back door. One common ploy is for the husband to insist on joint custody of the children of the marriage, which he abandons only after he receives his wife's concessions on the economic issues pertinent to the divorce. Here again a fixed rule for property division happily reduces the level of game-playing that is available, for it is no longer possible to link the two issues together in one negotiation. Here is yet another illustration of how simpler legal rules can produce more desirable incentive effects.

DAMAGES AND SPECIFIC PERFORMANCE

The problem of divorce illustrates a larger issue of remedial law under contract that implicates the now familiar combination of take and pay. A competitive market may offer parties a large choice of contracting partners, but once the contract is formed there is only *one* party to whom each side can look for performance. If one side decides to renege, where else should the other turn? It is precisely because the market is unable to secure performance that some legal remedy must be supplied in the first place. Ordinarily, we do not dwell heavily on the remedial question because reputation and the prospect of continued dealings lead to a high level of performance wholly without regard to the threat of legal sanctions. But where the prospect of breach arises, then the two parties stand in a bilateral monopoly relationship with each other. I may choose to lend money to anyone of a thousand persons; I can only collect the debt from my debtor.

In these circumstances, do we stick with the rules that require strict performance or do we adopt some just compensation formula?[6] The first response parallels that given in Chapters 4 and 5: let the parties choose the remedies; do not impose remedies as a matter of law. But what remedies should the parties choose if they advert to the problem, and what remedies should be supplied if they do not? Here the basic choice is between one solution that gives strong protection to contract entitlements and a second that treats the party in breach as having an option to perform *or* pay damages—where the so-called expectation damages are damages calculated to give the innocent party benefits equivalent to those that would be gained from the expected performance.[7] This last remedy is one that allows A to take B's property right (that is, his right to receive the goods under contract) upon payment of just compensation. In form and in structure, the choice of remedies is identical to that advocated in the problems addressed above.

To see what is at stake, assume that A and B have a contract whereby A will sell B widgets for $1,000, and that thereafter A gets an offer from X for $1,500. Can A walk away from the contract if he is prepared to pay B the $200 it will take for her to procure the widgets from another supplier at $1,200? Or must A obtain B's release from the contract? Requiring a release allows B to play dog-in-the-manger and refuse to release A unless he forks over to her a large chunk of his anticipated $500 in additional profits, say $400. The danger of B's holding out could lead to a collapse of the A-X transaction, for the bargaining costs could well consume the entire $300 in potential gain.

An expectation measure of damages averts this difficulty only by creating the inverse problem: what if the provable losses to B are only $200, but the intangible costs of dislocation are twice that amount? Socially it is better for A to perform, because his $500 gain is smaller than B's $600 loss. Yet the low level of provable damages will induce what has been called, perhaps misleadingly, an "efficient breach" of contract. In choosing between remedies, the ultimate trade-off is one that compares the cost of renegotiation of a release with the costs of incomplete compensation when only damages are required. With cases involving land sale, specific performance is the norm; for labor contracts, where performance is not easily compelled, damages are awarded, but the breaching party sometimes may be enjoined from working or performing for a rival. These solutions are simple and serviceable, but they are not uniformly robust; so many contracts contain explicit options that allow A to withdraw on some payment, set (usually for reasons of simplicity) at some specific dollar figure or easily calculated by some express formula. Thus one reason we can be confident that take and pay solutions are a necessary part of any system of law is their voluntary incorporation into contracts to obviate what might become major coordination problems.

DAMAGES AND INJUNCTIONS

The potential use of just compensation rules also arises in remedial settings under the tort law. In their justly famous article on the subject, Guido Calabresi and Douglas Melamed captured much traditional learning by distinguishing between what they called *property rules* and *liability rules*.[8] Property rules are those which are consistent with the first four of our simple rules. The owner of entitlement loses that entitlement only by individual consent, save in those circumstances where he is guilty of committing a wrong. A liability rule offers weaker remedial protection for the initial entitlement in that its holder is entitled to damages only if the entitlement is either taken or destroyed. Specific performance is a property rule in the world of contract remedies; expectation damages are a liability rule. In both tort and contract contexts, the defining feature of a property rule creates a holdout situation where the holder of the property has monopoly power. Yet by the same token, a liability rule allows the taking of property upon payment of just compensation.

The situation is simpler where the property has already been destroyed, so that all that remains is the question whether the plaintiff is entitled to compensation. Calabresi and Melamed introduced their distinction between property and liability rules to deal with the problem of threatened and uncertain future harm. Such cases arise most notably in disputes between neighboring landowners, where a choice of remedies has to be made, analogous to the choice between expectation damages and specific performance. One possibility is to prevent the defendant from operating, say, his factory so as to eliminate any possibility of pollution. If that is done, the familiar bilateral monopoly problem crops up because the only person from whom the factory owner can purchase relief is the neighbor who might suffer pollution. Alternatively, a court might allow the factory to operate, subject to an obligation to compensate for any losses thereafter sustained. As with the other cases involved, it is necessary to figure out which of these two remedial systems outperforms the other.

Although the setting is quite different, the relevant considerations are similar to those involved in cases of confusion and accession. If the potential damage is to barren and unproductive land of no distinctive value, then the loss is like the deprivation of a fungible piece of wood: accordingly, money damages should be the preferred remedy. It seems better to allow the defendant's activity to go forward so long as the capacity to make full compensation for future losses is assured. Similarly, if the probability of harm is low, the damage remedy instead of the injunction is likely to minimize the costs of error: why prevent any action which 99 percent of the time will not cause any damage if compensation can be paid for the 1 percent of the time where it does? As one court put it in denying an injunction against the operation of a copper-smelting plant in Tennessee brought by the owners of "thin mountain land": "Shall the complainants be granted, in the way of damages, the full measure of relief to which their injuries entitle them, or shall we go further, and grant their request to blot out two great mining and manufacturing enterprises, destroy half the taxable income of a county, and drive more than 10,000 people from their homes?"[9] More precisely, the question is whether the defendants will be forced to buy out the injunction at some astronomical price, given the holdout question. It is easy to guess the court's answer from the tone of its question.

By the same token, however, when the size of the plaintiff's loss becomes larger, when the nature of the interests are more difficult to evaluate (as in a case involving a nature preserve), and when the probability of harm increases, the balance of equities tends to change: now compensation is more likely to be needed, and more difficult to measure, but less likely to be available, and less likely to be sufficient. At this point, the property rule seems to create fewer dangers; so consent of the neighboring owner is required before the activity can go forward. Between these two extremes lurks a thousand intermediate possibilities, many of which take the form: "defendant may use his lands so long as some conditions on time, place, and manner are observed and so long as damages are paid for any residual harm." But beneath the welter of relevant considerations, the best general solution probably is to grant the injunction unless the plaintiff's expected harm is minor relative to the defendant's forgone gains. That solution in effect uses the strong set of absolute entitlements to set the baseline norm, and allows deviation from it only in those cases where the holdout problem is likely to be pronounced.

So is this solution a simple rule, or is it rather more complex given the number of intermediate cases that have to be arrayed along a single axis? It is a little bit of both. The individual cases on the balance of equities and convenience are sometimes close to call and difficult, although often, as in the Tennessee case, they are easy. In this regard, looking only at the decided cases overstates the frequency of difficult cases, since the easy cases are either never brought or are resolved long before trial. Only the hard ones remain. Viewed over the full domain of cases, then, the day-to-day operation of the law is far simpler than the occasional borderline case would suggest: the number of cases that squeeze through the sieve are quite small. Most ordinary uses of land do not count as nuisances. For many that do, the bare threat of a damage award will drive out the offending use. For the few cases that remain, the injunction will often issue as a matter of course. Only at the end of a very long journey do we come to a subset of cases in which the choice of remedy remains difficult even after all factual disputes are resolved. Nonetheless, some comfort can be taken that the variations are themselves so difficult to foresee that no private party could hope to take advantage of the lingering ambiguity before the fact. When private parties stop trying to beat the legal system, it is time to call for the legal system to call it quits on further doctrinal refinements. The simplicity of legal rules makes it easier to deal with complex factual situations. But it does not eliminate the complexity altogether.

MONOPOLY AND ANTITRUST

The analysis of necessity and bilateral monopoly has presupposed a set of problems that arose from circumstances beyond the power of the parties to avoid. Yet what should happen if the number of independent players on one side of the market is reduced by voluntary agreement in transactions that are designed not to provide goods and services within the market, but to prevent competition that otherwise would take place between rival suppliers? Such collusion would normally reduce the supply of goods below that found in a competitive market. Similar collusion could take place in labor markets, since either employers or employees could seek to fix wages below or above competitive levels, respectively. It would be a mistake, however, to assume that any resulting changes in price and wage levels is simply a transfer from consumers to producers. Real allocative losses take place because the change in price level forecloses some mutually advantageous transactions that would take place if prices or wages were set at competitive levels. There are thus social losses that result from the change in market structure. In principle, if there were no coordination problems whatsoever, all consumers could band together and *pay* producers money to remain competitors, leaving both sides better off than before.[10] Yet the difficulties of coordinating individual behavior make this response wholly unlikely. The question then is, what is the second-best solution? In particular, should some restrictions be placed on mutually beneficial voluntary transactions because of their systematic negative effects on third parties?

To respond to this problem it is necessary to deal once again with the trade-off between incentives and administrative costs. One possibility is for the legal system to do nothing at all. Within this environment, any given contracting party can rely on self-help, and insist by contract that any potential suppliers not collude with each other. At that point, bid-rigging and price-fixing become contractual wrongs remedied in the normal contractual fashion. This is the flipside of asking workers to sign "yellow dog" contracts—to agree not to join a union while working for the employer. The point of the system is to allow employers to use self-help to fend off a labor monopoly. Prohibiting the employer from demanding this minimal assurance of loyalty reduces the likelihood of a private cure for the monopoly problem. Voluntary arrangements to fix prices and wages will quickly fall apart, because monopoly pricing will invite the entry by new parties with low prices—a possibility not present in the necessity cases. Within markets, firms can bid up the price of wages; and new workers, even if denounced as "scabs," can undercut union power—but only as long as state power is not used to bolster monopoly positions.

It is possible, however, to take a somewhat more aggressive stance toward these collusive arrangements. The most obvious course of action is to adopt the classical common law approach, which renders legally unenforceable all horizontal arrangements (that is, arrangements between parties on the same side of the market), notwithstanding the general presumption in favor of enforcing voluntary agreements.[11] This strategy differs from the do-nothing approach in that it expedites the process of new entry by allowing members of the cartel or price-fixing arrangement to cheat on their own collective agreement by expanding their output beyond their allocated quotas. As the number of cartel members increases, the likelihood that at least one will cheat increases. Since the threat of new entry from outsiders remains undiminished, the pricing arrangement is likely to disintegrate speedily. The administrative costs are again low, and the potential for government mischief is sharply constrained because there is no Federal Trade Commission or Antitrust Division to go astray in an excess of administrative zeal. The only risk is that courts cannot distinguish between cartels with market power and ordinary firms, a risk that is faced even in the most minimal of antitrust regimes.

This system of nonenforcement does not touch the set of horizontal mergers and acquisitions that could in principle result in an increased concentration within the marketplace. Quite simply, when two separate firms agree to combine their assets into a single legal entity, the question of contract enforcement is obviated by the permanent change in corporate structure. But it is unwise to think that any system of government review can distinguish corporate combinations that increase market competition from those that do not. Often these mergers take place in a world market, so that the number of potential rivals remains large enough to ensure effective competition even if the number of active firms is diminished by one. In addition, mergers and other corporate combinations differ from simple price-rigging arrangements in that they often have beneficial as well as harmful third-party effects. The takeover may allow the expertise of one firm to exert effective control over the productive assets that lie in the control of another firm. The size of these efficiency gains could be very large, even if the parties to the transaction are unable to identify and quantify these gains for skeptical regulators who themselves have little incentive to make the right choice. And even if one could show that some undesirable increase in market concentration more than offset the efficiency gains in the abstract, the costs in administration, error, and delay are likely to exceed any possible gain that one could achieve by stopping the merger or acquisition from going forward. As before, the best protection against illicit concentration is the removal of restrictions against entry into national and international markets; and the tedious, expensive, and unreliable process of reviewing mergers may only retard that desirable practice. The best rule is again the simple one: if the parties are prepared to incur the expense of some permanent corporate rearrangement, no legal force should oppose them.

Thus it is desirable to have a more restrictive role for the law of antitrust than is now the common practice, which allows aggrieved third persons to attack the monopoly arrangement as the commission of a tort and to claim damages for the losses that they are said to suffer. Such is essentially the approach of the 1890 Sherman Act, which prohibits combinations in restraint of trade. This approach has many champions.[12] Still, on balance, it too represents an excess of regulatory controls, which should be avoided, here by the repeal of the basic statutory framework. The increased administrative expense of this approach is evident, and the costs are scarcely reduced when elaborate regulatory boards must give preclearance for mergers or other corporate adjustments.[13] And the allocative gains of this approach are either negligible or nonexistent. It is too easy for administrative prohibition or private suits to be directed against contractual practices that are themselves unexceptionable, as when a manufacturer allocates separate territories to its various retailers; and much of the antitrust policy before 1980 did represent an excess of zeal, both by government and by private parties.

All this is not to say that there are in principle no gains from a restrained and sensible antitrust policy. But by the same token, it should never be assumed that any ideal antitrust policy will survive unscathed the hurly-burly pressures of a political environment, in which the incentives for individual actors often cut at cross-purposes with the one sensible objective of an antitrust law. Quite simply, it is too easy in a political setting to forge an antitrust law that is more intent on protecting the position of marginal competitors than on ensuring the preservation of open markets in which large and small firms can compete for business on equal terms. A healthy measure of skepticism is always in order about any public enforcement mechanism as long as free entry remains available to undercut collusion.

Unfortunately, too often legislative intervention violates the first principle of government action: do no direct harm. Far from preventing collusive practices, government tampering risks underwriting these harms by requiring licenses, imposing tariff barriers, encouraging voluntary quotas, or passing antidumping regulations—all counterproductive steps that impose heavy administrative costs while undercutting the effectiveness of competitive markets.[14] At every turn, there is an insistence that some form of "competitive injury" justifies the restriction on exchange. Yet in each and every case, the right answer is that the gains to the consumers offset the ostensible losses to producers, who now have an additional incentive to produce lower goods at better prices and who benefit from a legal regime that affords them the advantage of competitive prices when seeking inputs into their own productive process. The harms from monopolies created, supported, and protected by government intervention are greater in extent and more difficult to expunge than the harms created by private monopolies. The simple per se rule that regards all competitive injury as noncompensable fits the bill. It is imperative to avoid succumbing to the power of physical imagery by treating the myriad forms of price-cutting and predation as tantamount to ordinary aggression. And there is little reason to muster heavy ammunition to dissolve cartels that are likely to collapse quickly of their own weight. The necessity principle scarcely requires the erection of a complex body of antitrust law that is far too likely to go astray.

7

Take and Pay

In the last chapter I showed how the theme of take and pay plays a powerful role in all sorts of private contexts. A new measure of complexity is injected into the system when this principle is applied to the state and to its power to take, regulate, and tax land.

OCCUPATION AND REGULATION

Often the government needs to obtain material resources from individuals in order to supply services to the public at large. In some cases, it can purchase those goods from individual members of the public in competitive market transactions, and does so because a system of voluntary exchange is cheaper to operate than one that relies on forced requisitions from unwilling vendors. But holdout and coordination problems preclude that consensual solution for certain key assets, such as specific parcels of land needed for the construction of a fort or a public road. This problem is best met by government taking with payment of just compensation. Ideally, the individual citizen is left indifferent to the loss because of the compensation paid, and the public at large reaps the benefit of state action, a benefit in which the individual citizen whose property is taken shares as well (which is one reason to be especially leery of the use of the eminent domain power against foreigners or citizens of other states). This solution has a familiar pedigree, for it tracks the rules governing expectation damages in contracts and remedial damages in torts.

There is today relatively little disagreement on the obligation of the government to pay full compensation for the value of land that it occupies and uses for public purposes. Yet here the lurking difficulties with damages in private settings must be attended to as well. Recall that with expectation damages, the major risk was undercompensation—that intangible losses to the innocent party would not be reflected in the awards. Yet too often the modern rules of just compensation raise the prospect of undercompensation to an exquisite art form. Moving costs, assessor's costs, loss of business good will, and the profitable prospect of a renewed lease are all disregarded in calculating damages. First the government throws someone off his land, and then it treats the cost and inconvenience of his forced exit as though they were voluntarily incurred by an owner eager to abandon his own property. This indefensible pro-government bias explains why the prospect of condemnation is greeted with dread by those who lie in the path of the public bulldozer: they bemoan their fate even after they receive what the government, but no one else, calls full compensation.

Worse still, these distortions in compensation schedules create social dislocations as well. The just compensation awards set a price schedule for the state; if set too low, the price operates as a subsidy that induces state condemnation where the gain to the public is below the private losses to the owner. The social upshot is too much condemnation. The simple rule that requires full damages in tort or contract should apply with remorseless force in cases of government taking precisely because it alone possesses the broad power to determine which persons and which property are subject to its condemnation power.

The law of eminent domain would be relatively uncomplicated if the only question is whether the government has to pay for land that it occupies. Under this view, all regulation of the rights to use and dispose of land (be it by sale, barter, lease, or mortgage) would lie within the power of the state to impose or not, as it chooses. This rule has the advantage of an evident simplicity. As long as the same party is in possession of the land before and after government action, no challenge to its constitutionality could be raised. But that same rule has catastrophic incentives effects on both government officials and private parties. The moment it is said that the state may allow an individual the bare right to walk on his land, or the far more comprehensive right to build an office building on it, someone, somewhere and somehow, will seek to influence through the political process the uses that will be allowed for the land. The owner of a nearby high-rise building or shopping center will spend resources to convince local government officials to shut down a project that poses a competitive threat even if it generates substantial benefits to the community at large. The political cycle of intrigue that follows will consume extensive social resources while degrading the overall decision process.

The only way to end the political struggles is to create a legal regime in which government officials do not have the power to create or destroy fortunes with a stroke of the pen. Accordingly, it truly would be a mistake of monumental proportions to confine protection under the takings clause of the Constitution to cases of outright dispossession. Although the modern law of takings is typically hostile to the claims of property owners, even it does not take the extreme position that equates private ownership rights with the bare possession of property. Instead, it explicitly recognizes that some forms of regulation on use and disposition may be imposed only if compensation is provided. Indeed, today the burning issue of modern takings law involves the definition of these "regulatory" takings: what rules should determine whether compensation should be paid where the government limits the owner's power to use or dispose of private property, but does not enter into possession of that property for its own benefit? The modern view is to say that government regulation of use is not a taking, for which compensation is payable, unless and until government restrictions go "too far."[1] Yet it now appears that this point is never quite reached unless the state imposes a *complete limitation* on land use. As long as any beneficial use is left to the owner of the land, the courts will not inquire into the reasons for the regulation or demand compensation for the loss of value that the restrictions impose. The rind of property remains with its owner, but its juices are sucked out by the state.

The constitutional rules will heavily influence state behavior. In the most well-known of the recent takings cases, Lucas v. South Carolina Coastal Council,[2] the issue turned on a South Carolina statute forbidding any construction of new homes close to the beach. Two stated justifications for the restriction were to increase tourism in the state and to improve the leisure activities of South Carolina citizens. Under that statute, South Carolina prohibited David Lucas from building ordinary single-family homes on either of the two lots that he acquired for a total of nearly $1,000,000, even though a similar home was already perched on the lot between his two newly acquired ones. The Supreme Court ordered the Council to pay Lucas full value for both lots since the restrictions had rendered them worthless. Lucas finally recovered $1,500,000 in compensation (the lots had risen in value since their initial purchase), but virtually all of his profit went to his bankers and lawyers. South Carolina was forced to take title to the lots, which it promptly resold, naturally, for development as single-family homes. The aftermath of the case shows the wisdom of the compensation requirement, for the noble intentions of the Coastal Council were wholly dependent on someone else's footing the bill. At every level, and in every context, government looks far closer at restrictions that it must fund than at those which it funds out of the hide of one of its hapless citizens. Even governments demand less when they have to pay more.

Equally important from a theoretical point of view, Lucas's settlement was a fluke that turned on the categorical prohibition against all new beachfront construction that was contained in the South Carolina statute. The message of *Lucas* is clear. No government will ever go that far again: better for it to restrict 99 percent of ordinary uses for no compensation than 100 percent for full compensation, and the revised South Carolina statutes reflect that point of view.[3] Viewed in marginal terms, the constitutional rule that routinely condones partial restrictions on land use abandons the only sensible policy in the area—the more you take the more you pay. A constitutional rule that provides no compensation until the last step, and then full compensation at the last step, makes that last step very expensive—indeed, so expensive that no state in its right mind will take it.

Yet why use a different set of compensation rules for regulation than for occupation? The rule that the more the state takes, the more it pays works well with occupation, where it prevents strategic behavior by government. Why then does it fail with regulation? Both the common law and the civil law reject the view that bare possession of land is equivalent to its ownership: all private law systems recognize the need to locate use and disposition in the hands of the party in possession. Why are these concerns irrelevant in evaluating government behavior? Surely no private party could prevent as of right the uses of property that did not constitute the commission of a tort, whether trespass or nuisance. Why should the government be vested with a set of powers to restrict private behavior that it cannot derive from the powers vested in its individual citizens? It may be said that regulation is necessary for the modern state to survive; for the connection between, say, rent control and the preservation of civil order is hardly discernible to anyone who has seen the structural inefficiencies and massive inequities of the New York (or Cambridge) rental markets. And if some regulation is necessary for governance, too much regulation is destructive of liberty. Both risks must be guarded against in working out the appropriate constitutional design.

REGULATING THE REGULATORS

The current law fails to limit the use of government regulation under the principle of take and pay. A new start is needed, one that does not have as its mission preserving from constitutional attack as much of the large regulatory state as is possible. The gap between regulation and taking must be bridged in ways that treat the former like the latter, not the latter like the former. At the risk of being dogmatic, I will assert that the *only* correct position is to recognize that *all* forms of regulation are subject to scrutiny under the takings clause. By design this position is meant to subject every form of government restriction to constitutional scrutiny. If the state relaxes the rules of trespass, so that some persons can make entry onto the land of a property owner, a takings question is raised. If it imposes a tax on the land, or limits the rental that can be charged a tenant, or imposes minimum lot size, setback or side yard restrictions, or density requirements of any sort, it must run the gauntlet set by the takings clause. Any form of regulation thus requires compensation in cash for the losses inflicted (1) unless the regulation is necessary to prevent the kinds of losses that neighbors could enjoin under ordinary tort law principles, that is, those set out under rule 4, or (2) unless some compensation *in kind* is furnished to the party whose property is taken.[4]

The Police Power

Both of these elements require a bit of elaboration. Test 1 captures the *police power,* a phrase that appears everywhere in constitutional discourse even though these precise words are found nowhere in the Constitution.[5] If A is about to attack B, B may disarm A without compensating him for the loss of his weapon. The act of aggression triggers the right of self-defense. Yet one major purpose of government is to eliminate the desperate need for self-help, and the police power allows the state to intervene to protect B under circumstances where B is entitled, but unable, to defend herself. The power also may be invoked where she is able to defend herself, if only to curb the risk of escalated conflict that is inseparable from the private use of force.

In principle, B is entitled to protection against more than the naked use of force. Damages and injunctions are routinely awarded in private lawsuits to control common law nuisances. In this setting, state action may be appropriate, especially where the diffuse nature of a potential harm places many people in a position analogous to B's. A's plant could spew pollution over an entire neighborhood. If B and her cohort privately could enjoin A's activities without compensation, the state may do so as well when acting as their agent. The state power allows intervention (by taxation and police protection) where the coordination problems for the innocent individuals preclude any system of effective private suit or self-help. The major limit on this exercise of state power stems from the familiar fear about overprotection from exaggerated harms. Yet here too the private law analogies on balancing equities in setting remedies provides a workable road map for government action. The possibility of error is inseparable from any use of state power: all that can be asked is that one minimize the alternative risks of over- and underdeterrence.

The weaknesses of modern law apply to both the ends and the means. Today judicial accounts of the police power are said to embrace virtually any kind of concern. To block the view of a neighbor and to fill in a ditch on one's own land are treated routinely as private wrongs that the state may prevent as of right, without payment of compensation. On matters of means, the most fanciful connections between an individual act and some ordinary harm may limit the use of private property. The assertion that construction of a house on a beachfront lot may alter the patterns of drainage or the configuration of a dune is regarded as a sufficient reason to ban or forestall construction, without any showing that these private actions will alter the mighty forces of nature, which are constantly active. In *Lucas*, for example, the dunes have moved hundreds of feet over the years. Although these shifts might destroy any house that is poorly situated, it is most unlikely that the construction of a home, in an area that is already developed, will alter in any appreciable way the structure of the dunes. Yet time after time a worst-case analysis allows visions of the apocalypse to color judgments about the desirability of social action. And all the while ostensible concerns about environmental degradation are allowed to mask other concerns, whether they be the control of competition or the suspension of all growth and development within a given region. Just as the tort law can operate properly only with a narrow conception of compensable harms, so too the constitutional law must embrace that conception to prevent the police power exception from swamping the basic substantive protection of property rights. Two simple rules would work a welcome revolution in this area: confine the ends of the police power to common law nuisances, and insist that there be a reasonable connection between means and ends.

In-Kind Compensation

Test 2 involves a requirement of *in-kind compensation,* which needs a bit of elaboration. In many cases, regulation (like dispossession) is focused on a single person who sustains all the losses and obtains very little, if any, of the resulting public gain. In such cases, no return compensation is possible. But other regulations sweep more broadly, and these may promise "the average reciprocity of advantage" insofar as *all persons are benefited and burdened in equal proportions.* If so, then the benefits that each party receives when like restraints are imposed *on others* constitutes compensation for the losses sustained.

Suppose a local ordinance says that all landowners must have side yards of at least fifteen feet in width. That rule may well be for the mutual benefit of all landowners, in which case no cash compensation is required. It is pointless to incur the administrative costs that collect taxes that are then repaid in equal proportion to the parties so taxed. But when local land-development restrictions are imposed by statewide ordinance, then the average reciprocity of advantage is wanting: the benefits are statewide but the burdens are local, so cash compensation is in order. That appears to be the result in *Lucas,* where state regulation of all local development was justified in an incautious moment as a means to advance the statewide interests of leisure and tourism. Some cases may produce mixed result: some portion of the local burden may be matched by a local benefit and some may not. If so, then the compensation should come in two forms: part in in-kind compensation and the rest in cash. Yet no matter how Byzantine the system of state regulation, the ultimate question is always whether the net effect of the scheme of regulation is to impose an implicit transfer of wealth from one individual or group to another. If so, that regulation should be blocked unless cash compensation is provided. In contrast, regulations that advance the welfare of all simultaneously should be allowed without cash payments, for these schemes are likely to replicate the condition of a positive-sum game normally obtained from voluntary agreement.

At this point, yet another simple test, that of *proration* of benefits and burdens, becomes, by proxy, the measure of just compensation whenever the benefits and burdens of regulation are not amenable to direct calculation. At a minimum, rules with selective burdens or explicit facial discrimination are always suspect, unless the heavy burdens are imposed on those who receive the greater benefits in exchange: a special assessment for a local street should be financed from local taxes if the road is primarily for local residents, but a superhighway built through the neighborhood benefits outsiders and should be funded by tolls or from general revenues. Formal equality becomes an important consideration not as an ad hoc consideration, but as a minimum condition for just compensation.

In practice, however, formal equality is not enough, for often formal rules do have (and are intended to have) a disproportionate impact on various people. A rule that prevents any development of agricultural land may impose identical restrictions on the conservation society and the land developer, but the formal equality conceals the enormous implicit wealth transfer that takes place between these two parties, for the developer chafes under restrictions that the conservation society has lobbied fiercely to impose. The value of the developer's holdings thus decreases while that of the conservation society increases, all under a formally neutral rule that conceals its massively redistributive consequences. Unless the restriction imposed is in fact justified as a device to prevent external harms under the nuisance criterion of test 1, cash compensation must be paid.

The constant refrain of just compensation is not a ploy to protect the rich and famous, although it will sometimes have that effect. Yet often its consequences are quite the opposite. The massive system of land-use regulation that the state of New York has imposed on its Adirondack Mountains (which includes a minimum lot size for private homes of forty-two acres) reflects the interests of the rich and powerful of New York City and the state, who use state regulatory mechanisms to destroy the value of local property (which is then taxed to provide additional funds for the highways used by tourists in the region). Here the just compensation restrictions are needed to stem Leviathan, so that the enormous human advantage of the common law system of property rights does not become a footnote to history in the ever-expanding regulatory world. The state needs an eminent domain power to overcome coordination and holdout problems. That power will be properly exercised only if the "agreements" imposed by the state replicate the essential properties of those agreements that are obtained by individual consent. Common advancement, not partisan political gain, is what a sensible construction of the takings power can supply.

Unfortunately, on this critical issue the inexorable judicial tendency is to abandon any serious efforts to match benefits with burdens. A landmark preservation scheme in New York City places a heavy burden on the owners of the affected buildings without affording them comparable benefits, yet the lack of proportion has been treated simply as one factor to be taken into account, and not as a powerful barrier against regulation without compensation.[6] Statements of principle are abandoned in favor of "ad hoc" inquiries that in the end bend to accommodate the exercise of state power. In practice, the in-kind compensation requirement receives the same extravagant interpretation that is given to the police power. All comprehensive schemes produce some tiny benefit for the net losers. If the courts remain steadfast in their refusal to examine the size of the benefits received by each party subject to regulation, an ounce of benefit will be thought to justify a pound of burdens. The "presumed benefit" *to* a regulated party coupled with the "presumed harm" *by* a regulated party has thus worked to render virtually all land-use restrictions immune to constitutional attack.

The current constitutional regime of "anything goes" unleashes a whole set of unwelcome political and economic consequences. The relentless pattern of judicial decisions has reduced the constitutional protection of property to a guarantee of bare legal possession. Virtually all the rights of use and disposition are subject to political veto. The current constitutional vacuum thus creates a fatal schism between power and responsibility that a sound system of property rights seeks to avoid: when only one side may use, but the other may veto, stalemate becomes the order of the day. The takings clause, designed to overcome holdout and coordination problems, has been made to atrophy as these problems multiply. Power expands to fill a vacuum, and legislatures continue to stretch the limits of the law and conjure up new forms of restriction, seeking to come ever closer to the threshold that calls for them to pay compensation without ever crossing that line. Without just compensation, private losses to owners are left off the social ledger, so that large losses are systematically created for the sake of small gains.

No one doubts that a constitutional system that allows the government to do whatever it wants by way of regulation and restriction is simpler than one that subjects that government to some form of constraint. Yet by the same token, no one doubts that a rule that allows private individuals to do whatever they want is simpler than one which imposes limitations on the use of force. In both cases, some simple prohibitions may generate powerful incentive effects that offset the modest administrative costs imposed. Preventing aggression generates benefits that outstrip the taxes needed to fund that effort. Likewise, application of the just compensation principle imposes at modest cost much needed limitations on the abuse of state power, and allows us to reach a responsible middle position between political domination and total anarchy.

TAXATION

The arguments for using the just compensation principle to constrain state regulation apply with equal force to the area of taxation. After all, a tax is only a threat to take specific property unless its owner pays a certain portion of income or wealth to the government. The reason for taxation in this large and complicated world is that we can never achieve unanimous consent about the funding of necessary public services, such as national defense and the maintenance of law and order. The same form of necessity that undergirds the control of monopoly—a massive coordination problem—again overrides a system that allows only for voluntary exchanges.

The first objective of a system of taxation is to make all citizens better off after taxes are imposed than they were before. Carrying over the just compensation principle from the cases of necessity and regulation to taxation provides the essential clue to understanding the system. As a first approximation, the organization of a tax system should mimic sensible patterns of regulation, so that the individuals taxed receive in exchange government benefits worth more than their exacted contributions. Here, while the individual surrenders cash, the government does not give cash in return, but does provide a bundle of services notoriously difficult to value in the individual case, and likely to differ in value across persons who at first blush appear to be similarly situated. (Two workers may live near the interstate highway that one takes to work and the other never uses.) But where the basket of public services is extensive and randomized, the odd imbalances that appear in individual cases will tend to balance out in the long run.

It is exceedingly difficult for a court to second-guess the political process to decide whether or not the public—that huge aggregation of separate individuals—demands or needs any particular set of services. Likewise, it is not possible to attach a meter to the skulls of unsuspecting citizens to measure the benefits that people receive, either from government expenditures in general or from some particular appropriation. The inability to measure benefits and burdens directly, however, is not a mandate for constitutional paralysis with taxation any more than it is with state regulation. The just compensation principle, with its corollary of proportionate impact, is able to create sound institutional incentives for taxation: match taxes and benefits. By this one simple test, judges could reduce the flood of implicit transfers that occur when burdens are skewed in one direction as benefits are skewed in the other. The proration constraint leads quickly to flat taxes on income, sales, and property. No longer is it possible to single out airports, gasoline, hotels, jewelry, nursing homes, soft drinks, yachts, or even beer and tobacco for special taxation, without showing that their use correlates with the creation of some external harm. When people know that to tax their neighbors is to tax themselves, their appetite for larger government and complex taxes will be reduced. The flat tax constraint does not place, nor should it place, any explicit constraint on overall levels of public expenditures. But it knocks out many of the opportunities to spend political capital for partisan gain. Flat taxes stack up well against the two tests for any legal system: the costs of administration are low, and the incentives for responsible political behavior are great.

Today the principle of proportionate taxation lies in the constitutional dustbin. Freed of any external constraint, legislatures seek the endless set of special taxes referred to above, without the slightest concern for matching revenue with expenditure. The process quickly spins out of control, as interest groups are locked in pitched battles for partisan advantage. The imposition of an excise tax (one measured by the quantity sold, not the price) on bottled water, alcoholic beverages, or soft drinks could well require the reprograming of every cash register in town, often at a cost of thousands of dollars. A change in the general sales tax level reduces that cost and limits endless rounds of political intrigue. Yet special taxes have become the vogue even though the path of least political resistance often leads to economic stagnation.

A constitutional regime of flat taxes will not solve all problems. But the relevant question is not how to achieve perfection, but how to achieve improvement, and this is one area in which massive simplification should have desirable social and economic consequences. No form of coercive government activity should ever be evaluated under a presumption of its correctness. The principle is universal: whenever the state acts, it should show either that it combats some recognized evil or that it provides compensation in cash or kind to those whom it taxes or regulates.

At this point, there is a sense in which the system of simple rules is complete. It starts with well-defined rights to individual labor and talents. It adds to that a strong system of property rights that permits the intelligent use of natural resources and facilitates gains from trade in competitive markets. The rules of contract organize exchange, and the rules of protection ensure that the ownership of property does not become a club with which individuals beat, pollute, or defame their neighbors. The necessity principles and the just compensation principles are but different sides of the same coin; both allow a sensible social response to the coordination problem without running roughshod over the rights of those persons whose resources are needed for social purposes but whose consent is not forthcoming.

If we stick with the six basic principles that I have outlined, the overall level of complexity will be reduced and resources will be freed from the multitudinous legal tangles imposed on them by thousands of boards, bureaus, regulations, and controls. Of course, no one can devise a system that will not spawn its fair share of complex cases: facts have a habit of becoming complex. Nor can all complex issues be avoided: even an optimal antitrust policy leaves unsolved some genuine difficulties. But even with these disputes and gray areas, simple rules give us a leg up. Complex rules for a complex world are an invitation to disaster. Yet that is just what we have today, when all players hire their expert advisers, political analysts, and their sophisticated lawyers, both to play high stakes poker and to cut their political deals. Across the globe billions of dollars go to transfer payments across interest groups, undermining morale and sapping productive energies. Success in politics gives the winner as high a return as honest labor, but it imposes heavy costs on losers that are unthinkable in a system of trade. John Kennedy said a long time ago that a rising tide raises all boats. What we ought to try to do is assure increased general productivity by reducing the legal complexities that hamper its growth. That is not possible if the law-making industry is the most robust growth industry of them all.

REDISTRIBUTION OF INCOME AND WEALTH
The Perils and Allure of Redistribution

The elaboration of the takings principle, and indeed of all six rules, thus far has taken little note of one of the most salient themes of social life both in the United States and elsewhere: the redistribution of income and wealth through state action. The four initial rules are designed to establish a system of strong individual rights in person and property and to facilitate voluntary exchanges that leave all parties better off than before. The subsequent discussions of necessity, eminent domain, and taxation then marked a strategic retreat from a strong libertarian position that imposes obligations on individuals only for wrongful conduct (whether that be promise-breaking or aggression). The supplemental rules of necessity, taxation, and eminent domain are not designed to redistribute income or wealth from rich to poor, or indeed along any other axis, such as from city dwellers to farmers, or the reverse. Rather, these principles are all designed to overcome the coordination problems that block socially desirable solutions. In principle, the model leaves no room for the high degree of political discretion routinely exercised in any redistributivist system.

Instead, ideally, the rate of return received by each citizen is made, to the extent feasible, proportionate to his or her investment in the common social venture. The overall strategy is to direct as much effort as possible to improving social welfare, thereby avoiding wasteful squabbles over the division of the surplus.[7]

Using government to maximize the total size of the pie without altering the relative size of its slices offers a complete program for political and social action. But this plan refuses to accommodate today's enormous social impulse for redistribution of wealth, even at the cost of some shrinkage in the size of the pie. Even a full-throated defense of redistribution in the abstract does not imply a commitment to the redistributive programs now in place. Thus it is not apparent why farmers should subsidize consumers, or consumers subsidize farmers; or why consumers should subsidize unions; patients physicians, or physicians patients; or taxpayers subsidize students; or one set of businesses subsidize another. The freedom with which programs of subsidy and regulation are created is indicative of a world in which redistribution has run amok—as it easily can. What case is there for redistribution that entrenches the privilege of the well-to-do and politically adroit at the expense of the poor and the uninitiated?

Countless programs of redistribution have these perverse effects, but income or wealth redistribution from rich to poor lays a far greater claim on the social conscience and cannot be dismissed in a cavalier fashion. Although many theories have been advanced to explain the redistributive sentiment, at root it rests upon *one* powerful perception—that a unit of wealth is worth more to a poor person than a rich one. It is thus generally thought that taking wealth from the rich and giving it to the poor will increase overall social *utility* if wealth remains constant. In principle, redistribution may increase utility even as it reduces the total amount of social wealth. Behind this vision lies the idea that it is possible to make social comparisons of the benefits of wealth to different persons, to make interpersonal comparisons of utility. Although rigorous economists frown on the conceptual ability of any person to make these subjective comparisons, they are in fact routinely and confidently made: if some conceptual inability blocked the process, we should be hard-pressed to explain the enormous numbers, and predictable direction, of voluntary charitable activities that are commonplace in all organized societies. Only tribute, not charity, moves from poor to rich.

A vast gulf, however, still separates a system of voluntary redistribution from state-coerced redistribution. The former system is one that is perfectly consistent with the basic set of rules developed thus far, for voluntary charitable gifts ought to be as much protected as voluntary exchanges. The recipient clearly gains from them, and if the donor thought them self-destructive, he need only stop giving. The private gains between the consensual parties are clear, and it is hard to see how anyone else loses. Without losers, no one should be in a position to veto these transactions any more than he could veto the voluntary exchanges of others. Yet the legal enforcement of gifts is the least of a donor's problems, especially when we move outside the obvious class of interfamilial gifts. As the social distance between donor and recipient increases, it becomes more difficult to pick out deserving recipients from operators milking the system for all it's worth.[8] Nor is it easy to determine either the proper form or the amount of the transfer: Is the transfer in cash, in kind, in food stamps? Can it be spent anywhere at any time? The necessary judgments on this score cannot rest on any inflexible standard of the proper minimum level of support, for much depends on both the wealth of the donor and the needs of the recipient. Even advocates of voluntary assistance programs worry about their incentive effects, and constantly look for levels and forms of support sufficient to benefit those in need without undermining their willingness to do productive labor. Out-and-out gifts, no questions asked, are rarely made even by generous donors. Specialized forms of assistance, training programs, and support services are very much the order of the day.

The difficulties that beset voluntary redistribution are largely self-correcting, for if a program fails consistently, its champions eventually abandon it. The *precarious* nature of charitable giving is one of the features that make it most effective. Yet it is also the one feature that subjects it to sustained criticism by those who believe that individuals have an affirmative right to receive support that must be made secure by government intervention and guarantees. The systems of public welfare are in many instances unable to perform nearly as well as the private systems that they displace. Taxpayer cries for supervision of public officials and their charges rule out the informal systems of control available to many charitable endeavors. Instead, public welfare programs must rely on impersonal bureaucrats, always subject to norms and proofs, which are utterly impervious to undocumented forms of common knowledge and common sense, no matter how reliable. It is very difficult in practice to translate the restrained moral impulse for assistance and support into a detailed and comprehensive administrative program.

The problems here, however, go beyond the specification of welfare recipients and benefit levels. Systems of public redistribution suffer from built-in structural handicaps that cannot be eliminated by careful planning. These programs score low in terms of both their administrative costs and their incentive effects. First, it is difficult to give money, goods, and services away to the poor. Too often powerful interest groups rake off a substantial portion of the revenues from the top. Even when redistribution is channeled to the proper persons, the state incurs major administrative costs in monitoring the recipients' behavior, a task that requires extensive manpower and an inclination to snoop.

Worse, incentives for production under redistributive taxes are necessarily dulled, both for those who pay the taxes and for those who receive the benefits. Redistributive taxes reduce the private return of productive individuals and hence reduce their overall level of production. The specter of redistribution (for ends they cannot control) also encourages them to fight new taxes that provide them with no benefits, direct or indirect. It is difficult in the abstract to say how large these disincentive effects are, but it is doubtful that they are negligible, and far more likely that they are substantial. Parallel incentive effects are at work for recipients. It becomes more profitable to use the political process to obtain support than to engage in productive labor.

Redistribution is also likely to lead to futile efforts to stamp out poverty, since the demand for redistributive services always outstrips its supply. Thus we cannot assume that the number of people in need of support is going to be constant regardless of the legal regime that is introduced to support them. The recent experience with the homeless in New York City has led to widespread public frustration and disillusionment. Good intentions and public funds are not sufficient to ensure, or even promote, the success of welfare programs. The effort to provide more humane treatment to homeless people has *increased* the number of the homeless, because the marginal incentives on people to take care of themselves were reduced in every way when other people showed their eager willingness to take on this responsibility. The forces of self-interest are strong, in some instances stronger even than the forces of self-respect. If the state provides welfare benefits in excess of wage levels, some number of people will simply decide not to work at all. The moral hazard principle (adverse outcomes that are insured are more likely to occur) typically operates with underappreciated force in collective aid programs: the more that is given the greater the number of people who will need it. The forms of misbehavior so easily recognized in the activities of politicians, business people, and professionals to enhance their income are also practiced by the poor and their advocates. No one is immune from the temptations that only government can make available.

The Technique of Redistribution

It may well be that these obstacles are so insuperable that we should contemplate a radical dismantling of the welfare state on the simple ground that it can never deliver what it promises. But I do not intend to insist on that categorical proposition here. Instead, I want to assume that some level of redistribution is socially appropriate, and then ask the question of means: how should that system be implemented given that it cannot be accounted for by these six simple rules?

The first approach is to seek to redistribute wealth by altering the third and fourth simple rules, that is, those which relate to protection of liberty or property or of the exchange relationship. A huge amount of effort along these lines routinely is expended nowadays. But it largely fails because precious little redistribution in the desired direction actually takes place. Once people realize what is going on, they figure out how to avoid or mitigate the consequences of the legal restriction. Thus any such effort, for example, the attempt to redistribute wealth through a minimum wage law (which redistributes from the poor below that level to those just above it), is likely to have perverse effects. Most obviously, unemployment will increase because employers will cut back as higher wages lower their return. Yet even here the reduction in employment (typically estimated at 0.15 to 0.25 percent for each percentage increase in the minimum wage) understates the aggregate level of private response to the minimum wage.[9] In addition, movements take place on other margins: split shifts for workers can replace the single shifts that they previously had; tasks on the job can be made more onerous; fringe benefits can be subtly reduced; and on-the-job training can be curtailed. The object of the employment contract is to maximize joint gains between the parties. The minimum wage law, with its redistributive impulse, seeks to impose costs on one side of the relationship but ignores the private responses to the challenge, and so ends up hurting both sides. Systems of price control reveal the same persistent pattern of shortages, intrigues, and queues. It is simply not possible to justify inefficient systems of regulation by their ostensible redistributive benefits.

A second avenue for redistribution is through various systems of mandated benefits. It has become ever more commonplace for government to insist that employers provide all their employees with certain packages, such as health insurance, as a condition of employment. Similarly, rent control requires that landlords provide an implicit subsidy to their tenants by allowing them to renew their leases indefinitely at below-market rents. And federal government regulations now routinely require that state and local governments provide special education programs, public accommodations for the disabled, and, most important, medical benefits for the poor. Even when federal funds are earmarked for the task, they are insufficient to cover the cost of the obligations that Congress has decreed. The common feature of all mandated benefit programs does not lie in the nature of the benefits mandated. Rather it lies in the technique of off-budget financing that is used to supply those benefits: the legislative body that dictates the expenditure does not pick up the entire bill. Redistribution no longer represents a collective acknowledgment of a collective social responsibility. Instead, a political majority (itself a complex coalition) requires group A to provide benefits to group B. It is, as Leo Durocher said, a case of "Let's you and him fight." The separation of financial responsibility from political control inexorably leads to an excessive level of benefits and to poorly designed programs.

In order to forestall these difficulties, the seventh simple rule therefore takes a conditional form: *if* there must be public redistribution, then it must be financed out of general revenues collected from the same group of individuals that votes the program into place. If the government wants to subsidize health insurance, then let it do so on the budget. It can impose general taxes and then give employers supplements to offset the additional costs that the program imposes. If the government wants to have a rent control program, it can use general tax revenues to lease apartments from landlords at market rents, and then relet these apartments at below-market rents to the class of intended tenants.[10] Now the difference between the market and the rental price is made explicit and placed on the public record. If the government wants to provide health insurance to AIDS victims, it can take competitive bids from companies that write the insurance to see who will provide the required coverage at the lowest possible price. Although hidden subsidies of such great magnitude may survive, explicit subsidies are more likely to wither in the glare of public scrutiny.

More than a simple distribution of the tax burden is at stake in choosing the method of financing. When the expenditures are made explicit through the budget process, the public is better able to make an informed choice about the costs and benefits of the program. Rational ignorance of government behaviors becomes a less desirable policy for ordinary individuals to pursue. Where all persons have to pay, it is far more difficult for a political majority to deflect the costs of some benefit program onto groups that are unable to protect themselves through the electoral process. The feedback mechanism thus reduces the level of redistribution that will take place and increases the likelihood that only those programs that enjoy strong public support will survive.

But even with public support, redistribution has to be financed. Some portion of it could doubtless be funded by a flat tax, that is, a tax proportionate to income. But it is also likely that additional revenues will be sought. Here it is imperative to avoid the proliferation of special taxes that fall on certain groups or activities, for these taxes also divorce political control from financial responsibility. But the most difficult question is whether, once redistribution is admitted into the system, redistribution should be funded by flat or progressive taxes.

There are three advantages to the flat tax. First, it eliminates a destructive dimension of political discretion that always exists with a progressive tax. The flat tax leaves the government discretion on how much revenue to raise for its budgetary commitments (including redistribution), but gives it no discretion in choosing the form of the tax. Progressive taxation allows the government discretion to determine both the amount of the tax and its incidence. There is no unique progressive tax; there is only a *family* of taxes that share the characteristic of increasing marginal rates. The system could be heavily skewed to allow marginal tax brackets up to 90 percent, as happened in the United States during the 1950s and 1960s and continues in many

European countries today. Or its highest bracket could be around 30 percent, as was the case during the Reagan years. There is no strong theory which indicates which schedule is optimal. If the progression is steep, the total income subject to the tax will shrink, given the negative incentives on production. If the rate of progression is gradual, the income base will remain largely intact, but the additional taxes collected will be small. All that can confidently be said is that government control over rates introduces a level of political discretion and class struggle whose effects on overall wealth production are likely to be negative. Indeed, if progressive taxation is adopted, it would be best to limit the difference between the bottom and top brackets by constitutional amendment. It is better that a progressive schedule be arbitrary and fixed than merely arbitrary.

The second major disadvantage of the progressive tax lies in its administrative costs. An income of $100,000 to one person yields a tax that is far greater than if the same income were shared by two separate persons, each in a lower tax bracket. It becomes necessary therefore to police a wide variety of transactions (gifts, trusts, family partnerships, incorporations, exchanges) to determine whether the fruit is taxed to the tree on which it grew. The incentive to mislabel the source of taxable income is removed if there is no private gain from assigning it to a fictitious source. A huge chunk of the Internal Revenue Code is solely in place to police end runs around progressivity. Similarly, allowances have to be made for the receipt of income. If you earn $100,000 in each of two years, the tax is far lower than from earning $200,000 in one year. Hence the tax laws need to make provision for income averaging to reduce the sting that is imposed when an annual accounting period gives a false impression of individual wealth. Another set of complex carry-over provisions is the result.

The third major disadvantage stems from the incentive effects of the tax. Higher marginal brackets mean less production from the most productive people. They mean that married couples (whose income is pooled under joint returns) face disincentives when the second earner, usually the wife, seeks to return to the labor market. These brackets also funnel real resources into elaborate schemes to avoid the tax collector's bite. In the end, progressive taxation faces this paradox. It is surely a better way to finance redistribution than any direct tinkering with the ordinary rules of property, tort, and contract. It is also superior to any system of mandated benefits or special taxes that can be devised to finance redistribution. But even so, its has costs of its own that cannot be ignored in any social calculus. Redistribution there may be, but its effects should be moderated by placing some constraints on the modes of collection even if few are imposed on the patterns of disbursements. Accordingly, the seventh simple rule, that of income distribution, assumes its final shape: all redistributive programs should be financed by flat taxes.

III

The Rules in Action

8

Contracting for Labor

Worldwide, the regulation of labor markets has created a legal edifice of stunning complexity. Protective laws abound on every conceivable aspect of the subject: health, safety, wages, pensions, unionization, hiring, promotion, dismissal, leave, retirement, discrimination, access and disability. The multiple systems of regulation now in place often work at cross purposes with each other. Unions, for example, may be given protected status under a collective bargaining statute, while being subject to suit under an antidiscrimination law. The law designed to preserve access for the handicapped will make it more difficult to hire and promote members of minority groups by gobbling up resources that would otherwise be available for such programs. The protection of both will typically work to the disadvantage of aliens (themselves often minorities) who, not having the vote, are likely to be disadvantaged in political markets relative to economic ones.

The volume of regulations, rulings, and cases on each of these bodies of law takes a treatise to summarize fully, but even the most meticulous exposition will reveal the enormous amount of discretion that is left within the interstices of the system. Liability rarely rests upon clear rules which can be known in advance and relied on by employers and employees alike. Instead, there are grand statements that make liability turn on the failure to make "reasonable accommodation" (except in cases of "undue hardship"), or on proof of "improper motive," or on the inability to establish "just cause" for dismissal. But the critical concepts on which liability rests are not easily rendered operational, even by example. Instead, all too often, they are an open invitation to volumes of obscure regulations which create at least as much confusion as they resolve. The *Federal Register* today thus contains reams of material on the various forms of antidiscrimination law—all novel branches of law inferior to the standard rules of contract that they consciously and systematically displace.

In the face of this mind-numbing complexity, we cannot accord any presumption of legitimacy to today's status quo, which has been created by a set of elaborate legislative compromises and political deals. It has been fueled by the perception that employers dictate the terms of employment to their workers in their relentless pursuit of the bottom line, but at the same time are so irrational, so subject to whim, caprice, and prejudice, that they cannot be allowed to set the employment rules for their own places of work. Most assuredly, adoption of the current legal arrangements has not been driven by any systematic examination of first principles. The present law may embody the correct set of social responses, but if it does, it does so by happenstance. The present legal regime has not been legitimated by a long and harmonious tradition of voluntary interaction. It is not the result of a customary or a spontaneous order. By the same token, it is both too dangerous and too easy to dismiss the current structure out of hand, given its dubious pedigree and the inordinate complexity that has become its calling card. The prudent approach therefore is to look at labor law without the benefit of any presumption one way or another.

In this chapter, I shall apply the simple rules to the regulation of labor markets. For this project, the first four autonomy-based rules are sufficient to organize the field, for there are no situations of necessity, either public or private, that justify any system of forced exchanges or restrictions on voluntary ones. Faithfully applying these four principles offers, I believe, the key to the radical simplification of labor law. The additional administrative costs imposed by the current systems of regulation are used to purchase a legal order that interferes with individual freedom of choice and the productive social use of human resources. And these higher administrative costs create inferior economic incentives. In the end, this rising tide threatens to sink all boats.

PRIVATE CHOICE AND DEFAULT RULES

Thus far I have celebrated the power of a few simple ideas to account for elaborate social arrangements, and have consistently adopted the view of the social observer to the exclusion of the stance of the market participant. But there is another task related to the first which requires that I descend from my lofty perch as lawyer-cum-economist and assume the role of market participant. In that capacity, what contract should I choose to enter into given the wonderful freedom that the law has allowed me? At this point, the inquiry turns from contractual freedom to contracting strategy—how do self-interested persons formulate their labor contracts with other self-interested persons? More concretely, what kind of devices do, and should, contracting parties use to ensure that today's welcome agreement remains viable over time? If A performs first and B ends up with both the money and the services, only to turn around and flee, then we do not have a contract that creates reciprocal obligations to mutual advantage. Instead, the breach by B, after the performance by A, turns out to be nothing more than a refined species of theft. Knowing of this risk in advance, a prudent party will seek out strategies to ensure that contracts designed for mutual gain do not generate profits for one party and losses for the other. The problem of securing contract performance remains acute even after the legal regime is committed to the principle of freedom of contract.

A successful regime of contracting must also overcome a second obstacle. The number of possible permutations under any employment contract between A and B is very large. There are all sorts of sudden and unforeseen bends in the road, and it is often impossible or too costly to specify in advance ways of coping with them. It is very expensive to negotiate every contingency for every contract term. Most of those expenditures will be wasted because many of the remote contingencies will never come to pass. And even if all contingencies did receive full and complete treatment, changed circumstances are likely to call for renegotiation anyway.

In light of this persistently imperfect knowledge, much of the business of the common law is to develop a set of *default* provisions designed to imitate what a typical or model person in a particular role would want under certain sorts of circumstances. Fashioning the right set of default provisions cannot be achieved by taking refuge in the useful abstractions of A and B. Now it is necessary to draw on (or to acquire) a powerful experiential base within a trade or business, or to rely on a shrewd sense of economic theory, to predict how rational contracting parties in certain characteristic roles (employer and employee; buyer and seller; landlord and tenant; creditor and debtor) will bargain in general. Sometimes there are implicit conflicts between what customary practice requires and what economic theory predicts, and it is very difficult to choose between them. But rather than stress the difficult situations where rival cases are in tension, it is better to give a bit of the flavor of how common practice and economic analysis usually work in tandem.

The systematic study of ideal default provisions pays substantial dividends for dealing with the general question of regulation and markets, and it ties in well with the general theme of simplicity that lies at the core of this book. Where there is good reason to believe that a set of default terms makes sense, there is no compelling case for forbidding parties to adopt those terms expressly as part of their agreements. In addition, there is good reason to believe that simple rules within a contractual setting often do a good job of serving the twin objectives of reducing administrative costs and of setting desirable incentives for both parties. My major purpose in this chapter is to show that the common law rule which treats contract at will as the default contract in labor arrangements makes good sense on both the above counts. In the broad run of cases, this contractual form is far superior to the other forms of labor contracts that are often offered in its place, namely, judicially imposed rules countenancing suits for wrongful dismissal and statutory institutions for collective bargaining. But before turning to so fundamental a task, I will examine the interaction between explicit provisions and default rules in connection with another recurring issue in labor contracts, that which governs the sequence of performance between employer and employee. The clarification of approach in this noncontroversial area casts important light on the importance of freedom of contract in all areas of labor relations.

SEQUENCE OF PERFORMANCE

One major problem in contracting concerns the sequence of performance. Thus the ordinary labor contract raises the question of whether work precedes payment or payment precedes work. This simple question gives rise to that exotic and underappreciated body of contract law called the law of "conditions." In a world of sequential exchanges, how is that order of performance determined? The right way to analyze this issue is to begin with the presumption that any express agreement between the parties should be respected. Thus if the contract calls for "payment in advance," the work need not be done if the payment has not been tendered. In many cases, however, the contract will be silent on the sequence of performance, in which case the custom of the trade should control, which in the example given usually calls for the work to be performed before the contract wage is paid.

The function of the customary rule is to select that sequence of performance which minimizes the likelihood of breach by either party and thereby yields the greatest gains to both parties under contract. In normal situations, a fairly powerful argument can be made in favor of a regime that has labor perform first, with the employer obligated to pay in full only on the completion of the work. (The contracting issue gets very messy if there is a partial performance that has value to the employer, who nonetheless must cover from some other source.) It should be clear why it is desirable to take this approach, even though it exposes the worker to the serious risk of nonperformance on the other side.

One possible explanation depends on the theory of exploitation that I criticized earlier. The worker, it may be said, always gets the short end of the deal. But I think that this explanation is mistaken, for there are two more powerful explanations that are consistent with the general theory of contracting for mutual benefit outlined above. Thus one relevant question is, which way is the risk of *insolvency* greater? If the employer has great wealth, then that wealth works to the advantage of the worker by providing a fund that makes any private settlement or legal judgment collectible in the event of an employer's breach. But if the employer pays a worker who does not perform, there is a more serious risk that the worker's wealth will be dissipated before any suit could be brought for breach. In addition, the remedy of the worker is easy to determine: it is the wages owing. But the loss to the employer is far more difficult to measure because the value of the work that should have been performed is not a fixed sum. The remedial system works far better with employee suits than it does with employer suits.

Reputation also has to be factored into the equation. Often an employer has to be in the market all the time. The requirements of the business are such that it is not just a question of hiring A or B or C. It is a question of hiring many workers at the same time. If the employer gets a reputation of not keeping promises, the business risk he faces is not so much legal suits from disgruntled employees as it is the inability to find people willing to work without being paid in advance or at a premium rate. The reputation of being an untrustworthy employer spreads quickly by word of mouth, and it translates quickly into dollar and cents losses. The employer who faces reputational losses labors under constraints that do not bind as powerfully for individual workers. Ironically, the larger the firm, the more effective the constraint. Leaving the worker with the residual legal risk therefore will usually make sense, and an alteration in the underlying wage rate could compensate the worker for the residual loss. If the reverse sequence of performance—pay now, work later—is desirable, it can be adopted explicitly in particular cases, or perhaps by industry custom and practice. For still more complicated cases, such as long-term construction projects, a system of progress payments—a certain percentage of cash is paid when a certain percentage of work is done—can be used to split the risks between the parties. But the law cannot create anything close to the ideal payment schedule by default rule, and it should not try. When all is said and done, some shipwrecks will take place even with the ideal default rule. But it is the rate of failure, not the fact of failure, that is critical in choosing the right legal rule. The task is to minimize the risk of contract breach. But that risk can never be driven to zero no matter how ingenious the contractual strategies.

The Contract at Will

The basic logic of sequential performance in contracts is, I think, pretty widely accepted today. A far more controversial application of the same general approach arises in connection with the so-called contract at will.[1] Now what a contract at will basically says is that neither side needs to offer any public justification for the termination of a contractual relationship. The employer can fire a worker without offering any justification. It is only necessary to say, "You're fired." By way of a set-off, and it is a critical set-off, if a worker doesn't want to stay on the job, she is not required to give a long song and dance routine either. All that she has to say is "I quit," and the relationship is forthwith terminated.

The rule is surely a simple one, but it is under prolonged siege today, for the central legal question facing both legislatures and courts is whether a contract of this sort ought to be permitted. There is, to be sure, a school of thought that generally says that private choice should always be curtailed, so that the only serious social options are whether certain practices should be prohibited or required. There will be nothing that people are just allowed to do. I think that it is necessary to escape that double bind and to recognize that while a contract at will may not be appropriate in many circumstances, there will still be many cases, the lion's share of cases, where it turns out to be the value-maximizing solution for both employer and employee.

As before, we should not make that judgment in the naive belief that there will never be a shipwreck, for cases will occur (and these are the ones most likely to be brought into court) in which the results under an at-will contract will appear to be unfortunate and unjust. But there are enormous risks in trying to tailor the entire law of contract to forestall the occasional case of disaster. It is not possible in advance simply to prohibit the contract at will solely in the cases where it does not work. We do not have the luxury of hindsight at the time of contract formation. Instead, it will be necessary to alter the entire fabric of contract law and to create a legal environment that makes it more difficult for good employers and good employees to structure their relationships. An unjust dismissal law is always intrusive, for it exposes every decision in labor markets to second-guessing by either a court or an administrative agency.

So what are the advantages of the contract at will? Paradoxically, the first is that, notwithstanding its apparently precarious nature, the contract provides both sides with a *secured* obligation. The point sounds strange given that one side can quit and the other side can fire, without any explanation. For most people, the idea of security connotes a mortgage or a lien on some form of property—the home mortgage is perhaps the most familiar example. But it is appropriate to expand our horizons on this point. The employer who decides to fire a worker has to pay a price, that is, he will no longer be able to reap the benefits of the worker's labor. Conversely, the worker who decides to quit will no longer be able to command the wage. Each obligation is held hostage to the other. Before quitting or firing, one has to make a hard decision about whether the benefit forgone is worth the labor or the wages that can now be retained. But once a decision to sever the arrangement is made, the security on the other side is instantly realized, without the formalities and delay of foreclosure proceedings. The worker instantly recovers her labor, and the employer his cash. Knowing the efficiency of the security arrangement, people will move with caution, given that it is always costly to exercise the right to quit or to fire.

The unquestioned right to quit or to fire has powerful and desirable incentive effects. In particular, it serves as an effective check against the advantage-taking open to either side in a continuous relationship. Thus if the employer tries to chisel the worker, her threat to quit becomes more credible because she has less to lose from quitting given the greedy behavior on the other side. The argument also holds in reverse. The lazy worker is easier to fire because she has that much less value to the employer. The party that tries to take too much of the cooperative surplus—the joint gain from the employment relationship—runs the risk of losing the entire gain to an unreviewable and unilateral decision by the other side. These moderating influences lend a certain durability to the contract at will that contrasts with its fragile legal nature. Employers who spend enormous amounts of money in training workers for particular jobs are not eager to see them depart. Similarly, workers whose training is job-specific are not eager to leave. The contract at will is thus a versatile legal arrangement that is compatible with a wide range of business practices.

The utility of the contract at will is also strengthened by reputational forces. The employer with a large workforce is constrained in dealing with any particular employee. Firing the first worker for reasons that other workers perceive as unfair will have powerful ripple effects throughout the firm. Other workers will become uneasy and in consequence will reevaluate their own prospects: the job that once looked good will not seem as good as it did before. The best workers may be the first to leave, since they have the best opportunities elsewhere. Consequently, the decision to fire one worker, if unwise, can come back to haunt the employer and affect adversely his relationships with the 8, 20, or 1,000 workers that remain in his employ. In practice, it is a lot harder to fire a worker under a contract at will than it is for a worker to quit, for there are often convenient personal reasons to explain why workers come and go. It is therefore a great mistake to stress only the legal modes of enforcement when the social ones are at least as powerful and important in practice.

Another major advantage of the contract at will is the ease of its enforcement. The legal position is this: I quit, or you fire me; judgment for the defendant. The entire system takes about two words to explicate in the standard case. "Anything goes" within the legal system precisely because anything will not go in the business setting. Simplicity has its dividends, for both sides can share in the administrative savings in the form of higher profits and higher wages. Only the lawyers lose when the contract at will is fully respected.

Wrongful Dismissal

No one can claim that the contract at will never results in any miscarriages of justice. But again the benchmark of a legal practice is not perfection, but the next best alternative. To see what that looks like it is necessary to ponder for a moment the law of wrongful, or unjust, dismissal, the major rival to the contract at will. The one feature that the "just cause" rule has in common with the at-will rule is that both can be captured with a verbal tag that is only two words long. But while "at will" is a phrase that gets the courts out of the business of overseeing employment contracts, a state-imposed "just cause" immerses them in an endless variety of litigation. There are any number of possible ways in which an employer may be said to misbehave. Where there are industry standards and common conventions to evaluate for-cause dismissal, there will usually be experienced arbitrators to see if individual cases fall within these well-known categories. The very fact that the contract used this standard is good reason to think it efficient in the particular circumstances of its adoption.

There is, however, a broad gulf between the "for-cause" rules that might be developed in some private settings and the for-cause rules that are imposed on contracting parties by a legislature or a court. The for-cause requirement imposed from without is designed to override contractual intentions, even arrangements that were explicitly formed on an at-will basis. Almost by definition industry practices will offer no guidance for the judicial for-cause rules. If the employer fires a worker some five months after he has asked her out for a date, is her refusal to accept his invitation the reason, or even a reason, why she was fired? Does it make a difference whether they associated with each other outside work in the interim? Or before? Or if the date was requested by a coworker or a foreman? The variations on this one theme resist any easy classification, but they are repeated countless times in litigated cases.

Similarly, in many cases the most important element for the success of a business is cooperative effort, which depends heavily on attitude and morale. Yet these are often the most difficult elements to explain to an outsider, especially after the fact. Success in business depends on an ability to anticipate big problems before they occur and to make adjustments in the composition of the workforce that are critical from the inside but almost impossible to explain to outsiders. Unjust dismissal cases often partake of the worst features of Socratic dialogue. The employer or manager who knows his reasons for action is not able to articulate them in ways that are persuasive to outsiders; in consequence, all local and specialized knowledge is removed from the case, even if it is a surer guide to practical conduct than some abstract theory of sound management behavior: how does one prove to a jury that a salesman has lost some spring to his step, even when it may be critical to replace him *before* accounts are antagonized or lost? The intangibles that matter on a daily basis are always discounted within a formal litigation setting. Yet beneath it all, the defenders of wrongful dismissal actions give no explanation as to why it is in the interest of firms to fire able workers and to retain incompetent ones. The mass of evidence introduced in individual cases is far less reliable than the simple background presumption that it displaces.

The law of unjust dismissal also places great pressure to give some global account of just cause: Is there just cause to dismiss a worker whose assignment is inconsistent with her religious beliefs? Is there just cause to dismiss a worker because her division has been closed down, because the firm's cost structure is too extensive, or because a product line has been discontinued? Each of these questions has been the source of extensive litigation, and the most that can be said of any of them is that the decision made must be "reasonable under the circumstances." The upshot of this structural indecision is that virtually any dismissal for whatever reason, from redundancy to manifest incompetence, may well be subject to legal challenge. The message will not be lost on employers, who will be slow to hire and slow to fire in order to minimize their exposure to liability under the unjust dismissal laws.

Nor does the problem stop with dismissal, for the insidious effects of the "regulatory pyramid" are at work in this area as in so many others. Once dismissals are subjected to judicial scrutiny, an employer may be tempted to reduce the worker's pay (say to a penny a day) or to assign her boring and unsuitable tasks. Yet the law cannot stand by and tolerate these "constructive dismissals" if it is to guard against wrongful ones. So these substitute responses of employers have to be regulated and supervised as well. But once they are, then all transfers, pay reductions, and demotions must be reviewed as well, because there is nothing in the unjust dismissal law to limit its application to cases of manifest abuse. Thus the system grows of its own weight, and judicial intervention becomes not the exception but the rule.

There are powerful theoretical reasons to believe that no matter how hard the law tries, its for-cause requirements can never work with anything like the precision of a market. The explanation is simple. Descriptively, there comes a point when there is a diminishing rate of return to all things, including labor. An employer who has 100 employees may find that the 101st is not worth as much to him as the first one. Yet the salary paid will be constant no matter how many employees are hired. Any rational employer who is not encumbered with the complexities of the unjust dismissal law will decide, "Look, I will hire employees up to the point where the last dollar spent is justified by the revenues I receive. As market conditions change and employees become unattractive to keep, I will fire them, because the wages and other expenses of retaining them are greater than their value to me."

Under a wrongful dismissal law, a court must decide whether to allow these constant marginal and incremental adjustments. Unfortunately, no court standing outside a contractual relationship has anything like the kind of detailed information necessary to decide whether the marginal benefits of hiring a given worker exceed or are exceeded by its marginal costs or how an employer ought to restructure his business to improve employee utilization. Since courts cannot make these marginal decisions about redundant employees, they will tend to move to very extreme positions. One approach is to leave the entire question to a jury, whose decision becomes unreviewable law in the case. Or if particular standards are outlined, courts may insist that, with a case of redundancy, dismissal is justified only by showing that retaining the employee in the business will throw the firm into bankruptcy or insolvency. That rule may provide a short-term victory for any given worker, but its long-term consequences are as catastrophic for workers as a class as they are for management.

When courts refuse to allow any firm to rationalize its workforce before falling into bankruptcy, the fear of legal sanction prevents gradual adjustments in the size and wages of a workforce in response to external market changes. Therefore, instead of the firm's being able to dismiss a single worker today and another tomorrow, it will be subject to changes in employment levels that are uncertain and discontinuous. The firm may now be forced to let go an entire team or division because there is no way to pay them. The legal limitation on dismissal therefore says in effect that it is better to fire 100 workers later than one worker now. The legal system will induce the class of dramatic failures that workers and employers both should strive to avoid. It may well create yet a second generation of complication—plant-closing laws that give notified workers time not only to find other lines of employment, but to organize political opposition to the firm's proposed course of action.

Nor will this legal intervention improve the long-term job prospects of employees as a class, given the influence of the rule not only on firing but on hiring as well. An employer who knows that dismissal on grounds of redundancy will be impossible short of bankruptcy will be very reluctant to expand staff, and will often prefer to respond to increased demand by more capital-intensive activities or by keeping existing staff and expanding overtime opportunities. Choosing this route allows the employer to escape the heavy costs of an overexpansion of the workforce. The entire regulatory process shows the constant preoccupation with the direct effects of decisions on named persons, without regard to the vastly greater indirect effects on other persons similarly situated. The effort to preserve a single job for one discrete, named individual results in the nonformation of numerous jobs for other people. The law on dismissal will act as an effective deterrent to making new hires.

COLLECTIVE BARGAINING

Wrongful dismissal laws are not the only legal attack on the contract at will. It is commonplace today, at least in the English-speaking world, to introduce by statute elaborate legal and administrative regimes that call for collective bargaining between an employer on the one side and a group of workers on the other, represented by a union, typically chosen by majority vote.² Under these collective bargaining arrangements, the employer is under a duty to bargain in good faith with the employee union, and the union is usually given the right to strike when and if bargaining reaches an economic impasse. One dominant feature of this system is the necessary abrogation of the contract at will, for an employer is not allowed to dismiss any worker for engaging in union activities or expressing union sympathies. This system is typically justified by an appeal to ideas of economic duress, employer exploitation, and inequality of bargaining power, which have been considered and rejected in Chapter 4. Here I want to discuss briefly the effects that collective bargaining has on the operation of labor markets.

The Firm versus the Workers

Whether the field of conflict is education, transportation, or manufacturing, negotiations under collective bargaining often lead to tense and protracted struggles between management and labor. On many occasions there is extraordinary bitterness and division, which frequently lead to recriminations and sometimes to violence. This bitterness is not necessarily endemic to the relationship between employer and employee; rather, it is a function of the legal rules that structure the negotiations between the two parties. Many problems with collective bargaining arise because legislation creates monopoly positions on both sides of the market, a state of affairs exactly the opposite of what a sound law should strive to achieve. Within the straight competitive situation, both employees and employers take the same market wage. No party has political leverage to improve its position beyond what it can get in ordinary market transactions.

Introduce, however, a single employer bargaining agency and a single employee union, and the law creates the same bilateral monopoly situation that the fifth and sixth simple rules sought to obviate. The benefits normally obtained from a thick market, including a higher level of trust, all too quickly disappear when unions are made exclusive bargaining agents for their members. Now negotiations are mano a mano, one against one. In this arrangement, there is no unique wage. The bargaining process could generate a wage as high as the monopoly wage, as low as the competitive wage, or anywhere in between. As a consequence, both sides have enormous incentives to spend real resources solely to achieve a private distributional gain. What one side gains, the other side loses. Indeed, even this scenario is too optimistic, because both parties have to incur the additional expenses of negotiation, so that the size of the total pie shrinks as the impasse continues. One need only witness the prolonged strikes and labor impasses at organizations as widely diverse as major league baseball, Caterpillar Tractor, the *New York Post,* Northwest Airlines, and the Chicago public schools to see how a strong set of bargaining incentives can overwhelm the otherwise robust cultural and attitudinal traditions of very different industries. The present legal arrangements frustrate the process of civil, nonproblematic negotiations. Rather, people on both sides engage in bluster and bluffing, force, deception, and, in some cases, coalition or intrigue. The net result is that everyone bargains with somebody whom he has every reason *not* to trust, an attitude as true on the one side of the market as it is on the other.

There is nothing inherent in the behavior of employers or employees that requires these unsavory personality traits to dominate contract negotiations. But as behaviors of this sort become commonplace, the law places a pie of fixed size on the table and says that it can be divided only with the mutual consent of both parties. At this point, strategic behavior dominates productive behavior. Those individuals within the business will have to change their style in order to do well under the legal rules. Over the long run, the market will be overrun by those confrontational personalities best attuned to the demands of their positions. The division of spoils brings forth enormous efforts by labor and management alike to get the largest possible share for themselves, and induces both sides to engage in conduct that may be obdurate, devious, or worse.

The precise division of the spoils, however, depends critically on the substantive commands of the different labor statutes. Under the National Labor Relations Act (NLRA), an employer may lock out workers and employees may strike with legal impunity when economic bargaining reaches an impasse. The strength of their relative positions depends on the ability of each side to weather the storm. The traditional rule, now under legislative siege, that allows management to hire permanent replacements in economic strikes is perceived as one advantage for firms determined to rid themselves of union involvement.[3] Whatever the rule on permanent replacements, in labor disputes involving industrial unions either side is allowed to break off relations with the other as long as it is prepared to pay an economic price.

The bargaining outcome often turns out quite differently under the Railway Labor Act (RLA), which since 1936 has applied to air transportation as well, where the current agreement remains in place through an interminable statutory process unless both sides agree to its alteration.[4] At this point, the statute creates the worst of the bilateral monopoly holdout problems that I examined earlier in Chapter 6. The inability of management to fire workers in effect gives workers a disguised legal ownership position in the firm—this is what makes it so difficult to remove featherbedding firemen from diesel locomotives. It also explains why in airline renegotiations the common response of management is to offer part ownership of the firm's stock to the employees in exchange for concessions on wages and work rules. A prime example is the protracted negotiations of Northwest Airlines with its multiple unions as it teetered on the edge of bankruptcy. By virtue of the default rule under the RLA, the workers own part of the firm in any event, so that the explicit "recapitalization" of the firm only makes explicit the ownership position conferred on employees by the RLA.

Unfortunately, the RLA embodies the worst imaginable response to the bargaining problem. Transportation is, or at least could be, a competitive industry. Competition is possible between firms in the same line of business—trucks or planes, trains. And it is unavoidable across the different forms of transportation. The case for regulation is thus at a low ebb. Even so, the RLA was adopted on the mistaken assumption that unions needed some way to equalize their bargaining position with management. Strikes could not be allowed, for while it is possible to stockpile steel in anticipation of the strike, and thus insulate consumers from immediate adverse consequences, no one can stockpile the morning 6:55 run from Albuquerque to St. Louis. The upshot is that strikes must be banned in transportation industries lest disputes within the firm have adverse third-party consequences that would dwarf those arising from the smooth operation of a competitive market. The system of confrontation that is built into the law fails because it ignores the clear implications of the simple rules.

Conflicts among Workers

Ironically, however, it would be a mistake of massive proportions to assume that the only conflicts that arise under collective bargaining agreements are between management and workers. It is also common to find serious conflicts between different workers who are represented by a single bargaining agency.[5] Since labor unions cannot function if they are required to have the unanimous consent of all workers within a unit, the legal system in the United States allows a bargaining representative chosen by a majority of workers within a firm to select the single representative for all workers within the business. Oftentimes, however, skilled workers have interests at variance with those of unskilled workers. Similar conflicts can arise between older and younger workers (owing to the seniority and the age discrimination laws), blacks and whites, men and women, and so on. Some workers may want full-time employment and others part-time employment. Some may want extensive medical coverage, but others may want shorter hours or more vacation pay. With standardized agreements, these individual variations in tastes and demands among workers are difficult to respect simultaneously. The most that can be asked of any harried union representative is that he act in good faith to juggle the competing interests, but no one has been able to develop any powerful set of guidelines to determine the order and level of sacrifice when these interests conflict. Yet by the same token, disappointed workers are often reluctant to leave the bargaining unit, both because they must sacrifice their uncertain share of the monopoly gains and because their entrance into other industries may be blocked by sitting unions of great economic power. This second set of conflicts also does not arise in competitive markets, which on this score as well operate with far less friction than their unionized rivals.

The social consequences of this bargaining system have been largely debilitating. One set of consequences has been that the labor statutes made it particularly difficult for black workers to maintain their economic power in the face of white-dominated unions which represent them against their will. Under the Railway Labor Act, for example, the level of black labor force participation within the workforce systematically declined after 1926, even after the Supreme Court announced that union representatives owed a duty of fair representation to their minority workers, a duty that was far easier to state abstractly than to enforce concretely.[6] There is little doubt that the older version of American labor law, enforced as it was by constitutional norms, did a far better job of protecting the interest of minority workers than the modern law of labor relations.[7] A system that allows the employee freedom to deal directly with an employer or to join a voluntary union of his own choosing is far superior to a system in which the state selects the "bargaining unit" under the usual set of complex and indeterminate criteria, which always work against the interests of a political minority. The difficulties of developing an ideal set of voting rules in congressional and local elections should serve as a warning to those who think that the democratic model is ideal for labor relations. The grotesqueness of carving out electoral districts to protect incumbents, on the one hand, and to respond to the interests of minority groups (often defined on lines of race or color), on the other, is evident to anyone who has watched congressional districts snake along an interstate highway.[8] There is no ideal solution when enormous powers are conferred on political institutions. But there is no reason to adopt voting mechanisms at all when market institutions are able to generate desirable social outcomes.

The Decline of Unions

The dislocations imposed by collective bargaining laws do more than influence the outcomes in particular cases. They also account for the long-term decline in union power. Any new firm that contemplates entering the labor market will be deterred by the prospect of collective bargaining, because it will not see a market moving smoothly. By way of analogy, international currency markets have only apparent stability when exchange rates are fixed by government decree. Similarly, in labor markets sharp discontinuous crises, such as strikes, become an irreducible risk, not only for unionized firms but for others who depend on unionized firms as suppliers or customers. There will accordingly be some effort to shift resources away from these regulated markets. Capital will replace labor, and smaller independent contractors will displace regular employees under aggressive outsourcing programs. Regulation will induce firms to gravitate to otherwise inefficient means of production and intensify the pressure to move to alternative modes of production that have for reasons of cost and technology become more desirable.

The declining role of unions in the labor force, then, is not simply a matter of a weak string of union leaders or a series of unanticipated losses in close union elections. It is a direct and predictable response to the changes in the means of production that allow firms to escape the limitations of an inferior form of labor organization. Assembly lines are relatively easy to organize because the conflicts among line workers are normally of manageable limits. But when boutique firms operate in niche markets, the days of the old industrial union are numbered no matter what legal rules dominate. There is nothing which says that the ratio between employees and independent contractors must be constant under some inarticulate rule of nature. As the employee relationship becomes more burdensome, independent contracting will become a more plausible option. It is no surprise, and constitutes no crisis, that the percentage of unionized workers has dropped from around 35 percent forty years ago to under 15 percent today. Even with state support, a unionized workforce finds it ever more difficult, whether in steel, construction, or transportation, to compete with leaner firms with a more efficient internal governance structure.

All these factors, it should be stressed, offer no argument for rendering collective bargaining agreements illegal in the private sector. If an employer finds it in his interest to insist that all or some of his workers be members of a designated union, then more power to his. The "closed union shop" arrived at by consensual means is as valid an institutional arrangement as any other, including the yellow dog contract, whereby workers are told explicitly that working for the firm means forsaking union membership. Each of these contractual forms may have its use in particular settings. The yellow dog contract may protect employers against a sudden loss of their entire force of skilled labor at a critical point in the production cycle—a problem that could pose a grave risk with the rise of "just-in-time" systems of inventory control. It also allows employers to sue a union for inducement of breach of contract if it tries to organize their workers.[9] The closed shop may well provide the employer with benefits that exceed any costs that unionization imposes. The union may have advantages over the firm in selecting abler workers or in monitoring their behavior. The union may also make certain critical concessions in order to retain its pride of place. But as before, the question is often not what arrangement is adopted, but whether it is adopted through voluntary choice or external compulsion. The case against mandatory collective bargaining therefore rests on the system of public coercion that undergirds it and that introduces a legal structure vastly more complicated and unstable than the simpler contract at will.

There is a moral here with which it is useful to close. The contract at will is widely used for positions of great power and positions of small consequence. It is used for chief executives and for day laborers. (One common exception is tenure for university professors, itself a complex subject that cannot be discussed here, but that depends largely on the fact that universities are not owned by shareholders, so that control is divided between boards of trustees, administrators, and faculty, where the last group needs tenure to preserve its governance position.) The ubiquity of the contract at will in unregulated markets should be treated as a sign not of widespread corruption but of widespread utility. To go against common practice, one needs to have enormous confidence in his own judgments about right and wrong. Typically, those who know most about the subject are aware of the subtle variations between individual cases and are least willing to intervene in the affairs of others, no matter what organizational form they adopt. But for those who have not faced the challenges of running a business, it is easy to disparage practices that are not understood. The law and economics of labor contracts and labor markets is a complex business, whose outlines have only been well explicated in the last generation. Imperfections are the order of the day in all markets. Anyone who thinks that the legal system can be operated without substantial error and cost is unduly optimistic about the power of law in general and of regulation in particular. But as we learn more about labor markets this universal law should apply: those who know the most seek to govern least.

9

Employment Discrimination and Comparable Worth

In this chapter, I turn to two further forms of assault on the contract at will, and by implication the broader doctrine of freedom of contract: the principle of comparable worth and the antidiscrimination laws. With both these conceptions, the focus shifts away from the theory of employer domination, used by some to justify wrongful dismissal laws and collective bargaining arrangements, to perceived injustices across various classes of workers. Under a theory of comparable worth, or pay equity, the question is whether the wages that women receive for work in predominantly female professions are equal to the wages paid for work of comparable value done by men, or at least to the wages paid in comparable professions that have been dominated by men. Under an antidiscrimination law, the gist of the offense is the failure or refusal to hire someone or the decision to offer that person less favorable terms because of some characteristic that the law forbids employers to take into account. Race and sex were traditionally at issue, and they have been joined as of late by more modern and controversial grounds, namely age, handicap, and, under some local laws, sexual orientation.

The themes here are familiar. Listen to any defense of an antidiscrimination law, and it is as though the principles of scarcity and self-interest no longer apply to ordinary social affairs. In the course of the debates, two themes will always come out. First, employers do not know their own interests, and hence are likely to respond to base prejudice or to fall victim to their own irrational and self-destructive calculations. Second, the costs of complying with the antidiscrimination norm can be shown to be so low that the state compulsion should be regarded as improving the economic operation of the system. The 1992 implementation of the employment discrimination titles of the Americans with Disabilities Act has brought forth countless reiterations of this theme, as though a single ramp or a modest enlargement of computer typeface sets the upper boundary on the typical adjustments that firms are required to make for their workers, thereby ignoring all other costs of implementation (overall planning, compliance, litigation, lower output, reduced flexibility of plant and personnel, morale of other workers) that rightly belong in the calculation.

I believe that both of these newer forms of intervention are mistaken and misguided. At the broadest level, the argument is identical to that I advanced in the previous two chapters. As long as people know their own self-interest, contractual bargains advance the joint welfare of the parties without having, on balance, harmful external effects, and should therefore not be disturbed. As before, the account of external effects looks past the disappointment that individual applicants always sense when passed over for any reason they regard as improper, and focuses on the highly positive overall outcomes for the system. The expansion of opportunities for employment is universally the best response to the threat of employer misconduct. But since the range of arguments in favor of these laws differs somewhat from those previously encountered, it is perhaps best to devote some closer attention to them. I shall begin with the more established antidiscrimination laws and then turn to the more recent proposals concerning comparable worth.

Antidiscrimination Laws

The consensus in favor of some antidiscrimination laws in the United States and throughout much of the rest of the world is so powerful today that it may seem flippant and foolhardy to call for their repeal.[1] There are many significant divisions between common law and civil law systems, and many differences in the organization of the common law as it has emerged in the United States, England, and the Commonwealth. It is also noteworthy that none of these systems developed an antidiscrimination law through incremental judicial decisions. In each instance, the laws were put in place by statutory enactment. The shift in sentiment over time has occurred in legal systems that on other matters differ widely in their attitudes and approaches to legal problems. Nonetheless, the convergence toward imposing some prohibition against discrimination in employment markets is well nigh complete.

This modern convergence could be taken as the strongest confirmation of the soundness of the employment discrimination laws. Why should anyone speak out against a set of laws that are widely accepted by all parts of the political spectrum? But consensus is always a two-edged sword. In some cases, the powerful social consensus that a practice is improper counts as a strong argument for making it illegal. But in other contexts, the existence of a consensus should lead to exactly the opposite conclusion. The preoccupation of Hobbes and Locke with the control of the use of force rested on the perception that no one could be free to order his own life if others were at liberty to kill or maim him. The overwhelming consensus against the unbridled use of force thus supplies the reason for using the coercive powers of the state and for positing consent to laws that prohibit such force. But a widespread consensus that certain styles of dress, music, and speech are appropriate is hardly a good reason to allow a majority (however large) to impose its will on a minority, and thereby to stifle any and all criticism and innovation. In these contexts, the sound social instinct is that any minority of one is entitled to protection even if the rest of the world takes offense at what he or she does. That is why a state antimiscegenation law constitutes a frontal assault on the ordinary liberty to marry a person of one's choice. Similarly, the toleration of polygamy and same-sex marriages is difficult to oppose in principle, no matter how awkward anyone might feel about interacting with people who engage in these practices.

The upshot should be clear. It is not possible to find any lockstep connection between social consensus and useful legislation. In all situations, the question to ask is, what general social consequences follow if one person or group is allowed to defect from the dominant social convention? If one person defects from the agreement not to use force, chaos could easily follow. If one person innovates in literature or business, others may profit from her successes or learn from her mistakes. A uniform prohibition on the use (or threat) of force advances social welfare; a uniform prohibition on freedom of thought and action in other spheres does not.

There is, then, a vast gulf between a unique political solution and a cultural consensus. Political power allows a majority to impose its will on a minority or, in a world of factions and coalitions, even vice versa. A cultural consensus must continuously reinvigorate itself to meet the threat of constant erosion. It gains strength precisely because those who disagree with the consensus are free of legal compulsion when they choose to strike out on their own. A strong political consensus is not a sufficient condition for enacting those preferences into law. The widespread adoption of certain laws may only demonstrate that it is possible to make the same type of legislative mistake in different cultures, given the constant tension along the boundary line between the market and politics. The spread of these laws could well reveal a defect common to democratic politics with its entrenched majoritarian institutions. While swimming against the political tide, I shall try to summarize the case for the repeal of antidiscrimination laws.

Recall the basic framework of this book. Any law that increases the complexity of the legal system has to justify itself by showing how it improves the overall efficiency of the system. A rule that expends resources to enforce contracts as made meets this test because it expands the gains from trade by facilitating novel forms of agreements that might not otherwise be feasible. Without legal enforcement of future promises, only spot transactions (that is, those completed immediately) are feasible and even they can be made only with difficulty.

The antidiscrimination laws increase the costs of operating the system, usually by a considerable extent. The first and most obvious change is in enforcement: there is no simple external observable test remotely comparable to "I quit" or "You're fired" that indicates whether an employment decision is in conformity with or in violation of the law. To show that the firing took place only begins the inquiry; it hardly ends it. In each case, it is necessary to delineate some less obvious boundary line between the legal and the illegal rupture of the relationship. The inquiry is likely to prove relevant, moreover, not only in the six thousand or so employment discrimination suits that are on average filed in federal courts each year, but in the more than fifty-five thousand other complaints that are brought forward each year for administrative review in the federal system, in the additional complaints in the state system, and in the larger number of cases still in which the threat of suit induces settlement or alters the pattern of employer behavior.[2] As long as improper motives may expose an employer to substantial risks of liability, the effects of litigation will filter back throughout the system.

This question of motive lies at the core of the *least* intrusive form of antidiscrimination law, the so-called disparate treatment test: did the employer fire (or refuse to hire) the employee "because of" some forbidden ground? In each case the "ground" is always present: people have a race, a sex, or an age—and that characteristic might have been taken into account in making the decision. Yet in each case lurks the possibility of a potent rejoinder: the employer insists that some other legitimate reason explains the dismissal. The incompetence of the worker is one obvious ground, which shares only one characteristic with race and sex: it can never be ruled out of bounds in principle. But there are other reasons as well. The business has contracted, so some employees have been laid off. The business has changed its strategy, so employees with different skills are required. The employer dislikes the worker because of some other personal characteristic—boisterous conduct, undue reticence, or fussy lifestyle—that is not on the statutory list of forbidden grounds. There are doubtless a huge number of dual motive cases, where some level of forbidden motive and some judgment about competence (or workforce reduction) may account for a particular decision.

It is commonly said that no antidiscrimination law prevents an employer from firing a worker for incompetence. Literally understood, that claim is true, but in practice it is manifestly false given the risk of erroneous rulings. In most cases, the employer may claim that the dismissal was due to incompetence, and may document that claim with an extensive file that shows when a worker has been late, how he has been disciplined, and the like. But evidence of this sort may be disbelieved, so except in the rare cases of factual certainty, incompetent workers may seek to hide behind claims of discrimination even if their conduct has been subpar in every way. Owing to this routine uncertainty, even the simplest form of an antidiscrimination law therefore has to set out elaborate burdens of proof, first to winnow out cases of permissible from cases of forbidden motive and then to determine whether liability will be imposed when both motives are present in varying degrees.[3] The range of employment decisions to which these complex arrangements must apply is exceedingly large, for it is not sufficient to regulate decisions to hire if decisions to fire, promote, demote, and transfer are left unregulated. The original drafters of the employment discrimination laws knew that they could not be content with only a narrow coverage provision. All personnel decisions had to fall within the scope of the statute if it was to have any chance of keeping up with the possibilities for evasion.

Some fear that the most robust enforcement of a disparate treatment standard will still leave many cases of discrimination undetected. In order to reach these cases, the law today (most notably in cases of race and sex discrimination) resorts to objective measures, namely, those which show disparate *impacts* on the members of two different groups—men and women, blacks and whites—which are thought to offer circumstantial evidence of discrimination.[4] The use of these statistical disparities could be rendered consistent with the less controversial disparate treatment tests except for one critical reason: The employee's disparate treatment case is normally overcome if the employer can establish legitimate grounds for dismissal. But in the American context at least, the critical question for disparate impact cases is not motive and pretext, but whether some "business necessity" may be demonstrated to account for the perceived differences. The precise verbal standards on this matter have shifted over time, and it does not appear—quite—that business necessity will be used to sustain only those practices strictly necessary to avert bankruptcy. But notwithstanding the doctrinal confusion, one important feature has nonetheless remained constant: evidence of good motive is not allowed to explain away the observed differences in hiring percentages for various groups. Since pronounced and significant statistical differences endure with many standard hiring practices, including most forms of employment tests, a formidable array of expert testimony is constantly placed on the record.

Now what is gained, if anything, by the use of so formidable a legal structure to attack the problem of discrimination? The answer is nothing, except social unrest and economic dislocation.

The antidiscrimination laws ignore the power of the market to deal with the most invidious forms of discrimination. The basic point goes back to the fundamental distinction between the use of force on the one hand and the refusal to deal on the other. The threat of force requires each person to make peace with those persons who are his worst enemies. It will, moreover, do no good to make peace with only one if others lurk in the wings ready to inflict mayhem. There must be an elaborate set of treaties with some aggressors and extensive private defense associations to ward off the others. As long as transaction costs remain prohibitive, it is doubtful that any person could secure protection against bodily invasion by a set of private contracts, however cleverly conceived and executed. The social contract theories of Hobbes and Locke were both directed at the control of private force, to which no network of private contracts could provide an adequate answer.

With discrimination, however, the constellation of choices and outcomes facing each individual is far different. The state already provides protection against the use of force, so that no individual has to engage in a web of contracts to achieve the personal security necessary to undertake voluntary transactions. Now the prospective employer or employee has a far more manageable task: to search the other side of the market in order to find the trading partner that will offer her the *best* deal. In this environment, a large number of individuals may be prejudiced against her, but the point is of diminished consequence, for the task is to find only that person who will make the highest offer for her goods or services. All the action involves that select group of individuals most favorably disposed to the worker—*not* the worst enemy or the median voter. Moreover, the employer who sacrifices economic welfare for personal prejudice will pay for her preferences on the bottom line. By forgoing superior labor in order to hire inferior workers, she will sacrifice resources to indulge consumption choices, and will be at a systematic disadvantage relative to employers whose economic motivations are more rational.

On this view of the subject, the element critical to success for members of minority groups is not the ostensible protection of an antidiscrimination law, but free entry of firms and workers into an open market. One recent study of the trucking industry deals well with the relative ability of civil rights legislation and open entry to deal with persistent forms of discrimination.[5] That industry, which was long closed to blacks, was covered by the Civil Rights Act of 1964. Yet the percentage of black drivers along the preferred routes scarcely increased during the first fifteen years that the civil rights statutes were on the books. But in 1979 deregulation came, and with it new entry and a sharp and substantial increase in the level of black participation in the industry. With the old barriers cast aside, new firms could compete in an industry whose cozy practices wrongly insulated incumbents from competition. New entry within the industry carried with it no administrative costs, but instead peeled away another useless layer of government regulation. Yet its results were far more dramatic than those brought about by the Civil Rights Act, which did nothing to touch entry restrictions.

Open entry will do much to change the composition of a workforce within an industry, but it does not follow that it will necessarily change the levels of discrimination within each firm. All forms of discrimination need not be unwise. Many small businesses, or departments in larger businesses, may find it cheaper to operate if they hire all members of a single racial group or only men or only women. But for this strategy to be successful, it must generate some cost savings, which will be passed on to outsiders in the form of lower prices for goods and services. There is, moreover, no need for the state to decide which forms of discrimination are invidious and which are cost-justified. The survival of the firm will have a lot to do with the soundness of its choices. As long as contracting practices are protected against various forms of physical duress, the situation will be under control. Even the legal prohibitions against fraud and misrepresentation, both highly desirable, are less critical in the grand scheme of things. Choosing the right trading partners will avert much of the risk of fraud and thereby reduce the relative importance of legal protection.

It is possible, moreover, to identify some reasons why some forms of discrimination are rational. Firms are complex social organizations that cannot turn to legal enforcement to resolve the continuous stream of ongoing disputes. The "relational" nature of employment contracts requires informal mechanisms of enforcement and adjustment, which in some instances are best put in place by paying close attention to the internal composition of the workforce. If workers come from the same neighborhood, attend the same churches, belong to the same clubs, it will be harder for them (and their employer) to escape the reputational consequences of poor behavior, and easier for them to enjoy the benefits of good behavior. The informal network of support and sanctions could allow the firm to function as a cohesive unit, and not just as a group of atoms each in search of its own local advantage. In addition, where workers are drawn from the same backgrounds, communication within the group is easier, and the collective choices that the firm must make about internal collective governance come more readily. There are likely to be fewer disagreements about how the common aspects of the workplace—décor, hours, food, music, vacations—are to be resolved. Widespread consensus within the firm helps reduce the evident stress that would otherwise be placed on any governance mechanism, however expedient or just. It is not that all firms have to be organized in this pattern or that there are no offsetting benefits to diversity within firms. Rather, it is that some firms, or some departments within some firms, may find that homogeneity works to their advantage. If it does, then they should be allowed to have their way.

In response, it may be said that these explanations for firm behavior are too benign and that an antidiscrimination norm is most needed when blind social prejudice is strongest. But when the antidiscrimination law is most needed, it is also least likely to obtain legislative approval, for few people have such lofty and bifurcated sentiments that they will lobby in some "public" capacity for legislative action that will curb their private prejudices. Thus the political action on discrimination that came at the height of Jim Crow in the South (and similar sentiments elsewhere) did little to help persons already disadvantaged in economic markets. Instead, it imposed additional burdens on blacks and other outsider groups. The crude forms of exclusion under Jim Crow included the aggressive use of enticement and loitering laws to prevent out-of-state employers from bidding up the price of black labor.[6] The local domination of the political system and the extensive set of land-use controls freely available to state and local governments could also be turned against any local or out-of-state employer that might wish to buck the dominant social convention. And everywhere the threat of private force (perhaps with a smirk or assist from the local sheriff) made free entry by outsiders a practical impossibility.

Other constraints worked to keep black workers hobbled in the labor market, even outside the Old South. The Depression era (1931) Davis Bacon Act, by requiring that all laborers receive the "prevailing" local wage, made it impossible for itinerant black construction workers to undercut their more established (white) union rivals in the North—which was the initial and explicit intention of the act. The Railway Labor Act of 1926 reduced many black railway workers to subordinate status by forcing them under the thumb of white-dominated unions. An open market prevents any group from being shut off. Conversely, legislation allows any victorious coalition to push its position to the limit.

Just that has happened, in reverse, under the American civil rights legislation in the post-1964 period. The original statute, the Civil Rights Act of 1964, was designed to ensure a "color-blind" regime in which it was impermissible to discriminate against *any individual* "because of such individual's race, color, religion, sex, or national origin." The often-stated rationale for the statute was that only the "merits" should be taken into account by rational employers and that all else should be ignored. The statute was designed to protect blacks and others against discrimination but not to grant them any favors under law. Dream on. This lofty conception could not—and did not—last, for no one has been able to identify a durable public concept of merit that operates independent of the characteristics specified in the initial civil rights legislation. The insistent contemporary outcry for diversity marks a widespread social determination that race, sex, and national origin *should* be relevant to hiring decisions at all levels of the market. In a market system they would be taken into account, in proportion to their influence, without any prod or guidance from the center.

Once the civil rights laws are on the books, however, implementation of diversity and affirmative action takes a very different course. The United States Supreme Court has responded to the inexorable pressure by adopting an explicit double standard in the teeth of the unambiguous color-blind language of the basic act. It is permissible for employers to engage in "voluntary" discrimination in favor of groups protected under the statute, even though the most rigorous disparate impact tests are used to monitor discrimination against members of protected groups. The Supreme Court has treated the question of disparate impact on favored groups as though it were in a different economic and social universe from affirmative action,[7] but only a determined legal formalist could fail to note that the overall incentive structures generated under its two-tailed interpretation of the act depend on both the carrot and the stick.

In some sense, the Supreme Court's repudiation of the color-blind version of affirmative action is an accurate reflection of broad-scale political sentiment. When pushed to the limit, very few if any institutions want to use a combination of test scores and grades to determine the composition of their university or their job pool. One great weakness of the 1964 statute was that it froze into law a set of sentiments on the color-blind question that have proved more time-bound than eternal. The forces for diversity and affirmative action are simply too powerful to be denied. Precisely because they are so strong, the strong hand of government is not needed to give them a boost. If the matter of discrimination were left to the market, the same political forces arrayed on behalf of affirmative action could still find their voice inside private organizations. But the legal stick for affirmative action would be removed. Its neutralization in turn should moderate some of the genuinely invidious discriminatory behavior directed toward the main nonprotected group, white males (not all of whom are gifted), who now face forms of discrimination that are more open and pervasive than they would have been in the absence of any civil rights statute at all.

Judgments about diversity and affirmative action are intrinsically matters of degree, which require a trade across different types of concerns—most crudely, considerations of merit, past injustices, equal treatment, and diversity. No one has a monopoly of wisdom on the relevant trade-offs. When politics overrides the market, the majority takes virtually the entire pie instead of its proportionate share, for there is no system of self-correction to slow things down when the costs of government action get too high. The situation is far more stable, and socially desirable, if shifts in sentiments are allowed to express themselves only incrementally in the ordinary marketplace. Indeed, one of the greatest advantages that markets have over politics is that they force interested actors to make the painful marginal calculations of how much they can have of a good thing before it becomes a bad thing. The enormous shifts in public sentiment over the past forty years would not have gone unheard in a world devoid of legislation. But with its differential response to the various forms of discrimination, the civil rights acts have fostered more discord, more discrimination, and more preaching than they have eliminated.

The problems with the statutes do not arise only at the interface of law and politics. They are also legion regarding matters more purely economic. The chief problem here concerns the appropriate definition of the term "discriminate." At one level, it might be assumed that the term refers to any effort to distinguish or classify individuals on the basis of a characteristic forbidden by statute. But rafts of critical issues are missed if the emphasis is placed on form to the exclusion of substance. In ordinary economic areas, when the question of illegal price discrimination arises, the inquiry does not stop with an observed difference in prices or wages. The second inquiry asks whether some *cost justification* accounts for the difference. If it costs more money to serve client A than client B, the question is whether the price differential reflects the underlying difference in costs. If some excessive monopoly profit is concealed by the price differential, there is illegal discrimination. But if not, the price differences become necessary to prevent the distortions that normally result when one customer is subsidized by another.

The exact same ambiguity in the meaning of discrimination surfaces under civil rights law, where it receives exactly the wrong answer. Early on, it was understood that the 1964 Civil Rights Act would be a dead letter if it reached only explicit and overt discrimination. But with the movement to disparate impact theories, the drafters overlooked a point that in practice has proved even more important: what should be done if two workers present the employer with identical packages of benefits but different packages of costs? To take a simple example, suppose male and female workers are able to produce X widgets per day. Further suppose that the injury rate, and hence the workers' compensation premium for the women, is three times what it is for men. Must the male and female workers be paid the same wage, to avoid the sting of Title VII, or should—perhaps even *must* under the law—there be an adjustment in the wage level for men and women so that the full cost (wages plus premium in this simplified model) is the same for both groups of individuals? Only where that condition is satisfied should an employer be indifferent to the sex of the worker who is hired.

The unchallenged rule today calls for equal wages regardless of differences in collateral costs. The theory is that if cost differentials are taken into account, the statute will become a dead letter, which, while true enough, is as it should be. But there are adverse social consequences that flow from turning a blind eye to relevant cost information. In an economic sense, the statute, in the hypothetical given, requires the employer to discriminate against men, with all the market inefficiencies that follow. The implicit subsidy makes the employer more reluctant to hire women for whom the statute now requires, systematically, an above-market wage. It leads to resentment among men, whose wage levels are correspondingly reduced and who in some

environments where team work is critical (heavy construction comes
to mind) may be exposed to higher risk of injury by virtue of working
with women; men may also object when money that could be spent
on wages must be spent on expensive sanitation facilities of great benefit to women, but of little benefit to men. It is no wonder that the
undercurrent of resistance to antidiscrimination laws is so strong in
certain occupations, but not in others: there are often perfectly rational industry-specific reasons for many employers and workers to oppose them.

The popular statutory account of discrimination has of late been
carried over into the treatment of disabled persons. Thus the Americans with Disabilities Act (ADA) takes the same forensic stand of earlier civil rights legislation. It condemns any differences in treatment
attributable to disability, and specifically requires employers to ignore
cost differences necessary to allow different employees to work at certain levels of efficiency. The ADA recognizes that nothing can be done
to make the blind see or the deaf hear, but short of demanding the
impossible it demands all "reasonable accommodations" that do not
result in any "undue hardship" for the firm. In any market setting,
certain firms will seek aggressively to hire handicapped workers whose
limitations are of relatively little consequence for their work. Phone
companies and law book publishers, for example, have extensively
courted handicapped workers and have invested substantial sums in
facilities to accommodate their condition. But the current law insists
that all firms take the same steps, even if the social return from their
investment is far lower for some firms than for others. The ADA has
been celebrated as an emancipation proclamation, but scant attention
has been given to the deterioration in wages and working conditions
for other workers that will inexorably follow if its commands are me-
ticulously carried out. (The early returns suggest that widespread
stonewalling has greeted this statute.) The mandate of expensive
changes in the way in which business is done will not generate net
benefits in excess of the costs entailed. In this context as in others, the
separation of legal control from financial accountability will lead to
excessive and wasteful investments, with the prospect of escalating litigation.

The problem of cost-justified discrimination is not confined to various terms and conditions within the workplace. The entire network
of pensions and insurance is heavily dependent, for example, on sex

classifications. As above, these formal discriminations survive in the marketplace because they take into account the differences in costs that are correlated with sex. Women as a group live longer and should therefore pay lower insurance rates—the sweet—but receive a smaller annual pension payment for any given contribution—the bitter. Pregnancy is an expensive condition to treat medically, and when covered by insurance it leads to dramatic differences in medical rates between men and women. But in the decided cases the cost justifications for these distinctions are willfully ignored, with the same resource misallocations as above.[8] An employment discrimination statute that starts out trying to remove irrational forces from the marketplace ends in entrenching a form of implicit subsidy that could not be sustained in a market setting. Again, the formal definition of discrimination is utterly incompatible with the more accurate economic account.

A similar approach is taken under the ADA, which refuses to allow employers to inquire about any preexisting conditions of an employee in deciding whom to hire.[9] The effect of this provision will in many instances be far more dramatic than that caused by the significant differentials that are ignored under the sex discrimination laws. Health insurance premiums for an AIDS patient are, for example, at least twenty-five times as great as for a healthy worker. Other conditions—diabetes, epilepsy, or emphysema—may also impose major costs on otherwise stable insurance pools. The ADA does not mandate that employers provide their workers with any set level of insurance; it only requires equal levels of insurance regardless of differences in levels of risk.[10] Employers will therefore have a strong incentive to cut back on the levels of coverage for both healthy and sick workers or to eliminate group insurance altogether, notwithstanding its enormous efficiencies in unregulated markets. And the further unraveling of the private insurance markets will be chalked up not as a consequence of regulation but as yet another unexplained failure of the marketplace, which in turn will only increase the pressures for complete state control of the health system. Here as elsewhere, the ADA works on the implicit assumption that it is possible to improve the lot of some without compromising the position of others. There are many strong arguments for providing public grants or tax credits to handicapped persons or the firms who assist them. But there are none for doing it through clumsy systems of direct regulation that only conceal the social costs of what is undertaken.

The dictatorial nature of the antidiscrimination laws runs deeper, for the enforcement of the nondiscrimination principle requires employers to ignore, except when affirmative action is at issue, the preferences of their customers, employees, and suppliers. Often there is little concern with the race or sex of an employee. But the common sentiment is not necessarily a universal one: in the case of physicians and nurses, lingerie sales personnel and ski instructors, personal attendants, and a thousand other jobholders, race, sex, and ethnicity often make a key difference. Do we really want to lecture a woman anticipating childbirth on the importance of hiring a male obstetrician if she desires otherwise? Do we really think that the preferences of people across the world are so uniform that all will exhibit preferences for the same select group of white males when they come from such different backgrounds and cultures? The totalitarian risks of trying to reshape individual preferences should be apparent to us all. If they are, then the best thing to do is to stay our collective hand and allow each person to go his or her separate way on these critical matters of choice. The people who lose in one set of transactions are apt to gain in another, and the burden of this selection is not likely to fall on disadvantaged groups, given that huge portions of the institutional discrimination, especially in education and employment, cut overtly in their favor. In every other area of life, the function of markets is to satisfy customer preferences at low costs, and not to change them. But with the civil rights law, the state is so confident in its collective view of right and wrong that it is willing to force its judgments down the throat of those who dare to want otherwise. I confess to having no corner on moral wisdom either, which is one reason to allow all people to choose their trading partners on whatever grounds they see fit.

Yet another irony of the civil rights laws deserves some brief mention. There is no natural limit to the number of protected classes, and no clear principle that indicates how to resolve conflicts between members of different protected classes. It may seem straightforward enough to protect black against white, or male against female, but the arguments become more complicated when a dispute pits black males against white women, or blacks against Hispanics, or both against Asians. In these cases, we discriminate both for and against protected classes, and the good that is said to be done on the one side is offset by the harm inflicted on the other. Matters only become more complicated when discrimination on grounds of age or handicap is added to the list of forbidden activities. The ability to entrench older workers in key jobs (which will prove to be a major drain on research universities now that tenured faculty members at universities may work indefinitely past the age of seventy) will impose a far greater harm upon all younger workers than any civil rights law can rectify. The entire system is therefore a massive crisscross of disguised transfers that in sum are a net tax on the operation of the system as a whole. We are better off as a nation by eliminating the administrative costs that magnify allocative distortions.

It may be said that all this is a matter of pure theory alone and that the laws have actually done far more good than harm. But the empirical evidence, albeit incomplete, cuts clearly in the opposite direction.[11] Initially, it is difficult to estimate the total costs of compliance with the civil rights laws, but it surely must be in the billions of dollars, even if we take into account only the direct costs of litigation and the substantial costs of teaching millions of employers and employees what the law requires. The distortion of behavioral incentives addressed above only adds to the overall bill. Any possible justification for the statutes must rest on their ostensibly favorable distributive effects, and these are very hard to find. The most telling measure of the effect of the civil rights laws on race, for example, is the ratio of black to white wages in employment. This figure improved in the years immediately after the passage of the 1964 Civil Rights Act, as it had improved in the twenty years before the passage of the statute. But since 1975 that ratio has remained roughly unchanged, despite the vigorous enforcement of the Civil Rights Act and the extensive use of affirmative action programs, some of which would have occurred even in the absence of any statute.

Voluntary affirmative action should in itself account for some improvement in the ratio, so if matters are largely unchanged, the coercive side of civil rights enforcement is likely to have had negative effects. The explanation is not hard to find. As in other areas of human endeavor, regulated firms have found ways, through plant location, advertisements, job classifications, and capital investments, to escape (at some positive private and social cost) the clutches of the civil rights acts long before the first employee walks into the hiring office. Yet that firms take these evasive actions does not mean that they will not also resort to quotas and other inefficient hiring devices in order to reduce the risk of liability in settings from which it is too costly to flee. Worse still, the roughly constant ratio of black to white wages is consistent with a *declining* standard of living for both groups. Much the same story can be told about the closing of the gender gap, most of which is attributable to a decline in male wages, not a rise in female ones. When the full record is examined, it should be clear that the substantive case for the civil rights laws has not been made on the traditional grounds first used to justify the statutes.

At best, one might point to a set of symbolic benefits. Statutes do not speak in univocal terms. If the civil rights acts are said to represent a national commitment to aid the weak and the powerless, they often convey other messages as well. Thus they encourage groups, no matter what their success in the political arena, to maintain a position of victimization lest anyone think that an improvement in social circumstances might justify a relaxation in the partisan enforcement of the civil rights statutes. The original arguments in favor of the statutes spoke rightly of the formal legal barriers to markets, of the overt and systematic prejudice that supported those barriers, and then proposed color-blind rules to prevent these forms of abuse. Yet the radical transformation in the cultural and legal landscape has done nothing to quiet the clarion call to arms. Today the enemy is hidden and unconscious forms of discrimination that require a massive national commitment to diversity and affirmative action—done of course at the collective level. By so retooling the civil rights law everyone now has some excuse for failure. Those who are outside the law's protection can point to the overt discrimination that leaves them there and insist that it is not justified by any misconduct on their part. Yet those who benefit from the programs can point to their very existence as compelling testimony to the pervasive and irradicable nature of invidious discrimination. At every stage, the institutional failure to achieve numbers and targets will be regarded not as evidence of the sad state of the supply side of the market (for instance, a lack of black Ph.D.'s in mathematics and the sciences) but as evidence of institutional corruption that requires still more stringent acts of public enforcement, acts that can only prove as unsuccessful as those that have preceded them.

There is one last irony. The enforcement of the civil rights laws consumes public resources that could go elsewhere—toward the maintenance of law and order. I believe that the billionth dollar spent on the recruitment and training of police, prosecutors, and judges yields a far higher social payoff than the first dollar spent in the enforcement of the antidiscrimination laws. The principles of scarcity are not suspended while the government makes new forays into unregulated areas of social life. The best and the brightest are now diverted into an enterprise that rewards intellectual cleverness and mathematical sophistication, but it soaks up able people whose efforts are better directed at curbing the unbridled use of force. I do not think that it is mere happenstance that the level of crime and violence has increased hand in hand with the rising commitment to civil rights enforcement. The civil rights laws treat discrimination as though it were tantamount to the use of force, and then consume resources that are better devoted to traditional forms of law enforcement. A principle of the conservation of outrage applies: if we treat discrimination as tantamount to force, then why should we be surprised by the erosion of the moral prohibition against the use of force?

The employment discrimination laws, then, show more clearly than one might suppose the importance of keeping to the simple rules that govern the operation of a sound social order. On all matters, both great and small, the opposite of freedom of contract is always a form of social domination by whichever group holds political power. The idea of a social order based on individual freedom and the control of force and fraud is indivisible over its various domains. When it is compromised in the name of civil rights, it is compromised everywhere.

COMPARABLE WORTH

The system of comparable worth envisions a level of government control that, if anything, is more expansive than that imposed by an antidiscrimination law, for at its heart comparable worth requires pay equity not only for workers who perform the same job but for workers who perform different jobs that are judged by some government panel to be equivalent in their social value.[12] Like the antidiscrimination laws, comparable worth is proposed as a kind of painless pill. There is said to be some inequity inside the marketplace immune to correction by voluntary means, even though there are literally thousands of people who are trying to hire labor that is underpriced in its current use. The correction of that ostensible inequity is said to allow us to achieve simultaneously the best of both possible worlds: greater fairness and greater efficiency. As with the antidiscrimination laws, it seems clear that this promise is unfulfillable. The greater administrative costs wrought by a system of comparable worth must be justified by the creation of superior incentives for productive labor. But comparable worth statutes go astray because the incentives they create are wholly perverse. The violation of the simple rule of voluntary exchange comes at a very high price.

In dealing with these statutes, it is imperative to be aware of what hinges upon the choice of a term. When somebody says that the statute is concerned with "pay equity," the threshold question is what is meant by "equity," or "fairness." There was a time when I thought I understood exactly what the term implied. A system of fairness, as I understood it, was always one that was based upon individual autonomy and individual consent. A theory of fairness was one that allowed people to have zones in which they could make their own decisions and that required them to honor the promises they made. When the dust settled, the preoccupation with fairness led to the same system of freedom of contract that in so many contexts has fallen prey to government regulation. But today the term "fairness" has been co-opted into an antimarket standard, attainable only by purposive government action. The Fair Labor Standards Act of 1938 is not a charter for individual freedom.[13] It is the statute that authorizes the administration of the minimum wage laws and a host of other restrictive labor laws as well, including restrictions on labor within the home. Similarly, the National Labor Relations Act does not designate as unfair labor practice the use of force, intimidation, or fraud in forming or maintaining employment relationships; instead, it dictates the entire system of mandatory collective bargaining, which renders illegal any agreement whereby an employer and employee seek to bypass an elected union representative.

It turns out that these competing conceptions of fairness within the legal arena are in many ways mirrored by larger philosophical disputes over what it means to talk about fairness between individuals in some original position, some sort of a state of nature. Under the first of the simple rules, each person initially owns, and is entitled as a matter of right to own, the talents and endowments which he happens to receive either by genetic endowment or through social circumstance. In contrast, the very powerful modern conceptions of fairness or of equity, as developed at length by John Rawls in his *Theory of Justice*, insist that this natural distribution of talents is essentially arbitrary, and that the major function of the state ought to be to take whatever talents one person has and make sure that the fruits of those talents are shared in some just social form with all other individuals. So a claim of fairness that talks about private property and individual self-ownership clashes with a claim of fairness that is predicated on the collective ownership of labor and by easy extension of all the means of production.

It is wise to be wary about an idea of fairness so protean, so rich, and so filled with different meanings that everybody can place her own particular political program under its capacious mantle. The critical question about "pay equity" is whether there is any precision in the term—something that decides that equity is going to be a collective determination or, alternatively, that equity is going to be determined by individual, subjective valuations as expressed in the marketplace. The critical question thus turns on the relationship between labor and value.

In this context, there are two rival conceptions of value, one objective and the other subjective. The common conception of objective value holds that, notwithstanding the way people behave in their day-to-day lives, some neutral or impartial observer can make an objective determination of what is worth having, and can quantify that vision with sufficient clarity to be able to override the subjective preferences individuals display in ordinary, private transactions.

The alternative conception, which I favor, is intrinsically subjective. Each person has her own conception of what the good life is; each person thinks that certain resources are better spent in one way than in another. There is no public commensurability with respect to satisfaction; it is impossible to put a ruler against satisfaction of wants and say that there is so much here and so much there. There is, in effect, no objective, independent observer who can tell exactly what counts as value to any individual. There is a combination of political biases and intellectual predispositions so thick and interwoven that to try to institutionalize them is, in some sense, an exercise in folly. The key word is "institutionalize," for it is evident that people do make private interpersonal comparisons of utility all the time, as with charitable giving. But it is one thing to decide these matters for yourself; it is quite another to devise institutions that can make these judgments by a collective deliberative process, where the ebb and flow of political forces and the political clout of the potential recipients will dominate the process. It is best to regard these judgments as subjective in order to insulate them from the forces and vagaries of the political process.

Under the simple rules developed earlier, value is determined from an initial position of self-ownership (rule 1) by a system of voluntary exchange (rule 3). Within that framework, value is not determined by the estimation placed on a person's labor by any random member of society or by some hypothetical person who attaches an average value to that labor. It is assigned by the person who attaches the highest value to that labor. The exchange becomes socially desirable because it is desired by both parties to it. The guarantee of value stems not from any objective or social certification of the wisdom of the transaction but from the mutual consent that generated it. If 99.99 percent of the population regarded a person's labor as worthless, the market could still generate a high wage from the remaining 0.01 percent.

What happens when the government resorts to objective measures of value? Now some person, some bureaucrat, will have to come up with a collective determination of the value of labor, a task that can be accomplished in only one of two ways, both of which by definition must ignore the ordinary constraints of supply and demand. The first of these rests upon a Marxist conception, the labor theory of value, which holds that the value attributable to any particular good is determined by the amount of labor put into it. The difficulty with this system of valuation should be immediately apparent. The widget that takes two hours of labor to produce is said to be worth twice as much as the identical widget made in a single hour. The system is like a nightmarish self-fulfilling prophecy. The more labor that is invested in a particular good, the greater its ostensible value. Yet is coal more valuable when it is mined from the ground with a teaspoon? The theory may gain some modest plausibility because the goods that we see produced in a market system are on average worth more than the labor needed to produce them. But that is because those projects with substantial labor and little value are culled out of the system by the demand constraint, which plays no part in the labor theory. Goods that cost enormous amounts to produce but that have little value are not produced at all. The absence of willing buyers constrains the overall level of production and provides a stern warning not to engage in heroic ventures to produce goods of no value. The goods that survive the market constraint are worth the labor it takes to produce them.

Under the system of "pay equity," however, employers and consumers do not determine the value of labor. Instead, the market test is regarded as a poor surrogate for assessing value, which then must be determined by some other criterion. Since demand does not count, the only available strategy is to determine value by setting out some cost function—no simple task even for the expert consultants paid to do it. This process entails, for example, figuring out how many years of education it took to acquire a particular skill, how many hours of labor it will take to do certain sorts of tasks, what kinds of risks are associated with the venture, until some valuation is reached for the labor in question.

But it is not sufficient to do this task with respect to one job. It must be done with respect to all jobs, and there must be some internal coherence in the rankings. Job A can be compared with job B, which in turn can be compared with job C. Some A-C valuation can then be made. But A can also be compared with D, which in turn can be compared with C, or A can be compared with C directly. To strive for "fairness" between, say, nurses and truckdrivers is to place massive administrative and institutional demands on any system of comparable worth. For the system to function, the entire network must be perfectly aligned; otherwise, the ostensible conclusions will be determined de facto by the path of comparison. We cannot have a system in which the comparable worth of line employees is thought to be greater than that of the supervisors, for the net effect will encourage people to accept demotions in responsibility in order to increase their take-home pay. Why adopt a system that promises such weird anomalies? Matters are made no easier when new technology creates new jobs in new industries. The system of centralized planning will be overcome by the details and end up perpetually lagging behind current reality.

The additional levels of complexity brought on by this system are defended in the name of fair distribution. But it should be evident that they will have massive adverse effects on matters of production. The administrative costs of the system are far greater than those of ordinary markets, and their incentive effects will be largely self-destructive. The bureaucrat, the union, the pay commissioner, or the arbitrator may set the comparable worth of any particular job, but none of them will be able to coerce any particular employer into hiring a certain number of units at the fixed price. We can expect positions to go begging where the wages are below what the market demands, and to have a glut of applicants, waiting in line or searching for favors, trying to obtain those few valued positions where the wages are set above the market level. It is unlikely in the extreme that any firm faced with a relative wage scale will reconsider its former practices, confess its own error, and announce that its own practices have marginalized or devalued the contribution of women to its workforce. No order from above will lead to a transformation in the demand schedules of the regulated firms. The far more likely outcome is that the employer will adopt strategies designed to mitigate the effects of the law, regardless of the social dislocations that follow.

Why would any person want to create a system with such mind-boggling complexities? The most frequent answer is that government coercion is necessary to stop what is thought to be a pervasive form of sex discrimination within markets. Because of that discrimination, the argument runs, something has to be done to make sure that the value that women have in labor markets is equal to that of men. But this argument has clearly gone astray if the case for a general anti-discrimination law is as weak as I have argued in the first part of this chapter. The perceived wage gap—men make about 30 percent more than women in the United States—may be accounted for by a whole host of explanations. These include the number of hours worked, labor force commitment, choice of jobs, and commitment to marriage, children, and family, to name just a few. In the end, we should expect that once these other factors (plus additional ones of which we are only dimly aware) are taken into account, sufficient explanations for the wage differentials will emerge. The best empirical work in the area supports this position, for there is no evidence that more than 10 percent of the wage gap is not accounted for by the known explanatory variables. No system of regulation as comprehensive and cumbersome as comparable worth could ever hope to close that gap without making both men and women (and their families) worse off than before.

Once again, the basic logic of the market mechanism bears restatement. If there were large numbers of women who received wages that were below their market worth, some new entrant could reap enormous returns by hiring in that sector.[14] It is quite clear that markets are never in perfect equilibrium, for new opportunities and new perils constantly arise, and these require instant and powerful adjustments. But by the same token, it is a mistake to assume that they are usually out of equilibrium. Some one will enter to fill the gap. In the end, therefore, the same basic analysis applies to all three forms of regulation of labor markets: collective bargaining, unionization, and pay equity. All of them are more expensive and less effective than free entry in securing the benefits of full employment opportunities for all.

10

Professional Liability for Financial Loss

The problem of professional liability for financial loss spans the continents; it is a major issue today in all common law jurisdictions: the United States, Great Britain, and the Commonwealth. The area is rife with massive litigation. Some firms are reluctant to provide accounting and other professional services to their clients, fearing the enormous tort liabilities that could follow in their wake. Yet they are often powerless under the law to change the scope or magnitude of their liability by contract. This is another case in which the simple solution—contract—has been undermined by judges whose affection for complex solutions knows few doctrinal or institutional limitations.

TORT OR CONTRACT

Until thirty years ago, the standard common law rule both in the United States and the Commonwealth held suppliers of gratuitous information responsible for losses only in the event of fraud. The key decision was by Judge Benjamin Cardozo in the 1931 New York Case of Ultramares Corporation v. Touche.[1] Its fact pattern has been repeated countless times since then. The defendant accounting firm conducted an audit of its client. The audit failed to uncover the client's concealed liabilities or inflated assets. The defendant thus confirmed the audited firm's value of its business, and that confirmation was relied upon by the plaintiff, a purchaser of the stock or assets of the business who

194

discovered to her sorrow that what she had bought was worth only a fraction of its purchase price. No one doubts that the buyer has her action against the seller, for fraud and for breach of contract. Yet the seller (and its shareholders) cannot be found, or have spent the proceeds of sale. In desperation, the buyer then turns to the auditing firm and claims that its negligence in the examination of the seller's business led it to make misrepresentations that overstated the seller's worth. The upshot of the defendant's lack of prudence was the plaintiff's improvident purchase of an overvalued business. Her request for damages equal to her loss from the purchase quickly follows. The negligence of the auditing firm is said to make it a guarantor of the buyer's losses.

Judge Cardozo held that claims of this sort could not be brought unless the disappointed buyer could show that the auditing firm had participated in the fraud or had had knowledge of the fraud which it then failed to disclose. The requisite fraud and knowledge might easily be inferred from reckless behavior. But ordinary negligence was not a sufficient basis for imposing liability in the absence of contract. "We doubt," he concluded, "that the average business man receiving a certificate without paying for it and receiving it merely as one among a multitude of possible investors, would look for anything more."[2]

There matters remained for over thirty years. Then in the English case of Hedley, Byrne & Co. Ltd. v. Heller & Partners Ltd. the older consensus was challenged when the House of Lords suggested that liability for economic loss in these three-party situations could indeed be predicated on negligence.[3] The case itself presented a variation on *Ultramares.* An advertising firm provided services on credit to its client on the strength of a credit report that it had received from a merchant banker. The report overstated the assets of the client, which was liquidated before it paid the advertising firm for the services it had rendered. The advertising house then sued the merchant banker for its unpaid debts even though it had no guarantee for that obligation.

The transactions at issue in *Ultramares* and *Hedley, Byrne* exhibit small differences. The first transaction was a purchase of assets; the second was a provision of services on credit. In the first case, an accounting firm was hauled on the carpet; in the second a merchant banker. But both cases ask the question of what liability should attach when an auditor makes inaccurate representations, perhaps negligently, about its client to a third party which then relies on those representations to its detriment. In order to analyze this situation, it is best to begin with a problem of characterization that is ordinarily put to one side in the decided cases: are we dealing with an issue of contract or are we dealing with an issue of tort?[4] In answering that question, the law, following some influential language used by Lord Atkin in the 1930s in a product liability case, has generally opted for the tort approach and has treated the disappointed creditor as a stranger or "neighbor" who has been injured by the accountant's or bank's mistake. This equation sounds odd to the ear, for a neighbor is normally thought of not as a stranger, but as the person who lives next door, to whom some special, reciprocal obligation of neighborliness is owed. But Lord Atkin gives a rather different reading of the subject, for in one of the most famous passages in English law he wrote: "The rule that you are to love your neighbour becomes in law, you must not injure your neighbour; and the lawyer's question, Who is my neighbour? receives a restricted reply. You must take reasonable care to avoid acts or omissions which you can reasonably foresee would be likely to injure your neighbour. Who, then, in law, is my neighbour? The answer seems to be—persons who are so closely and directly affected by my act that I ought reasonably to have them in contemplation as being so affected when I am directing my mind to the acts or omissions which are called in question."[5]

That the application of this neighbor principle was not limited to cases involving strangers becomes clear from his application of the principle to the relationship between the manufacturer of a product and the product's "remote" consumer: "[A] manufacturer of products which he sells in such a form as to show that he intends them to reach the ultimate consumer in the form in which they left him, with no reasonable possibility of intermediate examination, and with the knowledge that the absence of reasonable care in the preparation or putting up of the products is likely to result in injury to the consumer's life or property, owes a duty to the consumer to take that reasonable care."[6]

Lord Atkin's generalizations, however, are exceedingly dangerous because his invocation of the neighbor principle lumps together two distinct types of situations. The first class of cases contains only cases involving harms to strangers where one person engages in actions that cause harm to someone with whom the actor is not connected, either directly or through intermediates. That set of issues is not relevant in this context because in all cases of misrepresentation the communication from the defendant passed to the plaintiff, which then made a decision on whether to rely on the information or not. The second class, relevant here, encompasses cases involving a network of persons linked together by a series of contracts. These cases can involve only two parties, as with buyers and sellers; or they can involve three (or more) parties linked together by contract: landlord, tenant, subtenant; manufacturer, dealer, and consumer; general contractor, subcontractor, and employee.

Lord Devlin, a great common law judge, applied Lord Atkin's neighbor principle to the commercial transaction before him in *Hedley, Byrne*. After his own exhaustive examination, he concluded that in the gratuitous transaction before him, it would be a mistake to saddle the defendant with a heavy financial liability, especially since the plaintiff advertiser was free to purchase more precise information before undertaking the work on credit. In this case, his intuitions seem right on the mark, and in fact conform closely to what Cardozo had concluded in *Ultramares*. But Devlin's task would have been far simpler had he started with the explicit disclaimer of liability that Heller & Partners had included on its transmittal of information. The no-liability result was dictated by contract, without all the Herculean labors that led him astray.

The failure to begin with the explicit contract is but one symptom of an error into which both Lord Atkin and Lord Devlin fell: the willingness to use the same principles in both stranger and consensual settings. I believe that this conflation between strangers and traders is fundamentally wrong. Recall for the moment the logic of liability in cases involving strangers. Without the imposition of some liability, the actor keeps all the benefits from acting while externalizing part of the cost. The net effect was to encourage the performance of certain actions that produced private gain and social loss. The purpose of the liability system was to force the actor to treat the losses of the other party as though they were his own. A rule of strict liability achieved that result by forcing the actor to pay for those losses, no matter what level of care he took. A rule of negligence forced the actor to take those losses into account by allowing the injured party her action where an actor failed to take reasonable care. In some cases, the victim might be in a better position to take precautions against the loss, and in those circumstances her negligence could be used to reduce or bar her recovery. The important point for these purposes is that the dynamics of the professional liability cases, and the business expectations they generate, do not respond very well to the logic used in stranger cases.

CONSENSUAL ARRANGEMENTS

To analyze the consensual situation, it is useful to consider the problem in two stages. The first looks at the simple case that involves only two parties, where the defendant-seller makes a representation to the plaintiff-buyer about the financial condition of the business he owns and is offering for sale. Once that case is understood it is then possible to turn to the more difficult and controversial three-party situation of professional liability for economic loss, where the defendant, as in *Hedley, Byrne,* makes a representation about the financial condition of some third party with whom the plaintiff wishes to deal.

The Two-Party Case

In order to understand the two-party case, it is critical to recall that the problem presented is not that found in the ordinary stranger case. One actor has not forced losses upon another without his consent. Within the context of a misrepresentation case, that problem disappears, for all such cases involve two individuals coming together in a joint enterprise. To the extent that a defendant wishes to impose losses upon a plaintiff, the defendant will have to pay for that loss. Some term of the basic contract will have to be altered to reflect the loss that will be left for the plaintiff to bear, whether by price or by some other mechanism (such as time or quality of performance) collateral to the underlying arrangement. Even under conditions of uncertainty, exchange will only take place when each party perceives itself to be better off with the deal than without it. What is more, the parties will not settle for just any exchange that improves their initial position. They will continue to tinker with the terms and conditions of that deal until they find the best possible arrangement for both.

In working through the implications of this model, we should not presume that the parties will choose a regime that requires the defendant who has made a negligent representation to compensate the plaintiff in full for any ensuing loss. The business problem of the two sides requires them to balance a number of independent variables, and when all of these are taken into account, that one-sided solution—all loss falls to the negligent defendant—seems highly unlikely. Let me mention a few of the central complications, which once again highlight the interaction between administrative costs and legal incentives.

Levels of Precaution

The first relevant variable concerns the relative cost of the precautions that can be undertaken by either the recipient or the producer of the information. It is a very common assumption in American law, and I dare say elsewhere, that individual consumers are "powerless" to prevent various kinds of losses from occurring. But that categorical judgment does not describe reality, because it proceeds as though, no matter what the level of cost, individual behavior will be unchanged: it treats response as perfectly indifferent to stimulus, saying that people in no way, shape, or form respond to incentives. Yet that is a fundamentally mistaken way to conceive of the effects of legal rules. If the legal regime clearly and unambiguously states that a party takes the information and relies on it at its own risk, then the level of recipient precaution—how that information is verified and used—will be far higher than it would be if the supplier has warranted, or is required to warrant, the soundness of what has been conveyed.

Accordingly, there are two distinct ways to increase the level of recipient precaution. The first is to reduce the level of care required under the warranty. The supplier of information can be held responsible only for a failure to take reasonable care, or perhaps only for giving out information he knows to be false. Alternatively, the damages recoverable in the event that the supplier of information fails to meet his obligation can be limited to some fraction of the recipient's loss. A maximum dollar limitation is one way to achieve that result; denying compensation for certain classes of business loss (such as potential profits) is another. These two approaches can be combined, for example, in a provision that allows limited damages but only on proof of negligence. But no matter what approach is used to cut back on liability, more of the task of loss prevention will fall on the plaintiff, who is better able to discharge it, a socially desirable result.

Administrative Costs

Administrative costs are also of great importance in the context of professional liability. Suppose that customer precaution against a given form of peril is more costly than producer precaution. An accounting firm may do a better job of ferreting out errors and fraud than the firm it audits. It still does not follow under those circumstances that liability, with full tort compensatory damages no less, ought to be imposed on the accountant. Administrative costs may loom very large. If the legal rules necessary to rectify error are costly to apply, the voice of wisdom says that certain kinds of errors are best left unrequited. In other words, if the defendant can prevent a loss for $50 less than the plaintiff, but it costs $100 in administrative costs to ensure that the defendant does its job, it is better to leave the plaintiff to fend for itself than to impose the liability. That conclusion need not be imposed on the parties, because at the time of agreement they can reach it themselves, and where they do, their judgment should not be questioned. No one can assume that liability should be imposed on a defendant solely because it is the cheaper cost avoider. Some good things are too expensive to require.

Reputation and Deterrence

A third critical variable in these situations is reputation. Liability in a consensual universe does not turn only on compensation once something goes wrong. Instead, compensatory damages are one tool used to secure the proper level of deterrence so that wrongful activities do not occur in the first place. In working out the balance of advantage, it is always a mistake to assume that an injured party has no effective remedy if it is unable to invoke the legal machinery after the fact. There's a regrettable tendency among lawyers to say that if there is no legal remedy, there's no constraint on human behavior at all. Social sanctions cannot be ignored in determining the institutional value of any legal arrangement. No one is a socially free agent where others depend on him, and customers should not be treated as strangers whose preferences are to be disregarded simply because they are unable to win a lawsuit. Lawyers could learn a lot from one of their own number—John Donne.

Virtually everybody involved in business recognizes the enormous importance in business affairs of preserving a reputation for fair and honest dealing. If a firm badly monitors its accounts, or badly constructs its buildings, it is at financial risk, even if it doesn't have to pay a single dollar to the injured party. When bad information is revealed, the firm's losses are devastating because that information will reduce its likelihood of maintaining its sales at the former level. People bond themselves to do reliable work by being repeat players in a given market. Where the reputational bond is strong, the legal bonds may be weak, because the incentives for good conduct can be secured without having to incur the extensive administrative costs of any system of liability.

Advantages of Regulation by Contract

With all of this said, it follows that there's absolutely no presumption that the regime of full compensation so often applicable in cases involving strangers ought to carry over to the two-party consensual arrangement. Typically these consensual cases involve the joint production of information; typically these cases involve the joint prevention of loss; and typically these cases entail high administrative costs. Under these circumstances, all sorts of loss-sharing devices are likely to prove superior to the rigid, tortlike, full damage rule. Under these circumstances, it is as plausible to have a default rule which holds that the plaintiff takes the risk of inaccurate information unless either the information has been acquired for a fee or it was supplied fraudulently. This rule parallels many of the nineteenth-century common law rules for gratuitous undertakings that have dominated such areas as medical malpractice involving indigent patients, liability for the destruction of chattels stored without payment, and the occupier's liability for guests injured on the premises. *Ultramares* is foursquarely within this tradition, and even though that decision has been frequently attacked, its rule requiring fraud has had as of late a modest but welcome revival.[7]

That cautious approach makes good sense. Given the complexities of the situation, there are major risks to external regulation through the tort system that seeks to fix once and for all either the standard of liability or the measure of damages once liability has been found. This conclusion holds true in either of two possible states of the world. Notwithstanding the differences between firms, if it turns out that the same liability regime is appropriate across the board, the danger is that regulation (driven by a powerful set of anticontractual motivations) is apt to fix on the wrong rule across all firms and all cases. If, however, it turns out that the variations across separate cases are important, any uniform rule is certain to ignore or misunderstand the variation between cases and their significance. Large auditing firms may, for example, have one kind of problem, and small auditors have another kind. Those differences could relate to their capacity to self-insure (diversification is more likely when a firm has many clients), to their capacity to monitor, to the nature of the businesses of the audited firms or to their reputation, which may vary with particular submarkets or over time.

Either way, the gap between the optimal and actual liability regimes will, more often than not, be great. One advantage of markets is that they allow uniform solutions to spread quickly if appropriate, while allowing diverse solutions to emerge (somewhat more slowly) when required. A range of contractual solutions may be tailored not to the generic relationship, but to the particulars of each case. In contrast, regulation through the tort system invites comprehensive judgments that are likely to be wrong, and then kills off access to the information that might facilitate the correction of the initial mistakes.

The Three-Party Case

This same framework of analysis carries over to the three-party case, where the professional defendant misrepresents the status of a third party to the plaintiff, causing economic loss. It is in precisely this situation that Cardozo's basic presumption of liability only for fraud better comports with business requirements than Devlin's presumption of liability even in cases of ordinary negligence. To sort out the basic picture, it is necessary to make a few preliminary economic observations.

Collateral Gains and Losses

To begin with, in any three-party case, the villain of the piece is insolvent or otherwise beyond the reach of the law. The case therefore concentrates on the allocation of loss between the two parties that remain. In thinking about how to allocate that economic loss, we must distinguish between two types of cases. In the first class, the losses sustained by one party are unaccompanied by any collateral gain to the other side. In the second, the losses that are borne by one side are offset, either in whole or in part, by gains obtained by the other side. As an illustration of the first case, consider a situation in which corporate assets are destroyed by flood or fire—a clear loss to the company without any offsetting gain to a third party. In contrast, the typical case of an accountant's liability involves a takeover of a company whose assets are revealed after the fact to be worth less than the price paid by the acquiring corporation. Further examination reveals that the value of the shares of the target corporation was overstated by the professional accountant for the target corporation, on whose figures the acquiring corporation relied. The seller received a substantial gain. In view of this fact, what are the social losses of this standard transaction?

First, there are substantial losses to the acquiring firm, which may have paid $100 a share for assets worth only $50 a share. The sense of grievance is clear enough. However, the seller has received that $100 per share, which it will not have to disgorge. So at least as a first approximation it looks as though the gains on one side are matched perfectly by the losses on the other side.

Unfortunately, that assumption is wrong, for reasons that will presently become clear. But for a moment treat this crude calculation as correct and then ask the following question. If the direction of the accountant's error is unknown—whether she would overstate the value of the shares or understate their value—and the buyer and seller in this transaction could get together with the accountant beforehand, what kind of liability would they want to impose on the accountant? As a first approximation, they would not want any liability at all. To the extent that each of them had a 50 percent chance of an overcharge and a 50 percent chance of an undercharge, their expected value from the deal would be exactly the same as if the valuation were perfect. Therefore, neither party would be willing to incur any administrative costs in order to put a system of liability in place, either between themselves or against the accountant. Since all errors cancel, all are ignored at the planning stage in determining the level of precaution. A system of no liability is superior to all others, for it increases the gains to both sides.

That conclusion is at manifest odds with the current system, which states: "Let's ignore the gain to the seller and only take into account the loss to the buyer, and worry about its prevention." Starting from this unsound assumption, the law then creates a systematic and expensive divergence between the private and social costs of erroneous information. The private costs to one side are offset by the private gains to the other, so that the social costs generated by overpayment for stock are (as a first approximation) zero. Yet the legal system treats the losses of the acquirer as though they were social losses, by systematically ignoring the associated gains of the target corporation.

Distributional Consequences

Unfortunately, the convenient assumption that the social losses generated by misevaluation are zero is in fact wrong. To state the matter in its most general form, it is incorrect to assume that distributional decisions have only distributional consequences. These decisions also have strong incentive effects that impinge directly on the total level of output generated by the legal system.

Two different types of cases illustrate the basic point. In the first, the transaction would have gone forward but the price would not have been set at $100 a share: it would have been set at $50 per share if the asset value had in fact been overstated, or at $150 per share if that asset value had been understated. When any misevaluation is discovered, the consequences at the time do look largely distributional, because the parties on both sides of the transaction are saying, "We want to go ahead with this deal, and the only thing that separates us is the total amount of the consideration that is going to be paid." But often this assumption is not going to hold. If, for example, the target is rickety and has uncollectible key accounts, an outsider may well decide not to purchase the target's shares *at all*. Or, if the purchase does go forward, it may assume a radically different form, so that certain kinds of residual risk will be placed on one party instead of the other. Once these sorts of complications emerge, misinformation not only has distributional consequences, but clearly will encourage the completion of some transactions that should not take place or induce people to adopt the wrong contractual terms for those that do take place. These scenarios do reveal important allocative losses stemming from the accountant's valuation. When these are present, it becomes worthwhile to do something about the mistake, even at some additional cost.

Worse still, the accountant's errors are not likely to be randomly distributed, with a nice bell-shaped curve that forms neatly around the true value. The usual pattern of audit error is that the accountant hired by a prospective seller or borrower overstates the value of the assets to be sold or offered as security for a loan. Once that systematic bias is identified, it is likely that the losses will be borne by the outsider (the purchaser or lender) rather than by the insider (the seller or the borrower). Armed with that general information, outsider lenders and purchasers are rightly going to be very wary in their business dealings. They will take expensive precautions of their own because they perceive themselves to be dealing not with a random draw but with a stacked deck. A seller or borrower will seek to counter these pressures by saying: "Look, in this setting information is more easily acquired for your use by us than by you. But I know that you will only credit any information we supply if we warrant to make good your loss (or at least some fraction of it) in the event that the information we have supplied turns out to be wrong."

But the seller or borrower may find that the offer of a (limited) warranty will be insufficient to ease the concerns of the doubting buyer or lender. After all, what assets stand behind that warranty? If the transaction aborts, the seller or borrower may have few assets to make good on the promises given. But the need for reliable information still remains, and the third-party professional may be hired to bond the statements made by the seller or borrower. It is from just this logic that the case for some professional liability is born. The immediate parties to a transaction will hire the services of some third party in order to reduce the overall social loss generated by inaccurate information.

But what will be the extent of that professional liability? The critical point to remember is that, even though losses will occur, they will not be equal to the losses that the disappointed purchaser or lender suffers after the fact. Rather, the losses will always be limited to some fraction of that total. But what fraction? If it turns out that the economic losses suffered by the plaintiff are, say, $50, do we really think that the social losses are $10, $20, $30, or $40? It's very hard in the abstract to make the appropriate estimation, however critical it is to the design of the overall liability package. If we think that the social losses and the private losses are roughly the same, then having a viable remedy for professional negligence on the model of the decision in *Hedley, Byrne* is the appropriate legal response: the professional banker or accountant may well be held liable in full for the economic loss of the buyer or lender, even if there is no direct contractual arrangement between them. The fees paid by the seller or borrower will provide the necessary funds to buy the insurance. But this conclusion is utterly misguided if the social losses from misinformation are lower than the share price or loan value. In these settings, the strong tort model with full compensatory damages for negligent misrepresentations leads to an expensive purchase of the wrong type of insurance.

Consequences of the Dominant Legal Approach

Unfortunately, the important legal decisions on this subject do not address any of the issues outlined in this analysis, even when they reach the right conclusion. Instead, the dominant judicial position assumes that whenever there is a sale or loan of any substance, the buyer or lender desires to purchase an expensive insurance policy against economic loss, at least in the event of professional negligence. It is no longer possible to hire an accountant or auditor whose sole function is to provide auditing services. Yet these services have long been demanded, even in an age when accountants and auditors had a virtual de facto immunity from liability for professional negligence.

The modern legal regime, however, *ties* the service function to the insurance function, so that it becomes quite impossible to purchase one without the other. That insurance is very expensive, because it has to cover the expected payout once liability is established and the enormous expenses associated with determining both the existence of negligence and the extent of the associated financial losses. Owing to the complexity of the issue, few if any cases can be resolved by some expedited procedure, such as summary judgment. Given that legal state of affairs, the business judgment quickly becomes: are the gains from the auditing business sufficiently large to offset the losses from the insurance business? If they are, the transaction will go forward, with less net gain to all its participants. If not, the sale or loan will fall casualty to the unwise legal rules that govern the auditing and counseling functions.

The complexity of the transaction therefore requires the professional banker or accountant to raise his fees to his own clients, who in turn seek to recoup them from their potential buyers or lenders, the ostensible beneficiaries of these legal innovations. But now the familiar question about mandated protection arises yet again. Is a lender or purchaser better off with a legal order that reduces legal protection after the transaction in order to reduce the cost of protection beforehand? At bottom, the three-party situation thus yields the same conclusion as the two-party situation. No one gains when the law requires the parties to spend $100 of their private funds in exchange for $50 of net value.

The Contractual Alternative

In light of the difficulties with this mandatory regime, why not allow the auditor and client to contract out of the tort liability? The auditor normally deals with a single client. She should be in a position to decide whether she wishes to offer an extensive or limited warranty. Once the warranty is selected, the client can make its terms known to the class of potential lenders or purchasers, to evaluate as they see fit. Where the class of third parties is small and concentrated, some of them may come back to the auditor's client and demand greater protection. At that point, a mutually beneficial three-way exchange can be negotiated whereby the auditor provides additional protection for an additional fee in a direct contractual setting. Alternatively, the client could seek independent advice from an accountant of his own choosing. To be sure, with public offerings, the class of third parties will be broad and diffuse, so that the terms of trade must necessarily remain on a take-it-or-leave-it basis. In this context, the level of protection for third parties will be fixed by the negotiations between seller or lender, and their professionals. If that protection is set too low, the offering will be undersubscribed. Either way, the contract approach should induce auditors to offer optimal terms for their services.

Under the present tort-based regime the public and the private offerings are treated as polar opposites. It is generally said that there is no liability for negligent misrepresentation where the offending statements are made to the world at large. In the famous language of Judge Cardozo, liability for negligence is to be avoided because it "may expose accountants to a liability in an indeterminate amount for an indeterminate time to an indeterminate class." The common law takes its cue from this famous aphorism: if there is a representation to a single person, or a small group of persons, negligence liability may be imposed, in light of the "specific reliance" undertaken by these third parties. There is no parallel liability for public statements.

But in point of fact the distinction is odd. The key questions in both contexts are two: First, what is the expected liability from negligent audits or reports? Second, what is the relative efficacy of contract and tort solutions? On the first question, the indeterminate scope of liability to the public at large need not translate into extensive liability for either the seller or the auditor. The public offering may be directed toward many persons, but all of them cannot accept the offers for a limited number of shares. The uncertainty to the seller and the auditor lies therefore in the *identity* of the potential claimants, not in the anticipated level of financial exposure. Negligent misrepresentations in large closed transactions could dwarf the potential liability from negligent misrepresentations to the public at large in some smaller deal. There is no categorical line between the two classes of transactions.

Nor is there any reason to believe that tort solutions are preferable to contract ones in either the public or the private setting. In both contexts, the auditor and the original client have powerful incentives to set the right terms of trade. In a public offering, the sure knowledge that potential investors cannot counteroffer should lead both parties to adopt the respective liability provisions that will encourage these parties to come into the market, lest the offer be undersubscribed. In the private setting, a second round of negotiation could correct any mistakes in allocation contained in the original offer. The renegotiation possible with the private offer makes it more likely that such contracts will be more finely tuned than public offerings. But it also gives the seller and auditor incentives to save those renegotiation costs by making a suitable offer the first time.

Once it is recognized that there is no necessary fit between some idealized tort rule and the joint expectations of the parties, the parties have some incentive to experiment with new contractual terms. The universe of potential warranties need not be limited to two—no liability or full tort liability. It is possible for some sellers to say, "We understand that you are nervous about my rendering services without any financial exposure, so we'll tell you what we'll do. We will put up a bond equal to three times the fee that we have received for the services in question. That will give us a powerful incentive to protect against losses on all sides, even though it won't provide you with full compensation if this deal fails. Anybody who wants to rely on this report will now not only get the report but also on top of it will get the damage schedule, which shows exactly what reliance is worth to that firm."

Other variations are possible as well. One tack taken by a seller, for example, might state: "If you want more protection, there are two things you can do. One is to come right back to me, the auditor who has done all the work. You want to have protection? Now you pay a separate premium based upon the dollar value of the transaction." There's no reason to rely upon *Hedley, Byrne* or any other abstract principle of tort law. The institutional structures make it possible to write a direct contract between a prospective buyer and an auditor if that is desired by both sides.

But then again the buyer may not want to rely on the seller's auditor. After all, the auditor has been hired by somebody else, and if she missed the problem the first time, she may miss it again. So now that buyer could take that auditor's report, complete with its well-crafted disclaimers, to his own people for evaluation. There is no law that prohibits two independent audits on a big deal or cooperation between auditors. This solution places heavy reliance on the victim's precaution, which duplicates the seller's precautions, but even so it may well be cost-effective if it reduces the frequency and severity of any expected future litigation. Once the problem is transferred from the courts to the marketplace, the players will have better incentives to generate reliable information, wholly without regard to the underlying legal rule.

Given the range of trade-offs between administrative costs and incentives, the courts should never assume that they can capture the optimal standard of liability in a single word, and keep it there. The current emphasis on "foreseeability" of loss as the touchstone for potential negligence liability would quickly disappear from the scene in any contractual setting. The foresight of loss is common on both sides, and while it alerts everyone to the problem at hand, it gives no clue as to the contractual arrangements that minimize its consequences.

So once again the fatal step in the foreseeability approach is the first: the willingness to make law for private parties that are capable of making law for themselves. From this assumption it is an easy inference to the ordinary principles of negligence. Yet once they take hold they are hard to root out, for the same courts that do understand what contract arguments should control are reluctant to accept any disclaimers of tort liability, no matter how common they are in practice. The process of private correction of judicial errors is thus all too often frustrated by judicial regulation. There are some welcome signs today that liability for accountants and auditors is slowly abating, but doctrinal confusion and legal uncertainty are a poor substitute for a consistent regime of contractual freedom.

11

The Origins of
Product Liability Law

In dealing with labor contracts and economic losses arising from the rendering of professional services, I have argued that the simple common law conceptions of private contract do a far better job of regulating these relationships than the complex judicial or statutory arrangements that government all too often forces on the contracting parties. This comparison between private agreement and public ordering is not, however, limited to those types of cases. It also embraces many cases of physical injury, including the damages that result from the use, or misuse, of the many products routinely placed into the stream of commerce.

The question of product liability has quickly moved to the forefront of the debate during the past generation. The massive expansion in liability is by now an oft-told tale: The number of cases and the number of dollars transferred have vastly increased since the rise of modern product liability law somewhere around 1970. Thus total insurance premiums for product related lines were about $1.650 billion in 1970, but over $19 billion in 1988.[1] Likewise, the number of product liability lawsuits commenced in federal court as late as 1975 (the year before the first insurance crisis) was 2,393, a figure that increased to 16,166 in 1988 before tailing off to 13,408 the next year, and remaining roughly constant thereafter. Probably a somewhat greater number of suits were filed in state courts, and doubtless many other cases were settled before suit under threat of litigation. Yet even these

211

numbers understate the level of litigation, because certain key suits, such as the test litigation over the liability of tobacco companies for lung cancer, are test cases that consume huge resources even though they do not appreciably increase the number of filed cases.

With all this flurry of activity, no one has been able to establish any correlation between the level of litigation and the level of product safety. It is clear that overall accident rates have fallen in the past generation, in large part because overall improvements in technology and wealth have made homes, workplaces, and roads safer than they had been before, hardly changes attributable to any innovations in product liability law. In many categories of product-related injuries or deaths, however, it appears that the accident rate has *risen* just as the number of lawsuits has intensified: injuries requiring emergency room care were up for such products as playground equipment, ladders, power lawn mowers, swimming pools, and chain-saws, often by as much as 100 percent, even in the face of general technological advances. For motor vehicles, there appears to be a more or less uniform decline in the rate of accidents per mile driven that is uninfluenced by any important legal changes.

Two of the most important milestones in the regulation of automobile safety were the passage of the National Traffic and Motor Vehicle Safety Act of 1966[2] and the entry into product liability law of the crashworthiness doctrine, which was introduced in 1968 and spread quickly thereafter.[3] Yet anyone who looked at the death rates per million miles driven could not figure out when these statutory interventions took place or gauge their possible effect. The overall death rate dropped from 8.8 in 1947 to 2.2 in 1989. Over 10 percent of that drop came in 1948 (8.8 to 8.1), and the drop was nearly as large in the next year (8.1 to 7.5), probably as a result of the retooling from the wartime to the peacetime economy. Thereafter the rate declined to 5.0 and stayed steady throughout the 1960s. Then there was another sharp decline in the early 1970s (from 4.9 in 1970 to 3.5 in 1974), followed by five straight years of no change at 3.3 in the late 1970s. By 1989 the rate had declined to around 2.2.[4] It is clear that the long-term trends are driven by overall changes in technology in the construction of both roads and vehicles. The isolated bursts of improvement could be attributable to all sorts of exogenous factors, including the percentage of teen-age drivers, the price of gasoline, and so forth.

But there is surely no obvious connection between innovations and regulation or liability and these changes in the death rates.

The institutional story is the same as the statistical one. It seems clear that what happens in lawsuits does not affect what is done in the design or manufacture of products. Adverse verdicts are treated essentially as random noise that does not reflect badly on any party connected with the design or production of the product, a pattern that is common with medical malpractice cases as well.[5] Litigation often takes place after a product line has been modified or discontinued. Jury verdicts either say nothing about what should be done to make a particular product better or give inconsistent recommendations. So garbled a signal cannot serve a powerful deterrent function.

Whatever the success of the product liability system, it is clear that legal changes of the magnitude involved have profound social consequences, even if they are brought about by judicial decisions that are largely oblivious to them. The revolution in the courts has thus prompted many calls for legislative reforms, which in turn have provoked equally impassioned defenses of the new judicial order. On balance, it appears that the struggle over reform has not quite proved to be a stalemate. The frequency of product liability litigation and the extent of damage awards have stabilized over the past four or five years. In part, some legislative reforms have restricted the scope of liability or have reduced the permissible levels of damages; and in part, recent judicial decisions, while far less restrictive than those rendered before 1970, have cut back on liability or at least have curtailed its further expansion.[6] The area, however, promises to be one in which intensive activity on all fronts will continue in the years to come. However, the vast range of things that count as products—food, machine tools, pharmaceuticals, chemicals, automobiles, ladders, nuclear power plants—makes it very difficult for anyone to formulate a single uniform set of legal doctrines to cover all the cases that fall within this body of law. As might be expected, the interplay between the two central themes of this book assumes a prominent part in the overall tale. The rules of product liability law are like poorly designed all-purpose screwdrivers—ill-suited and far too complex and convoluted for the many tasks that they must perform. And the source of this complexity is the familiar one—the inveterate tendency to use complex collective, or tort, solutions in preference to contractual ones.

As with professional liability of all sorts, the threshold choice is whether liability for defective products should be governed by private contract or by public control, through tort. Today, in practice, the answer is as it was elsewhere: the common law, both in the United States and other countries, treats the physical damage to person or property resulting from the use of a defective product as part and parcel of the tort law. Clearly, the nature of the injury—not the nature of the relationship between the parties—was dispositive on the question of legal classification. But in principle the result should be the opposite. Tort law should cover all injuries to strangers, and contract law should cover all injuries that arise out of any preexisting consensual arrangement between the parties. Public regulation is necessary to deal with externalities, not with physical injury or property damage as such. Choosing the right principle of classification therefore is no idle exercise, for it carries with it important substantive consequences. The readiness to apply rules of tort to a given area usually means that there will be greater judicial regulation and less contractual freedom in allocating physical injury and property losses.

Note, however, that the tendency to treat physical injury and property damage cases as falling in the domain of tort has deep roots in the common law, where for a long period of time these cases did not lead to social and economic dislocation of the sort they are charged with today. In this regard, product liability followed on the heels of other common law doctrine. Judges deciding the early cases involving property that was lost or misused by a bailee (that is, a person to whom property is delivered with the intention of redelivery at some future time) tended to regard the question as one of tort law. A different set of standards was developed to determine what standard of care was owed by what kind of bailee. A higher standard was often imposed on those who received goods for their own use than on those who held them for the convenience of the owner. Similarly, in the early medical malpractice cases, which sharply limited the liability of physicians and hospitals, judges also treated the issue as one of tort law and not of voluntary contract. Over and over again, the law of tort involves so many special relationships between different classes of people (bailee-bailor, landlord-tenant, employer-employee, physician-patient, common carrier–shipper) that it seems safe to say that elements of contract law intruded into the basic legal doctrine only by indirection—by shaping the defendant's basic standard of care or by allowing a defense based on the assumption of risk for the accident in question. Yet the resulting common law rules were, if not perfect, often quite sound, notwithstanding the shaky conceptual foundations on which they rested.

The same basic attitude has permeated the history of product liability law. But although product safety has always been regarded by judges as a fit subject for direct government regulation, some other explanation must be found for the massive expansion of liability in the United States, a development which for the most part has not been imitated in either the European Community or the British Commonwealth. To understand what is at stake in the various views of product liability, it is necessary to trace with some care the historical evolution of the applicable legal doctrines. There are many verbal similarities between traditional and modern product liability laws, but a major transformation of the subject has taken place from within.

The major doctrinal changes in product liability law make it important, even at this late date, to compare the logic of the older product liability law with that of the new. This inquiry requires a study of four separate periods: before 1850, from 1850 to 1916, from 1916 to 1968, and from 1968 to the present. Only then is it possible to judge which system should be preferred as a matter of principle, without regard to considerations of legal precedent. As with other areas, the basic relationship between administrative costs and incentive effects holds true. The major defect of modern product liability law is that it substitutes a highly expensive and indeterminate scheme for a simpler set of common law rules that had better incentive effects. It is another case of the double whammy: the legal system incurs greater legal expense in order to implement an inferior set of incentives. In this chapter, I will trace the evolution of product liability law until the modern period, starting between 1965 and 1968, and in the next chapter I will carry the story forward to the present.[7]

BEFORE 1850: TOUGH LUCK

Before 1850, product liability law could be accurately summarized in two words: "tough luck." An injury caused by a product was always the problem of the victim, never of the product manufacturer, or indeed of any supplier in the chain of distribution, including distributors and suppliers of component parts. Likewise, it appears that there were few if any actions for physical injury brought against retailers by their customers. But while to the modern eye there may appear to be little difference in the legal position between the manufacturer and the retailer, at common law there was an important difference. The retailer had direct contractual relationships with the purchaser of the product, and if that party were injured while using or consuming the product (many of the early cases involved foodstuffs), the denial of liability had to rest on some variation of the assumption of risk defense: you take your chances with all products—period.

With manufacturers and other suppliers who did not stand in direct contractual relationships with the buyer, the situation was different, and that difference carried over to the case where the buyer of goods gave them to someone else, typically a friend or family member, who was injured by their consumption or use. In these cases, recovery was denied on somewhat different grounds. All these cases were said to involve suits against a "remote" supplier of the goods, that is, one who did not for whatever reason have a direct contractual arrangement with the plaintiff, such as an intermediate wholesaler or manufacturer. It was as though principles of causation were unable to bridge the apparent gap between a product manufacturer and a remote consumer. The mere presence of the product in the hands of a third party was regarded as an act that severed the causal connection to the defendant manufacturer; or, in some formulations, it was said to render the accident unforeseeable to him. There could be no tort because of the missing causal link. Likewise, there could be no contract because the presence of that same third party precluded direct relations (or "privity") between the plaintiff and the defendant. Contract and tort were the only logical possibilities. Since both of them were blocked, there was no recovery at all.

The pattern of argument just outlined was not formally articulated in any common law case before 1830 or so. Instead, there was in the case law not a single hint of any doctrine exonerating these remote defendants from tort liability. Silence was the most eloquent indication of the dominant legal position. But as inventive plaintiffs' lawyers sought to expand the scope of tort liability, the issue had to be confronted head on. The first one hears of any successful action in product liability involved an unhappy situation where a boy sought recovery for an injury inflicted when an ill-made gun, purchased by his father, exploded in his hands while being discharged.[8] The decisive points for the judges in this 1837 case were two: first, the seller had represented that he was selling a safe gun made by an excellent gun-maker when he knew it was a dangerous gun made by an inferior gunmaker; and second, the gun was purchased by the father for use by the son, a relationship known by the seller at the time of sale. In essence, the case was one of physical injury that resulted from a care-fully contrived fraud, and the decisive precedent involved a bad loan that the plaintiff had made to a third party on the strength of the defendant's fraudulent representation. There was no willingness to ex-tend liability to any other person into whose hands the gun might pass without notice to the defendant.

The next question was how far the new line of potential liability for defective products might extend. Here the potential nineteenth-century doctrinal development was brought to an abrupt halt by the key English case of Winterbottom v. Wright, decided in 1842, which had enormous influence throughout the United States and the entire British Commonwealth.[9] In that case, the court refused to allow a driver employed by the postmaster general to maintain an action against a repairman to whom the postmaster general had entrusted the repair of the coach. The court barred the action because it fear-ed the most "outrageous consequences" would ensue if "every pass-enger or person passing along the road" could bring an action for injuries of this sort against, it was clear, manufacturers as well as re-pairers.

This general rule of no liability has been harshly criticized, virtually from the time of its birth, and is universally rejected today everywhere in the common law world. But lest we engage in an overhasty celebra-tion of the demise of *Winterbottom*, it is important to note its advan-tages over some more expansive system of product liability.

- The system is very cheap to operate, because it generates no liabil-ity against remote suppliers of any product.
- The system allows and perhaps encourages suits for personal in-juries to be brought against other parties who are in immediate control of the dangerous instrumentalities just before they cause injury. Injured workers can sue their employers; occupiers of real property, their landlords; and consumers, retailers.

• The absence of liability against remote suppliers induces a high
level of consumer care and precaution. The consumer without recourse against a product supplier pays a higher price for his own
carelessness, and thus will take more care to avoid accidents.

The familiar trade-off is again present in this legal regime. The manifest virtue of this system was its low administrative costs. Its implicit
price was that certain forms of misbehavior by manufacturers and
others up the chain of distribution were left uncorrected and unde-
terred. In principle, a manufacturer could be sued by the party below
it in the chain of distribution, and so on down the line, but the transactional obstacles (insolvency, jurisdiction, and joining all parties in
a single proceeding) made any such suit a rarity. This initial system
of no liability may not dominate all others, but it does create a useful presumption for understanding subsequent legal developments:
namely, the risk of loss should follow the possession of the product at
the time of injury. Hence with product consumers and users, the most
common result is no liability of any sort. Where liability is desirable,
the first person to fasten on is the party from whom the plaintiff purchased the goods. This framework makes it possible to carve out certain sensible exceptions to the tough-luck approach toward accidental
product injuries, and these slowly worked themselves into the law during the next period.

FROM 1850 TO 1916: MISREPRESENTATION
AND HIDDEN DEFECTS

The first exception to the tough-luck rule focused on misrepresentations of product safety made by a remote supplier of the goods.
Thomas v. Winchester, decided in New York a decade after *Winterbottom,* involved a druggist who filled a prescription for extract
of dandelion with the deadly but innocent-looking belladonna.[10] The
customer's wife took the drug in ignorance of its fatal characteristics,
and she died. The court held the druggist liable for her death even
though the two were not in privity of contract. Although there was no
fraud, the druggist's mislabeling had consequences that passed
through the husband to his wife, who also relied on the label. Rightly
understood, his misrepresentation overcomes the initial presumption
of no liability. Since the druggist was a professional, negligence is easy

to establish, if it is required at all. The key feature in *Thomas* was the radical asymmetry of information. The druggist had access to the true information while the user of the product, whether or not she was its purchaser, did not. The key distinction that should organize the law of product liability is the one between latent, or hidden, defects and patent, or obvious, ones.

In the years that followed Thomas v. Winchester, recovery for defective products placed into the stream of commerce was slowly expanded, not only from manufacturers but from other remote suppliers as well. If a defendant supplied a poorly constructed scaffold to a contractor from which the contractor's employee fell to his death, the employee could sue the supplier, notwithstanding the absence of any contract between them.[11] If a defendant who had manufactured a coffeepot sold it to a restaurant operator, the restaurant's customer could sue the manufacturer when the pot exploded, regardless of the absence of any contract between them.[12] In some of the early cases, there was a debate over whether suits for damage caused by latent product defects could only be brought if the products were "inherently dangerous," such as poisons or guns, or whether they could also be brought if the products were "imminently dangerous only if defectively made." By 1903 at the latest, it was recognized that liability could arise in both these categories, although with the second, courts still required some evidence of actual concealment of a known defect.[13] Here the simpler rule that held the defendant who created the defect responsible for the damage it caused was limited by additional complexities of no evident social value. The system had taken some substantial strides toward a sensible equilibrium, but had not quite reached it.

From 1916 to 1968: The Rise of Strict Liability

The next stage in the evolution of American product liability law involved a consolidation and extension of the earlier rules of liability. The critical step in this process was the famous 1916 decision of Judge Cardozo in MacPherson v. Buick Motor Co.[14] That case followed the usual pattern of cases involving products with latent defects that caused harm in ordinary use. Owing to defective wood, a wheel on a new Buick collapsed, injuring its driver, when the car was driven along the highway at eight miles per hour. Cardozo wrote as though he had taken a huge stride beyond the prior case law by setting the new presumption in favor of suit against a remote supplier, regardless of whether the defect arose from the inherent nature of the product sold, as with poisons or explosives, or from the defective or careless process of its manufacture, as with bad wheels. But the decision marked only a small shift in overall theory, and the additional lawsuits, if any, caused hardly a ripple in insurance or product markets, which is as it should have been. All that happened was that the defendant no longer needed to have any special knowledge of the hidden defective condition. What mattered was the gap between what had been represented and what had been sold. The type of the defect became immaterial. The fact of the defect dominated.

Another issue was whether it was still necessary to prove that the hidden defect was negligently created. The first overt move to strict liability came in Justice Roger Traynor's famous 1944 concurring opinion in Escola v. Coca-Cola Bottling Co. of Fresno, which involved a Coca-Cola bottle that allegedly exploded while the plaintiff, a waitress, was putting it into her employer's refrigerator for storage.[15] Justice Traynor insisted that proof of negligence only added expense and complication to the ordinary lawsuit. For him, it was sufficient for the plaintiff to show that the product was dangerous in its original condition and caused harm to the plaintiff when used in a normal and proper fashion.

His basic intuition rightly links liability to the presence of hidden defects. Thus if the condition that causes the harm is obvious, a matter of common knowledge or otherwise known to the plaintiff, there should be no recovery because there is no misrepresentation to trigger the liability. No one is under an obligation to purchase or use a product in the first place. So once the product is used with an awareness of the risk in question, the normal defense of assumption of risk should apply. No manufacturer will try to take advantage of this rule by offering inferior products for sale, for there will be few, if any, takers. The many products with known risks—farm equipment, heavy machinery, chemicals and drugs of all sorts and descriptions—will be sold, and knowingly purchased, because the feared harm is inseparable from the associated benefits. But manufacturers will have an incentive to minimize the expected frequency and severity of obvious defects, for the safer the product, the higher the price. Likewise, customers can make their own subjective comparison of known losses with potential gains. Only with hidden defects are buyers and users stripped of the mechanisms of self-protection; only there should the law intervene. The line between hidden and obvious defects may not be clearly discernible in all contexts—no line is—but it is recognizable enough across the broad range of institutional settings to provide the one simple distinction necessary to organize what has become an ever more complex and unruly body of law. As Judge Stanley Fuld said in the 1951 case of Campo v. Scofield, "[T]he stress has always been upon the duty of guarding against *hidden* defects and of giving notice of *concealed* dangers."[16]

Once the class of product defects is narrowly (and properly) defined, the analysis of the relative strengths of negligence and strict liability from Chapter 5 comes into play. There is no reason to trouble ourselves over the pervasive indeterminacy of cost/benefit inquiries— here captured in the question of how much care is "sufficient" to absolve a manufacturer or supplier from liability. It is just as easy and sensible to make negligence irrelevant to the determination of liability. In most of these cases, the manufacturer will be the party in the best position to avoid the harm, and thus the less innocent party. In addition, from a practical point of view (important, no matter how obvious), it is far cheaper to adopt a strict liability system, and to make liability turn on the fact of harm, not on the level of precaution. As long as liability is confined to hidden defects, manufacturers can choose the level of inspection to reduce losses to acceptable levels. The strict liability rule thus induces the manufacturer to minimize the sum of liability and inspection costs. There is no obvious conflict between the welfare of the firm and the welfare of the society at large. The rule is simple, easy to administer, and causes no dislocations in product or insurance markets.

Justice Traynor thought that his expanded strict liability regime had two other advantages. First, it would allow losses to be spread across the broad class of consumers, each of whom would suffer a modest cost increase. Second, it would, he thought, impose useful incentives on manufacturers to take imperative measures to ensure that their products reached the market free of defects. At this point, he left the secure enclave of simple rules, and mischief followed. Loss-spreading independent of incentives is not a sensible objective of any tort system. As long as losses are constant, they are more cheaply insured on a first-party basis as part of some comprehensive system of accident or health insurance. Coverage no longer is tied to complex questions of liability, and the level of coverage may be precisely set by contract and not left to the vagaries of the tort system.

Similarly, the incentive rationale is subject to two powerful objections. First, it works at cross-purposes with loss-spreading. If the manufacturer could fully pass his liability costs on to other customers in the ordinary course of his business, then he would be wholly unconcerned with the dangerousness of his products. Yet if customers bear all the losses, the manufacturer has no incentive to avoid any loss, no matter how severe. Perfect incentives and perfect loss-spreading can never be accomplished simultaneously.

In practice, of course, the passing along of liability costs is never perfect, for when a firm raises its prices, it must increase the attractiveness of its product to the customers or lose its sales. Marketing products with a bad loss experience is hardly the way to keep customers or raise prices. Justice Traynor also failed to note that firms faced with excessive liabilities could simply drop out of the market, leaving consumers with fewer alternatives than before. It was, and is, blind optimism to assume that firms will respond to changes in liability rules *solely* by altering their care in product design and construction or by increasing prices to cover costs. Sometimes firms will leave the market altogether, as has happened with manufacturers of several important drugs (such as Bendectin) and vaccines (against pertussis and polio) in the United States, so that the firms that do remain may receive the undeserved benefits of monopoly pricing.

These unfortunate consequences of a misguided product liability system did not materialize hard on the heels of *Escola*. For even though Traynor's rationales were broad, the actual rules of liability were narrow. The key sentence in his decision for day-to-day operations was the last: "The manufacturer's liability should, of course, be defined in terms of the safety of the product in its normal and proper use, and should not extend to injuries that cannot be traced to the product as it reached the market." Defects still had to be latent; intermediate parties (distributors, retailers, and so on) had to do nothing to increase the risk of danger to the ultimate consumer; and the user of the product could not recover damage where the use of the product was improper in any relevant respect. These three elements of the case are essential to the misrepresentation theories that should govern product cases.

The function of these three conditions is best understood by looking at the cases that they exclude. Cases of obvious dangers are outside the scope of the liability system because the product user knows what he is getting. The insistence that the product remain in its original condition excludes cases where the product design has been modified once it leaves the manufacturer's control. Manufacturers are quite powerless to prevent these modifications, which on durable products may be made years after sale, often by a purchaser on resale, with whom the manufacturer might have ongoing relations. These modifications often remove safety features in a product in the interests of speed and flexibility, so that the added risks are rightly attributable to the party who made the modification, and not to the original manufacturer. Requiring that products be in their original condition therefore excuses the manufacturer only for defects created by another. In principle, the result is no different from allowing a hunter in a shooting accident to say, "I didn't shoot the bullet that wounded you; someone else did." To be sure, in the odd case a product modification may improve product safety; and in some cases the modification has no effect on the initial product defect; and perhaps there are some modifications that substitute a new small defect for a larger preexisting one. But these situations are likely to be extremely rare. It is far more likely for a mechanic to damage a new tire by improper installation or excessive use, for a delivery person to store Coke bottles in hot conditions, for an electrician to remove electrical insulation, or for an employer to take a safety guard off a punch press. Traynor's initial defense seems sound today in the broad run of cases, and, if necessary, narrow exceptions of little institutional importance can be carved out of the basic framework for benign or useful product modifications.

The last condition of "normal and proper" use is aimed at the problem of consumer misbehavior. The topic is critical because in every product case the manufacturer is not using its own product; in most cases, the user is the plaintiff or someone closely allied with him. Given the downstream location of physical control, it is an invitation to social disaster to impose liability on the manufacturer for the misdeeds of product users. No private contractual arrangement would ever tolerate so pronounced a division between de facto control and legal responsibility. Indeed, ordinary consumer warranties, limited as they are to the repair and replacement of defective goods, are binding only for products that fail to perform in normal use. It is even more important to keep that condition alive in personal injury litigation with its vastly higher stakes. Traynor's insistence that the recovery be confined to cases of normal and proper use eliminates the prospect of forcing careful consumers to subsidize careless ones through the tort system. It also spares manufacturers from having to design products that protect the careless from their own neglect while making product use more awkward for diligent consumers. In a word, Traynor's third condition weeds out from the liability system all those cases where the product user is the author of his own doom. Just as a defendant may say "I didn't do it," so too he should be able to say to any plaintiff "you did it to yourself" when the defect is open and the injury avoidable.

Escola, perhaps unconsciously, developed a legal regime that targeted cases where manufacturer misconduct was the *sole* cause of injury. It had little to say about the complex cases of joint causation that can arise when a product is both defective in its initial condition and mishandled or misused along the way. Such cases of joint causation are likely to be few, at least if liability is confined to cases of hidden defects. As long therefore as the strictures of Traynor's original system were in place, the law posed no threat to the innovation and production of useful products. These constraints on recovery stayed in effect from the time of Traynor's 1944 concurrence until the late 1960s. But once Traynor's justificatory apparatus became part and parcel of the mainstream thinking, his constrained system began to unravel, as courts and judges took his expansive rationales for liability far more seriously than they did the conditions carefully preserved in *Escola.*

12

The Contemporary Product Liability Scene

The expansion of the scope of product liability from its halting inception in the mid-nineteenth century until the last third of the twentieth century was, in operational terms, very modest and for the most part salutary. Nonetheless, the tension between carefully delimited rules of liability and Justice Traynor's broad rationales for those rules could not survive indefinitely. Either the theory had to be narrowed to accord with the law, or the law had to be expanded to accord with the theory. Unfortunately, the latter outcome has occurred: the broad (if inconsistent) Traynor rationales for liability eventually led to the erosion of the twin requirements of latent defect in the original condition and normal use.

Changes of this magnitude reflect fundamental changes in outlook, here brought on by the close connection between academic writing and legal transformation. Time after time, the notable scholars of the day harped on the importance of the insurance mechanism for passing on losses, on the inadequacy of private contract for allocating risk, on the ignorance of consumers as a class, on the irrelevance of reputation as an instrument for securing product safety, and on the superior capacity of judges and juries to craft and apply rules that would sort out good products from bad ones.[1] There was in the 1950s and 1960s almost no academic writing in favor of maintaining the limited status quo. Most of the leading academics insistently advocated greater use of the liability system, both generally and in product liability cases.

225

Their writings worked themselves into the legal system soon after the adoption in 1965 of the Restatement (Second) of Torts (a project, in equal parts restatement and reform, undertaken by the American Law Institute).

This revolution rested largely on two theoretical assumptions, both of which could explain why liability should be expanded, but never why it should be limited. The first of these premises held that a manufacturer is *always* in a better position to prevent the harm than the consumer, regardless of how the harm occurs. This assertion treated the victim's precaution, an essential feature of the old order of liability at common law, as ineffective and irrelevant. The consumer became an automaton "powerless" to prevent the loss, behaving invariantly regardless of the information that she possessed, the dangers that she faced, and the incentive structures under which she labored.[2] In practice, those extreme and heroic assumptions could not be maintained in their full rigor, with the result that the plaintiff's conduct could bar or reduce liability in cases of extreme misconduct—but the shift from the earlier rules was very substantial indeed. Not wearing seatbelts, driving over the speed limit, driving while drunk, and not following instructions have in many places become "foreseeable" forms of misuse for which manufacturers and not consumers are accountable.

The second dogma we have already encountered: namely, that all losses can be handled by insurance, which has been belied in a thousand ways today, since litigation over insurance coverage (for everything from leaky plumbing to injury from asbestos) has cost literally as much as defending the underlying tort suits. Insurance affordability and availability have become seriously compromised, for insurance companies cannot price future risks for products sold years ago by sellers who cannot control or influence the conduct of persons now in possession of these goods. Already there have been two major convulsions in insurance markets, one in the mid-1970s and the other in the 1980s. Yet the same iron law for the underlying product markets applies also to insurance. Sometimes it is cheaper for a firm to leave a market than to remain in business under adverse conditions. Sometimes that departure is far from voluntary. Lloyd's of London was active in reinsurance for United States product risks during the 1970s and 1980s when the peculiar nature of American tort law was largely unappreciated by English insurers, who assumed blithely its similarity to their own. Their ruinous experience in the reinsurance market has left Lloyd's a mere shadow of itself, wracked by internal division and overwhelmed by external liabilities.[3]

These twin concerns about loss avoidance and loss-spreading have exerted a large influence on the basic contract/tort choice in product liability cases. Justice Traynor's opinion in *Escola* gives us good reason to believe that strict liability for hidden defects will work well in a broad range of circumstances if suitably constrained by rules that govern third-party and user behavior. But his educated hunch is not an inflexible truth, and if his preferred default rule is unsound for certain classes of products, manufacturers should be willing to enter into *direct* contracts with consumers in order to allocate risk. The privity barriers that loomed so large in the early law of product liability should thus become a casualty of the increased stakes associated with the sale of risky products.

Nonetheless, the contractual response has been effectively thwarted by the law, which views any disclaimers of tort liability with deep suspicion and distrust, especially as they apply to bodily injuries.[4] The issue today is regarded as so far beyond dispute that the American Law Institute's Draft of the Restatement (Third) of Product Liability law does not even pause to examine the question. Instead, it adopts the position of an unbroken line of cases when it provides: "Disclaimers and limitation of remedies by product sellers, waivers by product purchasers, and other similar contractual exculpations, oral or written, do not bar or reduce otherwise valid product liability claims for harm to persons."[5] The explanation for the provision is every bit as terse and unpersuasive. "It is presumed that the plaintiff lacked sufficient information, bargaining power, or bargaining position necessary to execute a fair contractual limitation of rights to recover."[6] There is no effort to sort out which of these explanations applies to what cases, or to indicate what is necessary to create a conclusive instead of a rebuttable presumption, or even what the terms of a fair contractual waiver might be, given that in principle these are assumed to have at least an ethereal existence.

The uncompromising position of the modern law is not without its adverse consequences. One of the most unfortunate of these has been to prevent private firms from issuing warranties to expand the scope of their responsibility beyond that now required by law. Thus when Uniroyal offered to repair or replace its tires free of charge in the event of blowout, as long as the tire was not punctured or abused, the firm voluntarily assumed a form of limited product liability without proof of product defect. In Collins v. Uniroyal, Inc., the New Jersey Court held the company's offer half valid: the expanded basis of liability stood, but the limitation on damages to repair or replacement was struck down as unconscionable and invalid. The upshot was that full tort damages were now recoverable without proof of product defect.[7]

The decision may have benefited this one consumer, but it effectively closed down any effort to expand warranty coverage while limiting damages, which would have benefited consumers as a class. To be sure, the New Jersey decision did not strike down a payment of $10,000 for anyone killed while driving on a Uniroyal tire, riding in a General Motors car, or taking a Merck drug. But what firm can take the chance that the doctrine of unconscionability will convert a useful warranty into a financial death sentence? As long as even *one* state (to which all injured parties could flock) might enforce the coverage while voiding the damage limitation, no firm will experiment with warranties that could prove far more ruinous than doing nothing at all. The road to contractual innovation has been effectively blocked by a decision that may not be followed. Yet the practical consequence of this and similar decisions is to reduce the level of information available to consumers by making it impossible for firms to supply the limited warranties that signal the expected failure rate of a product by the compensation they provide. The firm with a superior product can afford to fund a limited warranty that its inferior competitor cannot match. Once it becomes too perilous to supply that warranty, one obvious mark of product differentiation will be eliminated. It goes without saying that any contractual effort to limit liability for arguably defective products will be squelched as well.

The shift from contract to tort thinking converts default rules into direct judicial regulation. Since private contract can no longer correct judicial mistakes, judges and juries must articulate at least a plausible set of product liability rules. But again they face the familiar problem of making one size fit all. The basic rule of strict liability works well for most classes of construction defects, such as cases involving tin slivers in tunafish cans or pitted metal in fan blades. It also works well for mislabeled or contaminated products. But just as a strict liability rule is inappropriate in areas of medical malpractice, it is unsuitable in cases of voluntary agreements about the side effects of drugs (such as steroids and substances used in chemotherapy) that are part of the inescapable price of medical treatment. Yet it is eminently rational for consumers to accept substantial product risk in order to improve their chances of living. Sick patients will grab at a 10 percent chance of a fatal, even unknown side effect if the alternative is a 100 percent chance of dying from a deadly disease. It is thus critical in these cases that the baseline against which product success is measured is not some riskless world of perfect health, but the world of hard choices and hidden perils into which they have been cast.

Modern doctrine tries to accommodate these cases by removing strict liability for "unavoidably dangerous products" properly prepared and carrying proper directions and warnings.[8] But although that provision appears to be the soul of good sense, two weaknesses remain. First, the rule does not indicate how the adequacy of a direction or warning should be determined. Second, the rule presupposes that breaching this duty calls for full tort damages instead of some lesser remedy. Even a responsible and sensitive effort at direction from the center can have unanticipated and unwelcome consequences. So while strict liability is not some magic talisman, the broader point on contractual freedom is forgotten in a fog of talk about inequality of bargaining power, consumer ignorance, and (as will become apparent) regulatory neglect. All contracting-out possibilities were effectively foreclosed by the mid-1960s.

In and of itself, that judicial assertion of power does not guarantee an inferior set of social outcomes. But it changes the odds for the worse. The missing ingredient in the brew is a legal shift to solutions that voluntary agreements would supply. It is sometimes said that the key vehicle for changing the law of product liability was the 1965 Restatement (Second) of Torts, §402A, which adopted Justice Traynor's principle of strict liability for defective products in *Escola,* which he had persuaded his court to adopt in 1963. But on this score at least the Restatement reads like an echo of the past, not like the harbinger of the future. The real extensions of liability began after the Restatement was adopted in cases that it barely touched. Indeed, the critical expansions in liability had little to do with the acceptance of strict product liability, but can be traced to a number of other important developments in recent years. It is useful to consider three such topics here and their unification into the modern risk/utility formulation of product liability law.

The Present Synthesis
Open and Obvious Defects

The first doctrinal change of note was the abandonment of the earlier rule that a plaintiff could not recover if injured by an open and obvious defect.[9] By making this shift, courts abandoned the misrepresentation theories that animated the earlier system of product liability. Now courts had to instruct juries how to decide which open and obvious defects were sources of liability and which were not. The argument in favor of this new legal regime is often put in the form that no manufacturer should be able to increase its profits by making hidden dangers more obvious. But the incentives for the manufacturer are in reality much more complex. Once a danger is made more obvious, other parties downstream become alerted, whether or not the law calls this dangerous condition a product defect. If consumers' estimation of the risk increases, then their likelihood of buying or using the product will accordingly decrease. That result will hardly please the manufacturer, whose objective is not simply to minimize its liability once its products are sold. The manufacturer has to sell its products in the first place. Making some conditions obvious will make the machinery safer (so that the phrase "obvious defect" becomes a near oxymoron) by reducing the costs of precautions that have to be taken by the buyers and users of equipment: it is easier to neutralize a known condition than a hidden one.

The open and obvious rule thus creates a stable set of expectations for the parties and places the burden of modification and precaution on the employers who buy the product and the employees who use it. An employer can guard against the risk by customizing the equipment in light of its special knowledge of its own requirements. It can also alter the general conditions in the workplace—lighting, length of shifts, training, and instructions—to minimize risks. The employee for her part can take analogous precautions to minimize risk by carefully operating the equipment. (It is no surprise that many suits involving open and obvious conditions are brought by employees injured on the first day or so of work.) All in all, the open and obvious rule has the commendable virtue of passing the risk of liability along with the product in orderly fashion, where it can be allocated between employer and employee by contract or, as is more common today, under the workers' compensation system.

The moment the rule is abandoned, some court or jury will have to decide which open and obvious defects could be prevented by the manufacturer at cheaper cost than by the employer or worker, even though there is no metric for deciding whether it is cheaper for a manufacturer to install a guard when the product is first sold, or to have a second employee assist the first when some dangerous operation of cleaning or repair has to be undertaken on equipment while it is still in service. Once again, the older rule is more desirable because of the cheaper costs of its administration and its more desirable incentive effects.

Warnings

The second major expansion in tort liability took place with warnings, particularly those for drugs and chemicals. Contrary to the situation with machine tools and similar equipment, simple inspection is not likely to inform consumers of drugs and chemicals of the product risks. Simple warnings like a skull and crossbones might inform a person not to ingest a drug or chemical at all, but are hardly sufficient to tell consumers how to safely use those dangerous products that can have beneficial effects. Clearly, some warnings are required as a matter of common sense, and these are normally supplied by a manufacturer if only to satisfy consumer or professional demands.

But it is critical to ask whether the market response should be regarded as sufficient as a matter of course. Given that firms have some incentive to downplay the dangers of the products they sell, there is a respectable case to be made for some public control of warnings to counteract what might prove to be a serious risk of concealment or nondisclosure. But what technique should be used to supply warnings for goods that are produced on a mass basis? Starting with the polio vaccine cases of the 1960s and extending through the swine flu vaccine cases of the 1970s, courts insisted on a case-by-case review of warnings after the fact for products found (perhaps wrongly) to produce some disease or disability.[10] Ad hoc investigations of warnings are expensive and wholly indeterminate, and no global standard more precise than "adequate" or "reasonable" covers the disparate range of dangerous products. Oftentimes, the decisions seem heavily motivated by a search for the deep pocket. Thus one case allowed the plaintiff to recover for brain damage caused by a stroke brought on by birth control pills because the word "stroke" was not used in the Food and Drug Administration's warning, which ran on interminably about the increased risk of death and brain damage from the pill.[11] The current case law thus carries over its deep suspicion of the half-hearted nature of direct regulation, even though the levels of direct administrative scrutiny are high. "Nevertheless," the conventional position continues, "unqualified deference to these regulatory mechanisms is thought by a growing number of courts to be unjustified. An approved prescription drug or medical device can present significant risks without corresponding advantages."[12] Courts always regard mandated warnings as minimal, but not necessarily sufficient; consequently, the jury may reject the outcome of the administrative process and start over from scratch. There is no sense that the administrative process (as is surely the case with new drugs) might be too restrictive in allowing new products to reach markets and too cautious in selecting the required warnings and instructions.

The better solution adopts yet another simple, per se rule: *conclusive* weight should be given to warnings for standardized drugs and chemicals mandated by federal legislation—compliance with the administrative order ends the warning case, period. The difference between these two approaches is enormous. With the conclusive statutory presumption, few failure-to-warn cases ever reach the courts, for compliance with the law becomes a low-level managerial decision involving little or no discretion.

This simpler regime has a number of real advantages. Under the present law, a jury has a temptation to magnify the adverse outcome to the plaintiff before it while ignoring other cases in which the warnings have done their job. It has little incentive to consider the possibility that supplying alarmist warnings might well have deterred other people, now invisible, from taking prescription drugs beneficial to them. Similarly, the individual plaintiff has every incentive to insist in hindsight that any stronger warning would have changed her choice of drug or pattern of use so that the injury suffered would have been avoided. Those forms of dissimulation are not possible in an administrative setting where the adequacy of the warnings is decided before, not after, the product is placed on the market. Private individuals will now bear the harms of excessive warnings, and reap the benefits from accurate ones. They will choose to make an honest assessment of all forms of risk because they have to make their choices before the race is run, not after the results are posted on the leader board.

Bypassing the defects of the current system does not imply that the content of warnings should be left solely to private choice, given the possibility of deception and misstatement if manufacturers could never be held accountable for their warnings in any forum. Rather, this proposal calls for a shift in the relevant forum for decision. Those public interest groups and others who want stronger warnings can make their case through the usual administrative procedures, in a set-ting where the gains from stronger warnings can be weighed *ex ante* against their perils. (Complicated warnings may be discarded or mis-understood, and excessive warnings may deter people from using products with a net anticipated benefit.) This process worked in the birth control case, where the magic word "stroke" was added to the warning years before the litigation was resolved. Where no warning covers all bases, that fact can be acknowledged: the label could then recommend that physicians or other professionals be consulted before the product is used, or it could mandate special inquiries to see if a product that is safe when used alone becomes dangerous when used in conjunction with other products.

Some federal schemes have in fact been read to adopt just this ap-proach. Thus the Federal Insecticide, Fungicide, and Rodenticide Act (FIFRA) requires manufacturers to submit detailed warnings to the EPA, which then rules on them before they are placed into use. Once in place, the approved warning could not be altered by anyone. One early decision held that individual workers who claimed injury from the products covered by FIFRA could attack the warnings in state tort actions.[13] The effect of the legal regime is to subject these approved warnings to challenges of adequacy by juries in fifty different states operating under fifty different laws. But more recent decisions have taken the sensible view that once the EPA has approved the warnings, a second wave of attack through the tort system is blocked. Questions of adequacy can be settled before the agency once and for all, and not in scattered and inconsistent attacks after the fact.

Cigarettes afford another example of the interaction of federal warning labels and state tort actions. Today cigarettes may be sold in this country only in packets containing statutory warnings that are drafted by Congress itself and that have been revised and strengthened in 1969 and again in 1984. It matters little what the warnings say, since the generic risk of cigarettes is a matter of common knowledge that, if anything, is overestimated, not underestimated, by the general public.[14] Where, as has been held by the Supreme Court,[15] the statute is interpreted to preclude private attacks under the tort law on the adequacy of the statutory advertising and (it appears) labeling, major litigation costing millions is happily avoided. In addition, the courts will not have to figure out case by case what the warning should have been, and how much influence a warning would, over the life of a smoker, have over the choice of cigarette brand or the amount of tobacco consumed.

Cases of misrepresentation are most suitable for litigation where a single discrete statement induces detrimental reliance—say, in the form of an imprudent investment or loan. Litigation cannot work well where sprawling life histories and extensive social histories must be developed simply to decide what this plaintiff knew at that time. No one can assemble a set of evidentiary accommodations that can render sensible trials of individual cases of cigarette injuries, and no one should be allowed to try. Cigarettes are a generic product, and the differences in harms across brands (apart from dose-related responses, which the government warnings never address) are so slight, if they exist at all, that one single warning is sufficient unto the day. The tendency of academics is to decry the privileged place that cigarettes enjoy relative to other products. The correct approach is to do the reverse, and to make this statutory approach standard for other products, such as drugs and other devices that are currently regulated by the Food and Drug Administration (FDA).

A system of preclearance standardized warnings will not work for all products because for some (such as cosmetics) the risks may be so small that setting up the administrative apparatus will not be worth the costs. Nor is it likely to work for machine tools that differ from model to model and manufacturer to manufacturer. Here product-specific warnings may be required, and they should be evaluated with conscious awareness of the limitations of the judicial process. But for many risky products—drugs, chemicals, pesticides—federal administrative systems are already in place to set or monitor warnings. Nothing is gained by running a second-tier inquiry, where the factual complications of the particular case (was this immune disorder caused by normal disease or by another drug or chemical?) only cloud reliable determinations on the warning questions. In principle, everyone supports cost-effective warnings that will enable intelligent choices to be made by product users. But the modern insistence that any warning already vetted through the administrative process be subject to a second evaluation through the judicial process is perhaps the most important structural flaw in this area of modern product liability law. It is another illustration of inferior incentives at higher administrative costs.

Indeed, the current law of warnings seems so unsuited for its purpose that one often looks elsewhere to find explanations for its continued hold on the courts. One explanation is political in nature. The extensive system of liability for drug-related injuries could be regarded as a way station along the road to a no-fault system of compensation for drug-related injuries—or even a national health care system. Keeping the heat on the drug companies makes them a proponent of legislative reform as a means to escape their own tort liabilities. But judges have particular tasks and limited powers. If they cannot participate directly in such major legislative decisions as the formation of a general compensation system, let alone a national health plan, why should they put their thumbs on the tort scale in order to influence the political outcome? Worse still, the system smacks of cynicism, for unwarranted liabilities are used to enlist defendants in a battle that they would otherwise not care to fight. Worst of all, the argument reveals a naiveté about political realities. It is far more likely that drug companies will forsake certain high-risk parts of the market rather than undertake the struggle to reform either tort law or health care. Indeed, any reform effort will be resisted by the lawyers who profit from the present uncertainty. The far more likely outcome is the one we have today: a program of partial no-fault compensation for drug-related harms that coexists in some shadowy fashion with the tort right of action for injured plaintiffs, such as is mandated by the National Childhood Vaccine Injury Act.[16] But the funding of this statutory program, its stability over time, and the handling of individual claims are all up for grabs.[17] It is hard enough to get tort doctrines right when they are examined for their own validity. It is impossible to get them right if major hidden agendas lurk in the background.

Crashworthiness and Design Defects

Crashworthiness represents a third major expansion of product liability law. Before the modern period, design defect cases all fell into the well-worn pattern of latent defects in the original design causing harm in ordinary use. Thus the hapless driver of an automobile could recover for injuries if the gas tank exploded when he turned the key in the ignition or if an improper design allowed excessive gasoline to accumulate in the carburetor. Indeed, it is just for cases like this that callbacks for repair and corrections are made by manufacturers today. The crashworthiness doctrine vastly expands the class of contingencies against which a manufacturer must guard to encompass major collisions, including those brought about by the palpable misconduct of the driver or some third party. For these losses, liability could not be strict, for no automobile could withstand a head-on collision at high speeds with a Mack truck. So ordinary negligence principles apply.

Unfortunately, the difficulties in this area are a replay of those in the warning cases. Since there are no clear standards to decide which collision injuries are preventable and which are not, the best that the law can do as a general matter is to insist that a vehicle be "reasonably safe" or "not unreasonably dangerous." It is no longer enough to say that the risk of collision injury is obvious, and that the buyers can choose the level of risk that they are prepared to take by selecting a vehicle of appropriate weight and durability, equipped with the proper options. After the fact, the law converts judges and juries into ad hoc designers charged with evaluating the many trade-offs between safety, convenience, and price that go into designing and selling an automobile.

One recent cause célèbre in the crashworthiness genre was the celebrated case of Moseley v. General Motors, where the jury awarded a $105 million verdict for compensatory and punitive damages when a seventeen-year-old boy was burnt to death after his General Motors truck was struck by a drunken driver.[18] The case gained notoriety from an NBC program, orchestrated by the plaintiff's experts, that used concealed incendiary devices to guarantee an explosion on impact in a visual demonstration designed to illustrate that the car was the most dangerous vehicle on the road. But the elements of journalistic fraud and an unholy alliance between the bar and the media should not divert us from the central issue of the case: what evidence was there that this truck was dangerously defective? The plaintiff's charge was that the design was flawed because the gasoline tanks were located outside the protective sideframe rail of the vehicle. Yet the vehicle complied with all federal safety standards, and its rate of failure in side collisions was, contrary to appearances, the lowest in the industry (0.196 deaths per million vehicle miles).

The sharp contrast between intuitive hunch and base rate (deaths per millions of miles) information illustrates much of what is wrong with modern product liability litigation. Evaluating product safety on the strength of a single case is no better than running an elaborate statistical analysis based on a sample size of one case. All relevant base rate information can be easily overlooked or ignored after the fact, when the obvious defendant, often a drunken driver, is uninsured and broke. Nor does this problem arise in only one aberrant case. Gary Schwartz cast substantial doubt on the dramatic line of Pinto cases that were litigated with similar spectacular verdicts in the 1970s.[19] The evidence of fatal omissions and smoking guns was largely ripped out of context, and huge amounts of adverse publicity were heaped on a car whose overall safety record was comparable to that of rival models available at the time. Once again, litigation favors anecdotal evidence over systematic inquiry.

These criticisms of the common law system of monitoring design safety should not be regarded as an endorsement of the current system of motor vehicle regulation, for there is little reason to believe that any system of government regulation will do much to advance the level of vehicular safety. As noted in Chapter 11, there is no credible evidence of any sharp, or even perceptible, decline in the rate of vehicle accidents that can be traced to either the interventions of the National Highway and Traffic Safety Commission, starting in 1966, or the major expansion in tort liability ushered in shortly thereafter. The key process is the transfer of information about the safety characteristics of automobiles; for private monitors—insurance companies, consumer reports, trade publications, and informed consumers—are more responsive than government monitors.

But suppose that this critique is wide of the mark. The question then becomes what form of regulation should be used to overcome the information deficits of ordinary consumers. Here a system of direct regulation, for all its enormous defects, has several enduring advantages over the system of tort liability that now operates in tandem with it. One constant bias of ordinary trials is to give undue weight to the design feature involved in a particular crash relative to all others. The tendency therefore is to redesign automobiles after the fact to cope with the contingency that did occur, even though the proposed design changes, if adopted before the fact, could have increased the likelihood of accidents from a different source. A system of regulation that evaluates design and safety features before production is undertaken is less likely to unduly emphasize certain perils relative to others precisely because neither regulators nor consumer advocates can peek out from behind the veil of ignorance.

In addition, administrative design standards (even if misguided) can be complied with before sale, and such compliance would largely eliminate the enormous administrative expenses of modern product liability litigation. In principle, the law should then treat all nonconforming vehicles as defective, and allow suits for the injuries they cause. Yet the likelihood of noncompliance with a known standard is very low, and this yields safety evaluations that are both cheaper and more reliable—a hard combination to beat. As with warnings, once this system of federal regulation is in place, the critical question is: what social gains are obtained by superimposing upon it the additional system of tort liability? To be sure, some individual design errors are likely to slip through the cracks of any regulatory scheme. But the existence of these errors is offset by larger errors that are likely to run in the opposite direction. Safe and prudent designs are equally likely to be branded defective on the basis of hindsight.

One illustration of the problem is the protracted litigation over driver-side airbags in automobiles. The question has been thoroughly vetted within the administrative process at the federal level. The insurance industry in general lined up behind requiring airbags, chiefly on grounds of safety, while the automobile industry opposed it, chiefly on grounds of cost and effectiveness.[20] Years of wrangling led to an elaborate administrative compromise that allowed use of alternative passive restraint devices (such as seatbelts that automatically engage), and an explicit timetable was hammered out to phase airbags into new vehicles. In this picture, what is gained by allowing individual plaintiffs in state product liability actions to assail the very design compromises approved at the federal level, with a claim that insists that every automobile sold in the United States without an airbag since 1976 was defective?

Unfortunately, these claims were not obviously barred by the National Highway and Motor Vehicle Safety Act. Even though federal law trumps (or preempts) inconsistent state laws, the framers of the Safety Act inserted a provision that expressly preserves state tort actions, without thinking through the implications of that approach. Nonetheless, the courts have had the good sense to assume that the state tort actions preserved by this savings clause do not include actions that seek to overturn the comprehensive administrative solution that rejected the immediate installation of airbags, which the plaintiffs insisted was required.[21] But there is little wisdom in leaving the interaction between federal administrative action and state tort law to the mercies of judicial interpretation. The federal statutes should contain explicit provisions that block state tort law actions concerning automotive designs that comply with federal standards. Interim uncertainty and out-of-pocket expenses both could have been averted by this simple per se rule. In design as in warning cases, one bite at the apple is quite enough.

RISK/UTILITY, THE NEW SYNTHESIS

The proliferation of legal theories in the modern period quickly led to an effort to develop a comprehensive alternative to the earlier view, which rested on the dual pillars of latent defect and ordinary use. One such synthesis was proposed by John Wade in 1973, and it has since been adopted verbatim by many courts.[22] No longer does the distinction between patent and latent defects occupy center stage. Instead, the issue is whether a product itself is "unduly dangerous," which in turn is said to rest on a consideration of seven related factors:

1. The usefulness and desirability of the product—its utility to the user and to the public as a whole.
2. The safety aspects of the product—the likelihood that it will cause injury, and the probable seriousness of the injury.
3. The availability of a substitute product which could meet the same need and not be as unsafe.

4. The manufacturer's ability to eliminate the unsafe character of the product without impairing its usefulness or making it too expensive to maintain its utility.
5. The user's ability to avoid danger by the exercise of due care in the use of the product.
6. The user's anticipated awareness of the dangers inherent in the product and their avoidability, because of general public knowledge of the obvious condition of the product, or of the existence of suitable warnings or instructions.
7. The feasibility, on the part of the manufacturer, of spreading the loss by setting the price of the product or carrying liability insurance.

This list clearly marks a quantum leap in complexity in the area of product liability. At one level, the list possesses a certain degree of plausibility because as a matter of common business practice, we should expect manufacturers, buyers, and users routinely to take into account the factors included by Wade. The gains from the use of the product, the associated costs, the ability to prevent those losses by the various parties up and down the chain of distribution, and the ability to insure against losses constitute the same set of problems that all market participants had to face before the expansion of the product liability law and have to face today. Why then attack the law to the extent that it seeks to imitate the decisions made by the firms it regulates?

The answer to this inquiry comes in several parts. The most general answer addresses the nature and function of legal rules across a wide range of human endeavor. Here two alternative strategies could be adopted. The first uses law to create and defend separate spheres of influence and control for each person, and then allows people to exchange their entitlements for their mutual betterment. It is assumed that the transacting parties will have better information about the gains and losses than any outsider. If so, the older rules that keyed on misrepresentation are defensible as a means to ensure that exchanges generate mutual gain, in this case in labor or financial markets. Hence the critical distinction between latent and patent defects.

The Wade view does not change the factors relevant to the analysis, but it does shift the locus of decision from the transacting parties to the state. Under the rival modern conception, judges and juries are required after the fact to micromanage complex products in all areas of human endeavor. Today it is always open to a plaintiff's lawyer to say categorically that a new safety device on a machine tool may reduce production but save on accident costs, and thus is reasonable to install. And it is of course open for the manufacturer to say that this decision is better made at the plant level by employer and employee. So a constant system of second guessing after the fact has become the order of the day. No matter what is done, it is always possible for the aggrieved plaintiff to say that more should have been done. The private judgment of informed persons in the marketplace has been replaced by the public and unprincipled judgments of the state, acting through its judges and juries on a case-by-case basis. Community standards are battle tested in a way in which a generalized cost/benefit analysis is not.

This general point refers back to my central theme. Recall the basic assumption that increases in administrative expense can only be justified by improvements in incentive effects. On this test, the shift from the older to the newer standards of liability is clearly undesirable. To look first to the cost, any system that makes liability turn on seven factors of admitted relevance must be far more complex than one that stresses the distinction between latent and patent defects. The deposition of a single engineer in an individual case easily could, and often does, consume hours of time before all the possible permutations are exhausted.

Yet the collection of endless information about what might have been does not necessarily lead to agreement on what should have been done. How should Wade's seven factors be traded off against each other when they point in opposite directions? Consumer precautions are often a substitute for producer precautions, and third-party precautions (not explicitly mentioned on the list) could well be a substitute for both. The standard risk/utility test makes it appear as though these factors are all binary, that is, subject to a yes or no answer. Either there is a substitute product available at the same price with lower risk, or there is not. But the world is far more complex: often there is a product which may be safer in some ways, less safe in others, more efficient for some work, less efficient for others; more costly in some ways, less costly in others. Even before the fact, the parties may find it difficult to articulate the reasons that led them rightly to exercise one choice over the other. After an injury occurs, it is far too easy to pass adverse judgments on the entire process and to charge a firm with soft-pedaling safety. The standards are so malleable that a jury could defend any verdict from no liability to punitive damages after hearing the same evidence.

Further, inconsistent verdicts by juries need never be reconciled. One jury may well decide that a heavier assembly is necessary to keep the transmission in place, but it will not consider what compensating weight reductions, if any, should be made elsewhere. Another jury may decide that the gas tank is located too close to the passenger compartment, but it is not obligated to relocate it or to state what structural adjustments are necessary if it is relocated. Decisions about transmissions and gas tanks are never examined in relationship to each other to see whether both changes can be made simultaneously. The net effect is to impose totally unrealistic expectations on automobile manufacturers. About fifteen years ago I heard Charles Babcock, then in charge of product liability litigation at General Motors, describe the Babcockmobile that he had constructed to show the impossibility of complying with the inconsistent commands generated by design defect litigation. The composite car incorporated all the features that one jury or another had thought necessary to keep a car from being defectively designed. Babcock's composite car weighed about a ton more than any car then on the road, and could not move after all its improvements were installed. Doubtless it would have failed to meet other safety and pollution standards as well. If decisions on liability are designed to provide guidance for manufacturers, then surely the legal system has failed in one of its essential objectives.

The indeterminacy of the process has adverse consequences not only in the conduct of a particular case but in the operation of the overall system. What is a firm supposed to do with the information contained in an adverse or favorable verdict about its products? If the decision is adverse, there will be no indication of what the safe alternative is and therefore no clear message as to what alterations should be made. If the decision is favorable, there is no guarantee that a different jury, viewing a different injury, might not come to a different conclusion. Either way, the verdict is likely to be rendered long after the product has been discontinued, a victim of advancing technology and design standards. Thus no verdict can inform a manufacturer about the suitability of its new product lines, beyond reiterating what the basic tests for liability themselves say. What beneficial incentives can be produced by so fuzzy a signal? Better to ignore the information entirely, as is routinely done today. But then nothing is left to the deterrence rationales of the current law.

The case against the modern legal rules of product liability would be strong enough if the only adverse effects were on matters of litigation and judicial administration. But the effects are not confined to so narrow a legal compass. Front-loaded onto the cost of any new product is the price of its anticipated litigation. In the extreme, these costs could destroy the market for new products, as has largely been the case in the United States with the sale of small airplanes. Or the costs of potential litigation could delay the advent of innovation or increase the costs of the products that are sold. Here too the consequences are not simply distributive, but affect the overall level of safety in the marketplace. If new planes are not sold, older planes will continue to fly, carrying with them a lower level of safety than their newer substitutes. Yet ironically the original manufacturer may be able to show that the older products, although inferior to the new products that have not been manufactured, are still not defective when measured by a risk/utility test applied *as of the date* that the product was first placed into the stream of commerce. Or the manufacturer may show that the equipment was fatally modified by a subsequently intermediate reconditioner who has long gone out of business. By shutting off new innovations, the legal system increases the reliance on inferior products and perhaps the overall accident rate as well. Once again, good intentions produce bad results.

It may well be replied that we have to endure some of the weaknesses of ordinary product liability practice because the latent defect/patent defect distinction does not reach all cases of imperfect consumer information. No one can doubt that imperfect information is the order of the day, with or without information. But the critical question is whether cases of imperfect information look more like those of no information or more like those of full information. Generalizations on that issue are hazardous, but my own sense is that the initial rate of acquisition of information is higher than one supposes. In checking references, an employer learns a lot from a few phone calls. An experienced scout can rate most players very quickly. Most judgments in job interviews are made in the first five minutes. And if you want to know, for example, what makes a car safe, automobile weight is a very good proxy for overall safety, as most consumers intuitively understand even if they lack knowledge of the underlying physics.

But even if there is a problem with imperfect information, we should set the standards by administrative action and revise them when appropriate, but give them conclusive effects, just as could be done with warnings. This one modification of American law would reduce the frequency and difficulty of suits, and stabilize the expectations of consumers and manufacturers alike. But it has not happened because the savings would not be shared by the lawyers who operate the system, working diligently for plaintiffs *and* defendants alike.

In sum, the American experience with product liability law turned bad when judges and legislators lost faith in the ability of consumers to deal competently with the mix and quality of ordinary products. No longer is it sufficient to provide a consumer with enough information about a product to decide whether or how to use it, or indeed whether to inquire further before making that decision. If it were, we should expect the impact of product liability law to shrink even from its small nineteenth-century levels, because the private cost of transmitting information about most products has fallen, not increased. Advancement in technology does not mean complexity. It often means simplicity. It is easier to turn a key in the ignition than a crank on a motor, easier to operate my user-friendly Macintosh than my old Underwood typewriter.

Yet this opportunity to shrink the scope of the tort law has been spurned by modern judges and legislatures, who attach undue weight to second-guessing technical and business decisions about matters on which they have no competence. For even with the recent modest retrenchment in litigation, there has been no acknowledgment of the mistaken assumptions on which the modern edifice rests. Instead of seeking to supply information, product liability law, with legislative support, still seeks to govern production, but always after the fact and in a standardless way. In its former role, the law aided the operation of the market by helping market actors make informed decisions. In its modern incarnation, the law has powerful antimarket origins and consequences. The rules are designed to override consumer preferences and to allow judges and juries to assume the role of design and warning experts. They have not been good at their job; nor could we expect them to be. Here again, complex rules generate inferior allocative consequences.

13

The Internal Life
of the Corporation

The study of corporate law can be broken down conveniently into two parts. One part deals with external relations. It asks how the corporation, treated as a person or entity unto itself, deals with the rest of the world. The second part deals with internal relations. It asks how the corporation and its familiar cast of characters, its officers, shareholders, directors, and employees—and perhaps creditors—cohere and work together.

This division is critical for understanding the proper scope and function of corporate law. The question of external relations raises some distinctive problems, and I will deal with it in the next chapter. But before examining how a corporation relates to the rest of the world, we first must understand the rules that should be used to facilitate its internal self-governance. At first glance, the task seems daunting, for the term "corporation" is used to designate an enormous diversity of voluntary associations that adopt a single legal form. Some corporations are small family concerns with a few individual shareholders, many of whom work as employees in the business. Other corporations have large numbers of publicly traded shares held both by individuals and by large institutional investors such as pension funds and mutual funds.

This very diversity in the composition of corporate entities should inject a note of caution into the perennial debates over their regulation. Two corporations often function very differently even though they operate under identical legal forms. A standard set of regulations may prove innocuous for some of the regulated firms, but it is likely to be injurious to others. What benefit justifies the cost of another layer of regulation? With the rise of informed, full-time institutional shareholders and stock-optioned managers, the number of corporate failures should decline, and with it the need for state intervention. The richness and variety of business entities that operate within a single corporate framework are a sign of its own vitality. It is not a reason to impose limits on its use. Worse still, imposing one kind of regulation could create oddities and injustices that would be used in a second-best world to justify the next round of regulation, and so on down the line. It is far better to forestall that outcome by adopting a sound approach at the outset and hewing to it throughout.

On internal corporate matters, that sound approach only requires using the standard common law rules of property, contract, and tort that have been outlined in previous chapters.[1] Networks of simple contracts are the key to success for all long-term cooperative endeavors. Joint ownership of property, for example, requires covenants that spell out how the owners will deal with each other on such matters as selling, leasing, and mortgaging the property. The co-owners must also regulate the use of and access to the property for each owner. They must also specify rules that allocate the costs associated with taxes, repairs, maintenance, and improvements. Likewise, the now popular forms of collective ownership—condominiums, cooperatives, and homeowners' associations—all started out as systems for the transfer and ownership of interests in land or buildings.

Corporations are no exception to this general rule. Once the initial endowments of each player are established, the rules of contract allow for their endless recombination under the driving principle of mutual gain. The relationships among shareholders, officers, and creditors, each with a distinct role to play in a joint enterprise, is established by a network of agreements that knows no external limitations and controls. If the initial set of entitlements marks a Pareto improvement over the prior state of affairs (one that makes at least one party better off and no one worse off), then so do the subsequent contracts made by the corporation. From a distant perch, we may not know which set of terms is optimal before the venture starts, but we can learn what they are, for this corporation, by watching the way the process unfolds.

Within the internal corporate setting, the law of contract has two familiar functions. The first is to protect the contracting process from contamination by force, fraud, or incompetence. The second function is to set the distinctive default rules for corporate transactions while leaving the parties free to choose whatever skewed distribution of control, use, and cost they want, whether by conscious and detailed agreements or by an accretion of habitual practices that jell into custom over time. Where some members of a firm contribute different amounts and kinds of labor and capital, the corporation may not do well with a single class of common stock, but may well require nonvoting shares, preferred stock, options, and debt instruments of various maturities and kinds. Members of the firm will have to ask whether the improved incentives generated by, say, a new class of preferred stock are worth the administrative hassle that it creates. Because such a question does not have anything close to a unique answer, the law should facilitate, not ban, various types of transactions. The state should never impose upon the parties any regime of *mandatory* terms not waivable even with the parties' unanimous consent.[2]

Nonetheless, all ongoing organizations must confront their incomplete knowledge of future events. One response to uncertainty is simply to sell assets that are thought to be at risk in the future. But while that response will shift the question of uncertainty between parties, it will not eliminate it. All that can be inferred from the fact of exchange is the buyer's superior ability to respond to anticipated difficulties. The question still remains as to what steps any buyer or seller should take to preserve the property transferred. In this regard, it is clear that the documents transferring ownership often have dual responsibilities: the old one of transferring title and the new one of governing cooperative behavior. Thus the purchase of a unit of a condominium or cooperative commits the owner to an elaborate corporate governance structure whose function is to respond to future uncertainty. At this point, the critical questions are those not of title to land or apartment units but of governance of ongoing affairs, so that the cooperative, or the corporation, must face all the problems that exist in a political democracy. The theory of representative government allows some decisions to be pushed forward in time so that they will be made on the strength of more reliable information. Yet by the same token, the resulting delegation is possible only with an abandonment of the ideal of unanimous consent for all substantive decisions.

The very statement of the issue shows that the problem of corporate governance frequently parallels the problems of political governance. But it would be a major mistake to assume that the magnitude of corporate problems is necessarily equal to the magnitude of those faced by political organizations. Politics is organized on a territorial principle, where the state has a monopoly of force over all who live within the jurisdiction whether they consent to it or not. Except in the case of immigration, the state cannot select some people as citizens and reject others. The state owes a duty to all people born within its territory, those whose parents are citizens, or both. The lack of a clear consensual foundation means that the governance structure must bridge the gap between individuals whose natural inclinations are toward conflict, not cooperation. The antagonisms between rival groups create prospects for genuine abuse, and extensive safeguards must be included in any constitution that seeks to thread a path between the twin risks of government paralysis and majority domination. Even in a federalist system that allows individuals free movement across state boundaries, exit does not protect individuals against the expropriation of assets such as land and local business licenses that themselves are not portable across state boundaries. As the exit option becomes less viable, more elaborate safeguards have to be devised.

Similar problems haunt any private organization, but with lesser intensity, because corporations possess powerful structural advantages over their government counterparts. Unlike the state, a corporation is not an organization with total political power over its shareholders. For any citizen to escape the control of the state, it is necessary to leave the state's territory and to abjure citizenship. But for a shareholder to leave a corporation, it is necessary only to sell or otherwise dispose of shares. The shareholder need not sacrifice any separate asset or advantage in order to sever connections with the firm. In addition, a corporation has the power to *select* its shareholders. The power of inclusion and exclusion may (or at least should) be absolute; yet as with the contract at will, those who possess it are not likely to exercise it capriciously. Instead, the goal will be to bring together separate individuals whose financial and business objectives are relatively congruent in order to minimize the likelihood and severity of the inevitable conflicts that will arise down the road.

This contractual power of selection thus allows the corporation to obtain the unanimous consent of all the shareholders at the time of formation of the business. Accordingly, each person who acquires an interest in the firm will value it, at the time of purchase, more than the property or money paid to acquire that interest. In order to obtain unanimous consent the new arrangement must be Pareto superior to the prior state of affairs: everyone is at least as well off as before, and someone or (as is more likely here) everyone is better off than before. No state or national constitution is likely to satisfy that exacting condition for all its citizens.

The next question is, what form of contract should be adopted by unanimous agreement? Most people are aware of the distinction between spot contracts and continuous relationships. The former, exemplified by the cash sale, contemplates an immediate exchange, after which the parties go their separate ways. A partnership or corporate venture envisions not the once and for all exchange, but an ongoing relationship in which the welfare of each party is dependent on the actions of the others. How then should the parties structure their relationship to prevent abuses in the future?

Let us start modestly, that is, with firms that have only two members. Thereafter, we can try to figure out what will happen when three or more players are present. The gap between two and three is far greater than a single number. In theoretical terms, the two-party situation is one in which the major difficulty is hard bargaining between the players. It is impossible for the players to form coalitions. But with three or more parties, coalitions are possible, and in a three-party game an alliance of two against one is inherently unstable if all decisions are made by majority rule. Other safeguards beyond the vote will have to be included in the corporate arrangement, and these protective provisions can grow progressively more complex as the number of shareholders increases.

Within the two-party situation, there is perfect knowledge at the outset that any contracting device that is created will turn out to be imperfect in the future. To place the problem in its most generic form, the parties will have to worry about the *renegotiation problem*. Consider any deal made between the two. Although it was optimal when originally struck, the transaction in its initial form becomes suboptimal owing to a change of external circumstances (new opportunities, personal illness, changes in tax laws, death of a shareholder, or whatever). As circumstances change, the original shareholders (or their successors in title) may have different attitudes toward risk, different levels of wealth, or different skills to bring to the venture. What was once tried did not work. Or it worked too well.

If parties had perfect knowledge, the terms of renegotiation could follow the original plan, but precisely because the future defies prediction, an optimal renegotiation rule is difficult to devise. Yet generally speaking, one of two broad strategies is possible. Strategy number one allows change in the original contract only with the voluntary consent of every participant—two persons in the simplest situation, and more as we expand the number of shareholders in the corporation. Strategy number two allows some group (say a majority of shareholders by vote) to alter the structure of the deal without procuring the consent of the remaining shareholders, *but only if* they leave those outside the dominant group no worse off than they were before the proposed change was implemented. In the language of standard contract law, the second position allows the dominant group unilaterally to breach (or more accurately to transform) the contract as long as it pays outsiders full expectation damages, that is, money equal to the value that the minority shareholders had before the renegotiation was forced. The difference between the two approaches lies in the choice of remedy: either an injunction against changes in the first place unless the outsiders are bought off at a mutually agreeable price *or* damages assessed by formula. The issue harks back to the fifth simple rule: Does the contract allow for forced purchases upon payment of just compensation or not? As in the general case, the choice of rule depends on the relative severity of the holdout and the expropriation problem. Some cases show how pervasive this issue is within the corporate context.

VOTING

The first task for any organization is to choose its voting rules. One possibility is to insist that all subsequent decisions must be made by unanimous consent. Yet few corporations of any size could possibly survive the attendant risk of paralysis. At this level, the risk of holdout dominates that of expropriation. The need for quick action on the strength of current information requires some delegated powers, which may be used wisely or abused.

Another possibility is a simple majority vote, a rule of one vote per share. But is that system sufficient to set up adequate control mechanisms for the firm? At one level, the answer is clearly in the negative, given the risk of the minority's expropriation by the majority. A simple rule that says that all shares of a given class are entitled to the same dividends and sales represents one entrenched rule of corporate formation that goes a long way to quell fears of abuse. Similarly, systems of cumulative voting may give minority shareholders some seats on the board of directors, where their mere presence might effectively constrain the appetites of the majority. But even these rules might not provide adequate safeguards with respect to certain major corporate transactions, such as the sale of a major division or a merger with another firm. In these cases, some, but not all, firms might wish to remit the matter for direct shareholder approval (even by a super-majority) on either an advisory or a binding basis. Finding the optimal voting rules is no easy matter because the successful choice depends not only on the capital structure of the firm but also on the distribution of shareholder holdings within that firm.

DIRECTORS' LIABILITY

A second problem that calls for a contractual answer concerns the liability of members of the board of directors for misconduct in office. Directors make some mix of good and bad decisions. An ideal decision rule is one that maximizes the gains from good decisions and limits the losses from bad ones. The possible rules are familiar: directors can be held strictly liable for bad decisions; they can be held responsible for wrong decisions made with negligence, but not otherwise; or they can be held responsible only for gross negligence, reckless or deliberate fraud. Which rule should be chosen and why?

If the only goal of legal rules were to make compensation for the wrongful losses after the fact, the rule of choice should be strict liability. Yet that rule is the first to go. No director could work under a rule that allowed the shareholders to keep the benefits of all decisions, and forced the directors to compensate them for bad outcomes. No one bats a thousand: the director who did the best possible job could easily be wiped out by the costs of a single wrong decision. A basic rule of no liability for erroneous decisions treats the gains from the good decisions as shareholders' compensation for their losses from bad ones.

To illustrate, suppose a director makes 100 decisions: 90 correct, 9 incorrect but carefully made, and 1 incorrect and negligently made. Assume each decision is worth $1 million. A strict liability rule requires the conscientious director to pay $10 million in damages even though he has provided the shareholders with $90 million in benefits. The no liability rule prevents overdeterrence by knocking out all payment. But what about a bit of fine-tuning in the form of liability for negligence: liability for $1 million is not astronomical; it is merely crushing. No one will therefore take the position without insurance coverage for million-dollar losses, *plus* the costs of litigation and erroneous verdicts. So once again the need to induce responsible individuals to become directors in the first place countenances against a rule of full liability for negligent misconduct.

The most difficult case is that of deliberate wrongdoing or its close cousin, recklessness. If all such cases could be identified and punished without error, why not impose liability for corporate theft or conscious dereliction of duty? But again the risk of erroneous determinations has to be faced, and with it the incentives that will drive good people away from directorships. Prudence may call for contractual protection against suit, coupled with other sanctions, such as dismissal or fines, against corporate misconduct. Such efforts to open the door ever so slightly to claims for malice and fraud have generally proved unsuccessful: clever lawyers are masters at inferring fraud and malice when neither exists.[3]

Once again the obvious difficulties accentuate the need for contractual solutions. In addition to specifying the grounds on which directors may be held liable, contracts can specify the extent of director liability to aggrieved shareholders and the nature and the scope of the insurance coverage available to them. No system of liability eliminates all possibilities of abuse, and the litigated cases are likely to be those where the contracts work poorly after the fact. But the soundness of a contractual provision is not determined solely by looking at the cases that challenge its validity. It is also necessary to take into account the cases where the contract succeeds so well that it is never tested. No firm should be required to exonerate directors from threat of suit by aggrieved shareholders. But most firms will find that other systems of director control must be adopted as well to handle the recurrent problems of neglect or abuse.

INSIDER TRADING

The same overall analysis of contractual freedom applies to insider trading, which continues to dominate popular accounts of corporate wrongdoing with each new revelation of improper conduct. Yet on the analysis here, there is scant reason for any public prohibition against insider trading, notwithstanding the common assertions that public vigilance is necessary to ensure confidence in the stock markets, to prevent fraud on the market, and to allow a level playing field to emerge between large and small shareholders of corporate enterprises.[4]

To see why regulation is inappropriate, return to the beginning of the corporate life, to examine choices the promoters of the corporation face in setting the terms and conditions on selling shares, either privately or in some public offering. To maximize their revenue, promoters must respond to two conflicting tugs. First, they want to receive as much as they can per share of the venture sold—including the advantages of insider trading. But the more favorable the deal they keep for themselves at the outset, the less attractive the shares to the outsiders, and the lower the per-share price. The promoters therefore must maximize (the sum of) immediate revenues and long-term freedom. At the time of the initial offering, there is no conflict between the ideal terms for promoter and shareholders. Price adjustments can reflect the residual risks involved with the shares.

On this view, there is little reason to resort to public regulation to protect shareholders from insider trading. Any protection they want can be included in the original contract of sale. That contract could require directors and management to disclose in advance all trades in shares of the corporation; it could allow them to make only limited sales, and then only on certain occasions; or it could forbid the management team to allow its holdings in corporate shares to fall below some specified amount.

Nor is there any reason to assume that insider trading will be routinely allowed. Corporate managers routinely disclose sensitive information to their lawyers, investment bankers, and printers on the understanding that they (or their firms) will not trade on it. Why allow some to reap the entrepreneurial profits created by others? The abuse of inside information is thus effectively blocked by private arrangement. And most law firms and printers are willing to meet their clients more than halfway, by adopting internal rules that prohibit all forms of individual stock trading by their members. Investment houses obviously must make more carefully tailored arrangements.

A similar argument could be made against the use of inside information by the officers and directors of the firm. Quite simply, shareholders do not wish to compensate their directors by allowing them to use the inside information for personal benefit. Generally speaking, the insider's compensation is geared to the value of the services that are provided, and it would be odd (or so one could argue) for the amount of compensation tendered to an officer of the firm to be dependent on the size of his independent capital and his willingness to make large gambles on the strength of imperfect inside information. Shareholders may prefer that their officers and directors not trade on the inside information that they possess. But not necessarily so. Who is hurt by the use of the inside information? In part, the answer may depend on the kind of information that the insiders hold. If the information points to an increase in share value, those who sell when the insiders buy may well be prejudiced by their actions. But if a disclosure in the charter of incorporation puts everyone on notice of the right and warns shareholders to take perhaps an extra measure of caution before selling, who can object?

Insider trading should be regarded as legal as a matter of course not solely because all traders are forewarned in advance. It is likely that it performs some useful functions as well. Thus suppose that a firm is engaged in certain delicate transactions. To disclose the specific transactional information to the public may well increase the peril to the firm. For example, if the firm is entering into a sensitive negotiation to buy the stock of a small corporation, public disclosure of the target may well attract other bidders to the market and thereby reduce the chances of success. When the insiders buy up firm shares, they signal to the market the firm's favorable prospects without disclosing the confidential information in question: the rise in share prices should alert all investors to any improvement in the firm's prospects. If the insider trading brings stock prices closer to their true value, the market should be more and not less efficient, to the benefit of insiders and outsiders alike.

But what about sale by insiders? Some of the same arguments apply in reverse. Suppose that a potential lawsuit against the firm has a serious chance of success. If the directors of the corporation state in great

detail the reasons why they fear the suit, they may well compound the
risk by supplying their adversaries with critical information. By selling
shares, insiders can communicate their worries to the market without
pinpointing their source of concern. Yet selling shares is limited in a
way that buying them is not: the insiders who sell too many shares
may well lose control of the firm and thereby place their own insider
status in serious jeopardy.

Taken together, these illustrations highlight an important ambiguity
in the ethics of disclosure that is easily overlooked in discussions of
insider trading. Disclosure is a two-edged sword. One edge gives traders better information about the firm so that the trading price more
quickly converges with the underlying value. But the other edge simultaneously reduces the value of the firm by giving, free of charge, that
same valuable information to hostile outsiders. If the harm that this
information can wreak on shareholders is greater than the benefit
it can confer, it is best for the corporation's insiders to remain
mum—just as intelligence agencies keep mum even though the public
at large has a legitimate oversight interest. Insider trading is thus a
form of guarded communication by which shareholders can discover
changes in the firm prospects without being hurt by like disclosures
to others.

Whether this, or any other, advantage to insider trading exceeds its
cost raises a difficult question that admits of no categorical answer.
Given the difficulties of accurately evaluating common practices, the
familiar lesson of caution comes to the fore once again. The enforcement of the insider trading laws is no small enterprise. The government must maintain an elaborate computer watch on share trading to
detect any unusual patterns or levels of activity. Yet that activity itself
might not be evidence of insider trading, for anyone may investigate
the operations of a corporation and its market, and buy or sell in
large quantities on the expectation of a radical change in corporate
fortunes. It is just through that private evaluation of information that
markets remain efficient. It is therefore necessary for government in-
vestigators to weed out traders who have not flouted the insider laws,
an investigation that requires detailed and intrusive factual scrutiny of
all unusual activity. Thereafter comes the nontrivial expense of enforcement actions, along with the spectacle of criminal trials against
people who have beaten the system. Insider trading also imposes
heavy costs on firms, which must monitor their own employers for

compliance with the law. While the total administrative expense mounts, it is easy to lose sight of the distinction that matters: the difference between those who acquire inside information in violation of company rules and those who do not.

The present affection for expanded criminal and civil liabilities has a further vice: it ignores the various self-help remedies available when insider trading is legal. In the first instance, it seems clear that firms have to disclose whether they plan to tolerate the practice or not, and those that do not can then set whatever internal sanctions against it (including restoration of profits, imposition of penalties, recovery of litigation expenses, and dismissal from the firm) they choose. Once warned, investors could invest elsewhere, and just forgo a given opportunity. Alternatively, they could invest in mutual funds run by experienced traders who can try to take advantage of the insider trading. Or the investors could adopt a strategy of buying and holding a diversified portfolio, such as a stock index fund, in order to ride a particular stock down and up on the strength of insider trading. Few insiders will want to invest in stocks which have negative expected values, so that over the long run a buy-and-hold strategy could yield positive returns, with a minimum of supervision and personal expense. But whatever the private responses, the case for complex regulation is weak indeed.

GOING-PRIVATE TRANSACTIONS

The choice between rules that combat holdout and those that combat expropriation also arises in so-called going-private transactions, where a group of insider managers who hold some stock position in the firm wish to acquire outstanding shares held by people outside their circle.[5] Their reason for doing so is simple enough. They believe that they have the expertise to develop the firm along certain lines and do not wish to share those gains with passive shareholders who have nothing to contribute to the venture and who may stand in the way of its success. In the unanimous consent regime, the firm can only be made private if all the shareholders agree, and accordingly, there will be gains all around from a successful renegotiation. What is not known is the fraction of those gains that will be garnered by each shareholder. Yet adopting this strategy initially has a real drawback. The parties will expend substantial resources to obtain the lion's share of the surplus, and may well become deadlocked so that no deal is made at all. The transaction costs under this legal structure are very high, and tend to multiply rapidly as the number of participants increases. The structure that may work for two shareholders may be wholly inappropriate for a firm with a hundred.

But there is a second approach. Here the winners will be able to force the exchange and to keep all the gains for themselves. Just that situation arises where the insiders (if they command a majority of the shares) can invoke an appraisal remedy that in principle forces the minority of shareholders to surrender their shares in exchange for the prebid value of the shares—thus overcoming any holdout problem. In practice, the frictions of the process may allow the dominant faction to do a good deal better than that, leaving the minority shareholders worse off than if nothing had been done. While this outcome works wonders for the winners after restructuring, it does not serve their initial long-term interests, for people are far less willing to invest in ventures whose gains can be snatched by a process over which they have no control. But similarly, the parties should have reservations about requiring renegotiation for any corporate restructuring. If the parties anticipate gridlock when future decisions must be made, then they also will be less willing to invest in the venture.

The ultimate question here is, simply, which of the two strategies should be adopted to handle the renegotiation problem? The answer can be given in a single sentence: there is no dominant solution, that is, a solution that is necessarily good for all corporations in all circumstances. It is not possible to state categorically whether the problems with bargaining under a unanimous consent scenario are more severe than the problems with exploitation under a forced buy-out. Nor can we rule out the possibility that some third approach to the renegotiation problem is better than either of these standard approaches. (It might be possible to provide for a forced buy-out at 110 percent of valuation, which divides the surplus but prevents any buy-outs where the gains are smaller than 10 percent.) The members of individual firms have to make intelligent estimates of which approach is likely to prove best for them.

The correct answer then depends on the relative size of the transactions costs for the two (or more) alternative solutions. The number of shareholders, the distribution of their holdings, their interpersonal relations, their overall wealth, their attitudes toward risk, and a thousand other variables are relevant even if they are difficult to identify or quantify. In some settings, the shareholders may renegotiate to secure a pro rata distribution of the gain. In other cases, they may lean toward a forced buy-out to increase the likelihood of a needed corporate restructuring. So again the moral is clear. No default rule is likely to perform well, although the appraisal remedies have taken hold. Precisely because of our collective ignorance, the dominant solutions should be contractual. Independent directors may be asked to pass on the adequacy of bids. Outsider offers may be solicited. Yet no matter what is done, perfection is not attainable given the standard difficulty of organizing corporate-control transactions in highly uncertain situations.

Takeover Bids

Bargaining problems are also critical when takeover bids are made to acquire the shares of a public corporation.[6] What kind of regime should the shareholders of the target corporation adopt to respond to the outsider who is willing to pay a handsome premium in a tender offer for all or a substantial fraction of the target shares?

One possibility is to deny individual shareholders the individual right to tender or withhold shares. This position denies shareholders their normal right of alienation without the approval of their fellow shareholders, an indispensable condition for an organized market. But the justification for restricting individual choice is to allow the target's shareholders to realize a higher overall price by bargaining as one with the outside bidder. Just as the ordinary homeowner need not accept the first offer that comes her way, so too the ordinary shareholder need not show any indecent haste to sell. If all shareholders are forced to suspend their individual rights of sale, the outsider will not be able to pick off the individual shareholders one at a time, but will have to deal with them as though they were a single owner represented by management, which then can conduct an "auction" to extract the highest price from the competing bidders.

Yet this auction alternative runs the risk of forestalling attractive offers, for the prospect of having to face concerted and organized resistance may deter some bidders from entering the fray in the first place. Hence the impulse for a rule whereby the management of the target firm remains passive in the face of outside offers. That approach

260 The Rules in Action

can stimulate offers because the offeror can count on paying a lower price by making a lightning bid at a small premium that shareholders must accept quickly and without coordination. The tendering shareholders yield something in price in order to increase the probability of getting a good offer. Yet even here the shareholders have powerful protections, for many shareholders of public corporations have adopted buy and hold strategies whereby they ignore day-to-day fluctuations in market price and sell only if some personal or tax need requires them to reevaluate their position.[7] They realize enormous gains from free-riding on the wisdom of others. A handsome premium over the market price will normally be necessary to rouse such shareholders from their slumber, and thus both they and the active traders should be able to garner a substantial premium from a takeover bid even if their management is required to remain passive. The empirical evidence indicates fairly clearly that shareholders of the acquired corporation generally do far better than shareholders of the acquiring corporation, gaining on average a return of 50 percent, while the acquiring corporation shareholders break about even.[8]

In addition, the passive strategy will prevent the management from abusing its power to conduct the auction and entrenching its position inside the firm. If one reason for the tender offer is that current management is not responsive to new industry developments, or is hidebound in its ways, shareholders will not want to entrust their fortunes to this group. The conflict of interest between shareholders, who wish to maximize profits and move on, and managers, who wish to draw high salaries and perquisites, is too great to be ignored. Delay is one strategy that management could adopt, and it could lead to the rejection of desirable offers. But it is also possible for management to engage in other strategies that are still more destructive, such as selling off key portions of the firm either to render the asset-mix of the firm unattractive to the acquirer or to saddle the firm with prohibitive amounts of debt. Alternatively, the target firm could launch a bid for some of its own shares, except perhaps those already acquired by the tendering firm.[9]

Yet as in all trade-off situations, the argument for passivity is not decisive. If management has worked hard and effectively to create a desirable situation, a rapid sale by shareholders will result in exploitation in the opposite direction—of the anticipated gains of managerial excellence by the opportunistic acquiring shareholders. In this scenario, management control is the antidote to abuse, not its source. Given this possibility, we should perhaps look with far more favor on the "golden parachute"—severance pay contingent on a successful takeover—afforded key members of the management team. It represents a way to hire able managers in the first instance by assuring them a high payback for their efforts whether or not the firm is taken over. It therefore helps align the interests of management and the shareholders, for if both can gain from the third-party takeover, they are more likely to bring it about. Yet like all other strategies, it can fail badly on occasion, as when the parachute gives compensation to weak managers whom the firm would prefer to fire even if the takeover did not take place.

This tentative discussion of takeover situations is designed deliberately to indicate that there is no evident reason to expect the auction to dominate the passive approach or vice versa. But even from that straightforward conclusion, we can derive an important truth about the troubled relationship between contract and regulation. In any one case, the relative strengths of the alternative solutions will vary. Both the general analysis and the particular illustrations demonstrate one clear moral: where there is no dominant solution to a recurrent problem, a regime of mandatory terms should be avoided. The system is itself based on guesswork and is thus defeated by the heterogeneity of the situations to which by necessity it has to apply. The local knowledge that the parties are likely to have is superior to that which the regulators are likely to have, or even to acquire. At best, the regulators should fulfill their familiar office in contract-like disputes: they should supply a set of default terms that they think will work for the majority of cases in which the parties have remained silent.

Accordingly, statutes, such as the Williams Act[10] or state control laws, that seek to regulate the terms of tender offers are generally misguided. These rules are designed to give new bidders a chance to enter the market and to allow target shareholders time to consider additional offers. The Williams Act, for example, requires acquiring firms to file extensive reports stating their proposed investment in the firm and their anticipated plans when they have acquired more than 5 percent of the shares of a target corporation. It also requires that tender offers be kept open for thirty days and that bidders not buy and sell in the market while their tender offer is outstanding. Finally, the act requires that when tender offers are oversubscribed shares be taken not in the order that they are tendered, but pro rata across all tendering shareholders. State control laws might also "sterilize" the right of the acquiring corporation to vote its shares during the period of the tender offer or prevent the merger of an acquired corporation with the acquiring firm.

Both the federal and state approaches are misguided because they assume that the auction approach is superior to the passive management approach, and thus add regulatory cost and drag to the entire process. Any evidence that the premium for the target shareholders is greater under regulation is hardly evidence of its success, for it is consistent both with smaller gains from the shareholders of the acquiring corporation and with the prevention of small-premium tender offers that might have been made if management were forced to remain passive.

Similarly, it is a mistake to allow managers to intervene in the takeover process ostensibly to protect the interests of creditors, suppliers, and employees (to whom they have at most contractual, not fiduciary, obligations). The payoffs from different corporate decisions are likely to vary most widely for shareholders, which is why they normally are protected by the fiduciary obligations of trustees. The payoffs to bondholders are far less volatile, and these parties are better able to protect themselves through explicit covenants, including those that grant them the right to run the business should the equity in the firm be impaired or destroyed, at which time they would become de facto shareholders standing in a fiduciary relationship with a new set of directors. It is important, moreover, to make sure that the duty of loyalty owed by corporate directors and management extends only to shareholders, for if directors must be loyal to all the different parties, in practice they will enjoy the leeway of being loyal to none. Any expanded set of fiduciary duties will thus cloud directors' responsibility and reduce the willingness and ability of other players on the corporate scene to protect themselves by contract.[11] The key point is therefore to preserve the regime of freedom of contract even in these complex settings, for the ordinary logic of gains from trade applies with as much force to corporate transactions as it does to the ordinary sale of a home or a bag of groceries.

14

The Corporation and the World

So far, I have argued that the relationships that shareholders have with each other and with their corporation are in general best governed by the usual common law rules of property and contract. One recurrent theme of that system is that outsiders who want to deal with the firm should be given notice as to the structure of its internal constitution on matters, such as insider trading, that might influence their ability to protect themselves by contract. In some cases, however, the outsiders affected by a firm's behavior are not people contemplating contractual relationships with it. Ordinary individuals are involved in automobile accidents and exposed to pollution. The same is true of employees of corporations. The question then arises, what is the responsibility of the corporation for these external harms? Instead of property and contract, the operative principles in such cases are those drawn from the tort law. At one level, the responsibility of the individual actors should be identical to those persons who act on their own account. But no discussion of corporate liability can end with a discussion of individual liability. Instead, a complete analysis requires taking into account the role of two principles with opposite impulses. The first principle, that of vicarious liability, is invoked to hold the employer responsible for the torts of an employee arising out of and in the course of employment. The second principle, which cuts in the opposite direction, limits the liability of corporate shareholders to the capital that they have committed or promised to the corporate venture.

Vicarious Liability in General

The first question about vicarious liability is why we should have the doctrine at all. If an employee is fully responsible for the wrongs in question, the victim has one good remedy, to recover from the employee. What possible reason is there for a second remedy from the employer? There has always been a great deal of uneasiness about using this principle of vicarious liability—"vicarious" as in vicarious atonement—to expand the scope of tort liability because it seems to violate the basic moral principle that no individual ought to be responsible for the acts of another.[1] Whatever the dictates of abstract theory, the practical explanation for the persistence of the doctrine is as powerful as it is mundane. The employee may be insolvent, may have fled the state, or may be unidentified. The whole range of familiar enforcement problems may make the obvious remedy an incomplete one. The hard issue, therefore, is to select the second-best solution. Should the injured party be left with no remedy at all, or should the firm be required to stand behind its employee to give compensation to his victim?

As a matter of ordinary private law, the answer is clear: whatever acts an agent commits within the scope of his employment are chargeable to the principal on whose behalf the agent acted. Therefore, if the agent is poor and the principal rich, the latter places his full assets on the line for the misdeeds of the former. The employer no longer has an incentive to hire irresponsible employees or to delegate the riskiest work to the most financially strapped workers. The rule also spares outsiders the kind of complex detective work that is better handled inside the firm. A defective component of an automobile breaks and the car veers off the road. Should the injured bystander or driver be required to find out which of the manufacturer's employees was responsible for the glitch or which failed to conduct the inspection that might have detected it? Since all paths lead to the same employer, matters are simplified by allowing the injured party the direct action against the employer, who can then monitor his employees by whatever set of sanctions seem appropriate for the purpose. Screening, training, and inspections are practical methods of social control. In addition, normally nothing prohibits the execution of a second contract between the employer and the employee that calls for the employee to indemnify the employer (although in practice the usual indemnification requires the employer to back the employee). There is little doubt that where the injured party stands in a consensual arrangement with the seller, this full range of considerations leads to the routine decision that has the seller stand behind the work of his entire staff, given his greater ability to prevent the risk in question.

The legal acceptance of the vicarious liability rule in the case of injury to strangers imitates this consensual result. This one simple legal adaptation makes it far easier to do business in a complex world, and the rule has long been a staple of the common law. To be sure, there are exceptions, as when the employee acts out of personal malice or sets out on a "frolic and detour" of his own, and in these cases he does not function as an employee at all. No firm should be held liable when its nine-to-five employee causes harm while out partying with friends on a Saturday night. Pinpointing the boundaries between covered and not covered work is easy in most cases, but, inevitably, any distinction brings forward a body of complicated cases at the margin. For example, should the employer be held liable when the truckdriver deviates from the prescribed route to run a personal errand—a question to which there is still no uniform or acceptable answer, although minor deviations tend to fall within the scope of employment and major ones do not. But otherwise the rule of vicarious liability is deservedly strict. Thus any actions, even those explicitly forbidden by the employer, undertaken in the ordinary course of work, serve as a sufficient basis for vicarious liability. There are added measures of complexity that seek to temper the rule by a showing of careful hiring, adequate supervision, or careful inspection of the finished product.

It might be tempting to condemn vicarious liability as an improper subsidy of injured parties by hapless employers, but the normal inefficiencies associated with subsidies of corn or dairy products, chiefly their overproduction, are not present. The basic assumption is that the employee is already responsible for the injury, so that any improper conduct by victims has already been ruled out or taken into account. The remaining question is how to induce proper behavior by workers whose limited financial resources and possible personal anonymity are, if anything, formidable obstacles to recovery. The institution of vicarious liability does create some costs of its own, and it is therefore somewhat less simple than the rule of no liability that it replaces. But in its categorical form, the principle generates the proper incentives, and it is so straightforward to administer over the broad run of cases that it is easy to forget that the principle is necessarily invoked in every case of corporate liability. The principle of vicarious liability of the firm for its worker, when applied generally throughout society, appears to increase overall wealth and satisfaction without causing any skewed distributional effects across individuals. The powerful efficiency of the rule suffices to explain why it remains a bellwether of the common law, notwithstanding all of the philosophical objections lodged against it.

LIMITED LIABILITY AND THE EXTERNALIZATION OF RISK

Should this rule of vicarious liability, which works so well for employer and employee, be carried over to the somewhat different context of corporations and their shareholders? Here the governance structure is quite different from that previously observed. Typically, a firm has many different shareholders, often with different classes of stock. The individual workers in charge of day-to-day operations are, moreover, not directly supervised by the shareholders, who are by design passive investors in the firm, entitled to a financial return because of their willingness as shareholders to put their capital at risk. In this very distinctive context, the statutory rules of limited liability create a sharp limitation on the common law rules of vicarious liability. The shareholders of a public corporation act through their agents—the officers, directors, and employees of the firm—but they are liable only to the extent of their invested capital (plus any additional required contributions) in the event that these agents misbehave. The risk of agent misbehavior is thus transferred in part from the principal to the outsider. If the capital of the corporation is $1,000 and the harm caused is worth $5,000, the shareholders are wiped out to the extent of their original investment, but (in the absence of insurance) the remaining $4,000 in losses rests upon the outsiders to the firm, who are left to fend for themselves as best they can.

The question for analysis is whether the shifting of this residual risk from insider to outsider for corporate activities is a defensible deviation from the traditional common law rule of vicarious liability.[2] For the moment at least, I shall confine my attention to the case where the shareholders of the firm are individuals, and not other corporations, which themselves have the attribute of limited liability. Notwithstanding the strong presumption against the deviation from common law

principles, in this specific context the rule of limited liability is justified, even though in some cases it might appear after the fact to have
worked quite badly. But the story (not the rule, but the story) is a
complex one that requires a close assessment of the net advantages
and disadvantages of the rule. It is important in defending limited
liability not to make at the outset the illusory argument that it provides a perfect solution to all problems of external corporate relations.
Instead, the more modest task is sufficient for the purpose: to show
that the inconveniences positively caused by the rule are on balance
outweighed by its advantages.

Let us begin with the disadvantages. The chief drawback is that
the institution of limited liability creates a radical asymmetry in the
distribution of gains and losses from risky operations. In this context,
the phrase "risky operations" does not refer to the business risks associated with the failed venture. Some of those risks will be borne by the
shareholders themselves, who must therefore seek some contractual
protections against the misconduct of their own officers and employees. Yet some of these financial losses will be born by creditors of the
firm, who can protect themselves not only by executing a contract
with the firm but also, if necessary, by extracting personal guarantees
from the shareholders that are not defeated by any doctrine of limited
liability. The structuring of these commercial limitations is necessarily
complex (and thus a job for contract) because of the skewed nature
of the investment return. If the project is enormously successful, the
creditors will only get back principal and interest, just as they would
if the project barely broke even. But if the project goes belly-up, creditors can be wiped out. The creditors have a disproportionate share of
the down side, and the implicit conflict of interest may lead shareholders and corporate officers to prefer riskier financial projects than they
would undertake if they did not rely on borrowed capital. It is just
this risk that leads to the set of extensive covenants that lenders usually require of their borrowers—including those that address the purposes for which the funds can be used, the conditions under which
the loan can be called, and the security for the basic arrangement. Yet
these differences depend on the implicit conflict of interest between
borrowers and lenders. There is little distinctive about them in the
corporate setting.

The problem of limited liability, along with the asymmetry of returns that it creates, becomes more salient with a second form of risky

venture: tortious harm to third parties. Conceive of a corporate venture that can result in one of two outcomes: a high rate of product failure that results in extensive property damage or bodily injury or successful product innovation that brings high financial rewards. Under limited liability, the expected payoff to that corporation would be higher than the payoff to that same corporation if limited liability were removed and if the assets of the individual shareholders were made available to satisfy tort judgments against the corporation.

Suppose that the assets of the corporation are $1 million and it engages in a venture that promises with equal probability either $5 million in tort losses or $10 million in economic gains. (Assume for this purpose that the tort calculations are correctly formulated—an undertaking with its own fair share of difficulties.) Without the institution of limited liability, the expected return to the shareholders is $(0.5)(\$10 \text{ million}) - (0.5)(\$5 \text{ million}) = \$2.5 \text{ million}$. But with limited liability in place, the equation for the firm shifts so that its return is $(0.5)(\$10 \text{ million}) - (0.5)(\$1 \text{ million}) = \$4.5 \text{ million}$. In both these instances, the expected return to the venture is positive, and so the venture should go forward. But with limited liability, the firm creates an anticipated $2 million—$(0.5)(\$4 \text{ million})$—in uncompensated losses that must be borne by outsiders to the corporation, a source of evident unease if not downright unfairness.

More than unfairness is at stake, however, for a slight change in the numbers implies that limited liability will induce the firm to engage in ventures that yield its shareholders a positive expected return while producing a net social loss. Thus if the 50 percent chance of a gain of $3 million is offset by the equal chance of a loss of $5 million, the expected social return is negative, and is equal to $(0.5)(\$3 \text{ million}) - (0.5)(\$5 \text{ million}) = -\$1 \text{ million}$. It looks therefore as if the firm should not undertake the venture. Nonetheless, the shareholders will be induced to do just that because their private return equals is positive: $(0.5)(\$3 \text{ million}) - (0.5)(\$1 \text{ million}) = \$1 \text{ million}$.

The exact numerical example is only illustrative of a pervasive problem that does not disappear when the calculations become more complicated. As long as the poor outcomes of the distribution are kept from the shareholder by limited liability, some ventures of the firm will produce private gains and social losses—a divergence that is a recipe for social dislocations. As long as it is uncertain what the payoffs, positive or negative, will be, the problem will arise in a probabilistic sense in each and every corporate transaction. The sense of unfairness associated with the uncompensated losses to outsiders therefore has, as is so often the case, a perfect correspondence with the efficiency losses of limited liability, as measured by the excessive willingness to undertake risky ventures. It looks therefore as if the system of limited liability should be understood as a subsidy for risky ventures, which like other subsidies creates distortions between private gain and social loss. The problem with risk is acute with tort obligations where the outsiders cannot protect themselves. If the matter were no more complicated than this, limited liability should be understood as the faction-driven legislative fix that undermines the sound rules of vicarious liability developed at common law.

Now what is wrong, or at least incomplete, with this argument? Its shortcomings are revealed only when the nature of the corporate transaction is looked at from a second point of view. The inquiry thus far has focused only on the kinds of projects that will be undertaken by the corporation once limited liability is in place. The prior, and more subtle, question is whether this corporate aggregation of talents and capital could have been assembled if the institution of limited liability had not been made available in the first place.

The answer to that prior question has to be "no." In any assessment of individual behavior, it is not possible to change one term in the overall equation and then assume that everything else will remain the same. More specifically, if the protection of limited liability is removed, the nature of cooperative (we can no longer say corporate) ventures will radically change. Potential investors will recognize that the problem of entrusting their wealth to corporate agents, which was previously controlled in part by limited liability, will become more acute. An investor may be willing to risk $X of her fortune that she contributes to a firm, but she will be very reluctant to expose her full fortune of $10X to the vicissitudes of a venture that she does not control or oversee. Neither she nor her fellow corporate shareholders could relish the prospect of having an outsider sue her in a court far away from the firm's principal place of business. She will not have the knowledge to defend the firm effectively, and hardly anyone would savor the prospect of actions for contribution and indemnity being brought against fellow shareholders scattered all over the globe. Removing limited liability is quite likely to reduce substantially the pooling of capital in joint ventures.[3]

So what happens when the number of pooled ventures is reduced? To begin with, it is no longer safe to assume that the level of technological innovation will remain the same as before. Since it is no longer possible to fuse capital with labor on the same scale as before, the gains from trade in joint ventures will be reduced. New technology will take somewhat longer to develop. If the alternative were that no activities were undertaken which had net social harms, perhaps we would be happy to wait for new gains in order to forestall the divergence between private and social cost outlined above. But the alternative to the new technology is the old technology that is already in place, and it might pose still greater risk of tortious harm to outsiders. The same uneasiness with external harms that arose with limited liability will now manifest itself in a somewhat different guise. The risky business ventures will be undertaken by small businesses, with very few principals, who in toto have very limited resources, and who for that reason are quite unwilling to purchase insurance against tort liability. Limited liability will no longer be the source of the social risk or the feared asymmetry between gains and losses. Good old-fashioned insolvency will.

Once risky ventures are confined to individuals with limited resources, the same unresolved problem of external harms reappears in a world without limited liability. Indeed, that world may be inferior because it forestalls the formation of larger firms, which are better able to make the technological innovation that can reduce the risks of external losses. The mistake in the initial argument is that it assumed the wrong baseline: it proceeded as though the alternative to limited liability is a world with no uncompensated external losses, when in truth that alternative is external losses generated by the operation of small firms and isolated individuals. The right comparison requires us to trace all the adjustments that will be made in the formation and the operation of firms, and when that is done, the imperfections of limited liability may well yield a net advantage.

Another advantage to limited liability derives from its ability to enhance the *transferability* of shareholder interests in a corporate venture. The issue arises in an everyday setting with the transfer of real estate subject to a mortgage. Such transactions can take place in two forms. In the first, the original borrower, or mortgagor, remains liable for the original debt as a guarantor of the purchaser of the mortgaged property. The second arrangement is the so-called clean deal, in which once the mortgaged property is transferred to a purchaser, the original debtor is off the hook. The lender's sole recourse should the property prove to be worth less than the outstanding amount of the debt is to go after the personal assets of the purchaser of the property, not the original borrower.

In most business transactions, the clean deal is preferred to the deal that keeps the original borrower in the transaction. No one is very keen on being a guarantor responsible for picking up the debts of a total stranger over whose conduct he has no control. The risk of misconduct is too great. (Indeed, "nonclean" deals usually take place when the property is transferred from an individual to a closed corporation of which he is the sole shareholder, or in similar cases.) If the choice is between transfer with retained liability as a guarantor or no transfer at all, it is quite probable that many property owners would choose to keep the property even though they could find a buyer who otherwise would pay them a satisfactory purchase price. The incidence of liability heavily influences the transferability of the asset. The gain from sale may be overshadowed by the residual risk on the guarantee.

The same predicament could arise with joint ventures without limited liability. Limited liability, much like nonrecourse lending, allows the clean deal. It makes it possible for the original investor in a corporation to withdraw from the deal without bearing the residual liability of a guarantor for a firm of which he is no longer a part. Limited liability says that once a shareholder disposes of his interest, he no longer bears any contingent liability for any debts incurred while he held an interest in the firm. Accordingly, the buyer of the shares no longer has to calculate how to get redress from the seller of those shares in the event that she, the buyer, is held liable to a third party. The need for indemnification is thus eliminated. The advantages of this simplification in debt structure are evident even in the simple three-party transaction that was outlined above. They become ever more conspicuous as the frequency of transfers increases, which will occur over time as the original shares are retraded. The availability of a ready market to sell shares is not important only at the time of their disposal. It also encourages investment in new firms long before resale takes place.

Furthermore, it is possible to handle the problem of external harms even if limited liability is preserved. Contract creditors, as noted before, can protect themselves by taking guarantees from shareholders if they so choose. Tort creditors, for their part, can be protected by a law requiring the corporation, as a condition for keeping its limited liability, to take out insurance to protect outsiders against property damage or bodily harm. The level of insurance required can, if necessary, be calibrated to the anticipated level of harm. In addition, capital requirements can be imposed, as they routinely are, on the insurance companies to see that they can meet their own financial obligations. The system has the added advantage of allowing the law to set priorities should there be a great disaster that threatens or destroys the solvency of the firm. The tort creditors can have first (indeed exclusive) crack at the proceeds of the insurance coverage, and where those assets suffice, the priorities that the contract creditors have established among themselves—most notably the priority of secured creditors— can be respected.

The major difficulty with the insurance solution does not concern a matter of principle. It concerns a matter of amount. How much insurance should be required for certain types of activities? One vivid illustration of the problem concerns the Price-Anderson Act, whereby American nuclear power plants are required to keep $560 million in insurance in place as a condition for obtaining operating licenses.[4] The money is to fund compensation for external harms to person or property caused by a nuclear incident within the plant. The scheme itself conforms to the model that I have set out above, but there are two caveats. First, some portion of the premiums for the insurance is to be paid out of the federal treasury. The system of limited liability is therefore combined with an implicit subsidy for nuclear power, whereas the preferable arrangement is to require the utility companies to pay for the full cost of insurance themselves. Second, it may well be that the present dollar figure chosen for external protection—$560 million—may be too low, even though it has been increased from time to time by statutory amendments. But by way of offset, it is critical to note that insurance is coupled with the monitoring function of the Nuclear Regulatory Commission, which (in principle at least) reduces the likelihood of harm. The use of nuclear power is, moreover, not simply a source of external risk. It is also a source of external benefit insofar as it replaces the use of dirtier coal, with its own, typically uncompensated, pollution and health risks. On net, therefore, the adoption of limited liability in the nuclear power industry may serve to reduce the risk of external harm.

Finally, inherent in limited liability is an ultimate irony. Limited liability, by insulating individual investors from the full risks of external harm, has made it possible for successful corporations to accumulate billions of dollars in assets to answer for the external harms their activities create. No system of unlimited liability has ever been able to generate such substantial protections against external harms.

Accordingly, one should be leery of the rhetoric that is used to denounce limited liability. The principle deviates from the ordinary common law principles of partnership and agency, just as the rules of vicarious liability deviate from the ordinary rule of individual responsibility. Nonetheless, limited liability should not be thought of as a special privilege that allows the rich and the fortunate to plunder the poor and the helpless. Quite the opposite, it is a general protection available routinely to all who seek it that reduces the level of uncompensated risks to which outsiders are subjected. The proper view of limited liability is of critical importance, not so much because the soundness of the institution is in doubt—today it surely is not—but because it allows us to understand the proper role of government regulation with respect to the internal affairs of the firm. If limited liability were a privilege bestowed upon the undeserving, it might be legitimate for the state to say, "Since we have given you this privilege, we should be able to exact some special concession from you in exchange." Corporations could thereby be subject to special taxation of income, or be required to waive contract defenses against their creditors, or be required to make available free of cost their assets for public service work, such as advertising for charities or political campaigns. Just this peg has been used to justify, against first amendment challenge, state limitations on the power of corporations to lobby against special taxes on corporate wealth, a result that is especially ironic because corporations often have out of state shareholders who cannot vote in local elections.[5] But all these tie-in arguments are inappropriate, because limited liability is an institution that is justified in its own right. As such, it should never be used as a lever to justify either the regulation of the internal affairs of the firm or the imposition of special taxes or burdens. Those obligations must receive independent justification of their own, if they are to be imposed at all.

The situation with respect to limited liability might in principle be different where a parent corporation seeks to use the corporate form to insulate itself from the debts incurred by its wholly-owned subsidiary corporation. In this context, we no longer face the specter of having to protect a widely diffuse class of individual shareholders who might not otherwise choose to invest in the firm at all. Instead, the protection of limited liability now works to the advantage of the parent corporation, whose individual shareholders (if any there be) are already protected by the doctrine of limited liability at the individual level. In these circumstances, the willingness to pierce the veil of the corporation to protect strangers in pollution and automobile collision cases should be greater than it is for ordinary corporations, although cases on the point are few and far between. But however this question is addressed, the central point still remains. The doctrine of limited liability for individual shareholders is on balance a net benefit and not a net burden, which is all that one can ask of any general rule. It is a mistake to evaluate its effectiveness by looking at the cases that it does not handle well while ignoring the mass of routine situations where it does its job. The deviation from the common law principles of individual and vicarious liability is both profound and important, but the simplicity of the rule's basic structure is one of the strongest recommendations for the basic principle.

15

Environmental Protection and Private Property

Environmental protection was not a distinct field of law before 1970. Since that time, it has become a growth industry and has enjoyed widespread political support that only recently has shown signs of fraying at the edges. One characteristic of the modern environmental movement is its manifest distrust of private law approaches to environmental protection, which it finds insufficient to deal with matters of such moral, aesthetic, and cultural urgency. The result has been a collection of rules and statutes that quite literally defy convenient summarization. That complexity derives from the ad hoc nature of approaches to environmental protection, which conceal the enormous amount of logrolling, cross-subsidies, technological inefficiencies, and unholy alliances that drives much of the modern law.[1] Some complexity is surely to be expected on matters of detail. But most of the complexity found in the present law could be avoided if the simple rules outlined here were applied rigorously to matters of environmental policy.

Return for a moment to our roster of simple rules. The second rule, of first possession, outlines the basis of property except for those resources that are held in common (that is, resources where the costs of exclusion are greater than those of coordination, such as water). The fourth simple rule then offers protection against external aggression. The third simple rule allows for the voluntary exchange of these property rights as long as the harm imposed on third parties is not thereby

275

increased. The fifth and sixth simple rules, on just compensation and takings, allow for multiple exchanges of property rights when voluntary transactions are not feasible. The combined operation of these rules yields a system of environmental protection resistant both to private forms of abuse *and* to excessive government regulation and control, which very often marches under the banner of environmental protection.

THE PRIVATE PARADIGM

The starting point of my analysis is the common law of nuisance. A garden-variety nuisance involves neither the use of force against the person or property of another nor the entry of one person onto the land of another. Rather, a common law nuisance is intimately tied to "nontrespassory physical invasions," and its paradigmatic cases cover all forms of discharges of pollutants, wastes, fumes, gases, or other noxious substances by one person onto the land or into the water of another person or group of individuals. The wrong of nuisance is hardly novel; indeed, it dates back to the earliest common law periods as part of the general system for the protection of property rights. For my purposes, two questions arise: why extend the protection as far as it goes, and why not extend it further?

To start with the first question, why not allow everybody to discharge pollutants and wastes without limit? Once again the basic appeal is to a veil of ignorance argument. If you had an equal chance of emitting pollution or suffering from the pollution of others, would you prefer a rule of no liability or a rule that imposed at least some liability? Here our intuitions are not as uniform and powerful as with the use of force against the person, but as a general empirical matter— there are few deductive truths on matters of policy—the collective "we" is confident that the gains from pollution usually are smaller than the losses inflicted on strangers. Behind the veil we would opt for limitations on the practice. In most cases, the discharges are deliberate, especially those continuous discharges brought to the attention of the owner. For these harms, it is not necessary to make the difficult choice between negligence and strict liability. But even in cases of accidental release of pollution, a regime of no liability hardly seems more desirable than it does for personal injuries or other forms of property damages. The choice then boils down to strict liability or negligence, where the former is to be preferred, in this context as in other cases involving strangers, because of its relative simplicity. In all these cases, the underlying assumption is that pollution causes more harm than it is worth, for otherwise we should at worst be indifferent to it and, in some cases, might actively subsidize its creation.

As with other cases of liability, an important caveat must be observed in pollution cases. The mere fact that pollution causes physical harm does not mean that it necessarily constitutes some legal wrong. An individual who injures herself while biking or mountain climbing causes harm, yet commits no tort, for injurer and injured are the same person. The same constraint applies to environmental torts as well. The landowner who builds a house on a fragile dune in the middle of a large plot of land may be a fool if his house comes tumbling down before completion, but he has only caused harm to himself; he has not committed a tort against others. It is not as though his actions impaired the lateral support of someone else's property, and it is a rank form of environmental paternalism (and one commonly exercised by state departments of natural resources) to prohibit or regulate the use of the site. No externality, no tort.

The rules for pollution should follow the same principles: self-pollution may be a harm, but it is not a tort. The reason for this rule is not merely conceptual. Where pollution harms its creator, a built-in mechanism of self-correction limits its extent. The polluter bears both the benefits and the costs of pollution and has every incentive to maximize the net benefits from the use of the land. That impulse to self-regulation, however, is *not* tantamount to an impulse to eliminate all pollution, but is only an effort to maximize net gain. People are willing to inhale the smoke from the fires they need for warmth, cooking, and protection. But they have a strong incentive to scale back their activities when the next unit of production promises gains smaller than the losses from the associated pollution. Individuals therefore make ceaseless searches for intermediate solutions that yield the largest net advantage from productive activity—a vastly different approach from seeking to keep pollution below some fixed a priori level, much less to drive it to zero. The single owner has the incentive to find the ideal mix between development and pollution.

Nor do the owner's choices conflict with the rights of other members of society who have not been exposed to the pollution. If I am entitled to work myself to the point of exhaustion, why am I not entitled to exhaust my lands in the same way? In both cases, I am not likely to use my rights of self-control to achieve self-destruction, which is why the state ought not to restrain my behavior in either case. Others may not approve of my actions in both realms, but I may disapprove of their unwillingness to work hard or their refusal to drill for oil in their private wetlands when I think of the good that comes from reducing reliance on dirty coal.

The point here is not a novel one, but is yet another application of the more general tests of compensable harms in the law of tort. The offense that one person takes at the behavior of others does not generate the legal right to take action against them. This rule stands us in good stead on all issues of lifestyle and personal choice. It allows the religious and the nonreligious, the cautious and the bold, the laidback and the up-tight to live side by side in relative peace without undertaking a hopeless search for perfect harmony. It is only the tangible consequences of individual behavior—the use of force, the use of lies—that trigger the case for public intervention. Knowing what other individuals do, favorable or not, may occasion deep hurts, but the effort to give legal redress to these hurts is far worse than the original wound.

This same cautious approach carries over to environmental concerns. Some people believe that it is important to develop nature to the full, to overcome poverty and to ensure prosperity; others believe that nature should be left in its original condition to the extent that that is possible, even if that means a cutback in overall standards of living. It is not within the power of either side to convert the doubters to the opposite position, and coercive systems of regulation are the worst possible way to achieve uniform social outcomes in the face of social disagreement. The interconnectedness of what goes on in one place and what goes on in another cannot be presumed on some dubious theory of necessary physical linkage for all events. Pollution of the property of another must be demonstrated by the ordinary rules of evidence.

The situation becomes more complex when the gains from productive activities are enjoyed by one person and the pollutants *do* in fact injure another person, for now an externality is present and some form of public regulation may become appropriate, as long as the costs of regulation are lower than the costs of correcting the externality. To be sure, much of this difficulty would quickly vanish, no matter what the initial liability rule, if any imbalance could be corrected by some costless negotiation that allowed two parties to operate as one.[2] In that unlikely event, the patterns of production would be identical to those obtaining when one person owned both parcels of property. If the applicable legal rule allowed pollution as a matter of course, the pollution victim would pay the polluter to reduce the levels of pollution. If pollution were prohibited as a matter of course, then the polluter could, if necessary, buy from the victim an easement to pollute. These costless transactions would place no drag on the system and would lead to no difference in ultimate output. All that would change in response to the initial selection of a liability rule would be the distribution of wealth between the two parties. In a critical sense, therefore, the villain of the piece is not pollution as such—it is the transaction costs that block desired collective solutions. In this setting the widely shared empirical hunch that pollution (or at least extensive pollution) causes more harm than it is worth is critical, because it permits the adoption of a system of property rights that anticipates the usual results of voluntary negotiation.

The legal system thus assumes that generally the polluter has the greater ease of adjustment and control and sets its initial baseline in favor of the right of all people to be let alone. Liability for polluters thus induces them to minimize the physical harms to others in order to minimize the economic losses to themselves. The engine of self-interest works well because the private incentives are well aligned with social welfare. A rule that says "the polluter pays" is simple in form but powerful in effect. Even though it makes no explicit reference to rational cost/benefit calculations, it nonetheless induces private parties to make them on their own time. Where the damage becomes very great, the rule should shift to "do not pollute—above a certain level." By implication, if the pollution has taken place cleanup may be the preferred remedy. The law thus develops an effective set of rules directed to private resource management based not on any special concern for environmental issues, but on the traditional building blocks of private property, a ban on physical invasion, and a protection of voluntary transactions.

One question, however, still remains: how to determine the choice of remedies. The stakes are high. A damage remedy for loss inflicted could be trivial, while the cost of cleanup may be huge. (If the figures are reversed, then the choice is clear.) By the same token, a regulatory ban could impose enormous losses, again for small benefits. The answer to this question is not etched in stone, but a simple procedure gives a powerful clue to the remedy of choice. Ask this question: if the damage in question were caused by pollution from natural sources, would the injured resource owner choose to clean it up with his own money? The question is not trivial, for every pollutant, from carbon dioxide to dioxin to radon, appears in the environment from natural sources, and most of the time no one does anything about them. Yet the class of cleanup cases is not empty. No one doubts the need to purify drinking water that contains excessive quantities of minerals and poisons.

The purpose of this single-owner test is to ensure that pollution victims do not choose an extravagant cleanup remedy solely because an admitted wrongdoer must foot the bill. Thus if a chemical company sells fertilizers whose run-off leaves trace elements in a private well, the decisive question to ask about cleanup is whether the owner of the well would opt for the cleanup (and to what levels) at his own expense if the pollutants came from natural sources. On issues of this sort, courts should be reluctant to accept self-serving testimony. The far better behavioral test is to observe the level of cleanup that was in fact undertaken *before* this particular problem arose with other pollutants. When—and it will be often—this test is flunked, the remedy of choice should be damages for anticipated harms, calculated with an eye of tolerable generosity to the afflicted owner.

FROM TORT TO REGULATION

The practical problem is one of extension and elaboration of the private rights of action into the public sphere.[3] Private actions work tolerably well where a single manufacturer has emitted discharges that damage the farmer next door. But the transaction costs of bringing and policing private actions become prohibitive where the pollution causes large aggregate damages that are distributed in small amounts over many injured parties and that affect resources held in common, such as water and air. Sometimes the class action mechanism can be used to join the separate parties in a single case, but the mechanics of such suits are often prohibitively complex, for it is cumbersome to give notice to individual class members (even if they can be identified) and awkward to calculate individual damages for each class member.

The quest for perfect justice through private rights of action is likely to bog down in a legal quagmire.

The administrative problems of controlling pollution lead to the imposition of regulation, and the form of regulation chosen is critical to its success. As before, a sound system of regulation requires a showing that the additional administrative costs incurred bring with them better private incentives. One approach is to adopt a "command and control" strategy whereby the technology that is used in pollution controls is specified by regulation. But that system is widely (and rightly) discredited.[4] Even with technology held constant, nothing guarantees that a method of controlling pollution from one operation will work for another. Command strategies induce government administrators to use outdated information to pick the wrong rule, and then lack the courage to admit their mistakes. The cost of compliance with a given mandate may "vary by a factor of 100 or more among sources, depending upon the age and location of plant and the available technologies."[5] A preferred strategy therefore minimizes the tasks of government by having it set the allowable level of pollution, and then leaving it to the firm to select its compliance strategy. To meet its target, the regulated firm can change its product inputs, production timing, or technological responses, or, most critically, it can pay someone else to reduce pollution in its stead.

The initial allocation of pollution rights could be made by fiat but a bidding arrangement is preferable. But the key feature is to ensure that the rights to pollute are freely transferable within the applicable region.[6] At this point, we should expect private sales of pollution rights when buyers value them more than sellers or when buyers can reduce pollution to some specified level at lower cost than can sellers. As long as the total amount of pollution is not increased, there is no external harm beyond that already authorized. The class of potential purchasers for pollution rights should not be limited to industrial firms. Environmental organizations should be permitted to purchase these rights as well, and to retire them from use if they choose. Or they can lease or resell some fraction of these rights when changes in climatic conditions make that desirable. At all points, the benefits of exchange (as called for by the third simple rule) are coordinated with protection from external harm (as required by the fourth). The system of tradable permits makes some people better off and no one worse off; why then oppose it?

The use of a property rights system for pollution control is administratively feasible, without risk of government overload or perverse political incentives. Yet at most points, it has been frustrated by an insistence on stringent preconditions for trade, such as a requirement that pollution-control equipment be installed before trading can commence, or by the restriction of trade to a fixed period, a limitation imposed on the abortive trading scheme in the Fox River Basin in Wisconsin. Yet trades of pollution rights in the Tar-Pamilico Basin in North Carolina show signs of working. The cost of removing a pound of phosphorous from point-source polluters ranges from $860 to $7,860. The cost of removing that same phosphorous from agricultural run-off varies from $67 to $119 per pound.[7] Paying farmers to reduce pollution substitutes efficient precautions for inefficient ones. A sale of "bads" yields the same social gains as a sale of goods; the only difference is that cash moves to the buyer of the bads, and from the buyer of the goods. But who else should care?

Mobile pollution sources could be subject to similar regulatory regimes that tax in accordance with the levels of emissions and the harm that they cause. The present standards all too often depend on various forms of command and control regulation. Thus the law controls automotive pollution by regulating the design standards for automobiles—so-called tailpipe standards—and under the Clean Air Amendment Act of 1990 (CAAA) by regulating the content of fuel as well.[8] These nationwide standards do not discriminate between pollution in Los Angeles and pollution in North Dakota. The mandates are insufficient to meet the problem in the former, but largely unnecessary in the latter. A local tax, geared to the quantity of emissions in local areas, does a far better job of containing pollution at a much lower cost. Los Angeles could impose a registration fee on automobiles that increases with the age of the car and a gas tax that necessarily varies with usage. Private users could then make their driving decisions while taking into account the social costs of their actions. North Dakota will not do much of anything at all.

The CAAA does recognize that some local variation is critical insofar as it preserves the division of the country into 247 attainment and nonattainment areas. The CAAA then specifies more stringent antipollution regimes for the latter, including the Chicago metropolitan area. Unfortunately, however, the CAAA spurns the tax approach and reverts to a grotesque form of command and control technology that defies easy summarization. One part of the CAAA approach to pollution technology is to mandate that all the states require their large employers, defined arbitrarily as those with 100 or more workers at a given site, in a nonattainment area to conduct extensive surveys to determine how their workers commute to work.[9] In response to the federal mandate, Illinois, for example, has passed its own Employee Commute Options Act,[10] which establishes procedures to bring its own nonattainment areas into compliance with the federal statutes. (The word "options" is a form of newspeak, which refers to the different kinds of responses made available to unjustified public coercion.)

The first flaw in this system is that it relies on federal mandates that visit the costs of compliance on states who have no control over the articulation of the scheme. Power is separated from responsibility, leading to a fatal imbalance whereby the parties dictate obligations that they need not fund. At the state level this approach invites resentment and resistance, which take the form of government and business protests to the federal EPA for aggressively exceeding the scope of the initial federal mandate. Yet no matter how construed, these mandates miss the mark. The basic statutory scheme defines compliance by the average vehicle occupancy (AVO) of each automobile commuting to work. If that number is above 1.36, then an employer is in compliance and need only promise to hold to a steady course to preserve that ratio. But if the number falls below that level, the heavy hand of the state strikes the noncompliant firm, which is then asked to choose from a menu of statutory strategies, including car-pooling, van-pooling, increased use of public transit, walking or biking, alternative work schedules, telecommuting, clean-fuel vehicles, and the elimination of employee parking spaces or privileges. The smallest variation in ratios could trigger a huge difference in compliance costs. But at no time is it asked whether the employees of one firm could find it easier to move from 1.40 to 1.50 than the employees of a second firm could find it to move from 1.30 to 1.40. The whole issue of costs at the margin is ignored when legal sanctions can vary enormously depending on which side of an arbitrary line a particular firm happens to fall. A tax on pollutants avoids these embarrassing discontinuities.

This coercive statutory regime also has the undesirable effect of introducing another layer of land-use regulation (itself subject to countless abuses at the state and local level) by a regulatory authority that lacks any incentive to take into account the dislocations that it creates

in local relations. Thus the remote federal hand may upset many delicate local treaties whereby permits for new businesses or the expansion of existing ones are granted on the condition that off-street
parking places be created to reduce neighborhood congestion. The
preemptive force of a federal rule (which always takes precedence over
an inconsistent state or local rule) could mandate fewer parking
spaces as an "indirect" method to reduce the number of vehicles on
the road, and hence the levels of pollution. But only the foolhardy
would draw so bold and optimistic an inference from one lonely and
uncertain fact. If congestion increases the time of transit or the search
for parking places, the pollution levels could be increased as individual trips take longer, consume more gasoline, and create more pollution. But the CAAA simply turns a bureaucratic cold shoulder to the
possibility of any adaptive responses by assuming that the actual consequences will be only the desired and intended ones.

The willingness to impose so powerful a level of federal control
depends, moreover, on some finding that the individual employer is
in some loose sense a source of pollution in the first place. But this
weighty determination rests on flimsy employee surveys that are themselves models of scientific misinformation. One obvious point is that
air pollution is attributable as much to cars driven by employees of
small firms as to those driven by employees of big ones. A uniform
gasoline tax covers all classes of business driving without discrimination. It also encompasses other activities, such as shopping trips and
driving children to school, that are often combined with commuting
to work and weekend jaunts that are not. Yet even for the designated
firms, the survey data are worse than worthless because they focus on
a number, the dreaded AVO, that is itself of little significance in the
battle against pollution. The ultimate question is not the number of
occupants per vehicle, but the amount of pollution per employee commute. A workforce of drivers that lives close to the work site may do far
less polluting than one that commutes long distances, even if there is no
car-pooling in the first setting and extensive pooling in the second.
Without detailed evidence as to the length of the drive or the costs of
alternative ways of getting to work, the assembled data are useless.

The CAAA stumbles in a second way because it chooses inept survey techniques to measure its own flawed objectives. Each target firm
must conduct its survey in a single week chosen almost at random,
and then use its findings to mirror the behavior of the firm over the

entire year. This survey technique necessarily ignores variations attributable to vacations, out-of-town meetings, seasonal employment hiring, weather, and a host of other unidentified factors. In each case, employees could lie with virtual impunity or adopt approved modes of commutation for that week and that week only. The CAAA seeks to take account of difficulties in the survey process by prescribing penalties for false reporting and by refusing to allow any form of sampling. If the compliance rate falls below 90 percent—an unheard-of response rate for most surveys—it will assume that all nonrespondents commit the worst possible commutation sin—driving to work in a single vehicle. The effort to coerce compliance (it is illegal under state law to withhold wages for failure to fill out surveys) overemphasizes the likelihood of noncompliance. It therefore inspires costly countermeasures, even when no pollution problem exists. With all these failures, it is not surprising that in the one place where the program has run its course—Los Angeles—no discernible improvement in automotive air pollution has been found, notwithstanding the massive investment of public and private energy.[11] Yet the painful collection of information in Los Angeles was made instantly obsolete by the major earthquake in January 1994, which disrupted the freeway system and forced changes in commuting and living patterns far greater than any system of federal regulation could impose. It is an inveterate habit of government planners to assume that if one system of regulation or taxation is good, then two or more systems must be better. Yet here the sad and obvious truth is that better and more reliable control of pollution is obtained by simple licensing (by age of vehicle) and taxing (by gallon of gas) than by the expensive mischief required by the CAAA.

Misguided forms of environmental intervention do not fall within the exclusive province of federal regulators. State systems often exhibit a similarly misguided determination to force technology in the name of controlling pollution. To cite just one example, California law requires that by the year 1998 2 percent of its fleet of new cars (roughly forty thousand) be zero-pollution (read electric) cars.[12] The program requires the high costs of a crash technology, costs that must be recovered by increasing the costs of other new vehicles. The overall effect is to reduce the rate of replacement of older vehicles, which through both older design and imperfect maintenance have far higher emissions levels than do new automobiles sporting the ordinary inter-

nal combustion engine. The object of the pollution exercise is to reduce total pollution from all sources to its lowest total level for any
given level of cost. It is not to reduce the pollution from some tiny
subset of automobiles if that reduction is more than offset by increases
in pollution from other sources. Who needs the false symbolism of a
zero-pollution vehicle when the overall effect of the program is to expend additional social resources to distort a sane set of antipollution
incentives? Once again a single simple approach outperforms the more
complex regulatory initiatives that are often in vogue today.

FROM REGULATION TO PURCHASE

One implicit assumption of the struggle over pollution is that the state
may use its coercive powers, including the power to tax, to prevent the
infliction of external harms on others. No external necessity, however,
confines the class of legitimate environmental objectives to the sup-
pression of pollution. The public's demand for certain important environmental amenities need not remain unsatisfied just because it goes
beyond pollution control. Just as it is possible to *purchase* lands for a
national park, so it is possible to *purchase* covenants over land to
restrict its use, again through the political processes under the sixth
simple rule of take and pay. The public can have its way if it is prepared
to pay for it. The decision to regulate will no longer wipe out the
regulated parties. Political majorities can no longer run roughshod
over political minorities. The basic test for just compensation—no
disproportionate impact in funding public improvements—can be
honored in the environmental area as it is everywhere else.

   Nor is this a matter of simple fairness between the state and its
citizens. Favorable allocative consequences attach as well. Since an
economic price has to be paid, the champions of regulation will be
forced to compare the regulation's tangible costs with the package of
benefits, tangible or aesthetic, that it wishes to acquire. Just as some
lands are not acquired because the costs are too high for the public to
bear, so too some regulatory initiatives will fail because of the difficulty of justifying large expenditures for transitory or imaginary
gains. And it is a good thing too, for there are no free goods in environmental areas any more than there are anywhere else. No government is omnipotent; no government is free of the influence of factions.
Only perfect governments should have a free hand in deciding whether

to regulate or not, and no government is perfect. The just compensation solution offers the best compromise between excessive government and private rights in the environmental area, as it does generally. Take and pay should be the exclusive approach when the state does not act to tax or enjoin some common law nuisance.

The proper basic approach to environmental protection thus stresses three related components. The first is to regulate not simply environmental harm in the abstract, but externalities. The second is to ensure that some sensible system of regulations is put in place when the harms are external. The third is to set up compensation systems when they are not. Too often these constraints are ignored in practice. It is useful to divide the concrete cases into two categories. The first deals with regulatory schemes that expand the definition of private wrongs beyond the common law of nuisance. The second deals with a system of public remedies that deviates from the optimal set of common law rules on the same subject.

THE NEW GENERATION OF PRIVATE WRONGS AND PUBLIC RIGHTS

Strip Mining

Suppose that land contains coal deposits located relatively close to the surface. The cheapest and most efficient way to remove the coal is to remove the top level of topsoil and vegetation in order to gain direct access to the coal. Afterward, the earth that has been removed can be used to fill in the hole. The private owner quickly recognizes that any effort to preserve a single tree on top of that strip-mined field will be both costly and unsuccessful. The best approach is to remove the coal quickly and cheaply and to worry about the land's restoration later.

Strip mining could be the prelude to serious physical harms to others. Any alteration of the configuration of the soil and the pattern of discharges may make the flow of water, often contaminated by pollutants, far more dangerous than before. The private nuisance action for damages and/or injunction is surely appropriate for these losses, as it has been for centuries. But in many cases, state intervention should be more aggressive. The damages caused may well be irreparable, and it may be hard to identify the landowner or landowners responsible for pollution in the first instance—an inescapable matter of detective work in all pollution cases. Instead of relying on a ragtag assortment of private suits against the mining operation, the government, as *parens patriae,* may enjoin certain kinds of action so as to stop the losses before they take place.

However, restoring mined land to its *original contours* is not necessary to combat these ills, even though federal law today requires that restoration.[13] The hills and slopes present when the mining began must be replicated on its completion. But why? Often it is highly expensive to restore land to its original contours, especially if fresh supplies of earth and gravel have to be transported to the site to make up for the volume removed by the mining operation. This expensive operation offers no increase in the total value of the land, and it does not protect other parties from any further risk of pollution. It is doubtful that the owners of nearby land, if given the mined land free of charge, would be so moved by aesthetic concerns that they would use their own funds to restore the land to its original contours, even if they might be willing to take extensive steps to remove observable aesthetic blight. Indeed, the risk of further pollution may be increased by the additional labors needed to restore land to its original contours. It is often more sensible to fill the hole, add some topsoil, and sell the land to a forestry company for reforestation.

One piece of evidence supporting this view is that private contracts for mining usually require a lessee to restore the site after the minerals are removed; but rarely do these contracts require restoration that costs the mining company more than the gains to the landowner. Why pay $10X for $X benefits? If the legal regime set out above were law (and it decidedly is not), the same result would apply with public regulation. The state could command an owner to restore lands to its original contours only if it were prepared to compensate him for the additional cost and only if it were prepared to compensate neighbors for the additional discharges resulting from that restoration. At that price, there would be few if any takers because the price is too high for the weary taxpayers asked to pay it—another illustration of the discipline instilled by a rule of take and pay. Alternatively, if state officials want to block development altogether, they could condemn the land outright (paying the full market value in compensation) and resell it at a lower price to miners willing to abide by whatever restrictions are imposed by contract. Either way, there will be no willingness to undertake costly programs for chimerical public gains. People collectively will demand less of those resources for which they must pay, and they will be more selective in the resources they choose. They will now, through the tax system, have an incentive to make the sound *marginal* calculations of relative value that are totally missing from any coercive regulatory system.

Nor can this policy be attacked on the ground that it exalts the private over the public interest. The public interest is no disembodied good, but the sum of the interests of all members of the public, *including* the private owners subject to regulation. The public interest is *not* served if the interests of any member of the public are ignored in the social calculation. Ironically, a strong insistence on compensation is more consistent with a comprehensive view than the current law, which excludes those with private holdings from the social calculus.

Wetlands

These insights about strip mining carry over to wetlands regulation. The leading judicial decisions on the subject allow extensive state regulation of wetlands under the police power. There is no requirement to compensate an owner for the loss of use, no matter how great. Within this set of incentives in place, political aggrandizement becomes the order of the day.[14] The inexorable goal of most environmentalists is "no net loss" of wetlands, regardless of the scarcity of the resources that are withheld from development. The policy in question is backed by constant references to the fragility and uniqueness of all ecosystems, as if none has ever survived the ravages of hurricanes, cyclones, volcanoes, forest fires, and the thousand other natural perils that wreak far more havoc than the occasional golf course or shopping mall.

Wetlands do not define themselves, and come in all sizes and degrees. Anything that ever gets wet can be called a wetland, with the result that the upper edge of the wetlands moves higher and higher up the hillside, and the kinds of restrictions placed on the harvesting of timber, the mining of minerals, and the development of land are far greater than would be the case if the price mechanism operated through the just compensation clause. I have worked on one case in which the Michigan Department of Natural Resources (DNR) attached the wetlands designation to an undulating doughnut inside a squarish fifty-seven-acre parcel of land adjacent to Highway M-59, reducing a prime commercial business site to a largely worthless wasteland.[15] Compensation was ordered by the trial judge, but the matter is subject to spirited appeal by the Michigan DNR, which takes the position that as long as some scrap of value has been left to the owner, massive losses in value are of no legal consequence. The case is just one of many illustrative of the fundamental difficulties in this branch of law. The question of whether compensation is owing is incorrectly measured by what is retained, not by what is taken. The result is learned disputes about whether the landowner has realized a small gain from an unrelated sale of some portion of an integrated parcel prior to the wetlands designation, or about whether reduced economic development of the land is possible given the regulation, and the threat of more to come.[16] The law therefore always asks the wrong question, and encourages rampant overclaiming by the government under a system of wetland protection by designation that allows it to act as though landowner losses are no part of the social calculation. There is no even division between those who own lands at risk of acquiring this dubious designation and the political forces that control the designation process. It is therefore much too easy for one group to claim some public benefit at the expense of the members of some other group.

To see the point, note that political debate over wetlands would assume a very different form if wetlands were evenly distributed over the country. To illustrate, suppose each of 100 individuals owned 10 acres of land, only one of which was eligible for a wetlands designation. Any comprehensive wetland regulation would, at least on its face, require equal sacrifice from all members of the community. A statute of this sort would be more difficult to pass by majority vote than if all 100 acres of potential wetlands were located on the property of 10 owners, who could lose by a 90–10 vote in the political process. Proration reduces the gains from legislation and forces each landowner to ask whether her private gains offset the loss in uses from the wetland designation—a close choice that could easily come out either way. Knowing how proportionate effects dull the demand for regulation, we should always be aware of the far greater dangers of *selective* designation when these lands are not evenly distributed. Indeed, one function of compensation is to equalize the burdens of wetland designation when the lands themselves are not evenly distributed, and thereby to reduce the wasteful jockeying that now takes place under the loose and arbitrary definitions of wetlands.

All this is not to say that pro rata designation is free of pitfalls, for nothing says that even when the wetlands are distributed pro rata, all 100 landowners will attach equal value to wetland preservation. Environmentalists may be more willing to accept restrictions than others: recall that formal proration is only a rule of minimum constraint for fair outcomes, and it cannot fully respond to the subjective elements commonly present in each case. At some point, therefore, untoward consequences may make it wise to expend resources for more precise valuations. Finding that optimal point is a difficult question on which it is easy for differences to emerge. But the critical task is to create the right set of structural incentives in the huge number of easy, but important cases.

These right incentives cannot be obtained once the government is freed from the obligation to compensate landowners. The current system of permits required for wetlands development is open to all forms of bureaucratic excesses. People have been sent to jail because without permits they undertook development involving the cleanup of old tires previously dumped on private lands, or they built wildlife sanctuaries on private property, or they brought clean builder's sand onto designated wetlands.[17] The permit system thus appears to be an end in itself wholly divorced from any sensible system of social control, in which the sanctions are directed not at those causing environmental harms, but at those who defy bureaucratic imperatives. Yet that is exactly what should be expected. Once the baseline shifts from "no nuisance" to "no development," the unstated assumption is that state control of all resources dominates private ownership of these same resources. The older problem of tension at the boundary lines is replaced by massive problems of coordination and control. The collective ownership of the means of production has proved to be a failure for manufacturing, so why should anyone expect it to perform better with regard to environmental issues?

Endangered Species

The analysis of the protection afforded endangered species follows the same lines. The current law protects endangered species from any form of private shooting, trapping, or capturing, but without compensating aggrieved landowners.[18] But again the public benefit has been treated as a sufficient reason to deny them compensation.[19] Yet in principle it only offers a justification for the invocation of the takings power *with* compensation. In the absence of any state regulation, private individuals could capture wild animals, and they certainly could protect themselves from the harms that these animals could cause to land or to livestock. The prohibition against capturing wild animals is often appropriate without payment of cash compensation in order to prevent the exhaustion of the common pool. But if the federal government wanted to feed grizzly bears live animals, it would have to acquire these by purchase. It is hardly clear why it should be able to escape this obligation by stripping ordinary landowners of their rights to defend their property from external aggression, so that the bears are able to choose their own dinners. By placing a mantle of protection over these animals, it has denied landowners their exclusive rights of possession, and should pay for that privilege, just as if it wanted to develop rare species of flowering plants on private lands. It is hard to see why the rules should differ when the state wants to preserve (often in the most ham-handed fashion) the species that it finds there in the first place.

The separation of power from responsibility has the same consequences in managing endangered species as it does anywhere else. It allows government officials who are secure in their high purpose to wield power in counterproductive ways. The best illustration of this that I have encountered involves the Cuyamaca meadow-foam, a small white flower recently placed on the endangered species list.[20] Galvanized into action, the Fish and Wildlife Service (FWS) required at least one rancher to postpone letting cattle onto his own fields until those areas with the highest concentration of the Cuyamaca could be fenced off from grazing cattle. It did not matter that both cattle and flower had coexisted in the same fields for nine years. But this high-minded government intervention quickly turned into yet another illustration of the law of unanticipated consequences. The flowers in the fenced-off area did not flourish because the surrounding high grasses blocked the sunlight. The flowers in the unprotected areas flourished even though some of them had been eaten. The intervention of the FWS took into account only one of the multiple perils to the plant, and thus brought nearer (at substantial private expense) the very result that it sought to prevent.

It is difficult to scour the pathless fields of anecdotal jurisprudence to know exactly how frequently episodes of this sort have taken place. But the number can hardly be small given the determination with which the Endangered Species Act is enforced. The basic incentive structure created by the act—the state acts, the citizen pays—is an open invitation to public actions that impose high costs on individual landowners in the pursuit of minor public gains. No one claims that species preservation is not a public purpose. But by the same token, no one should be allowed to claim that this public purpose does not take land and animals from private use and bring them into the public domain. Once compensation is required, then it will fulfill its familiar twofold office. It will prevent the unfairness of placing heavy burdens on certain landowners for the benefit of the public at large. And it will force public officials to decide which endangered species are worth preserving, in which habitats, and at what price. Without some constraint on public excess, nothing will prevent the definition of a distinct species from being sliced thinner and thinner, so that each subspecies—such as the red squirrel that held up the construction of Mount Graham Observatory in Arizona—will be said to require separate protection unless clear and convincing proof is shown that it exists elsewhere. The overclaiming problem will not cease because unique species are always at risk of destruction—such has long been the way of the world. It exists precisely because species extinction is so common a phenomenon that it should not be used as a club to defeat all rival uses of our natural resources.

Habitat

The problem with protecting habitat is closely related to the problem encountered in the preservation of endangered species, and is subject to a similar analysis. Where government officials can designate certain wildlife habitats as protected, they have no incentive to determine whether the public gains are worth the private losses. Worse still, that grant of state power creates perverse incentives for the landowner who discovers a valuable habitat on her property. Her immediate reaction is one of gloom, even though the social value of the land is higher with the habitat than without it, for her ordinary private uses of that land may now be restricted without compensation. The greater the social value of the land, the less its value to her, at least under the current law. Owing to the aggressive intervention of the state, her response is likely to be socially counterproductive. The well-advised landowner is *better off* destroying the habitat before it becomes public knowledge. "Shoot, shovel, and shut up" becomes the order of the day. Similarly, the current legal position makes it an act of rash heroism for a landowner to improve idle land so that it becomes, say, a habitat for a bald eagle, given that the government may thereafter prevent any gainful use of all lands near the nest site. But if the state must pay compensation to preserve the newly discovered or newly created habitat, the landowner has an incentive to bring that habitat to the attention of public officials in order to attract a price. The funds that are today spent on bitter litigation and habitat destruction are better spent buying habitat protection from landowners.

Typically, the bargain could be struck without any invocation of the eminent domain power. Indeed, one striking advantage of the contractual approach is that it encourages multiple uses of land, since both sides have an incentive to economize on what they desire. The same pattern of behavior should, and does, result regardless of who is the initial owner of the land. Oil companies, for example, could gain by revealing special habitats on their leased properties; and by the same token the Audubon Society can negotiate oil leases in its Rainey Wildlife Sanctuary in Louisiana; in fact, it did so, taking a lower royalty in exchange for a higher level of precautions, and then invested the proceeds elsewhere.[21] Yet when the Society directs its attention to public lands, it demands single uses because it can no longer reap the benefit from side payments. Cooperation turns to confrontation, not because of any change in human nature, but because of the change in the incentive structures under which all parties operate.

It might be asked why the government should be required to purchase habitats, which could be treated as a public resource to begin with. Alternatively, the landowners' behavior could be deemed a nuisance to the wildlife dependent on a given habitat for survival. But this extension of the nuisance argument goes far beyond the discharge of pollutants into waters owned by the public at large or other private landowners. Here the wrong in question is the refusal to allow the continued use of the land for the storage or cleansing of water which are the functions that wetlands perform. But to say that land is of value to others is not to say that those others own the land or have an interest therein. If I wish to store my oil on your property, normally I have to pay a fee for storage. If I want my birds to forage on your land, I must purchase rights as well. Why then is water purification any different simply because it is important?

Apart from purchase, the government might also claim that it has acquired rights to habitats on private property by long use, under the legal doctrine of prescription. That doctrine allows an individual who has openly, continuously, and notoriously used a portion of a neighbor's land as a path to obtain legal title to that path after the requisite number of years have passed. But the doctrine is so limited that the only continuous uses that support prescriptive rights are trespasses and similar wrongs, which the owner could have enjoined from the outset of the prescriptive period. My precarious enjoyment from viewing your English gardens does not prevent you from plowing them under. I had no right in the gardens to begin with, and could not acquire any by prescription simply by looking at them—a behavior that you could never have enjoined in the first place.

There is no reason to deviate from these general principles in dealing with questions of habitat. The habitat may have been used for years by certain animals. But that pattern of natural behavior does not shift the legal balance between state and private owner, whether the use was known to the owner or not. In no other context is the doctrine of prescription given so broad a construction. Yet once the government is allowed to assert such claims to habitat without compensation to the owner, it necessarily usurps private development rights in the face of settled expectations that have long run in the opposite direction. Once again, the discussion is not solely about matters of fairness, for questions of efficient utilization of land are at stake as well. What reason is there to encourage landowners to block off the views that their neighbors have of their lands in order to preserve their own future rights of development? By far the better approach is to protect the right to develop without forcing development to take place. The private landowner who wants permanent protection can purchase the land or a covenant that restricts development. The government that wishes to preserve habitat can purchase selected sites. With the present coercive system, anyone who creates habitat voluntarily may well bring himself within the scope of powerful government regulation. So efforts to drain clogged ponds or plant attractive vegetation could easily redound to the regulatory disadvantage of people who have undertaken social betterment at private expense. A system of coercion cannot avoid these pitfalls. But a system that requires the government to pay for the habitats that it takes encourages voluntary creation and preservation of habitat by private owners.

PUBLIC REMEDIES FOR ADMITTED NUISANCES
Liability and Cleanup

The difficulties of environmental protection extend beyond the expansive definitions given to public rights and to private wrongs. They often extend to the methods that are used to control admitted forms of pollution. All too often (as is the case with wetlands) admitted sources of pollution are granted special exemptions from the general rule: what sense is there in allowing farmers to escape all liability for extensive run-offs of fertilizers into public waters? The relaxation of the common law rules of nuisance to protect industry or farming is no better than the extravagant expansion of liability in other settings.

But just that sorry course of action takes place under the current Superfund law, which makes every major mistake imaginable in setting the liability system to control toxic wastes and spills.[22] There can be no quarrel with the strict liability features of the statute. But its other provisions are far more destructive. Most critically, the law spurns the obvious solution of making the owner of a dumpsite the sole party responsible for discharges from it and requiring that he post bond or obtain insurance to cover potential losses. Instead, the statute holds jointly and equally responsible all persons with any connection to the dumpsite, no matter how slender their contact: dumpsite operators, generators of waste, shippers and haulers of waste, lenders, and prior owners are all possible defendants (or "potentially responsible parties," in the current argot), especially if they have deep pockets. The resulting overkill on liability severs any connection between the severity of a party's wrong and the price that he has to pay. The imposition of retroactive liability for acts completed prior to the passage of the statute dashes settled expectations without creating any incentives for pollution reduction. It also makes it an act of heroism to purchase a site or, worse still, to accept it as a charitable gift. As regards the future, a party that reduces his pollutants by 99 percent receives virtually no benefit from his labors, for he can still be held fully liable for the sins of countless others who co-inhabit the same dumpsite. The legal wrangling makes it quite possible to join as defendants hundreds of separate parties, each of whom has an incentive to settle early and escape regardless of the seriousness of his own conduct. Millions for litigation but not a cent for cleanup is only a slight exaggeration, but sensible cleanup is routinely deferred until the protracted disputes over liability are resolved. Of the $30 billion spent on the program in the last thirteen years less than a third went to cleanup work and nearly the same amount went for lawyers.[23] Yet once cleanup is begun, it is likely to be carried to excessive lengths, for no one asks the critical question: if these losses were caused by natural disasters, would it be worth expending public funds to pay for the cleanup? Attempting a return to the original condition (as was the case, for example, with the oil spills from the *Exxon Valdez*) not only ignores the law of diminishing returns but also increases the risk of pollution from the powerful chemicals used in the cleanup.

Dirty Coal/Clean Air

Superfund teaches the lesson that a valid environmental end does not guarantee sound environmental legislation. That lesson is taught anew with the regulation of sulfur emissions under the Clean Air Act of 1977.[24] Eastern coal mined in West Virginia and Ohio is far dirtier than the western coal mined in Wyoming and Utah. A system of tradable emissions rights yields an enormous price advantage for the western coal with its lower sulfur content. Properly implemented, this regulatory regime would depress both the use and the price of inferior eastern coal, improving overall production but dramatically shifting wealth from east to west. The clean air/dirty coal coalition was an ingenious (if corrupt) alliance between environmentalists and eastern coal miners. Instead of using the tradable emission rights (or even explicit limits on the amount of coal emissions), the Clean Air Act, passed at their instigation, required a constant percentage reduction of the level of sulfur regardless of the initial sulfur content of the coal. In practice, compliance with these standards required the installation of plant scrubbers (a form of command and control technology). Nothing was done to tax the residual levels of pollution after compliance with the statute.

The overall effect of the statute was to reduce pollution, which the environmentalists desired. But that reduction came at an unnecessary social cost. Under the legislation, private costs of reducing pollution from 100 to 10 were identical to those for reducing pollution from 10 to 1, even though the social gain from the first action far outstripped the gain from the latter. The regulation therefore *broke* the connection between public harm and private cost by preserving the *relative* prices of clean and dirty coal. This regulatory strategy therefore eliminated any gain for end users from the purchase of low-sulfur coal—which is what the eastern producers desired. The scrubbing remedy dictated by the percentage approach is wrong from both sides: clean coal does not need it, and the dirty coal, when cleaned, is still too dirty. The transfer of wealth from western to eastern suppliers comes at an over-all social cost measured in billions of dollars for virtually no environmental benefit.

Other forms of unwise environmental regulation replicate the same mistakes. Too often new plants are postponed by environmental litigation even though they would operate at lower pollution levels than the plants that they would replace. This perverse outcome could not happen under a system of transferable quotas, but can easily happen if preconstruction approval is needed for every new plant. Why encourage a game of chicken in the hope that the old plant will close down while the new one remains unopened? Transferable rights help avoid this brinkmanship by allowing both the new plant and, or for that matter, the environmentalist to purchase quotas from existing plants. In other cases, major regulations are used to control the level of dangerous emissions when cheaper precautions may be available. Consider, for instance, the case of acid rain, which has been wrongly blamed for too many ills.[25] The local damage is often attributable to local causes, and most of the harm, regardless of its source, can be neutralized by small doses of limestone. The situation hardly calls for the imposition of major financial obligations under the Clean Air Act to reduce the level of sulfur dioxide emissions.

The question is what can be done to control the failures of the political process: exhortation, exposure, and recrimination will not do because the stakes are too high, and the forces of interest group politics are too strong, for these to exert any discernible effect. Only a constitutional solution has any chance of long-term success. Recall that the police power justifications for state regulation of private property are at their highest with respect to pollution risks. But the police power also requires that the state choose means reasonably appropriate for the stated end. That second requirement is never met when the techniques chosen reflect the complex interest group deals that dominate so much of environmental legislation. The state may have wide discretion in whether it wishes to start with sulfur omissions or nitrous oxide, but there is no rational basis for preferring an expensive system that produces little pollution reduction when a cheaper alternative offers greater reduction. The percentage reductions of the Clear Air Act should be struck down on constitutional grounds, for the only permissible ground of discretion is whether greater costs should be incurred for greater reductions in pollution outputs. Likewise, it is not possible to sustain the retroactive imposition of liability under Superfund or the grotesque rules of liability that charge one ostensible polluter with the sins of another. At the very least the state should be asked to tie taxes or liability to the approximate levels of harm caused.

Constitutional invalidation of these statutes will upset many complex legislative deals, but will hardly lead to any political or environmental disaster. Common law remedies, by way both of damages and injunctions, are still available, and the state retains broad abilities to pass sensible legislation targeted to the pollution risk: any form of tradable emissions program, for instance. But until the Supreme Court reverses its current stand of extreme deference to legislative judgment on all matters environmental, the constitutional rectification of the current situation will remain as elusive and unattainable as the political one. It is such a pity when the simple rules needed for effective social control are so close at hand.

Determining the Use of Public Lands

Issues of environmental protection also arise in the management of public lands now held by federal and state governments. At the most abstract level, the shift from private to public ownership does not alter the ultimate objective: to maximize the net value of all land uses, taking into account the environmental losses attributable to productive activities. But the techniques for reaching that social end are of necessity quite different. In dealing with private lands, two major bodies of law, the common law of nuisance and the constitutional prohibition against takings, afford workable guidelines for achieving sensible social solutions. These techniques, however, do not take the analysis very far with public lands. To be sure, the state should not be permitted to create nuisances on the lands that it owns and operates. Likewise, the state can bring nuisance actions when its lands and waters are polluted. But in most cases, the critical question goes to the mix of uses on state lands, all within the confines of nuisance law. Now the government is the owner, not some uninvited outsider trying to horn his way in. As the ultimate insider, it must make sensible decisions about resource use. Just as nuisance law provides little help, so too the constitutional protections for private property are of no real assistance in determining the use of public lands: the state cannot take from private parties what it already owns. The great temptation is to let the state as owner do what it will.

Yet this analogy between private and public ownership is deeply flawed.[26] The key difference lies in the identity of the owner: the single private owner can make, subject to the external constraints of tort law, decisions that maximize his private value. Self-inflicted harms call for no legal intervention because that owner, bearing all costs and receiving all benefits, has the right incentive to make sound decisions.

That optimistic conclusion, however, does not carry over to public lands, which are not owned by a single individual, but rather are held by the state in trust for all the members of the public at large. On public property, the government as such never acts. Rather, all its actions are undertaken by individuals, none of whom have definite rights in the property, either singly or jointly. But this evident lack of clear ownership rights among citizens does not magically reconcile incompatible land uses. Instead, it simply drives bitter disputes between individual users underground or into the administrative process, where it is difficult to decide which land use should be preferred and why. These squabbles between citizens can easily degenerate into pitched battles similar to those that arise among partners, shareholders, or ordinary joint tenants. The right to exclude strangers may be the hallmark of private property, but that principle counts for naught where no party has the right to exclude any other, and each has to respect the "equal rights" of others to occupy and use the land. Now that good fences no longer make good neighbors, disagreements can quickly escalate into confrontation when one owner wants to cut down trees that the other wishes to preserve—unless strong contract rights or substantial agreement keeps the co-owners working toward a common purpose. Finding an adequate default provision after disagreement erupts is often an exercise in futility, especially when changes in land use are contemplated.

The problem of coordination is exacerbated in the public sphere because the state is unable to reduce the scope of potential conflicts by selecting its joint owners or by allowing owners who disagree with the collective decision to sell their interests to others who do. Since citizens cannot switch, there is a greater tendency to fight. The public task therefore is to prevent overreaching when there is no obvious baseline for the fractional interest held by each citizen. When one person pollutes public lands, all other co-owners suffer; when one person makes certain uses of public lands, all others are excluded. As long as there is scarcity, there is conflict.

How should these conflicts be resolved? One approach recognizes the distinct preferences of the state's many citizens, and charges its administrative staff with the responsibility of collecting information about citizen preferences to figure out whether they are capable of simultaneous satisfaction, and if so how. The administrative process guides the collective choice. This process, however, carries with it the enormous disadvantage of inducing everyone to overstate preferences and understate costs. Since no one pays any price for an exaggerated claim, everyone should calculate, "I know my chosen ends; now the means to achieve it is to overstate the intensity of my preferences and to indicate that only one outcome is acceptable to me. If the other side does the same, then I have neutralized its tactics. If it does not, then I have secured a clear advantage." There is thus a single dominant strategy—an antisocial solution to this prisoner's dilemma game. All conservationists need only announce that they regard the environment in its natural state as sacred, and decry any form of alteration as tantamount to corruption. Developers and miners should take equally extreme positions on housing and jobs. Both sides will know that if they are successful the costs of their venture will be borne in part by those opposed to their position.

The continuing controversy over the protection of the spotted owl in old-growth timber on public lands in the Pacific Northwest illustrates the destructive dynamics of this debate. Is there a moral imperative to preserve a large habitat for spotted owls, even in the face of incomplete knowledge of their numbers and the minimal steps needed for the species' preservation? Or is cutting timber necessary for the continued vitality of the Pacific Northwest and its lumber industry? The political process leads to grandiose claims of environmental necessity and dire predictions of economic stagnation. The present process of decision making treats the value of the first acre of public land as the same as the value of the last, making it impossible to acquire information as to the *marginal* value of each acre in its alternative uses.[27] The result is a proposal that 6.9 million acres of virgin timber should be set aside to protect the spotted owl. There is no effort to distinguish between virgin tracts of old growth and other tracts that have been compromised by prior cuttings. There is no effort to examine whether second-growth timber might also provide a suitable habitat for the spotted owl. And there is a perverse incentive to underestimate the number of owls in the wild and their hardiness—because to do so would weaken the case for keeping the lands undisturbed. Unless there is a bid system—open to those who would save as well as cut—political failure is inescapable, regardless of the futile if attention-gathering gestures of presidential "Timber Summits" whose collective pronouncements are unacceptable across the board.

The high and sustained level of political rhetoric thus blocks mixed uses or moderate timber cuts. But suppose the cuts should be made: which acreage and why? Private owners have incentives to harvest that timber which is easy to replace and can be removed with little damage to other parts of their property. But the companies who harvest on public lands care little about the replacement value of the timber they cut. Worse still, since they do not own the land outright, they care little about the damage that their cutting causes to the forest itself. The same companies that harvest their own lands with an eye toward recreational use will take far less care in harvesting on public lands because they collect none of the gains of good husbandry and all of the gains from quick cutting. It is not enough to have mixed uses; the uses must be well coordinated.

Everyone else can also take advantage of lax and inefficient public land management. National parks make sweetheart leases of concessions to single companies without competitive bids. Camping fees and licenses are sold for a small fraction of their market value, so that wasteful queues reminiscent of the gasoline lines of the 1970s quickly form. Nor are the inefficiencies of public owners confined to economic issues of access and price. Our premier road builder, the U.S. Forest Service, is capable of wreaking serious havoc on religious practices as well. When the Forest Service built a road through the sacred burial sites of three Indian tribes (the Yurok, Karok, and Tolowa Indians), the Supreme Court, in Lyng v. Northwest Indian Cemetery Protective Association, brushed aside the tribes' free exercise claims: "Whatever rights the Indians may have to the use of the area, however, those rights do not divest the Government of its right to use what is, after all, *its* land."[28] The government is treated as the absolute owner of the property in question, endowed with a stronger right to exclude than that accorded today to private owners. The pronounced shift in the beneficial holdings is wholly suppressed, in part due to the traditional doctrine that long use generates no prescriptive rights against the government. It becomes clear that changes in the pattern of use, wholly without regard to changes in formal ownership, can result in huge windfalls (for loggers) and wipeouts (for Indians) on public lands, and these sudden shifts of fortune in turn invite unrelenting political pressures to redirect the use of public lands.

The preeminent status accorded to government ownership should not sit well with supporters of limited government. Private owners are normally given the absolute power to exclude only when the presence of rivals forces them to act in a market environment. The government conversely has a monopoly power to take that is not subject to parallel limitations, even though that entails far greater risks of misconduct or ethnic or religious insensitivity. At a constitutional level, it might be possible (although not in the present state of public opinion and judicial doctrine) to revitalize the classic public trust doctrine to undo the doctrinal shipwreck in *Northwest Indian*. Unfortunately, by a regrettable inversion, the public trust doctrine today is regarded as a limitation on the uses that private owners can make of their own land, which they are said to hold in trust for the public at large.[29] But more sensibly understood, the public trust doctrine should limit government uses of public lands. At the very minimum, it should require recognition of prescriptive rights and preclude sweetheart leases and sales of government resources. In a word, it should operate as a kind of reverse eminent domain clause—"nor shall public property be given to private users without just compensation." That doctrine would mandate privatization of public lands or facilities by competitive bid, instead of by public giveaway.

But obstacles would still remain. Resort to the market does not explain what assets should be put up for bid or how they should be packaged; the problem that the Resolution Trust Corporation faces in dealing with the assets of bankrupt savings and loan associations arises in this context as well. Is land to be sold in one large parcel or in several smaller ones? Someone has to hire a management consultant or investment counselor. Nor does privatization explain who should be eligible to bid. In one sense, it really does not seem to matter at all. If public lands are sold outright to oil companies, they can make deals with environmental groups to provide habitat for cash payments. In turn, environmental groups can follow the lead of the Audubon Society and sell drilling rights, subject to various restrictions but matched by a reduction in royalty payments. As long as subsequent transaction costs are low, water will find its own level.

But privatization by auctions might be opposed by environmental groups who claim to lack the financial resources necessary to bid against large corporations. As a factual matter the claim is disputable, for the budgets of the major environmental groups exceed $500 million per year, an amount that could be increased if money were spent on acquisition and not on litigation. In addition, many landowners are quite happy to convey property to conservation groups (the Audubon Society, the Nature Conservancy, and the Sand County Foundation are three such active programs) under deeds that exclude all development. But even if these private sources do not fully exhaust public sentiment for environmental protection, government support for environmental causes can still be combined with some form of market discipline by using the familiar "matching" plan—the charitable deduction. Qualified environmental organizations (groups that could be defined much as they are today) could compete for deductible contributions based on their programs for resource acquisition and management, including their willingness to trade assets, enter into joint ventures, and allow mixed land uses. (Museums face similar issues.) Using this system would help forestall the divisive politics of environmental decision making while simultaneously generating information about the intensity and distribution of public preferences. Some difficulties will creep into this revised process, but they could hardly be more severe than the shortcomings of the current political process. In the end, public management is more difficult than its private alternatives. Within the public sphere, the simple rules have some inescapable limitations that are best resolved by shifting the bias from public to private ownership of natural resources.

Conclusion

The Challenges to Simple Rules

The major mission of this book has been to articulate a point of view toward legal rules. Its basic message is spare: under the dominant constraint of scarcity, insist that every new legal wrinkle pay its way by some improvement in the allocation of social resources. All too often today's law does just the opposite: it makes more complex rules that hamper the productive efficiency of the society they regulate. The upshot is the simple rules identified earlier in this book: individual autonomy, first possession, voluntary exchange, control of aggression, limited privileges for cases of necessity, and just compensation for takings of private property, with a reluctant nod toward redistribution within the framework of flat taxes. The first four rules are designed to establish the basic relations between persons and their control of things, and the next two are designed to prevent the coordination problems that remain in a world of strong property rights and private contracts. The entire enterprise seeks to minimize the errors arising from these two sources. The system is one that stresses production and individual zones of choice and control. It designs its rules for A, B, and C and their friends, and has no patience with privilege or special interest. The protection of the rich because they are rich, or of vested interests because they are powerful, is no part of the overall plan. If people with great wealth and influence cannot continue to supply goods and services that others want and need, then they should, and will, find their own prospects diminished in a world governed by the

307

legal principles outlined here. Wealth may be inherited, but not privilege or success. This simple set of legal rules shows no favoritism.

This story as it has thus far been told contains many striking omissions. Here let me consider six common objections to this approach that have been raised before, and that doubtless will be raised again. These are charges (1) that the system is just too lean because it rests on an inarticulate notion of preference that fails to recognize that private preferences are not "given" or "exogenous" but are in fact shaped by the legal rules that regulate human conduct and thereby influence individual behavior; (2) that the system does not filter out illegitimate preferences; (3) that it does not satisfy the demands of justice; (4) that it overstates the role of atomistic individuals; (5) that it worries too much about calculation of gains and losses, and not enough about the place of virtue in any overall system; and (6) in a more practical vein that it ignores the complex issues of social change as it affects the nature of individual liberty and property rights. It is best to answer these charges in sequence.

ENDOGENOUS PREFERENCES

The greatest of the classic writers on political theory began their work not with legal rules but with accounts of human motivation and psychology. Hobbes's *Leviathan* does not propose the acceptance of an absolute sovereign until it develops a remorseless account of human self-interest and the turmoil that anarchy brings. Locke's treatment of the political economy in the two *Treatises of Government* follows his *Essay concerning Human Understanding,* devoted to psychology and epistemology. David Hume's *Treatise of Human Nature* likewise treats a sense of "self-interest and confin'd generosity" as the predicate for his three simple rules of personal obligations—the stability of possession, the transference by consent, and of the performance of promises.[1] And some seventeen years before he wrote the *Wealth of Nations* in 1776, Adam Smith in *The Theory of Moral Sentiments* stressed the dominance of individual self-interest in the conduct of human life.

It is no accident that these classic writers whose positions most strongly defend private property and freedom of exchange all start with the same uncomplicated view of the psychological mainsprings of human conduct. Nor is it an accident that the critics of market economies from Marx to the present all reject the twin postulates of stable preferences and individual self-interest, only to replace them with accounts of human motivation that are both more complex and less persuasive.[2] One influential strand of thought in this tradition argues that the content of rules shapes the nature of individual preferences, so that it is impossible to conceive of legal rules and social institutions as satisfying some predetermined set of human preferences in a world of imperfect information and high transactions costs. Over and over again, we are told that the advocates of competitive markets naively assume the stability of individual preferences when these preferences are in fact themselves shaped by legal rules.

For all its commendable philosophical sophistication, however, the contemporary preoccupation with endogenous preferences does nothing to undermine the case for simple rules. The first step in the counterattack is to notice the selective invocation of the theory. When the task at hand is to explain why aggression is bad, or why monopolies distort social welfare, no one resorts to complicated theories of human psychology. The robust assumptions of individual self-interest explain why these forms of behavior should be regarded as antisocial by showing how private gain translates into social loss. With aggression, the imbalance is evident, since the aggressor need not take into account the loss of his victim in deciding on the merits of his own action. With monopoly, the best defensive strategies of the potential buyers cannot eliminate the welfare losses when the monopolist sells above marginal cost. Remove the assumptions of individual self-interest and these arguments fall quickly into ruins, because private behavior is no longer predictable enough to account for social outcomes. Indeed, in this setting any appeal to endogenous preferences is downright dangerous if it undermines the firm social consensus that is otherwise achievable on these two critical questions.

Similarly, the theory of endogenous preferences fails as a descriptive matter as well. While it may be possible to find some experimental evidence that suggests instability in preferences in certain narrow settings, the predictive power of the standard theory of self-interest works quite well in explaining why common criminals seek to escape capture, why members of cartels wish to cover their tracks, why public figures of both parties are willing to engage in cover-ups to preserve their political careers, why local citizens will work to impose heavy costs on outsiders who wish to enter their communities, and why ethnic communities all too often react to outsiders with hostility escalating to the level of war.[3] The simple calculus of self-interest needs no refinement to explain these emotions.

What the theory of self-interest does need, however, is some firm foundations. It is not wise to look at it simply as a convenient first premise for economic inquiry or legal thought. Rather, it is far better to regard it as the consequence or conclusion of some other theory that has its roots deep in human nature. It is here that the wisdom of the classic writers, with their broad sweep from individual psychology to political institutions, bears its greatest dividends. The fatal flaw in these modern theories of social preference formation is that they downplay or ignore the powerful role of biological influences in shaping the patterns of human behavior. While a systematic language and great powers of cognition may constitute the mark that separates human beings from other, and lower, forms of life, the advent of these higher mental powers does not reduce the more primitive drives and emotions to some inconsequential portion of human behavior. Anger, love, hate, sympathy, resentment, and compassion, the differences as well as the similarities between the sexes, are as much a part of human nature as the habitual use of language and the appreciation of music or mathematics. These basic drives and emotions are not unique to human beings but exist in equal measure in other forms of animal life that find in conduct, not speech, the means to express a rich tapestry of mental and emotional states.

Behind the full range of emotions lies the dominant biological pressure toward self-interest, not in the simple sense of maximizing the individual's welfare, but in the richer sense of maximizing "inclusive fitness," wherein the perceived welfare of any person is tied not only to that individual's own success but to the success of offspring and other close relatives, discounted to reflect the level of genetic separation.[4] The parent values the welfare of the child as one half its own, and so on for siblings, cousins, and more distant relatives. Self-interest in this broader sense lies at the root of a huge range of human behavior, from feeding to fighting to mating and on to formal exchanges in the marketplace or informal associations within the family group. One key element that makes inclusive fitness work is the constancy of preference over time. If preferences were endogenous, the preferences of parents could easily change and the parents could be diverted from raising their young. But the consequences of such lapses of attention are likely to be fatal to those unable to protect themselves. For evolution to take place, it is necessary for the entire life cycle to reproduce itself, for the infants of one generation to become the successful parents of the next. The instability of preferences should be strongly selected against all species, including our own. And although it might be possible to find instructive cases where it is absent, any successful descriptive theory of human behavior has to recognize that much of preference structure is hard-wired, not socially determined.

Social institutions can, and should, direct these inborn drives and impulses into productive and creative channels, but they cannot destroy them. Kinship relationships may differ strongly across societies, but there is no society in which strangers are valued more than kin, in which aggression against kin is tolerated as a matter of course, or in which serious promises within the group may be broken with impunity. That the form of aggression or the content of the promises may differ within and across societies is of no moment for the general theory, which is more concerned with permissible forms of human action than with how certain individuals utilize the rights recognized.

The older tradition of natural law, so often deplored for its insistence on "prepolitical" norms, may be incorrect insofar as it assumes, as Justinian wrote, that "natural" laws are "ever fixed and immutable," and are known by some form of natural reason that relies solely on the rational faculties of all individuals. But the second part of the definition of natural law should strike a more responsive chord in those who take into account the biological mainsprings of human behavior. These rules *are*, as is claimed, adopted "by all peoples alike,"[5] in large part because of their utility for the members of all societies so governed. Individuals surely do differ from each other in the intensity of the preferences that they have for different commodities, which is one reason why trade is so important both within and across cultures. The very use, however, of the word "goods" as a synonym for personal property offers quiet but firm testimony to the proposition that there are few things in this world that have positive value in use for some portion of the population and negative value for others.

The theory of endogenous preferences is also too powerful for its own good. If preferences are as unstable as is supposed, then it is surely hard for selected people to know the preferences of their future selves. How then is it possible for persons whose own psychological make-up is so unstable to plan and direct government action to organize both their own lives and the lives of others? If the theory is true, then no one can intelligently assume the massive levels of power that are routinely assigned to government actors.

No similar doubt plagues the simple rules developed here. There is of course some doubt as to the intensity of preferences across various individuals, but that informed skepticism leads to an effort to create separate zones of influence and control—to create systems of personal autonomy and private property—that allow individuals to govern their own lives without having to account for all their actions to others. The exceptions to this basic situation involve only situations of necessity or the more complex issues of coordination necessary for the organization of political life. Even there, the role of forced exchanges is consciously limited to those basic steps which our general knowledge of human nature suggests are desired by all individuals, albeit in unequal proportions. It is for just that reason that the protection of life, bodily integrity, property, and the security of exchange are the limited objects to which the coercive power of the state are correctly directed.

Under state power so conceived, there is far less danger of oppression than under a regime where some individuals are authorized to say that others know so little about their own unstable preferences, and hence about their own "permanent" or "true" interests, that their own choices for leading their own lives should not be respected at all. Once this idea is unleashed, there is nothing in principle to prevent those who claim superior social knowledge from using political power to achieve their partisan ends. It is just to meet that dangerous totalitarian impulse that it is necessary to reaffirm once again one of the old standbys of liberal theory—the distinction between force and persuasion—that the simple rules reaffirm. Yet that distinction has become too easy to lose sight of in the constant calls for "restructuring" society from the center, by of course those who know better than the rest what the whole should be like. Each of us may urge others to change their ways, but none of us may compel others to change their behavior "for their own good." Within this world, no one comes into public debates in secure possession of the moral high ground, able to persuade but immune from persuasion by others. Anyone who wishes to teach others the errors of their ways has to run the risks that her own errors will be exposed publicly by others. But in that debate no one can use the ostensible malleability of someone else's preferences to establish the indubitability of her own.

LEGITIMATE PREFERENCES

The second charge against a system of simple rules unites a concern with preference evaluation with one for the demands of justice—social, distributive, or corrective. Over and over again, any analysis based on transaction costs, social welfare, or economic efficiency is said to be deficient because it rests on a fatally "thin" account of human nature that rates all individual preferences, or tastes, as equal, without any additional moral filter to determine which preferences are "legitimate" and which are not. The point is common to theories with very different political orientations. Libertarians and natural rights theorists, for instance, often insist that preferences for rape, murder, and theft are simply "illegitimate" and therefore can be ignored in determining overall social welfare. Their conclusion is correct, but their methodology is wrong. Their normative system has staying power precisely because its prohibitions remain strong *even if* these illegitimate preferences are taken into account and given their full weight. As before, the important question from behind the veil of ignorance is whether the gains anyone would obtain from aggression would compensate for the equal probability of his being its victim, and, as before, there are none for whom a good-faith answer is in the affirmative.

Of course, many people think that they are entitled to use force when their opponents are not, but the test requires them to give the same weight to the personal characteristics and preferences of other individuals as to their own. The religious Muslim, Jew, Christian, and pagan must all give equal weight to the others' religious feelings before deciding whether one faith or no faith should be allowed to repress the others. All may believe in the freedom of religion, but if so that freedom must in each case be subject to the same constraint on freedom of speech or action—that is, it must respect the prohibition against the use of force by others. The reason, then, that preferences for murder, theft, and rape are categorically illegitimate is that they are always outweighed by inconsistent preferences of greater weight and intensity: the desecration of another religion is not worth the equal chance that the same would happen to your own, especially when you don't know which religion is which. It is not that these preferences do not count at all, for *if* one could satisfy the murderer or the rapist without causing any harm to the victim (and the bigness of the "if" shows the idleness of the question), why not do so? It is that other preferences have so much more weight that a categorical rule is in question. Yet when there are special circumstances—unremitting pain, no prospect of recovery, consent to the withdrawal of treatment, or even the administration of fatal drugs—the utilitarian balance shifts in the opposite direction, which is why there is so great a struggle over voluntary euthanasia and assisted suicide today. The case now looks less like one of aggression against strangers and more like one of a consensual alleviation of pain—as long as the process of contractual formation controls the risk of undue influence or duress, as this basic framework provides.

It is not only the libertarian who appeals to the idea of legitimate preferences to short-circuit the global inquiry into gains and losses. Many modern social theorists are all too eager to deem certain preferences "socially constructed" (by the wrong people) and hence not entitled to respect by the legal system. The sets of preferences that can be ruled out of bounds, for example, are those which are thought to indicate racial bigotry and moral intolerance, which are then treated as no better than the preferences of the rapist or the murderer. Religious beliefs may or may not be on the list of illegitimate preferences, based on judgments as to whether they promote, for example, sound views on race or gender relations, or support views that the legal order should seek to expose or eliminate. No minimal state can achieve such ends. Instead, an entire system of education has to be oriented from the center to inculcate in children the "right" beliefs at the most impressionable age, often without recognizing that what is education for some looks like indoctrination to others. No one wishes to deny that parents are capable of miseducating their own children. But to the extent that all parents can control only the education of their own children, we can avoid the greatest peril of social life, the nondiversification of political risk, which occurs when any central agency is allowed and determined to set the agenda for the system as a whole.

Still yet another way to cut down on these preferences has been proposed by Ronald Dworkin, who made a well-known distinction between "personal" and "external" preferences. The former should be respected but the latter not because external preferences tie the success of one individual to the views that others have for him or for his way of life.[6] Dworkin thus posits some requirement of "equal concern and respect" as the linchpin of his entire egalitarian system.

At one level, the process looks innocent enough. Choosing between jogging and walking is a personal preference that is given full weight in the social calculus. But the gain from watching or making other people suffer is excluded. Yet Dworkin's distinction is quite hopeless as a way of sorting out the class of illegitimate preferences in that huge range of intermediate cases involving the interaction between persons. It may well be that I express an "external preference" when I want B not to enter into a personal relationship with C. Such strong preferences and moral judgments have surely been acted on in the ban on prostitution and same-sex marriages—where it hardly matters that the one is a cash relationship and the other is not. But in Dworkin's world it appears that the class of external preferences cuts far deeper, and concerns every person's own interactions with other persons. Indeed, it is the desire to rule out as morally irrelevant preferences based on race, sex, and age (subject of course to some slippery preference for affirmative action and diversity) that drives his distinction in the first place. His metaphor of "equal concern and respect" is used to suppress racist preferences that might lead others to undervalue blacks and to ignore their aspirations. And once those preferences are ruled out of bounds, it becomes a simple matter to discredit individual autonomy and the principle of freedom of association. The class of illegitimate external preferences is therefore said to cover all cases of associational choice and to reverse the ordinary rule that all individuals' fortunes should depend in part on reputation—that is, what others think of them. In controversial cases, Dworkin's desire to give these preferences no weight shrinks the class of personal preferences to choices that no one else cares about—not quite an empty set, but close.

Dworkin's extended conception of legitimate preferences quickly becomes the entering wedge of a totalitarian system. It is one thing to require people to respect the autonomy rights of other individuals, even if they do not respect or like them as persons. It is quite another to ask people to show and feel concern and respect for strangers as if they were family and friends. It is one thing to ask that people leave strangers alone. It is quite another to demand that they treat strangers as family and friends. Under Dworkin's freewheeling approach, the prohibition on external preferences becomes a club that allows the state (or at least the moral philosopher) to beat its (or his) way into every nook and cranny of human life—from courtship and marriage to child rearing, to education, to religious practices, to ordinary commercial contracting—in short, into every aspect of human culture and behavior involving possible connections and associations among individuals.

The great weakness of Dworkin's theory is that it does not provide a sieve to determine which forms of external harms should be controlled and which should be allowed to slide by. Worse still, it is not needed, for a faithful application of the veil of ignorance technique provides the essential protection against the use of force for both personal and associational freedoms. The Nazi, for example, is already barred from casting the Jew into the gas chambers and from passing rules that limit the private right to own property and to enter into contracts. The vote is open to all, and government is under a general duty of nondiscrimination toward all its citizens. So what if a Nazi decides solely in his private capacity to discriminate by not associating with Jews who are quite eager to return the favor? Does anyone think that Hitler could have engineered the Holocaust if these limitations on government power had been firmly in place? Or is that deadly outcome far more likely under the system of National Socialism (for which Nazi is a shortened form), in which all limitations on state power are regarded as archaic or inappropriate? The habitual reliance on big government comes at a terrible price.

Political institutions and legal rules have to function best when times are worst and moods are ugliest. It is not enough for the system to work well when in the hands of an enlightened statesman. It is also necessary to ask how it will operate in the hands of the quintessential villain. The smaller downside of a small government is perhaps its greatest virtue. So what if the worst lout can exercise his external preferences only by expressing his feelings about others and by refusing to deal with them? The first is an inescapable element of freedom of speech and the second an inescapable element of freedom of association. Why would anyone want a limitation on freedom of thought and action that is so intrusive into the thoughts, behavior, and judgments of others? And whom would we trust to draw up a list of the illegitimate preferences? The essence of living in a free society is learning to recognize that harms and offense are not always preventable, but must be borne to preserve the liberty of others—a far greater good. We do far better to control harmful external *acts* than to regulate external preferences generally. The theory of illegitimate preferences does more than suppress some preferences. It exalts, at great social peril, the hardy preferences that still survive. We need diversification in preferences just as we do in stock holdings—to limit the consequences of a bad draw.

THE DEMANDS OF JUSTICE

A similar critique can be made of any effort to insist that the simple rules should be supplemented by some additional principles of justice. It is far better to recognize that these principles cover the territory that any theory of justice should seek to govern. During the 1960s, Guido Calabresi introduced the fertile idea that the function of the tort law was to minimize the sum of administrative costs, accident costs, and the costs of accident prevention, *subject to* the constraint of justice. The first part of the formula illustrates the familiar tension between allocative gains and administrative costs. The constraint of justice was introduced to allow other values to be made part of some richer social account. But over time that strategy has proved a loser. A burgeoning law and economics literature assays the efficiency properties of various liability rules under a wide range of assumptions. But these other values of justice have played no independent or instructive part in any subsequent analysis of tort law. It is not a lack of imagination that has led to the poverty of discourse about justice, but a failure to appreciate the completeness of the original conceptual framework.

The key point is that many criticisms made in the name of social justice also can be made from within the system. Take, for example, the common legal prohibition that prevents A and B contracting to bind C. It is surely monstrous and unjust to allow anyone to engage in such a practice. But the case for injustice rests on the perverse consequences of allowing two parties to bind a third. If A and B may bind C, then C and D can bind E, and so on down the line. Each person therefore will be able to engage in the process of theft so long as he can enlist the aid of one other person with whom to divide the spoils. Viewed in the context of a single transaction, the proposition about not binding strangers to contracts may appear to be an intuitive matter of justice or fairness. But evaluated in light of its *repetitive* applications, the rule against binding strangers is an indispensable adjunct to the prohibition against theft. The converse rule, which allows A and B by contract to confer benefits on C, poses no threats to third parties, for those who wish to escape such obligations need only decline to make the appropriate undertaking in the first place. Thus, suppose the law says that if A makes a promise to B to pay C $100, C can enforce that promise. The rule is a useful expansion of the autonomy of A if C is not present when the agreement is made. But where is the social peril in allowing an action by C, since A can protect herself perfectly against C's suit in her bargain with B by refusing to make the promise in the first place? Hence the older rules that refused to recognize rights of action by third-party beneficiaries (persons in the position of C) were not consistent with social welfare, and the modern tendency to enforce these promises represents an improvement in the operation of the basic contract system.[7]

To be sure, problems may arise, for A and B may wish to rescind their agreement before C is paid. But these difficulties call only for a sensitive treatment of default rules, which might conceivably provide that unless otherwise agreed, C's right of action does not vest until some fixed date. As long as A's consent is a barrier to any obligation, the conditions under which a right of action is conferred upon C can be limited by the party to be bound. It is a very simple rule that bars actions of third-party beneficiaries, but one that is usefully jettisoned to increase the scope and power of commercial transactions. It is not always the case that older is better.

In other cases, where the allocative consequences of two rules are similar, moral intuitions about them turn out not to be very strong. Thus the long discussion about the choice between negligence and strict liability rules in Chapter 5 was so vexing precisely because, as a first approximation, the two rules have identical effects on wealth, utility, and accident prevention. What then is there to choose between them? Only by taking into account the more subtle effects of the administrative costs of the two rules is it possible to obtain some sense of which rule is better and why. The instincts about justice are so weak and ill-formed because the choice between the rival rules (relative, say, to a choice between capitalism and socialism) has such small social consequences that powerful instincts of justice are not likely to emerge.

Finally, in many cases a straightforward extension of these consequentialist arguments shows the same basic connection between common law conceptions of fairness and overall utility. The wrong of unfair competition usefully builds on the basic prohibition against misrepresentation. Where sellers falsely denigrate the goods of their rivals, they distort the relative price of substitute goods. When they attribute to their own goods virtues possessed only by their rivals, they also distort relative prices. In each case, the distortion of prices leads to a misallocation of resources by moving the market away from its competitive equilibrium by taking sales away from the party who would have them in a market with perfect information. The private gains of the duplicitous sellers are smaller than the combined losses of the disappointed rivals and the duped consumers. A set of practices that are rightly denounced as unfair also have untoward social consequences. Yet many consumers may not choose to sue if their losses are small relative to the cost of suit. But allowing actions by the rival seller economizes on the administrative cost while leading to the right allocative result. The basic analytical framework is thus able to put the law of unfair competition on a far more rigorous footing than it otherwise would enjoy. And it renders suspect any effort to treat competition as unfair when the element of misrepresentation is removed from the scene. All too many tariff and antidumping laws rest on a misguided conception that equates successful foreign competition with unfair trade practices.

There are other senses of unfairness that are also captured by these simple rules. In ordinary language, fairness connotes a worry about bias, favoritism, and selectivity: it is not fair for one person to obtain a benefit that is denied to another person similarly situated. Yet that requirement for even treatment flows directly from the simple rule on just compensation for the taking of property, where laws must have a proportionate effect on the subject population unless some good reason (such as the commission of a wrong under the fourth rule) justifies some differential treatment. The economic concerns behind this sense of justice are apparent as well. If both A and B are taxed equally, and the lion's share of the benefits goes to B, it is as though B has taken something from A. The dislocations to the economic system are not dissimilar to those that ensue when B takes A's property directly, by excessive lobbying for a lion's share of the gains.

The common conceptions of justice therefore are consistent with the basic theory outlined here, and indeed are required by it. Make way for Occam's Razor. If a smaller class of assumptions can be used to account for all the relevant results, why treat the intuitive sense of justice as the irreducible primitive of the system or even as an important side constraint? It is far better to regard the various conceptions of justice as deducible from this general theory of social relations with its more prosaic efforts to elaborate the systematic relationships between administrative costs and incentive effects. Adhering to the theory is not simply a matter of personal taste and intellectual elegance. Ideas of unfairness are dangerous when not moored to any substantive theory. I have already alluded to the use of tariffs to protect against "unfair" competition. Other examples abound. The 1931 Davis Bacon Act (which requires that all workers receive the prevailing—that is, union—local wage) was justified to prevent unfair "bootleg" and "cheap" competition from itinerant black laborers. Similarly, the complex structures of the National Labor Relations Act are designed to prevent "unfair labor practices" by management and labor, but in reality stifle the emergence of competitive labor markets. The federal minimum wage law was introduced under, of course, the Fair Labor Standards Act. In sum, there are no considerations of justice that can be set up in opposition to this theory, for the only enduring conceptions of justice are either the procedural conceptions of justice that undergird the theory or the substantive conceptions of justice derived from the simple rules.

THE COMMUNITARIAN IMPULSE

The defense of simple rules undertaken in this book is notable for yet another reason. It makes no formal effort to embrace those communitarian values of participation and connectedness so influential in academic circles today. Over and over again, we are regaled with the republican virtues of being public citizens, able to transcend our limited selves and to perceive the interactions each person has with the community as a whole. Too often, a theory of atomistic individualism, for which this surely qualifies, is regarded as weak, naive, and impoverished. The success of every individual is regarded as dependent on the health of the body politic as a whole.

Cries like this are familiar. Indeed, as Stephen Holmes has pointed out, these criticisms of individualism predate the modern communitarians and were part of the standard stock in trade of many of the "enlightened" fascist theories of an earlier day.[8] One does not have to impute terrible motives to modern theories to sound at least a note of caution about arguments that have traveled in such dubious company.

The attack on individual atomism is more than an attack on isolated individuals. It is also an attack on any form of voluntary association that is not validated by reference to some higher social end. Without the social construction of the sport of basketball, where would Michael Jordan have been—before baseball? (It is a sign of the times that basketball examples have shifted from the Wilt Chamberlain hypotheticals of a generation ago.) It takes more than superb physical or mental skills to account for the success of any single individual. No narrow utilitarian calculus of costs and benefits, we are constantly reminded, will take into account all the delicate connections that make a community and define its culture. We must give due weight to the duties that we owe to others as well as to the rights that we claim against them.

No sane person could claim that individuals arise Athena-like as full-blown members of society, independent of all influences from other individuals who live in society: parents, teachers, friends, and public figures of all sorts and descriptions. Nor could anyone doubt that some element of luck or caprice affects initial human endowments and the way these are utilized in market transactions. But this is an insight without a payoff, for the same point could be made with equal fervor about *all* societies, no matter how constituted and organized. Things could have been different, and those who are successful today may well have been unsuccessful instead, or at least less successful in a different environment.

So what of it? It is not possible to champion any system of social organization in a world of "it might have been otherwise." All that can be done is to try to maximize the opportunities available to all from the outset, for which diversification, not centralization, of power is the key. There is no reason why the presence of luck should lead to the rejection of the simple rules. A system of collective ownership of the means of production continues to limp under all its familiar disabilities even if individuals are linked to each other in communities. It is still hard to gather the information to decide how much of a good should be produced and who shall get it and at what price. It is still hard to encourage A to labor if B will pocket the gain. Luck—magnified by political caprice—will only loom larger in such a system with a strong central government than they both do in a market system, which rewards production more than political intrigue. It may well be that individuals are, inescapably, part of larger groups and associations and depend on each other for mutual aid, comfort, and support. But the question is, What rules best link them together? What rules best preserve the fragile accumulations of social good will?

It is at this juncture that simple rules show their strength. Thus start with the claim that the success that any individual enjoys is in large measure due to the social setting in which he is able to exercise his individual talents. From this observation it does not follow that those individual talents should be socialized. It is not "society" as some abstract entity that values those talents. It is a diverse group of other individuals that values them—a group that does not include everyone in society. Not everyone is captivated by the NBA finals or sits through Wagnerian opera. The individuals who do value these talents *receive* from any one person as much as they give to him. It is not that very successful individuals are necessarily parasites on ordinary people or that the limited success of ordinary people is caused by the success of their gifted comrades. Rather, successful people also *contribute* to their culture as much as, if not more than, they take from it. As a professional basketball player, Michael Jordan earned $25 (or was it $50?) million a year for his various exploits, but who's counting: he was cheap at twice the price in light of the worldwide satisfaction he generated. Are we really better off now that he has switched to baseball? Literally thousands of other athletes labor in relative obscurity, so why attribute his magnetism and success to some nebulous background conditions (a professional basketball league with a large following, a broadcast industry, a human penchant for excitement), but not to individual skills? The better social accounting recognizes that people who make fortunes in lawful occupations give *more* than they receive from them. Michael Jordan's basketball income could be expressed in pennies per fan; the satisfactions per fan, vastly greater. Successful people, no matter how rich, are part of the reciprocal system of cultural supports. They should not have to pay with cash on the barrelhead for the intangible benefits that they received from others, for they have made more than their own social contribution in the same coin, by creating a better environment for others.

There is a second response to the communitarian vision, which parallels the criticisms I made of theories of social justice. What is best in the communitarian tradition is already accounted for by the simple rules developed here. In this regard, it is instructive to refer to the

usual critiques of private property as promoting excessive individualism to the derogation of the social fabric.[9] But this point misunder-
stands how a system of private property works. Property interests are
not confined to possession of land and other tangibles. From early
times, the common law recognized and protected a broad class of "relational" interests—interests that emerge only when isolated individuals enter into gainful associations with others where the value of their
joint holdings critically depends on their mutual patterns of interdependence and reinforcement. These relational interests, moreover,
extend far beyond ordinary commercial arrangements, to religious,
social, recreational, and artistic affinities as well. In short, these relational interests—inchoate, informal, and diffuse as they are—are the
stuff of which vibrant communities are made.

Oddly enough, the strong governments envisioned by communitarians tend to destroy these *voluntary* associations. One particularly telling manifestation of this risk is the use of the takings power to condemn the land of entire communities in order to make way for a new
airport or even a new General Motors plant.[10] The grandiose projects
are supported by the usual alliance of business and labor groups, and
opposed by grassroots community organizations whose homes, businesses, and churches—private property all—are to be plowed under
in some (subsidized) redevelopment effort. Often there is a genuine
question whether any taking of these homes and businesses should be
allowed at all: is land for a General Motors plant taken for a "public
use," as the takings clause of the Constitution requires? No is the better answer, but put the point aside to concentrate on the other side of
the takings question: the amount of compensation for this admitted
taking. To facilitate and enhance the scope of government power,
modern judicial decisions have narrowly construed the class of private
losses for which compensation is required. When people are uprooted
from their homes, their relocation costs are solemnly held not to be
compensable, for the government, we are told, has to pay only for the
land taken, and not for the dislocations caused to those who stand in
the path of its bulldozers. The position represents a retreat from the
older and more sensible views of William Blackstone, which tied compensation to the injury sustained by the owner.[11] When people lose
the benefit of business and personal associations built up over years
in traditional communities, those losses are not compensable either

and for the same reason; the government actions may have destroyed business good will and a thriving social community, but the government did not take them for its own use.

This deplorable pattern of judicial decisions thus undervalues the loss *of those very things communitarians rightly praise* by acting as if property were only bricks and mortar and devoid of associational significance. In so doing these feeble compensation rules send out the wrong signals, which price the social costs of such government intervention far below their true level. The implicit subsidy creates the same form of distortion that is found in other markets, for it induces governments to embark on political projects whose total gains are far smaller than their social losses. These defective compensation rules place the brunt of the burden on the groups who are least able to withstand their burdens. What possible difference could it make if the losses that are ignored are called "private" for purposes of compensation or "communitarian" for purposes of philosophical deliberation? However described, these losses remain on the social ledger and lead to the very destruction of communities that communitarians deplore. Once again the patient application of the simple rules outlined here is far more responsive to any communitarian concern than the collectivist solutions normally advanced in their name. We do not need to ignore private property to reach results that advance and promote communities. We have to protect it for that very reason.

There is yet another reason to beware the use of communitarian arguments in a political setting. Just as large political societies are not families writ large, so they are not communities writ large. A community requires more than people who live side by side or individuals who owe allegiance to a single sovereign. It requires that people within the community show some concern for each other. Equal concern and respect cannot be rammed down the throats of people who wish to direct their emotional energies elsewhere. What is required is some willing acceptance and recognition of the communities by their members. Communities can be destroyed from without, but they cannot be created from without; they must be built from within. Thus any effort to use state machinery to create a sense of community is likely to backfire and to displace the voluntary groups that could otherwise be formed by free and independent people. A voluntary community also presupposes and protects the *exclusion* of some persons because they do *not* meet its criteria—whether described by ethnicity, religion, national origin, race, sex, or common interest, activity, or background. No one group or community can be all things to all people.

Within any political union it should be possible to have many communities that operate side by side and that live in peace and harmony with each other. But the constant history of slaughter for reasons of race, creed, and national origin should offer a sober reminder that even this modest ideal is one that fails far more often than it should. No one can prescribe the terms of union or separation that allow political states to survive when their citizens come from diverse backgrounds, form diverse communities, and have distinctive goals and aspirations. But one point should be clear: the more limited the scope of government power, the more likely it is that voluntary communities will be able to flourish side by side under its rule. The mechanisms of collective choice necessarily require some voting rule; and if property rights are weak and government is powerful, the winners in the political process will have their way no matter how grievous the losses inflicted on outsiders. The political union will be jeopardized by the constant struggle for internal favor and preferment. Where government has limited functions and confines its energy to providing those things—peace and good order, enforcement of contracts—that all people value, it no longer becomes the focal point of factional struggle. Government is then able to operate as a credible and neutral arbiter for people of different backgrounds and orientations. No one can expect miracles from a system of limited government—but the smaller the size of the government and the more disinterested its administration of the laws, the more likely it is that diverse communities can thrive under its rule. Communitarian values, rightly understood, are best served by small governments, not large ones. Again simple rules supply the best guide in a complex world.

Virtue

Another attack on simple rules comes from the tradition that emphasizes the importance not of social interdependence but of individual virtue. There has been very little talk in this book of compassion, of courage, of honesty, perseverance, integrity, loyalty, or any of the other personal characteristics that lend distinction and form to individual lives. You would deliver a feeble eulogy if all you said was that the deceased won over the admiration of a large circle of friends by avoiding criminal misconduct and by honoring contracts. Praise requires more than compliance with the minimum requirements of the law. People are often tested by a conflict between loyalty and self-interest, and it takes moral courage and moral wisdom to do the right thing. We honor people for what they do beyond the law, not for what they do in order to avoid the sting of legal sanction.

But why is a legal system that has nothing to say about the full catalogue of virtues thereby deficient? Law's stock in trade is the use of collective might, and the sanctions that it imposes must be reserved for the most serious of social violations—which typically involve using force and not keeping serious contractual engagements. A legal system is not a complete social system, and we should not reflexively invoke legal remedies to enforce whatever conduct we think to be socially desirable. The uncritical reliance on coercion drives out informal sanctions and curtails possibilities for displaying the personal virtues we all prize. The most that we can expect from a legal system is to create a domain that allows the virtuous a free sphere of action to do good deeds. These simple rules do that much: they constrain the use of force by others, and thus allow for each individual a field of unfettered action in which choices can be made without fear of legal sanction. The law therefore sets the stage, but a second tier of social norms defines the forms of conduct worthy of special approbation or disapprobation. Is it really possible to allow people to sue friends who do not stick with them in times of trouble? Or to sue people who are brusque and unkind? Is it necessary to create a set of legal rewards for someone who lends a sympathetic ear, gives a good piece of advice, or acts as a good Samaritan? To envision a society driven solely by legal and formal sanctions is to envision a society where bone is always rubbing against bone. We need to have some cartilage to soften the blow, and that can only come if the legal order is not so inclusive and intrusive as to destroy all informal systems of social control. The small-government attitude favored by a system of simple rules argues for a concept of legal control and legal freedom that recognizes the proper limits to law and to force—limits that are all too often ignored today.

SOCIAL CHANGE

One feature of modern social life is the rapid level of social and economic change. These simple rules are equal to that challenge. The central problems of the legal system are two: how to keep people at peace with each other; and how to allow them to join together in common ventures that promise mutual gain. Most forms of innovation require cooperative efforts, for which we should retain the traditional common law rules of contract that developed long before the advent of the laser and the computer. The content of contracts between parties will change to reflect the nature of the joint ventures, the costs of doing business, and the opportunities spawned by new technology. But amid these variations, the basic principle of gain through trade is a social constant.

Yet the dark side of contract law remains. No matter how exciting the business opportunities, the barriers to successful commercial transactions exert their tenacious hold: duress, fraud, advantage-taking, opportunism, double dealing, as well as misunderstanding, mistake, and incapacity. Against these persistent risks a whole range of precautions must be taken today just as they were centuries ago, when Aristotle first wrote that mistake and coercion each nullified all forms of voluntary action—including exchange.[12] The law of contract is able keep up with the most rapid-fire innovations, as long as it remains uncluttered with restraints that hinder or scuttle important commercial transactions. For all its minor differences, and with a little refurbishing at the edges, we could do as well with the Roman law of contract as we do with any modern system dedicated to the principle of freedom of contract, as our system too often is not.

A more important challenge to this static conception of common law comes in the area of property rights, whose proper definition facilitates the system of beneficial exchanges. Traditionally, wealth was concentrated in tangible forms of property: land, buildings, and chattels. Intangible forms of wealth were far less important even a hundred years ago than they are today, and were of little consequence before the age of the printing press. Whatever kind words might be uttered about the ancient principles of contract law, any modern system of property law must make peace with copyrights, patents, trademarks, broadcast frequencies, overflight easements, and computer software programs, of which the nineteenth-century (and of course the medi-

328   Conclusion

eval or Roman) property laws were wholly innocent. To tie the law of property to physical things is to ignore the important technological innovations of modern times and thus to risk "freezing" into place an archaic system of property rights that could do palpable damage to the social order. If ever there was an area for social innovation in legal rules, surely it is the property rights spawned by new technology.

This case for recognizing new forms of property rights is so compelling that it seems foolhardy to mount a defense of a legal approach that downplays the claims of modernity. But this point, while valid as stated, is *not* an objection to the system of property rights outlined here, for it misses the flexibility built into this basic system through the sixth simple rule: taking under conditions of necessity with just compensation. Although on its face this principle appears to apply only in static and prosaic contexts, as when land is taken for a post office, properly understood the principle also extends to more dynamic contexts. The takings principle allows for basic alterations in the system of property rights as long as these shifts promise substantial net benefits for society at large. The point is so fundamental that it deserves some elaboration and illustration.

To start with theory, the basic conception of taking is broad indeed: *any* modification of the traditional system of property rights, whether by taxes, by regulation, or by modification of the liability rules that protect private property, should be understood as taking some element from the bundle of rights—possession, use, and disposition over some discrete physical resource—that normally characterize the ownership of private property.[13] If therefore the basic principle of property law had provided that "no private property should be taken without the consent of its owner," a legal system wedded to this strong and comprehensive definition of private property could be fairly charged with freezing novel resources into an inefficient and outmoded system of property rights.

But the caveat on just compensation, in opposition to unanimous consent, adds the needed measure of flexibility to rebut that charge while still providing protection against the time-honored forms of expropriation and confiscation that (in a system of old property or new) always eat away at the productive power of any society. To be sure, *any* deviation from the traditional rules of property still constitutes a (partial) taking. But it does not follow that any such taking is illegitimate, for it may be compensated, not in cash but, as noted earlier, in kind. The parallel restrictions uniformly imposed on other individuals, as in the case of negative reciprocal easements, may be worth more to the property owner than the diminution of his own property rights. Whenever general, across-the-board modifications in legal rules (the ubiquitous principle of proration!) promise large overall gains, these gains supply the needed compensation for sacrifice of the traditional rights. With these two factors in place, no one should tarry over the distributional niceties, for everyone (to the extent that human institutions can devise these things) will be better off if the change is made than if society remains wedded to its older ways.

A number of examples illustrate the capacity of the just compensation rules to facilitate the creation of new property rights to meet changing technological demands. During the rise of commercial aviation in the early part of this century, the question arose whether airplanes were allowed to fly over lands owned by others. The traditional conception of property in land held (at a time when it was convenient to recognize such broad claims) that property extended from the center of the earth to the outer edge of the heavens, wherever that might be, but in any event far beyond the region of effective ground control. Under this rule, any small number of landowners could bring the entire system of air transportation to a halt by imposing stiff fees for crossing their air space. That holdout right is valuable only if it is held by one person or very few people. If everyone has it, then no one will be able to fly at all, and so all hold-out possibilities would vanish. Here the coordination problems are enormous, the externality problems minimal. Bilateral transactions cannot put the upper air space to its best use.

Yet the eminent domain power can. Just give any landowner this all-or-nothing choice: no flights anywhere or free flights everywhere. Which would he choose, knowing that in practice he could collect nothing from a private sale of rights under the first regime because others can make the same demands? This is not a case where one person's land is taken for a railroad, for which cash compensation is necessary. With high-flying planes, the full set of benefits, both direct (for example, you can fly yourself) and indirect (for example, cheaper transportation for goods or visiting relatives), affords all the necessary compensation. As a first approximation, the huge allocative gains swamp any ostensible distributional concerns. But for those who (like the owners of land taken for the railroad) suffer great damage from the overflight or noise of low-flying planes, explicit compensation can be (and usually is) provided so that they can share in the social gains of the overall enterprise roughly in the same proportion as their fellows.[14] Once made into a common, the upper air space can be regulated by three-dimensional rules of the road patterned on the well-established rules for maritime and highway traffic. The system of takings with just compensation thus meets the demand for innovation without allowing the state simply to "redefine" rights when a majority thinks it appropriate. Parallel arguments can be made for denying all landowners the right to exclude broadcast signals from passing over their territory.

Similar arguments explain much of what happens in the case of copyrights and patents, where the limited protection afforded authors and inventors necessarily interferes with the ordinary common law rights of people to use their labor and tangible property as they see fit.[15] Before the copyright law was passed, I could have set my pen to my paper to reproduce and sell copies of a Shakespearean sonnet the day after its initial publication. After the law's passage, I am stripped of that right, but I receive compensation in two forms: the increased production of great literature and the protection of my own works of art from copying and sale by others. Yet the refusal to extend copyright protection to mathematical theorems means that people who build on material in the public domain contribute to it as well. With information the coordination problems can never be ignored: free exchange of information in scholarly endeavors is often worth more than any system of exclusive rights. Properly understood, the just compensation system accommodates these variations on the main theme. The sole task is to figure out how to *maximize* the value from the social transformation, say, by setting term limitations on use or by creating a privilege (on grounds of necessity) of fair comment in reviews or in other scholarly works. The same principle of analysis can extend to new forms of computer software or genetic engineering. The difficult problem is not that of the conceptual framework, but that of the magnitude of the relevant trade-offs between open access (the coordination problem again) and the incentive to produce (sapped by external use).

The older framework, then, is no impediment to a system of social innovation. Properly understood, it supports it. By constantly testing any proposed innovations against the taking and just compensation requirements, the legal system offers protection against those pure forms of expropriation, so common throughout history, which diminish the material social base on which social progress and the alleviation of poverty depend. But the just compensation test is not so malleable as to allow all mischievous forms of regulation of the older forms of property such as land: rent control and most zoning ordinances do not pass muster. These institutions are proposed when voluntary markets are most robust and coordination problems are negligible. Accordingly, they result in diminution in overall wealth. Social change may be complex, but the simple rules, properly applied, are able to accommodate it. This last line of attack against the system, then, is misplaced.

UNFINISHED BUSINESS

There is, finally, one charge against the case for simple rules to which I do plead guilty. In this book, I have for the most part focused on common law issues of freedom and liability, particularly the rules of property, of contract, and of tort. But there are many issues today that raise questions that go far beyond the legal issues discussed here. I have said nothing about the problems of health care delivery; nothing of the relationship between church and state; nothing of pornography and obscenity; nothing of education at all levels; nothing about infrastructure, nothing about the military, nothing about scientific research—nothing, in short, about many of the issues that dominate political discourse today.

That omission is deliberate. And about it I will offer, without any defense, only these concluding observations. Many of the difficulties that we have in those areas rest on the willingness to arrogate to the public sector functions that are better performed by the private sector. Education is surely one primary example of the proposition, yet the resistance to a voucher system remains powerful indeed. Health care is another, and the insistence that it is an affirmative right of citizenship apart from contract will lead to further deterioration of the system at greater expense. Where these matters are dealt with by government, scant attention is paid to the just compensation principles that have proved so important in private areas: instead, everything is always up for grabs. Finally, it is best to avoid the mistake of thinking that nothing can be solved unless everything is solved. At some point, it is necessary to proceed in smaller steps and to recognize that pressing reforms in some areas should not be postponed until the day when all problems can be solved at once. The domains which I have addressed are important and worthy of consideration in their own right. When they are properly administered, they should improve the overall social situation, and thereby make it possible to attack many of the social issues that I have carefully set to one side. I suspect that even in those areas these simple rules would work far better than most people suppose. But be this as it may, there are large and complex domains of human endeavor in which simple rules should far outperform their more complex rivals. For these domains, the hard question remains: do we have the courage to try simple solutions when complex ones have failed?

Notes

Index of Statutes

Index of Cases

General Index

Notes

Introduction

1. See David Margolick, "At the Bar," *New York Times,* July 9, 1993, B10.
2. For the 1993 breakdown, see "The Am Law 100," *The American Lawyer,* July-August 1994. Five firms on the list have profits of over $1,000,000 per partner, with Cravath, Swaine & Moore topping the list at $1,450,000 per partner. The others with per-partner profits of over a million dollars are (in order of per-partner profits): Wachtel, Lipton, Rosen & Katz ($1,350,000); Sullivan & Cromwell ($1,275,000); Cahill Gorden & Reindel ($1,210,000); Davis Polk & Wardwell ($1,020,000). All these are New York law firms. It is worth noting that for the other firms on the list number 50 is at $380,000 per partner. Twenty-four firms have per-partner profits of over $500,000, and the lowest firm on the list is at $160,000.
3. Stephen P. Magee, "The Optimum Number of Lawyers: A Reply to Epp," 17 *Law & Social Inquiry* 667, 675 (1992).
4. For all the numbers and more, see Sherwin Rosen, "The Market for Lawyers," 35 *J. Law & Econ.* 215 (1992). For a more popular account, see "America's Parasite Economy," *The Economist,* October 10, 1992, 21.
5. Marc Galanter & Thomas Palay, *Tournament of Laws: The Transformation of the Big Law Firm,* 37 (1992).
6. Jonathan Rauch, "Suckers!" *Reason Magazine,* May 1, 1994, 21.
7. Robert C. Clark, "Why So Many Lawyers? Are They Good or Bad?" 61 *Fordham L. Rev.* 275 (1992).
8. Ibid., 284.
9. John Markoff, "Cyberspace under Lock and Key," *New York Times,* February 13, 1994, §4, 3.

10. See below, Chapter 13.
11. See Tamar Lewin, "Low Pay and Closed Doors Greet Young in Job Market," *New York Times,* March 10, 1994, A1, col. 1, noting the rise in temporary jobs to 24.4 million.
12. Clark, "Why So Many Lawyers?" 288.
13. Lisa Bernstein, "Opting out of the Legal System: Extralegal Contractual Relations in the Diamond Industry," 22 *J. Legal Stud.* 115 (1992).
14. For those who dare to enter these waters, as I do not, see Joseph Isenbergh, *International Taxation: U.S. Taxation of Foreign Taxpayers and Foreign Income* (3 vols. and supp., 1990). The question of complexity is duly noted in ¶1.13 and amply confirmed thereafter.
15. Lani Guinier, *The Tyranny of the Majority* (1994).
16. See Stephen P. Magee, William A. Brock & Leslie Young, "The Invisible Foot and the Fate of Nations: Lawyers as Negative Externalities," in *Black Hole Tariffs and Endogenous Policy Theory: Political Economy in General Equilibrium* (Stephen P. Magee et al. eds., 1989).
17. Stephen P. Magee, letter to the *Wall Street Journal,* September 24, 1993.
18. See, e.g., Charles R. Epp, "Do Lawyers Impair Economic Growth?" 17 *Law & Social Inquiry* 585 (1992), and Frank B. Cross, "Law versus Economics?" id., 653.
19. Magee, "The Optimum Number of Lawyers," 667.
20. See Jude Wanniski, "Taxes, Revenues, and the 'Laffer Curve,'" *Public Interest,* Winter 1978, 3–16.
21. For an account of why family leave legislation is likely to prove to be yet another unwarranted interference with the employment contract, see James V. DeLong, "Crass Act: Why Family Leave Won't Work: Family and Medical Leave Act of 1993," *The New Republic,* April 19, 1993, 14.
22. See, e.g., Tamar Lewin, "Low Pay and Closed Doors Greet Young in Job Market."

1. The Virtues of Simplicity

1. Friedrich Hayek, *The Road to Serfdom* (1944).
2. Peter Schuck, "Legal Complexity: Some Causes, Consequences, and Cures," 42 *Duke L.J* 1, 3 (1992).
3. See, e.g., Cipollone v. Liggett Co., 112 S.Ct. 2608 (1992), on the preemptive effects of the federal cigarette labeling statutes on state tort actions against manufacturers. The case involved both package labels and warnings and materials used in advertising and promotion. At issue were causes of action for defective design, failure to warn of dangerous side effects, overpromotion, implied warranty, ordinary negligence, and strict

liability, many of which were first established only after the initial passage of the statute in 1965.

4. See John Chipman Gray, *The Rule against Perpetuities* (1st ed. 1886). The most famous short statement of the rule is found in W. Barton Leach, "Perpetuities in a Nutshell," 51 *Harv. L. Rev.* 638 (1939). The case that exonerated the hapless lawyer from charges of legal malpractice was Lucas v. Hamm, 364 P.2d 685 (1961), and it was wrongly decided. The limitation to the first child to pass the bar is bad because all living children of A may die tomorrow, and a new child born after the gift may not pass the bar until twenty-one years after the death of A, the only "life in being" that makes it valid. The gift to the descendants of Queen Elizabeth is good because all those persons must be identified within twenty-one years of the death of Prince Charles, himself a life in being for this bequest.

5. The proposals for reform are legion and complex, and repeal is rarely on the agenda. For one summary, see Jesse Dukeminier, "A Modern Guide to Perpetuities," 74 *Cal. L. Rev.* 1867 (1986).

6. See the Model Penal Code (official draft, 1962).

7. See Richard A. Epstein, "The Utilitarian Foundations of Natural Law," 12 *Harv. J. L. & Pub. Pol.* 713 (1989).

8. For the first systematic study of optimal deterrence, see Gary S. Becker, "Crime and Punishment: An Economic Approach," 76 *J. Pol. Econ.* 169 (1968). The presence of an upper bound of punishment is one reason for a law making criminal unsuccessful attempts: if the severity of punishment cannot be increased for the completed offense, then the reach of the law can be expanded under the general second-best approach. See Steven Shavell, "Deterrence and Punishment of Attempts," 19 *J. Legal Stud.* 435 (1990).

9. Guido Calabresi, *The Costs of Accidents: A Legal and Economic Analysis* (1970). Calabresi made this judgment subject to a constraint of justice, on which see the Conclusion below.

2. The Enemies of Simplicity

1. The rule is in fact one portion of the 1677 English Statute of Frauds that has been adopted in varying forms in all states.

2. See Califano v. Goldfarb, 430 U.S. 199 (1977) (striking down the dependency requirement for male dependents of female employees).

3. See Craig v. Boren, 429 U.S. 190 (1976) (striking down different drinking-age limits for men and women).

3. Autonomy and Property

1. John Locke, *Second Treatise of Government*, ch. 5, ¶27 (1690).

2. John Rawls, *A Theory of Justice*, 73, 179 (1971). His first principle of

justice requires universal respect for the equal liberty of all persons. The second requires that all deviations from that principle benefit the least well-off in society.

3. The Orlando Magic won twice in a row with long shots. It used the first to obtain Shaquille O'Neal, and the second to get Chris Webber, who was dealt to San Francisco for Anfernee Hardaway and a number of high draft choices. Clearly, the lottery is a high-stakes business. But never forget that Michael Jordan was drafted third by the Chicago Bulls in 1984.

4. See generally Robert C. Ellickson, "Property in Land," 102 *Yale L.J.* 1315 (1993).

5. See Harold Demsetz, "Toward a Theory of Property Rights," 57 *Am. Econ. Rev.* 347 (Pap. & Proc. 1967) for the seminal account.

6. Gaius, *Institutes,* bk. II, 42–44 (Roman law). Frederic W. Maitland, *The Forms of Action at Common Law,* 16–26 (A. H. Chaytor & W. J. Whittaker eds., 1936).

7. Mary Battiata, "Issue of Seized Property Divides Poles: Ex-Owners' Prospects Founder in Financial Straits of the New Rule," *Washington Post,* May 5, 1991, A35, noting that claims for individual restitution in kind were rejected in order to avoid litigation and to stimulate foreign investment. See also Robert G. Kaiser, "East Europe: The Moral Muddle after Marx," *Washington Post,* May 19, 1991, D1, allowing some claims, even against owners who have improved property at their own expense; Peter Maass, "Hungary's Compensation Promise Proves Hollow for Many Claimants: Government Offers Bonds as Partial Payment for Seized Property," *Washington Post,* October 26, 1991, A14, bewailing the small amounts of compensation for communist thefts.

8. Justinian, *Institutes,* bk. II, title 1. For an extended discussion of these themes, see Richard A. Epstein, "On the Optimal Mix of Common and Private Property," 11 *Soc. Phil. & Pol.* 17 (1994).

9. For a convenient summary, see 3 Restatement (Second) of Torts, ch. 41.

10. Carol M. Rose, "Energy and Efficiency in the Realignment of Common-Law Water Rights," 19 *J. Legal Stud.* 261 (1990).

4. Contract

1. See, e.g., Robert C. Ellickson, "Property in Land," 102 *Yale L.J.* 1315 (1993); Max Gluckman, *The Ideas in Barotse Jurisprudence,* 75–112 (1965); and 2 Frederick Pollock & Frederic W. Maitland, *A History of English Law,* ch. 1 (2d ed. 1898).

2. For the most powerful discussion of the historical and pattern theories of justification, see Robert Nozick, *Anarchy, State, and Utopia,* ch. 7 (1974).

3. The case is Alaska Packers' Ass'n v. Domenico, 117 F.99 (9th Cir. 1902). For discussion, see Douglas G. Baird, "Self-Interest and Cooperation in Long-Term Contracts," 19 *J. Legal Stud.* 583, 586 (1990).

4. Clayton Act, ch. 323, 38 Stat. 730, 29 U.S.C. §§52, 53 (1988).

5. Torts

1. See, e.g., the celebrated cases of Bird v. Holbrook, 130 Eng. Rep. 911 (C.P. 1825), and Katko v. Briney, 183 N.W. 2d 657 (Iowa 1971).

2. United States v. Carroll Towing, 159 F.2d 169 (2d Cir. 1947). For the major defenses of the negligence system, see William M. Landes & Richard A. Posner, *The Economic Structure of Tort Law* (1987), and Steven Shavell, *Economic Analysis of Accident Law* (1987). For my early defense of strict liability, see Richard A. Epstein, "A Theory of Strict Liability," 2 *J. Legal Stud.* 151 (1973).

3. See, e.g., Wassell v. Adams, 865 F.2d 849 (7th Cir. 1989) (Posner, J., upholding a 97-3 split against the plaintiff's anguished challenge).

4. See United States v. Reliable Transfer Co., Inc., 421 U.S. 397 (1975).

5. See, e.g., Jones v. Chidester, 610 A.2d 964 (Pa. 1992).

6. The *T. J. Hooper,* 60 F.2d 737 (2d Cir. 1932). The case involved the ostensible failure of the shipping industry to use ship-to-shore radios. But it seems clear that Hand misunderstood the nature of the customary practices. See Richard A. Epstein, "The Path to the *T. J Hooper*: The Theory and History of Custom in the Law of Tort," 21 *J. Legal Stud.* 1 (1992).

7. See Helling v. Carey, 519 P.2d 981 (Wash. 1974).

8. On workplace injuries generally, see Richard A. Epstein, "The Historical Origins and Economic Structure of Workers' Compensation Law," 16 *Ga. L. Rev.* 775 (1982).

9. See Keeble v. Hickeringill, 103 Eng. Rep. 1127 (K.B. 1707). "One schoolmaster sets up a new school to the damage of an antient school, and thereby the scholars are allured from the old school to come to his new. The action was held there not to lie. But suppose Mr. Hickeringill should lie in the way with his guns, and fright the boys from going to school, and there parents would not let them go thither; sure the schoolmaster might have an action for the loss of his scholars."

10. New York Times v. Sullivan, 376 U.S. 254 (1964).

6. Necessity, Coordination, and Just Compensation

1. See, e.g, Mouse's Case, 66 Eng. Rep. 1341 (K.B. 1609) (general average contribution for admiralty losses); Ploof v. Putnam, 71 A. 188 (Vt. 1908) (privilege to enter in cases of necessity); and Vincent v. Lake Erie Trans-

portation Co., 124 N.W. 221 (Minn. 1910) (obligation to compensate for harm caused).

2. See Milton Friedman & George J. Stigler, "Roofs or Ceilings? The Current Housing Problem," 1 *Essays on Current Problems,* September 1946, reprinted in *Rent Control: Myths and Realities,* 87 (Walter Block & Edgar Olsen eds., 1981).

3. I thank David Lucas, who lived through Hurricane Hugo, for this example.

4. For the classical exposition, see Justinian, *Institutes,* bk. II, title 1, 25–36. The names have been carried over into the English law because the problems and the possible solutions are pretty much the same.

5. For the best account of this subject, see Lloyd Cohen, "Marriage, Divorce, and Quasi Rents: Or, 'I Gave Him the Best Years of My Life,'" 16 *J. Legal Stud.* 267 (1987).

6. For discussion, see Daniel Friedmann, "The Efficient Breach Fallacy," 18 *J. Legal Stud.* 1 (1989).

7. For the classic treatment, see Lon L. Fuller & William R. Perdue, Jr., "The Reliance Interest in Contract Damages," 46 *Yale L.J.* 52 (1936).

8. Guido Calabresi & A. Douglas Melamed, "Property Rules, Liability Rules, and Inalienability: One View of the Cathedral," 85 *Harv. L. Rev.* 1089 (1972). Their use of the term "property rule" should not be confused with a rule of acquisition.

9. Madison v. Tennessee Copper Co., 83 S.W. 658, 666 (Tenn. 1904).

10. See Fred S. McChesney, "Rent Extraction and Interest-Group Organization in a Cosean Model of Regulation," 20 *J. Legal Stud.* 73 (1991).

11. See Mitchel v. Reynolds, 24 Eng. Rep. 347 (K.B. 1711); Nordenfelt v. Maxim Nordenfelt Guns and Ammunition Co., [1894] A.C. 535; and William L. Letwin, "The English Common Law concerning Monopolies," 21 *U. Chi. L. Rev.* 355 (1955).

12. For a more complete account, see Robert H. Bork, *The Antitrust Paradox* (1977).

13. See the Hart-Scott-Radino Antitrust Improvement Act of 1976, Pub. L. No. 94–435, 90 Stat. 1394, 15 U.S.C. §18a (1976).

14. See, e.g., James Bovard, *The Fair Trade Fraud* (1991).

7. Take and Pay

1. Pennsylvania Coal Co. v. Mahon, 260 U.S. 393 (1922).

2. Lucas v. South Carolina Coastal Council, 112 S.Ct. 2886 (1992).

3. See the South Carolina Code, §48-39-290(B), with its incredibly detailed lists of conditions and exceptions.

4. I have defended this position at length in Richard A. Epstein, *Takings: Private Property and the Power of Eminent Domain* (1985).
5. Ernst Freund, *The Police Power, Public Policy, and Constitutional Rights* (1904).
6. See Penn Central Transportation Co. v. City of New York, 438 U.S. 104 (1978).
7. See Richard A. Epstein, *Bargaining with the State* (1993).
8. For some precautions against abuse, see Marvin Olasky, *The Tragedy of American Compassion* (1992).
9. See Richard B. McKenzie, *The Great American Job Machine* (1988).
10. See San Jose v. Pennell, 485 U.S. 1 (1988).

8. Contracting for Labor

1. For my defense, see Richard A. Epstein, "In Defense of the Contract at Will," 51 *U. Chi. L. Rev.* 947 (1984); for a comprehensive review of the literature, urging some intervention, see Paul C. Weiler, *Governing the Workplace: The Future of Labor and Employment Law* 49–103 (1990).
2. For my attack on collective bargaining, see Richard A. Epstein, "A Common Law for Labor Relations: A Critique of the New Deal Labor Legislation," 92 *Yale L.J.* 1357 (1983); for a response see Weiler, *Governing the Workplace*, 105–133.
3. National Labor Relations Act, 5, ch. 372, 49 Stat. 449, ch. 120, 61 Stat. 136, 29 U.S.C. §141 et seq. (1988). See also Labor Management Relations (Taft-Hartley) Act, ch. 120, 61 Stat. 136, 29 U.S.C. §141 et seq. (1988). For the origins of the permanent replacements rule, see National Labor Relations Board v. Mackay Radio & Telegraph Co., 304 U.S. 333 (1938). All current efforts to overthrow this rule have been beaten back in Congress.
4. Railway Labor Act, ch. 347, Title I, 44 Stat. 577, 29 U.S.C. §151 et seq. (1988). See, for a discussion, Katherine van Wezel Stone, "Labor Relations on the Airlines: The Railway Labor Act in the Era of Deregulation," 42 *Stan. L. Rev.* 1485 (1990).
5. For an exhaustive analysis of the difficulties of finding suitable decision rules within the bargaining framework, see Mayer Freed, Daniel Polsby & Matthew Spitzer, "Unions, Fairness, and the Conundrums of Collective Choice," 56 *S. Cal. L. Rev.* 462 (1982).
6. On the history, see David E. Bernstein, "Roots of the 'Underclass': The Decline of Laissez-Faire and the Rise of Racist Labor Regulation" (manuscript on file with the author, 1993). See also Steele v. Louisville & Nashville RR Co., 323 U.S. 192 (1944).

7. See Adair v. United States, 208 U.S. 161 (1908), and Coppage v. Kansas, 236 U.S. 1 (1915).

8. See, e.g., the unsatisfactory situation in Shaw v. Reno, 113 S.Ct. 2816 (1993).

9. See Hitchman Coal & Coke Co. v. Mitchell, 245 U.S. 229 (1917). *Hitchman* was rejected under the RLA, the Norris-LaGuardia Act of 1932, 47 Stat. 70, 29 U.S.C. §102 et seq. (1988), and the NLRA. The Norris-LaGuardia Act limited the power of the federal courts to issue injunctions in labor disputes; the RLA and NLRA make it an "unfair labor practice" to discriminate against workers because of their membership in unions or their participation in union activities.

9. Employment Discrimination and Comparable Worth

1. I have made the case more extensively in Richard A. Epstein, *Forbidden Grounds: The Case against Employment Discrimination Laws* (1992); for criticism, see John J. Donohue III, "Advocacy versus Analysis in Assessing Employment Discrimination Law," 44 *Stan. L. Rev.* 1583 (1992), containing data on the frequency and severity of discrimination suits.

2. For the federal figures, see Equal Employment Opportunity Commission (EEOC), Annual Report of 1989. About forty thousand of these claims are brought under Title VII, and about eleven thousand are brought under the age discrimination statutes. The Americans with Disabilities Act was not passed until 1990 and is not reflected in these figures.

3. McDonnell Douglas v. Green, 411 U.S. 792 (1973), is the first of many iterations of the problem.

4. See Griggs v. Duke Power Co., 401 U.S. 424 (1971). While *Griggs* was something of a thunderbolt on the legal horizon when it first hit, it has now, more or less, been codified in the 1991 Civil Rights Act.

5. John S. Heywood & James H. Peoples, "Deregulation and the Prevalence of Black Truck Drivers," 37 *J. Law & Econ.* 133 (1994). The seminal analysis of discrimination in competitive markets is still Gary S. Becker, *The Economics of Discrimination* (2d ed. 1971).

6. William Cohen, "Negro Involuntary Servitude in the South, 1865–1940: A Preliminary Analysis," in *American Law and the Constitutional Order,* 317 (Lawrence M. Friedman & Harry N. Scheiber eds., 1988).

7. See United Steelworkers of America v. Weber, 443 U.S. 193 (1979).

8. See City of Los Angeles, Department of Water and Power v. Manhart, 435 U.S. 702 (1978) (equal annual pensions for men and women regardless of life expectancy); and the Pregnancy Discrimination Act of 1978, Pub. L. No. 95-555, 92 Stat. 2076, 42 U.S.C. §2000e(k) (1988).

9. Epstein, *Forbidden Grounds,* 488–493.

10. Americans with Disabilities Act, Pub. L. No. 101-336, 104 Stat. 328, 42 U.S.C. §12101 et seq. (1988).

11. For a summary of the empirical evidence, see James J. Heckman & H. Hoult Verkerke, "Racial Disparity and Employment Discrimination: An Economic Perspective," 8 *Yale L. & Pol. Rev.* 276 (1990).

12. For the best criticisms of the proposed laws, see Ellen Frankel Paul, *Equity and Gender: The Comparable Worth Debate* (1989), and Paul Weiler, "The Wages of Sex: The Uses and Limits of Comparable Worth," 99 *Harv. L. Rev.* 1728 (1986).

13. Fair Labor Standards Act of 1938, Pub. L. No. 75-718, 52 Stat. 1060, 29 U.S.C. §201 et seq. (1988).

14. Victor R. Fuchs, *Women's Quest for Economic Equality* (1988).

10. Professional Liability for Financial Loss

1. Ultramares Corporation v. Touche, 174 N.E. 441 (N.Y. 1931).

2. Id. at 448.

3. Hedley, Byrne & Co. Ltd. v. Heller & Partners Ltd., [1964] App. Cas. 465 (H.L.E. 1963).

4. For a parallel argument, see Victor Goldberg, "Accountable Accountants: Is Third-Party Liability Necessary?" 17 *J. Legal Stud.* 295 (1988).

5. Donoghue v. Stevenson, [1932] App. Cas. 562, 580 (H.L. Scot. 1932).

6. Id. at 599.

7. See, e.g., Bily v. Arthur Young & Co., 834 P.2d 745 (Cal. 1992).

11. The Origins of Product Liability Law

1. For a general account, see W. Kip Viscusi, *Reforming Products Liability,* ch. 2 (1991). See George Priest, "Products Liability Law and the Accident Rate," in *Liability: Perspectives and Policy,* 184 (Robert E. Litan & Clifford Winston eds., 1988), for a more complete analysis of the figures excerpted here.

2. National Traffic and Motor Vehicle Safety Act of 1966, Pub. L. No. 89-563, 80 Stat. 718, 15 U.S.C. §1381 et seq. (1988).

3. See Larson v. General Motors, 391 F.2d 495 (8th Cir. 1968), a decision now uniformly followed in all states.

4. These figures come from the federal government's *Accident and Death Rates for Motor Vehicles, 1915–1988.* Death rates are customarily used because they are far more reliable than collision or injury data.

5. See Deborah Hensler, *Summary of Research Results on the Tort Liability System,* 10 (1986), and Paul Weiler, *Medical Malpractice on Trial* (1991).

6. See James A. Henderson, Jr. & Theodore Eisenberg, "The Quiet Revolu-

tion in Product Liability Law: An Empirical Study of Legal Change," 37 *U.C.L.A. L. Rev.* 479 (1990). The trends reported there held firm over the next three years.

7. For general histories, see Richard A. Epstein, *Modern Product Liability Law,* chs. 1–6 (1980), and George Priest, "The Invention of Enterprise Liability: A Critical History of the Intellectual Foundations of Modern Tort Law," 14 *J. Legal Stud.* 461 (1985).
8. Langridge v. Levy, 150 Eng. Rep. 863 (Ex. 1837).
9. Winterbottom v. Wright, 152 Eng. Rep. 402 (Ex. 1842).
10. Thomas v. Winchester, 6 N.Y. 397 (1852).
11. Devlin v. Smith, 89 N.Y. 470 (1882).
12. Statler v. George A. Ray Manufacturing Co., 88 N.E. 1063 (N.Y. 1909).
13. See Huset v. J. I. Case Threshing Machine Co., 120 F. 865 (8th Cir. 1903).
14. MacPherson v. Buick Motor Co., 111 N.E.2d 1050 (N.Y. 1916).
15. Escola v. Coca-Cola Bottling Co. of Fresno, 150 P.2d 436 (Cal. 1944).
16. Campo v. Scofield, 95 N.E.2d 802, 804 (N.Y. 1951).

12. The Contemporary Product Liability Scene

1. See George L. Priest, "The Invention of Enterprise Liability: A Critical History of the Intellectual Foundations of Modern Tort Law," 14 *J. Legal Stud.* 461 (1985), reviewing the contributions of Fleming James and Fritz Kessler.
2. See Greenman v. Yuba Power Products Co., Inc., 377 P.2d 897 (Cal. 1963), where the decision was written by Justice Traynor as the opinion of the court.
3. Richard W. Stevenson, "Lloyd's Offers Investors $1.3 Billion to Settle," *New York Times,* December 8, 1993, D5.
4. See Henningsen v. Bloomfield Motors, Inc., 161 A.2d 69 (N.J. 1960). The modern law usually allows disclaimers for economic losses, which are said to be the proper subject for contract warranties. See East River Steamship Corp. v. Transamerica Delaval, 476 U.S. 858 (1986).
5. American Law Institute (hereafter ALI), "Restatement of the Law," *Torts: Product Liability,* §8, 109 (1994).
6. Ibid., 110.
7. Collins v. Uniroyal, Inc., 315 A.2d 16 (N.J. 1974), cited with approval in the ALI *Torts: Product Liability,* 228.
8. Restatement (Second) of Torts, §402A, comment *k.* For the same view, see also ALI, *Torts: Product Liability,* §4, 57–59.
9. See, e.g., Micallef v. Miehle Co., 348 N.E.2d 571 (N.Y. 1976), overruling

Campo v. Scofield 95 N.E.2d 802 (N.Y. 1951). *Micallef* is approved in ALI, *Torts: Product Liability*, §2, illustration 3 (1994), 24.

10. See, e.g., Davis v. Wyeth Laboratories, 399 F.2d 121 (9th Cir. 1968) (Sabin vaccine), and Unthank v. United States, 732 F.2d 1517 (10th. Cir. 1984) (swine flu).

11. MacDonald v. Ortho Pharmaceutical Corp., 475 N.E.2d 65 (Mass. 1985).

12. ALI, *Torts: Product Liability*, §4, comment *b*, 62.

13. Ferebee v. Chevron Chemical Co., Inc., 736 F.2d 1529 (D.C. 1984) (allowing the state law damage action). The case contains its own Catch-22. The decedent was an agricultural worker at a government research center. The plaintiffs claimed that his pulmonary fibrosis was caused by the long-term exposure of his skin to the toxic herbicide paraquat, distributed only by the defendant. They argued that the official label did not warn of this risk. The company defended on the ground that the paraquat did not cause the fibrosis. If it is right on that question, as seems likely, then its warning has to be adequate, for there is no duty to warn of hazards that a product does not cause. On the preemption question, *Ferebee* held that it was possible to keep a distributor between a rock and a hard place: "Chevron can comply with both federal and state law by continuing to use the EPA-approved label and by simultaneously paying damages to successful tort plaintiffs such as Mr. Ferebee." Id at 1541. The decision has been uniformly rejected in recent years. See, e.g., King v. E. I. DuPont DeNemours, 996 F.2d 1346 (1st Cir. 1993).

14. See W. Kip Viscusi, *Smoking: Making the Risky Decision* (1992).

15. Cipollone v. Liggett Group, 112 S.Ct. 2608 (1992) (on which I worked as a consultant for Philip Morris).

16. National Childhood Vaccine Injury Act of 1986, Pub. L. No. 99-660, 100 Stat. 3743, §301 et seq., 42 U.S.C. §262, 300aa-1 et seq. (1988).

17. Enforcement of claims under the statute has been complex. The original funding provided for $80 million to fund claims prior to October 1988, a sum that has proved inadequate to meet the approved claims. For claims arising from vaccinations between October 1988 and October 1992, a $5 tax per dosage was used to build up the fund until it held some $600 million in February 1993. As of the end of September 1992, some 4,400 petitions had been filed, mostly for pre-1988 claims. Of those, the government has turned down 541 and accepted 502, for which $250 million has been paid. As of this writing, the original program has not been renewed: no taxes are being collected, and claims after February 1993 cannot be compensated out of existing funds. The tort status of post–September 1992 claims is not yet clarified.

18. For a powerful account of the case, see Walter Olson, "The Most Dangerous Vehicle on the Road," *Wall Street Journal,* February 9, 1993, A14.

19. Gary T. Schwartz, "The Myth of the Ford Pinto Case," 43 *Rutgers L. Rev.* 1013 (1991).

20. See, e.g., Motor Vehicle Manufacturers Ass'n v. State Farm Mutual Automobile Insurance Co., 463 U.S. 29 (1983)—only one of three independent appeals in the prolonged challenge to the airbag regulations.

21. See Wood v. General Motors Corp., 865 F.2d 395 (1st Cir. 1988).

22. John Wade, "On the Nature of Strict Tort Liability for Products," 44 *Miss. L.J.* 825 (1973). For judicial adoption, see, e.g., O'Brien v. Muskin, 463 A.2d 298 (N.J. 1983).

13. The Internal Life of the Corporation

1. For an extensive debate over this proposition, see "Symposium: Contractual Freedom in Corporate Law," 89 *Colum. L. Rev.* 395 (1989).

2. Frank H. Easterbrook & Daniel R. Fischel, *The Economic Structure of Corporate Law,* ch. 1 (1991).

3. Similar problems arise with questions of official immunity for government employees. For the old absolute immunity rule, see Barr v. Matteo, 360 U.S. 564 (1959); for the difficulties of a limited exception to the basic rule, see Harlow v. Fitzgerald, 457 U.S. 800 (1982).

4. See Dennis Carlton & Daniel R. Fischel, "The Regulation of Insider Trading," 35 *Stan. L. Rev.* 857 (1983); Frank H. Easterbrook, "Insider Trading as an Agency Problem," in *Principals and Agents: The Structure of Business,* 81 (John W. Pratt & Richard J. Zeckhauser eds., 1985); and Henry G. Manne, *Insider Trading and the Stock Market* (1966).

5. See Victor Brudney & Marvin A. Chirelstein, "A Restatement of Corporate Freezeouts," 87 *Yale L.J.* 1354 (1978), and Easterbrook & Fischel, *The Economic Structure of Corporate Law,* ch. 6, emphasizing the *ex ante* effects of *ex post* remedies.

6. The literature on takeover bids is enormous. See Easterbrook & Fischel, *The Economic Structure of Corporate Law,* ch. 7 (for passivity); Lucian Ayre Bebchuk, "Toward Undistorted Choice and Equal Treatment in Corporate Takeovers," 98 *Harv. L. Rev.* 1695 (1985) (favoring auctions); David D. Haddock, Jonathan R. Macey & Fred S. McChesney, "Property Rights in Assets and Resistance to Tender Offers," 73 *Va. L. Rev.* 701 (1987) (for management resistance); and Alan Schwartz, "The Fairness of Tender Offers in Utilitarian Theory," 17 *J. Legal Stud.* 165 (1988) (for passivity).

7. Lloyd R. Cohen, "Why Tender Offers? The Efficient Market Hypothesis, the Supply of Stock, and Signaling," 19 *J. Legal Stud.* 113 (1990).

8. Easterbrook & Fischel, *The Economic Structure of Corporate Law*, 194–195.

9. Since these matters were typically not regulated by contract in the 1980s, questions of their legality surfaced, on which see Michael Bradley & Michael Rosenzweig, "Defensive Stock Repurchases," 99 *Harv. L. Rev.* 1377 (1986).

10. Williams Act, Pub. L. No. 90-439, 82 Stat. 454, 15 U.S.C. §§78m, 78n (1988).

11. See, e.g., Pa. Cons. Stat. Ann. 515(a) (1992).

14. The Corporation and the World

1. For the classic criticism of the doctrine, see Oliver Wendell Holmes, Jr., "Agency," 4 *Harv. L. Rev.* 345 (1891) and 5 *Harv. L. Rev.* 1 (1891); Thomas Baty, *Vicarious Liability* (1916); and Young B. Smith, "Frolic & Detour," 23 *Colum. L. Rev.* 44 (1923). The best modern treatment of the subject is by Alan O. Sykes; see "The Economics of Vicarious Liability," 93 *Yale L.J.* 1231 (1984), and "The Boundaries of Vicarious Liability: An Economic Analysis of the Scope of Employment Rule and Related Legal Doctrines," 101 *Harv. L. Rev.* 563 (1988).

2. For the case urging repeal of limited liability, see Henry Hansmann & Reinier Kraakman, "Toward Unlimited Shareholder Liability for Corporate Torts," 100 *Yale L.J.* 1879 (1991).

3. For evidence, see Steven N. Wiggins & Al H. Ringleb, "Adverse Selection and Long Term Hazards: The Choice between Contract and Mandatory Liability Rules," 21 *J. Legal Stud.* 189 (1992).

4. Price-Anderson Act, Pub. L. No. 85-256, 71 Stat. 576, 42 U.S.C. §2210 (1988). The statute was upheld against constitutional challenge in Duke Power Co. v. Carolina Environmental Study Group, Inc., 438 U.S. 59 (1978).

5. See Austin v. Michigan Chamber of Commerce, 494 U.S. 652 (1990).

15. Environmental Protection and Private Property

1. For a good exposé, see *Environmental Politics: Public Costs, Private Rewards* (Michael S. Greve & Fred L. Smith, Jr., eds., 1992).

2. On this point the fount of all wisdom is still Ronald H. Coase, "The Problem of Social Cost," 3 *J. Law & Econ.* 1 (1960).

3. For a more systematic statement, see Richard A. Epstein, "Nuisance Law: Corrective Justice and Its Utilitarian Constraints," 8 *J. Legal Stud.* 49 (1979).

4. See Bruce Ackerman & Richard Stewart, "Reforming Environmental Law," 37 *Stan. L. Rev.* 1333 (1985).
5. Robert W. Hahn & Robert N. Stavins, "Incentive-Based Environmental Regulation: A New Era from an Old Idea," 18 *Ecology L.Q.* 6 (1991).
6. On emissions trading generally, see Robert W. Hahn & Gordon L. Hester, "Where Did All the Markets Go? An Analysis of the EPA's Emissions Trading Program," 6 *Yale J. on Reg.* 109 (1989), noting how difficult it is for these markets to emerge given EPA restraints on trade.
7. The material in this paragraph is drawn from David Riggs, Les Sease & Bruce Yandle, "Pollution Trading, Watershed Association, and Firm Governance" (manuscript on file with the author).
8. See Clean Air Amendment Act (hereafter CAAA) of 1990, Pub. L. No. 101–549, 104 Stat. 2399 (1990), codified as amended at 42 U.S.C. §§7401 et. seq.; for tailpipes, see 42 U.S.C. 7521; for fuels, see 42 U.S.C. 7545(k).
9. CAAA, §182(d)(1)(B).
10. P.A. 87–1275, 625 Ill. Con. Stat., Act 32.
11. David Ibata, "State Business Groups Urge Lawmakers to Fight Commute Rules in Clean-Air Law," *Chicago Tribune,* January 12, 1994, §2, 6, and David Ibata, "'Model' Smog-Busting Plan Flops: Local Firms Buck U.S. Law as Clear Air Deadline Nears," *Chicago Tribune,* January 7, 1994, §1, 1.
12. Alex Taylor III, "Why Electric Cars Make No Sense," *Fortune,* July 26, 1993, 126.
13. For discussion, see Hodel v. Virginia Surface Mining & Reclamation Ass'n, Inc., 452 U.S. 264 (1981), upholding against a takings challenge the Surface Mining Control and Reclamation Act of 1977.
14. See Just v. Marinette County, 201 N.W.2d 761 (Wis. 1972).
15. K & K Construction, Inc., v. Michigan Department of Natural Resources, File No. 88-12120-CM (November 11, 1992).
16. See, e.g., Ciampitti v. United States, 22 Cl. Ct. 310 (1991) (uplands and wetlands in a single parcel); Jentgen v. United States, 657 F.2d 1210 (Ct. Cl. 1981) (same); Loveladies Harbor, Inc. v. United States, 15 Ct. Cl. 381 (1988) (sale of a portion of a parcel with some wetlands).
17. Bruce Yandle, "The Assault on Property Rights: Which Way Out?" (speech delivered to the American Farm Bureau Association, based on information supplied by Margaret Ann Riegle, Chairman, Fairness to Land Owners Committee).
18. Endangered Species Act of 1973, Pub. L. No. 93-205, 87 Stat. 884, codified as amended at 16 U.S.C. §§1531–1544.
19. Christy v. Hodel, 857 F.2d 1324 (9th Cir. 1988), criticized in "Note: The

Endangered Species Act and Ursine Usurpations: A Grizzly Tale of Two Takings," 58 *U. Chi. L. Rev.* 1101 (1991).

20. See Mike Vivoli, "Putting People Last," *CEI UpDate,* November 1992, 13.

21. See Terry L. Anderson & Douglas R. Leal, *Free Market Environmentalism,* 90-94 (1991).

22. For the interest group politics, see Mark K. Landy & Mary Hague, "The Coalition for Waste: Private Interests and Superfund," in *Environmental Politics.*

23. Casey Buckro, "EPA Out to Clean Up 'Ridiculous' Situation," *Chicago Tribune,* April 11, 1994, §4, 1, 2. The story features a suit about the cleanup of a site in Kalamazoo, Michigan, in which 741 parties were joined as potential defendants. The EPA practice is to sue major corporations and allow them the unpleasant task of bringing in smaller third parties.

24. For the classic exposition, see Bruce A. Ackerman & W. T. Hassler, *Clean Coal/Dirty Air, or How the Clean-Air Act Became a Multibillion-Dollar Bailout for High Sulfur Coal Producers and What Should Be Done about It* (1981).

25. See Terry L. Anderson & Donald R. Leal, *Free Market Environmentalism,* 155–159 (1991), for a summary of the evidence, including the extensive report by the National Acid Precipitation Assessment Program.

26. On the differences between takings by and bargaining with government, see Richard A. Epstein, *Bargaining with the State* (1993).

27. See Donald R. Leal, "Unlocking the Logjam over Jobs and Endangered Animals," *San Diego Union-Tribune,* April 18, 1993, G-4.

28. Lyng v. Northwest Indian Cemetery Protective Association, 485 U.S. 439 (1988).

29. For an account of the evolution of the doctrine, see Lloyd Cohen, "The Public Trust Doctrine: An Economic Perspective," 29 *Cal. W. L. Rev.* 239 (1992).

Conclusion

1. David Hume, *A Treatise of Human Nature,* bk. III, §6 (L. A. Selby-Bigge ed., 1888).

2. See Jon Elster, *Ulysses and the Sirens: Studies in Rationality and Irrationality* (1979); Cass R. Sunstein, *The Partial Constitution,* ch. 6 (1993); and Cass R. Sunstein, "Endogenous Preferences and Environmental Law," 22 *J. Legal Stud.* 217 (1993).

3. David Binder with Barbara Crosette, "As Ethnic Wars Multiply, U.S. Strives for Policy," *New York Times,* February 7, 1993, §1, 1.

4. W. D. Hamilton, "The Genetical Evolution of Social Behavior," 7 *J. Theoretical Biology* 1 (1964).

5. Both halves of the definition are found in the earliest sources. See, e.g., Justinian's *Institutes,* bk. I, title 2, 1: "those rules prescribed by natural reason for all men are observed by all peoples alike, and are called the law of nations."

   Again, Justinian's *Institutes,* bk. I, title 2, 11: "But the laws of nature, which are observed by all nations alike, are established, as it were, by divine providence, and remain ever fixed and immutable; but the municipal laws of each individual state are subject to frequent change, either by the tacit consent of the people, or by the subsequent enactment of another statute." The theme carries over to more modern times.

6. Ronald Dworkin, *Taking Rights Seriously,* 255 (1978).

7. For the earlier view, see Price v. Easton, 110 Eng. Rep. 518 (K.B. 1833).

8. Stephen Holmes, *The Anatomy of Antiliberalism* (1993).

9. For one of the most thoughtful statements of this kind, see Mary Ann Glendon, *Rights Talk: The Impoverishment of Political Discourse* (1991).

10. See Poletown v. City of Detroit, 304 N.W.2d 455 (Mich. 1981).

11. 1 William Blackstone, *Commentaries on the Laws of England* *135 (1765). "But how does it [the legislature] interpose and compel? Not by absolutely stripping the subject of his property in an arbitrary manner; but by giving him a full indemnification and equivalent for the injury thereby sustained." This injury is far greater than the value of the property taken, for it includes loss of good will and the costs of relocation.

12. Aristotle, *The Nicomachean Ethics,* bk. III, ch. 1 (R. McKean ed., 1941).

13. For a defense of this comprehensive view of ownership, see Richard A. Epstein, *Takings: Private Property and the Power of Eminent Domain,* 57–62 (1985).

14. See, e.g., United States v. Causby, 328 U.S. 256 (1946).

15. William M. Landes & Richard A. Posner, "An Economic Analysis of Copyright Law," 18 *J. Legal Stud.* 325 (1989).

Index of Statutes

Americans with Disabilities Act, Pub. L. No. 101–336, 104 Stat. 328, 42 U.S.C. §12101 et seq. (1988), 183

Clean Air Amendment Act of 1990, Pub. L. No. 101–549, 104 Stat. 2399 (1990), codified as amended at 42 U.S.C. §7401 et seq.

Endangered Species Act of 1973, Pub. L. No. 93–205, 87 Stat. 884, codified as amended at 16 U.S.C. §§1531–1544, 292

Fair Labor Standards Act of 1938, Pub. L. No. 75–718, 52 Stat. 1060, 29 U.S.C. §201 et seq. (1988), 188

Hart-Scott-Radino Antitrust Improvement Act of 1976, Pub. L. No. 94–435, 90 Stat. 1394, 15 U.S.C. §18a (1976), 126

Labor Management Relations (Taft-Hartley) Act, ch. 120, 61 Stat. 136, 29 U.S.C. §141 et seq. (1988), 165

National Childhood Vaccine Injury Act of 1986, Pub. L. No. 99–660, 100 Stat. 3743, §301 et seq., 42 U.S.C. §262, 300aa-1 et seq. (1988), 235

National Labor Relations Act, 5, ch. 372, 49 Stat. 449, ch. 120, 61 Stat. 136, 29 U.S.C. §141 et seq. (1988), 165

National Traffic and Motor Vehicle Safety Act of 1966, Pub. L. No. 89–563, 80 Stat. 718, 15 U.S.C. §1381 et seq. (1988), 212

Norris-LaGuardia Act of 1932, 47 Stat. 70, 29 U.S.C. §102 et seq. (1988), 168

Pregnancy Discrimination Act of 1978, Pub. L. No. 95–555, 92 Stat. 2076, 42 U.S.C. §2000e(k) (1988), 183

Price-Anderson Act, Pub. L. No. 85–256, 71 Stat. 576, 42 U.S.C. §2210 (1988), 272

Railway Labor Act, ch. 347, Title I, 44 Stat. 577, 29 U.S.C. §151 et seq. (1988), 165

Williams Act, Pub. L. No. 90–439, 82 Stat. 454, 15 U.S.C. §§78m, 78n (1988), 261

Index of Cases

Henningsen v. Bloomfield Motors, Inc., 161 A.2d 69 (N.J. 1960), 227

Hitchman Coal & Coke Co. v. Mitchell, 245 U.S. 229 (1917), 168

Hodel v. Virginia Surface Mining & Reclamation Ass'n, Inc., 452 U.S. 264 (1981), 288

Huset v. J. I. Case Threshing Machine Co., 120 F. 865 (8th Cir. 1903), 219

Jentgen v. United States, 657 F.2d 1210 (Ct. Cl. 1981), 290

Jones v. Chidester, 610 A.2d 964 (Pa. 1992), 102

Just v. Marinette County, 201 N.W.2d 761 (Wis. 1972), 289

K & K Construction, Inc., v. Michigan Department of Natural Resources, File No. 88-12120-CM (November 11, 1992), 290

Katko v. Briney, 183 N.W. 2d 657 (Iowa 1971), 92

Keeble v. Hickeringill, 103 Eng. Rep. 1127 (K.B. 1707), 107

Langridge v. Levy, 150 Eng. Rep. 863 (Ex. 1837), 217

Larson v. General Motors, 391 F.2d 495 (8th Cir. 1968), 212

Loveladies Harbor, Inc. v. United States, 15 Ct. Cl. 381 (1988), 290

Lucas v. Hamm, 364 P.2d 685 (1961), 26

Lucas v. South Carolina Coastal Council, 112 S.Ct. 2886 (1992), 130

Lyng v. Northwest Indian Cemetery Protective Association, 485 U.S. 439 (1988), 303

MacDonald v. Ortho Pharmaceutical Corp., 475 N.E.2d 65 (Mass. 1985), 232

MacPherson v. Buick Motor Co., 111 N.E.2d 1050 (N.Y. 1916), 219

Madison v. Tennessee Copper Co., 83 S.W. 685 (Tenn. 1904), 122

McDonnell Douglas v. Green, 411 U.S. 792 (1973), 174

Micallef v. Miehle Co., 348 N.E.2d 571 (N.Y. 1976), 230

Mitchel v. Reynolds, 24 Eng. Rep. 347 (K.B. 1711), 125

Mouse's Case, 66 Eng. Rep. 1341 (K.B. 1609), 113

National Labor Relations Board v. Mackay Radio & Telegraph Co., 304 U.S. 333 (1938), 165

New York Times v. Sullivan, 376 U.S. 254 (1964), 108

Nordenfelt v. Maxim Nordenfelt Guns and Ammunition Co., [1894] A.C. 535; 125

Pennsylvania Coal Co. v. Mahon, 260 U.S. 393 (1922), 130

Ploof v. Putnam, 71 A. 188 (Vt. 1908), 113

Poletown v. City of Detroit, 304 N.W.2d 455 (Mich. 1981), 323

Price v. Easton, 110 Eng. Rep. 518 (K.B. 1833), 318

Shaw v. Reno, 113 S.Ct. 2816 (1993), 167

Statler v. George A. Ray Manufacturing Co., 88 N.E. 1063 (N.Y. 1909), 219

Steele v. Louisville & Nashville RR Co., 323 U.S. 192 (1944), 167

The *T.J. Hooper,* 60 F.2d 737 (2d Cir. 1932), 103

Thomas v. Winchester, 6 N.Y. 397 (1852), 218

Ultramares Corporation v. Touche, 174 N.E. 441 (N.Y. 1931), 194, 195

United States v. Carroll Towing, 159 F.2d 169 (2d Cir. 1947), 94

United States v. Causby, 328 U.S. 256 (1946), 330

United States v. Reliable Transfer Co., Inc., 421 U.S. 397 (1975), 100

General Index

Holocaust, 316–317
Hume, David, 308

Impersonal transactions, 48, 73–76
Incentives, 31–36; antitrust, 124–125;
common property, 67–68; endangered
species, 293; environmental losses,
300; medical malpractice, 105–106;
slavery, 55; private property, 62, 65;
product liability, 221–222; self-
interest, 78–79; taxation, 142–143,
146; tort, 96–97; wetlands, 291
Inclusive fitness, 310–311
Inequality of bargaining power, 84–86
Infancy and insanity, 81
Informal norms, 42–49; competition
with law, 8, 14
Injunctions, 121–123
Insider trading, 254–257
Intangible property, 327–328, 330
Intentional harms, 92
Internal Revenue Code, 27
International transactions, 10, 47, 110
Ius tertii, 66

Joint causation, 97–101; environmental
regulation, 286–296; juries, 242; social change, 328–329
Jordan, Michael, 321–322
Just compensation: contract breach,
119–120; in-kind, 134–137; and mistakes, 117–118; necessity cases, 114;
proportionate impact, 134–136; takings, 128–132
Justice, 317–320
Justinian, 70, 116

Labor, mixing property with, 116–118;
ownership of, 55–56, 60
Labor contracts, 151–170; conditions in,
154–155; for-cause rules, 159–160;
"relational," 177–178; sequence of performance, 154–156
Laffer curve, 13–14
Landmark preservation, 24, 136
Lawyers, 1–14; comparisons with doctors, 3; conflict of interests, 8; demand
for, 9; image, 1; income, 2–4; in gov-

ernment, 3, 12; jokes, 1, 8; optimal
numbers of, 11; percentages of GDP,
5–6, 11; popular dissatisfaction with,
2; practice of, 4; productivity of, 13;
statistics on, 3–4; in Washington, 3
Locke, John, 54–56, 60, 68, 172, 308
Lotteries, 61
Luck, 54–55, 321–322

Magee, Stephen, 11–13
Majority rule, 47–48, 163
Mandatory retirement, 28
Marx, Karl, 308
Medical malpractice, 102–105, 228
Melamed, Douglas, 121
Minimum wage law, 144–145
Misrepresentation, 81–82, 194–210,
318–319; product liability cases, 218–
220; three-party, 202–207; two-party,
198–202
Mistake, 116–119
Monopoly, 77, 78, 123–126
Mortgages, 270
Multiculturalism, 10
Mutual benefit. *See* Trades

National Childhood Vaccine Injury Act,
235
National Traffic and Motor Vehicle Law,
212–213, 237
Natural law, 311–313
Natural talents, 54, 57–58
Negligence and strict liability, 92–97,
102, 201–202, 264–265, 276–277,
318
Negligent misrepresentation, 195–210
"Neighbor" principle, 196–198
Nuisances, 123, 133, 276–280

Perfect justice, 37–42, 53
Police power, 132–134, 299
Political factions, 46–47, 136–137, 140–
141, 319
Pollution, 263, 274–286; clean-up, 280–
281, 296–297; electric cars, 285–286;
tradable permits, 281–282, 297–298
Pre-emption, federal, 25, 233–234
Prescription, 64–66